Writing and Reporting News

A COACHING METHOD

EIGHTH EDITION

Writing and Reporting News

A COACHING METHOD

CAROLE RICH

CENGAGE
Learning·

Australia • Brazil • Mexico • Singapore • United Kingdom • United States

CENGAGE
Learning·

Writing and Reporting News: A Coaching Method, Eighth Edition
Carole Rich

Product Director: Monica Eckman

Product Manager: Kelli Strieby

Managing Content Developer:
Megan Garvey

Associate Content Developer:
Rachel Schowalter

Media Developer: Janine Tangney

Marketing Manager: Jillian Borden

Content Project Manager: Dan Saabye

Art Director: Marissa Falco

Manufacturing Planner: Doug Bertke

IP Analyst: Ann Hoffman

IP Project Manager: Farah Fard

Production Service: MPS Limited

Compositor: MPS Limited

Text Designer: Anne Bell Carter, a bell
design company

Cover Designer: Studio Wink

Cover Image: Tim Brakemeier/dpa/Corbis

For product information and technology assistance, contact us at
Cengage Learning Customer & Sales Support, 1-800-354-9706
For permission to use material from this text or product,
submit all requests online at **www.cengage.com/permissions**.
Further permissions questions can be emailed to
permissionrequest@cengage.com.

Library of Congress Control Number: 2014943035

Student Edition:
ISBN: 978-1-305-07733-1

Cengage Learning
20 Channel Center Street
Boston, MA 02210
USA

Cengage Learning is a leading provider of customized learning solutions with office locations around the globe, including Singapore, the United Kingdom, Australia, Mexico, Brazil, and Japan. Locate your local office at **www.cengage.com/global**.

Cengage Learning products are represented in Canada by Nelson Education, Ltd.

To learn more about Cengage Learning Solutions, visit **www.cengage.com**. Purchase any of our products at your local college store or at our preferred online store **www.cengagebrain.com**.

Printed in Canada
Print Number: 01   Print Year: 2014

Brief Contents

Contents

PART THREE
Constructing Stories

PART FOUR
Understanding Media Issues

Preface

It's an exciting time to be studying journalism. "In my view the future of journalism can and will be better than its past," according to Richard Gingras, senior director of news and social products at Google. "I believe we are at the beginnings of a renaissance in the exploration and re-invention of how news is gathered, expressed, and engaged with. The media landscape is in the process of being completely transformed, tossed upside down; reinvented and restructured in ways we know, and in ways we do not *yet* know."

Although the development and delivery of news will continue to change, some journalism skills remain essential. This book teaches the basic skills of journalism as well as the skills for producing social and mobile media for digital delivery.

As in previous editions, the coaching concepts of this book are designed to help students acquire the writing and reporting skills they will need no matter which media field they choose to enter. The book also includes breakout boxes of social media, ethics and multimedia in every chapter. The chapters are written in a storytelling style to make learning a pleasant reading experience.

NEW MATERIAL IN THIS EDITION

This eighth edition of *Writing and Reporting News: A Coaching Method* has been revised to include more social media, multimedia and mobile media skills in every chapter. All chapters have been updated, more photos have been added and the following new sections have been added:

Chapter 1: Changing Concepts of News offers a new section on objectivity vs. neutrality.

Chapter 2: The Basic News Story contains a new section on objectivity and a new example of the basic news story.

Chapter 3: Social Media (was Chapter 4 in 7th edition) now includes new sections on verifying social media, curation, and a social media glossary.

Chapter 4: Sources and Online Research (was Chapter 5 in 7th edition) includes a new section on data sources.

Chapter 5: Interviewing Techniques (was Chapter 6 in 7th edition.) includes new information about the controversy in colleges over email interviews.

Chapter 6: Mobile and Multimedia Skills (was Chapter 3 in 7th edition.) is a major rewrite with expanded information on mobile media, new sections about multiplatform consumers, and multimedia innovation.

Chapter 9: Story Forms features a new lead focusing on the *Denver Post* Pulitzer Prize about the Aurora, Colorado, movie theater shooting and includes a new example for the question/answer story form.

Chapter 11: Broadcast News Writing features a new section on VOs and VOSOTs (voice-overs).

Chapter 12: Online Journalism offers another major rewrite with new examples from prize-winning college websites and a new section on digital first media.

Chapter 15: Media Ethics includes a new section on conflicts of interest.

Chapter 16: Multicultural Sensitivity features an expanded section on the Language of Multiculturalism with a new section on gender-neutral language.

Chapter 17: Profiles and Obituaries includes a new section on micro profiles (also called Twitter profiles).

Chapter 18: Speeches, News Conferences and Meetings includes a new lead and new examples.

Chapter 21: Disasters, Weather and Tragedies features new sections on the Boston Marathon bombing, Deadline Dangers, the Sandy Hook Elementary School tragedy and the role of social media in these tragedies.

Chapter 22: Media Jobs and Internships includes updated information using Twitter and social media and a new section on online portfolios.

For the first time a **Glossary** offers an alphabetical list of key journalism terms in the book. Also the inside back cover offers a quick **Glossary-at-a-Glance,** which features selected key journalism terms and social media terms.

HOW THE BOOK IS ORGANIZED

Although this textbook is arranged sequentially to take students through the steps from conceiving ideas to constructing stories, each chapter is self-contained so the chapters may be used in any order. While some material has moved to other chapters, the basic structure of the book has been retained:

Part 1: Understanding News: Part One contains chapters that explain changes in the media, the basics of a news story and the impact of social media on how we read and write news. This part will give students a greater understanding of the course they are about to take.

Part 2: Collecting Information: The three chapters in Part Two outline ways to collect the necessary information to write a story. Information includes types of sources available, online research, interviewing techniques and mobile and multimedia skills.

Part 3: Constructing Stories: Part Three covers tools to create stories in a variety of media. From writing leads to organizing stories, this section features techniques to help students whether they plan to pursue careers in print, broadcast, online media or in public relations.

Part 4: Understanding Media Issues: The chapters in Part Four discuss legal and ethical issues critical to understanding media today. The chapter on multicultural sensitivity covers topics that are more relevant and important now than ever before.

Part 5: Applying the Techniques: The chapters in Part Five apply techniques taught in the rest of the book to specific types of stories, from speeches to crimes and disasters. This section also features a chapter that teaches students how to apply for jobs by crafting cover letters and resumes in print and online formats.

ALSO AVAILABLE DIGITALLY

MindTap for Journalism, offering the ultimate personal learning experience, is now available with *Writing and Reporting News: A Coaching Method*, Eighth Edition. Fully integrated into one seamless experience, MindTap combines readings, multimedia, activities, and assessments into a singular learning path—guiding students through the course, maximizing study time and helping them master course concepts. Instructors can personalize the learning path by customizing Cengage Learning resources and adding their own content via apps that integrate into the MindTap framework with any learning management system. Also included within MindTap for this edition:

- **Learning Objectives** help students understand what they will learn in each chapter.
- **Getting Started Activities** engage students at the start of each part, motivating them to learn and collaborate via forums, voting and polling questions, and more.
- **Workbook Activities** reworked from the workbook that has always been offered, are integrated into chapter readings to help students practice as they learn.
- **Chapter Quizzes** help to gauge student understanding of the concepts in the chapter.
- **NewsScene Assignments** based on realistic news events. Assignments offer extensive source material, including videotaped interviews, telephone messages, official documents and database information, which helps students sharpen their writing skills for print, broadcast and online media.

To learn more, ask your Cengage Learning sales representative to demo MindTap for you—or visit www.cengage.com/mindtap.

SUPPLEMENTS

The **Instructor's Companion Website** is an all-in-one resource for class preparation and presentation for instructors. Accessible through Cengage.com/login with your faculty account, you will find the latest revision of the Instructor's Manual (description below), as well as a list of helpful weblinks that can be used to broaden students' learning experiences.

The **Instructor's Resource Manual** contains chapter-specific goals, teaching suggestions and answers to the textbook and workbook exercises. It has been revamped to include not only the News Scene IM, but also to also help instructors teach through the MindTap. The Resource Manual also includes examples of original stories. Because the Instructor's Resource Manual is an electronic document, the file is available for download at the Instructor's Companion Website, at *login.cengage.com*.

The **Student Workbook**, which will be available as a print-on-demand request for this edition, features several exercises in each chapter to reinforce the concepts taught in *Writing and Reporting News*, Eighth Edition. These include quizzes, exercises designed to give students more opportunities to improve their reporting and writing skills, and exercises designed to encourage critical thinking by asking students to critique news stories and analyze websites. This edition of the workbook also includes practice in using social media skills. Please contact your local sales representative to request the workbook for your students.

ACKNOWLEDGMENTS

I would like to thank many people at Cengage Learning who made the eighth edition of this textbook possible. They include: Kelli Strieby, Product Manager in the Humanities Division; Megan Garvey, Managing Content Developer; Rachel Schowalter, Associate Content Developer; Janine Tangney, Media Developer; Dan Saabye, Content Project Manager; Jillian Borden, Marketing Manager; Charu Khanna, MPS Project Manager and Heather Mann, proofreader.

I would also like to thank the reviewers, who contributed their time and advice for this edition:

Kwadwo Anokwa, from Butler University; Debra Tobin from The University of North Carolina at Charlotte; Richard Gaspar from Hillsborough Community College – Ybor City Campus; Huntly Collins from LaSalle University; Tina Lesher from William Patterson University; Carolyn Barta from Southern Methodist University; and Joshua Azriel from Kennesaw State University.

About the Author

Carole Rich has spent 25 years teaching journalism at four universities and coaching professional writers throughout the U.S. She has taught at the University of Alaska Anchorage and has served as chair of the journalism department at Hofstra University in Long Island, N.Y. She began her teaching career at the University of Arizona in 1985 and then taught journalism at the University of Kansas from 1987 to 1998 when she was hired as the distinguished Atwood professor in Alaska. Prior to becoming a professor, she worked for 16 years in the newspaper industry. She was a reporter for the former *Philadelphia Evening Bulletin,* city editor of the *Sun-Sentinel* in Fort Lauderdale, Florida, and deputy metropolitan editor of the *Hartford* (Connecticut) *Courant.*

Rich has been a visiting writing coach at newspapers throughout the U.S. and has conducted many writing seminars at journalism organizations, including a seminar for professional journalists in Spain. She is also the author of *Creating Online Media: A Guide to Research, Writing and Design on the Internet,* published by McGraw-Hill.

COACHING TIPS

Consider ways to present your story for **print, broadcast, mobile and online media.**

Ask yourself **how your story affects your readers.**

Consider whether your story needs a **photograph, graphic, audio or video.**

Plan to update your story for **online delivery.**

Use social media sites to connect with readers and viewers.

CHAPTER 1

Changing Concepts of News

We are very bullish on the future of high-quality journalism. . . . The distribution models are changing and the players producing certain forms of journalism are going to change. But it happens to be the most exciting time in journalism.

—**MARTIN T. MOE**, *Senior Vice President, AOL Media*

T'S SHORTLY AFTER 1 A.M., AND THE POLICE OFFICER'S PATROL IS uneventful, except for the man carrying a 5-inch-long rat on his shoulder. No crime; it was just a man who bought a rat at a pet store. At 5:42 a.m. a young mother wakes to the cries of her hungry 10-month-old daughter. At noon a homeless woman with a canister of pepper spray in her bra waits for lunch at the local soup kitchen, and as midnight approaches, three fraternity members celebrate the last day of classes by climbing on the merry-go-round at a shopping mall.

These are just a few of the stories and photographs that chronicle one day in the life of residents in Lawrence, Kansas. The project could be done in any community. When the *Lawrence* (Kansas) *Journal-World* tackled the subject, it created a "multi-media time capsule" by producing the story in the newspaper, on television and on its website with text, photos, audio and video.

Courtesy of Lawrence Journal-World

That's not unusual these days. Almost every news organization has done a 24-hour story, but what made this different was the participation from the community. In addition to reporting by reporters and photographers of the newspaper and its partner TV station, residents participated by sending in stories about their day in various forms: podcasts, blogs, video, photos and text messages via email.

This project was one of several innovative methods the *Lawrence Journal-World* has produced to interact with its readers and viewers in multimedia forms. And it is an example of how the nature of news is changing.

Readers are participating much more in producing and reacting to news through social media sites such as Twitter, Facebook, YouTube and others. Mobile media and tablet computers are also affecting how news is delivered.

"Americans are now fully into the digital era," according to a study by the Pew Project for Excellence in Journalism. More than three-quarters of U.S. adults own a laptop or desktop computer, and 56 percent own

LJWORLD.COM

See complete forecast

Marketplace   Jobs   Classifieds   Real Estate   Coupon

News   Sports   Arts & Entertainment   Living   Opinion   Multimedia

24 hours in Lawrence midnight–6:00am

Early morning in Lawrence
Police officer patrols city while others prepare for day ahead

Rise & Shine
Lawrence resident juggles family, work

City at its peak
So much to do, so little time. School counselor balances work, household chores

Calling it a day
Life full of ups, downs, surprises: Coach serves as mentor for team, family

Courtesy of Lawrence Journal-World

smartphones, according to the study. "News is a significant part of how people use these devices. . . . A mounting body of evidence finds that the spread of mobile technology is adding to news consumption."

Readers and viewers don't just receive news; they help collect and create it. They get the news when, how and where they want it on computers, mobile phones, tablet devices or social media networks. They contribute to traditional media outlets with news tips, story ideas and eyewitness reports in text, video and photos via Twitter, Facebook, Instagram, YouTube and other social media sites.

Definitions of news are also evolving, and economic factors such as mergers of media companies have changed the landscape of the news industry.

Declining newspaper circulation, increased competition from cable television news stations and access to millions of sites on the Internet are forcing news organizations to expand ways to interest readers and viewers. The days of writing for a single medium have ended at most news, public relations and advertising organizations.

MEDIA CONVERGENCE

Many of the skills you need to become a journalist are still grounded in basic reporting and writing principles, but in today's market you need to know how to present information for print, broadcast and online media. This mixture of media is called "convergence," "multimedia," "integrated media" and other terms.

In some types of convergence, a print news organization partners with a broadcast station to collaborate on a story. In other newsrooms the print and broadcast facilities are in the same building where journalists coordinate news coverage. Convergence can also be considered the merger of print, audio, video and interactive elements in an online form.

The *Lawrence Journal-World* was one of the first news organizations in the U.S. to converge its print, broadcast and online operations, which are housed in a 1906 brick building that belies the modern newsroom inside. In 2001, owner and publisher Dolph C. Simons converted a vacant post office on the National Register of Historic Places into a newsroom featuring a circular multimedia desk where editors coordinate information from print, broadcast and online media reporters. "We want to stay abreast of new developments and be able to deliver news and advertising, as well as other information, however a reader or advertiser might desire," Simons said.

These days many newsrooms at universities and news organizations all over the world have been reorganized to foster convergence of multimedia on a variety of platforms.

CHANGING DELIVERY OF NEWS

The increasing popularity of smartphones and tablet computers like the iPad is creating new venues for news companies to deliver their products. Mobile news delivery is the fastest growing trend for the media industry.

USA Today has completely restructured its newsroom to take advantage of distributing news on mobile and tablet platforms. The company disbanded its universal desk and reorganized the newsroom around 15 content areas such as travel, personal finance, technology and subjects that are geared to the audience and technology of mobile and tablet media.

These changes in technology have spawned an alphabet soup of terms related to forms of delivering news. Here are some common terms:

- **Blogs:** The term blog is short for "Web log" because blogs are posted on the Web. A blog can be a personal journal or brief commentary about any topic and can include audio or video.

- **Podcast:** This is digital media information in audio or video form distributed over the Internet for use on a portable media player such as an iPod, an instrument developed by Apple Inc., or an MP3 player. Pod is an abbreviation for "portable on demand." You don't need an iPod to hear or view a podcast; you can receive it on your computer with the use of software.

SOCIAL MEDIA

SOCIAL NETWORKING has transformed the media, according to Clay Shirky, a New York University professor who is considered an expert in this field. "We are living in the middle of the largest increase in expressive capability in the history of the human race," he wrote in his book *Here Comes Everybody.* "More people can communicate more things to more people than has ever been possible in the past, and the size and speed of this increase, from under one million participants to over one billion in a generation, makes the change unprecedented, even considered against the background of previous revolutions in communications tools."

Here are a few of the ways social media sites are changing journalism:

- **New job positions:** News organizations are hiring social media editors. They interact with their communities on sites such as Twitter and Facebook, train journalists in their newsrooms to use social media, and maintain and contribute blogs or tweets to company sites.

- **Reporting:** Journalists are using social media to gain tips and sources and to communicate with readers and viewers, especially during a breaking news event. Many government and community organizations and corporate communications agencies also post information on social media sites that reporters can follow to gain information.

- **Participation by readers and viewers:** News organizations are soliciting information from subscribers to their websites and social media sites for breaking news, eyewitness reports and feedback about stories and issues. And social media users share information about the news with each other, creating new types of communities. "The public is clearly part of the news process now. Participation comes more through sharing than through contributing news themselves," according to a report by the Pew Internet and American Life Project.

- **RSS:** These letters stand for "Really Simple Syndication," which is probably simpler to use than to define. If you want to receive certain blogs or podcasts regularly, you can subscribe to a site using a Web feed reader called an "aggregator" that will compile them and deliver them to you. You insert a link to the site into the aggregator software. Search engines such as Google or Yahoo! offer to deliver automatic updates of news via RSS feeds. These feeds, delivered to your account, contain headlines, summaries and links to the articles.

- **Aggregator:** This is software that compiles or collects certain websites that you want delivered to you regularly and pushes them to you via email or automatically downloads them for you into a portable media player. The aggregator is also known as a feed reader because it "reads" the sites it will "feed" to you. It checks them for new material and downloads updates to your account for easy access on your computer or portable media device.

- **Social media:** News organizations are using social networks such as Facebook, Twitter, YouTube, Tumblr and others to connect with readers and viewers. Social media is electronic communication where users share information, ideas, messages, audio and video content on websites designed to create online communities.

CITIZEN JOURNALISM

The concept of involving readers and viewers in reporting and disseminating news is called "citizen journalism," "participatory journalism" or "user-generated-content." The movement is an attempt by media organizations to increase their interaction with their audience. The contributors are often called "citizen journalists" because they are not staff members of the news organization, even though they may write blogs on a regular basis for the media website. Social media contributors sometimes perform the same functions.

Many of the citizen journalism sites are considered hyperlocal, providing local news and information for a neighborhood or small community within a larger area such as *The Oakland Local* (*oaklandlocal.com*). *The Twin Cities Daily Planet* (*www.tcdailyplanet.net*) is a successful hyperlocal site covering neighborhoods in the Minneapolis/St. Paul, Minnesota, area. The site has 100 media partners and bloggers.

A pioneer in the user-generated-content movement is a South Korean website called OhmyNews International. Oh Yeon-ho, creator of the site, said his motto is "Every citizen is a reporter all over the world." Since its inception in 2000 with 727 citizen reporters, the organization has grown to more than 62,000 contributors, with 70 full-time editors and reporters. The focus of the organization has changed to report more about citizen journalism than world news.

Courtesy of OhmyNews International

OhmyNews founder Oh Yeon Ho in the newsroom in Seoul, Korea.

This is how the company describes itself and its focus on citizen journalism: "We are a small team based at *OhmyNews* in Seoul, South Korea. We are international journalists. We know technology, and we are curious about the global progress of citizen journalism. And we adore coffee always. Grassroots journalism, citizen media, [and] crowdsourcing are all related terms that tackle the same question: How are regular people making and changing the news?"

ECONOMIC CHANGES IN MEDIA

The changing face of the media isn't just in the content and delivery of news; it is in the ownership of the largest media organizations. Economic forces created significant changes in major media companies at the start of the 21st century. Newspaper circulation was declining, and the large media companies listed on the stock exchange were under pressure because of sagging stock profits for their shareholders. Print and broadcast news organizations cut staffs and resources. Two of the largest media organizations, Knight Ridder Inc. and the Tribune Company, sold their newspapers and TV stations.

Journalists who got into the business years ago with the idealistic notion that the primary concern of media companies was content became disillusioned by the emphasis on economics, and many quit or retired. The times were changing and the news business was just that — a business that was supposed to make a profit. But journalists didn't disappear; many of them formed new online ventures and found news-related jobs in other publications, businesses, public relations organizations and government agencies. Good journalism skills have broad application.

Partnerships

News organizations that were once fiercely competitive formed partnerships to share news stories in print and video as a way to cut costs. In South Florida, *The Miami Herald*, the *South Florida Sun-Sentinel* and the *Palm Beach Post* began sharing stories, and similar arrangements were created among newspapers in Maine, Ohio and Texas. The nature of competition has changed.

Partnerships with university journalism departments are another way news organizations are expanding their coverage without expanding their staffs. *The New York Times* has a partnership with City University of New York in which journalism students write blogs to cover communities in Brooklyn and New Jersey; and with New York University journalism students to cover other communities within the metro area.

AOL has created a partnership with several universities called "PatchU," which offers internships and coursework as well as freelance opportunities at Patch publications, which are online sites that provide news and information in hundreds of communities. Students can write stories and cover local events in multimedia form and integrate social media for the Patch sites.

Pay Walls

Would you be willing to pay for online news that you currently can get free? That's a dilemma facing news organizations that are seeking ways to pay rising costs for their online publications. With advertising revenues declining and competition rising from other websites, news organizations have discussed charging for access to some or all of their online content. Several news sites have created pay walls, which wall off, or block access to, certain content. The cost of applications for digital delivery to smartphones and tablets will also affect the future of charges for online information.

CHANGES IN ONLINE NEWS

The Web has changed the nature of news in other ways:

Continual Deadlines When a news story breaks, reporters at many newspaper and broadcast organizations are expected to file the story immediately for the Web and update major stories online throughout the day. Twitter has changed the nature of breaking news as well. Reporters may tweet updates continually during a major incident or any breaking news story.

Interactive Content One of the main distinctions of online news is the ability to interact with readers. Web news stories often feature interactive content such as polls, chats and questions at the end of stories to prompt readers to express their views, as well as requests to comment on a news organization's social media site. More than ever, writers need to consider how their audience will be affected by the story, regardless of the medium.

Related Links Online news is accompanied by links to related information, so a news story may no longer be a single entity. Traditional print and broadcast news stories also refer readers and viewers to related online information. Social media sites such as Twitter also feature links to blogs, photos, videos and other media content.

Nonlinear Structure Print and broadcast news stories are written in linear order — to be read or heard from beginning to end as if in a straight line. Because the Web features links and multimedia features, it creates a nonlinear environment, meaning readers may access content in any order they choose. Although many online news stories are still linear, original Web content is organized in more related pieces. Instead of one story containing all the information, nonlinear news might be split into separate parts for background, profiles, timelines, databases and multimedia.

Databases Many news sites offer databases that you can search for information about health, school test scores, or crime statistics in your community. For example, *The Philadelphia Inquirer* (*www.philly.com*) offers an annual report card allowing you to search a database for public and private schools in Pennsylvania and New Jersey to find out about school test scores and related facts for schools in these areas. Many other news sites also offer searchable databases for crime statistics, school test scores and other community information.

Personalized Journalism In addition to blogs as a form of personalized journalism, online news sites are reaching out to users by asking them to contribute their personal stories on the organization's website or its Facebook or Twitter pages.

CHANGING VALUES

Several news organizations, such as the Radio Television Digital News Association, are developing special ethical codes for social media. With slight adjustments, these codes mirror the ones that apply to mainstream media. However, a study of executives from RTDNA and the American Society of Newspaper Editors revealed that these news leaders have some serious concerns about the effect the Internet and social networks are having on news values.

The study by the Project for Excellence in Journalism revealed that more than 62 percent of executives from print and 67 percent from broadcast media think accuracy is declining due in part to the speed of producing news and to social media. "I worry that journalistic standards are dropping in that blogging and celebrity gossip and tweets are being confused with reporting and editing that passes a rigorous standard," one broadcast executive wrote. A newspaper editor concurred and added, "There is too much emphasis, I believe, on getting information fast even at the expense of accuracy, thoroughness and fairness."

OBJECTIVITY

In the past, news reporting was expected to be objective or neutral, meaning that the story was supposed to be presented as factual and any opinions should be attributed. Many journalists and ethics experts have argued that objectivity is impossible because writers bring their acquired biases to reporting and writing; nevertheless, writers were supposed to try to be neutral in their reporting.

However, in the last few decades, news stories have contained more analysis to help readers understand the context of stories.

A study by Columbia University professor Michael Scudson and graduate student Katherine Fink revealed that in 1955, stories about events outnumbered other types of front-page stories nine to one. "Now, about half of all stories are something else: a report that tries to explain why, not just what," they wrote in their study.

PLAGIARISM AND FABRICATION THE CASE: (This situation is based on the case of Jayson Blair, a former reporter for *The New York Times*.) A reporter for your campus newspaper quickly becomes a star by charming editors and professors. His stories are filled with descriptive details and human-interest features that gain him a reputation as an outstanding writer. But the editor of the paper is concerned because several of his stories require corrections after they are printed, and the editor can't trace some of the sources. The editor and some staffers complain to journalism professors about this reporter's inaccuracies, but the professors dismiss the complaints as jealousy over this rising star.

The reporter lands a prestigious internship with a large daily newspaper and later is hired full time even before he graduates from journalism school. He shows much promise and gets assigned to major national stories, but during his four years at the paper his stories require 50 corrections, and one of his editors thinks he should be fired. However, the top manager at the newspaper excuses the reporter because he says that he has had several personal problems.

His trail of deception, plagiarism and fabrication is uncovered after the newspaper is notified that he plagiarized a story written by a reporter at another paper. The story was only one of at least 36 articles containing plagiarized or fabricated quotes and facts. The reporter resigns, and the newspaper publishes an extensive front-page Sunday story explaining the situation and apologizing to readers.

Dilemma

- What steps could have or should have been taken to prevent this situation from happening?

- Should a reporter be fired as soon as the first incident of plagiarism or fabrication is discovered?

- Should a reporter whose stories require numerous corrections be fired?

- What would you have done if you were the campus editor or his editor at that newspaper?

- What can be done to prevent plagiarism and fabrication in the media?

Ethical values: Accuracy, credibility.

Ethical guidelines: According to the code of ethics of the Society of Professional Journalists, "Seek truth and report it. Test the accuracy of information from all sources and exercise care to avoid inadvertent error. Deliberate distortion is never permissible."

Social media in the form of blogs and contributions from citizen journalists also affect journalistic impartiality.

QUALITIES OF NEWS

Definitions and delivery methods of news are changing. But these are some traditional qualities of news stories that still apply to print, broadcast and online media:

Timeliness An event that happened the day of or day before publication or an event that is due to happen in the immediate future is considered timely. In broadcast and online media, timeliness is considered "immediacy" and is even more crucial. When stories are posted online immediately after they happen or broadcast several times a day, you have to consider how to update them frequently. Some events that happened in the past may also be considered timely if they are printed on an anniversary of the event, such as one, five or 10 years after the incident. Timeliness answers the reader's question: Why are you telling me this now? The following story was timely because it was published the day after the accident:

> A bus loaded with elementary school children crashed head-on into a compact car in southwestern Jefferson County yesterday, injuring 24 students and the two drivers.
>
> — *The* (Louisville, Kentucky) *Courier-Journal*

If that story had been written for broadcast or online media, the angle would have been updated to report the current condition of the students and drivers.

Proximity An event may be of interest to local readers because it happened in or close to the community. This story has proximity to people in Scottsdale, Arizona, where the accident occurred and to readers in Kansas because the victims were from Kansas State University:

> Two Kansas State University football fans who went to Arizona for the Fiesta Bowl are in the hospital with serious injuries after being hit by a suspected drunk driver in downtown Scottsdale.

Unusual Nature Out-of-the-ordinary events, a bizarre or rare occurrence, or people engaged in unusual activities are considered newsworthy, as in this story:

Monitor lizards are an invasive species in Florida.

T. Campbell/U.S. Geological Survey

MAN TICKETED FOR WALKING HIS LIZARD

FORT LAUDERDALE, Fla. — Walking your dog along the beach here is illegal — and so is lounging with your lizard, Chris DeMango found out. Mortimer, DeMango's 20-pound purple-tongued monitor lizard, complete with matching pink doll sweater and leash, was out for exercise Monday. DeMango said a walk makes Mortimer more docile, but police said it makes him an illegal lizard — animals are banned on the beach. DeMango was ticketed, and his lizard law violation could cost him 60 days in jail and a $500 fine, said police spokesman Ott Cefkin. DeMango was not amused. "I would think that would be the most absurd thing, if I were to go to jail for this," he grumbled.

— *Tampa Bay Times/St. Petersburg* (Florida) *Times*

Human Interest People like stories about people who have special problems or achievements, or who have overcome difficulties. Human interest could also be described as animal interest stories because many stories about pets — especially missing or found pets — fit in this category.

Humans aren't the only ones who like to poke around their iPads. Now orangutans do, too.

When zoo keepers at the Smithsonian National Zoo were seeking ways to add more stimulation to the orangutans, they contacted Orangutan Outreach, a nonprofit organization that had success using iPads with apes at 12 other zoos in a program called "Apps for Apes." So they introduced iPads to six of the zoo's orangutans.

Their conclusions: Different apps for different apes. For example, "36-year-old Bonnie likes to bang on the drums, 16-year-old Kyle prefers the piano and 25-year-old Iris is content to listen to the soothing sounds of the koi pond while watching animated fish splash," according to a news release from the zoo.

"Apps for Apes fits perfectly in this new era of zoo keeping," said Becky Malinsky, great ape keeper at the National Zoo. "It's about changing up the day-to-day lives of our animals. We already vary their food, toys and social interactions every day, but the iPad offers another way to engage their sight, touch and hearing."

Richard Zimmerman, founding director of Orangutan Outreach, said the Apps for Apes program is designed to help people understand the need to protect wild orangutans from extinction. "We do that when we show Zoo visitors how similar humans and apes are, be it through observation, talking with wildlife experts or seeing the apes use the same technology we use every day," he said.

Conflict Stories involving conflicts that people have with government or other people are often newsworthy, especially when the conflict reflects local problems or, in this case, a national issue.

The Boy Scouts of America voted Thursday to end its controversial policy banning gay kids and teens from joining one of the nation's most popular youth organizations. . . .

Cpl.Lauren Kurkimilis/Courtesy U.S. Marines

Boy Scouts from Pack 77.

But the outcome of the historic ballot is not going to end the debate: Some opponents on the right said they would pull their sponsorships of packs and troops, and parents threatened to take their boys out of Scouting.

— NBCNews.com

Impact Reaction stories to news events or news angles that affect readers have impact, especially when major national stories or tragedies occur in any community. Newspapers often seek local angles by writing how people in their areas are affected by the news, as in this story following a school shooting in Connecticut.

SARATOGA SPRINGS, N.Y. — The sale and display of semiautomatic weapons and high capacity ammunition magazines will be banned at the upcoming gun show at the Saratoga City Center after City Council passed a resolution in the wake of a mass shooting in Newtown, Connecticut.

A gunman massacred 20 elementary school children and six educators at the Sandy Hook Elementary School in Connecticut by using a Bushmaster Ar-15-style rifle, a popular firearm.

The decision to ban the sale and display of these weapons is part of a compromise between the Sarasota Springs city officials, who wanted to cancel the event, and organizers of the gun show, who wanted it to go on as planned.

Some additional qualities of news to consider:

Helpfulness Consumer, health and other how-to stories help readers cope with their lives. Online news sites abound with helpful stories.

If your head spins at the torrent of medical studies that fills newspapers, magazines and TV, join the club. It seems that each day brings another round of studies contradicting last month's hot results.

One day vitamin E is found to prevent cancer. Next, it is suspected of causing it.

Margarine is good. No, it's bad.

One can almost hear a collective scream of frustration across the land.

Studies are the cornerstone of medical progress, showing doctors and patients the way to longer, healthier lives. But they can also lead us astray.

To try to help you through the hype and hustle, here's a basic outline of what studies are, how they differ, what they can tell us and where they can go wrong. Call it A User's Guide to Medical Studies. Or, How to Follow Health News Without Having a Stroke.

— PHILLIP E. CANUTO, *Knight-Ridder/Tribune News Service*

Celebrities People who are well-known for their accomplishments — primarily entertainers, athletes or people who have gained fame for achievements, good or bad — attract a lot of attention. But celebrity news has become so popular that some journalists are concerned it is displacing more important news and pandering to the public's desire for entertainment.

Ted Koppel, former anchor of the TV show "Nightline," said in a "Frontline" interview: "To the extent that we're now judging journalism by the same standards that we apply to entertainment — in other words, give the public what it wants, not necessarily what it ought to hear, what it ought to see, what it needs, but what it wants — that may prove to be one of the greatest tragedies in the history of American journalism."

Entertainment Stories that amuse readers, make them feel good or help them enjoy their leisure time have entertainment value. In a broad sense, many of the news features in sports and lifestyle sections can be classified as entertainment. These stories often involve celebrities or have human-interest qualities. But they are also controversial. The line between news and entertainment is not clear, especially in coverage of celebrities as stated in the previous item. However, this story combines qualities of human interest and unusual nature to entertain or amuse readers:

When Marjorie Clapprood opened her W-2 form from the state of Massachusetts, she was shocked.

The form said she was dead.

"Boy, when you're out, you're out," said Clapprood, a former state representative who lost her bid for re-election.

But she was by no means alone.

State W-2 tax forms mailed recently listed all 199 members of last year's Legislature as dead.

Some residents of the financially troubled state suspected that all along.

But members of last year's Legislature are taking exception to their recent demise, which was caused by a clerical error.

Clapprood, for one, said she isn't about to let the IRS consider her dead.

"They owe me money, I think," she said.

Corrected forms are to be mailed to the resurrected shortly.

— TOM TOROK, *The Philadelphia Inquirer*

Issues or Problems in the Community These stories usually include qualities such as conflict and proximity. This story is about an issue of interest to Californians, but it would also be of interest to people in other cities where homelessness is a problem.

Homeless people in California may be getting legal protection for sleeping, congregating, panhandling and urinating on public property.

Christopher Beland/Creative Commons

A homeless person sleeping on a street in San Francisco will have new rights under a proposed bill.

A San Francisco assemblyman has proposed a "Homeless Bill of Rights" to legally protect homeless people who are engaging in activities on public property. If passed by the Legislature, homeless people would have the right to sleep in legally parked cars, receive funds from public welfare programs and receive legal counsel if they are cited for infractions.

The measure is expected to be controversial in many cities, including Sacramento, which has battled tent cities for homeless people, and San Francisco, where local laws bar homeless people from sitting or lying on sidewalks.

Trends Stories may indicate trends, which are patterns or shifts in issues that influence readers' lives, such as increases in crime, social issues and other forces in society.

Many Milwaukee area public libraries no longer have strict "SH!" policies. Libraries are shedding their image as quiet, somber places for bookworms and students only. Instead, today's libraries offer a wide variety of materials and programs in an effort to appeal to more people.

— LAWRENCE SUSSMAN, *Milwaukee Journal Sentinel*

Hard News and Features

News falls into two basic categories: hard news and soft news. Hard news includes stories of a timely nature about events or conflicts that have just happened or are about to happen, such as crimes, fires, meetings, protest rallies, speeches and testimony in court cases. The hard-news approach is basically an account of what happened, why it happened and how readers will be affected. These stories have immediacy.

Soft news is defined as news that entertains or informs, with an emphasis on human interest and novelty, and less immediacy than hard news. For example, a profile about a man who designs model airplanes or a story about the effectiveness of diets would be considered soft news.

MULTIMEDIA COACH

TRAIN YOURSELF
to think for multimedia.

- Compare online news stories with those in your local newspaper. Are they the same, or do they offer links, polls, questions and other related features? If your local TV news station has a website, compare that site with the newspaper's website.

- Learn to think interactively. Analyze interactive online features such as polls, games, message boards and databases in your local websites or others, such as CNN (*www.cnn.com*).

- Plan to update stories. Analyze how major news sites continually update their stories.

- Consider the role of blogs and social media comments. Analyze blogs for their news or entertainment value. Check journalists' blogs at *www.cyberjournalist.net/journalist-blogs*.

- Consider the nature of your audience.

- Become a visual thinker. Compare the visuals for a news story covered in your newspaper, on TV and online. Consider visuals for the stories you will produce.

Soft news can also be stories that focus on people, places or issues that affect readers' lives. These types of stories are called "feature stories." A story about the growing number of babies suffering from AIDS could be considered a soft-news story. It isn't less important than hard news, but it isn't news that happened overnight. However, a feature story can be based on a news event. Instead of being just a factual account of the event, it features or focuses on a particular angle, such as human-interest reactions.

If the action or event occurred the same day as or the day before publication of the newspaper, the event is called "breaking news." Here is an example of the lead of a breaking news story from a Saturday edition:

Damage to a home in Kansas from a tornado.

Tornadoes rapped Topeka and southeast Shawnee County Friday afternoon, damaging seven homes and sending residents scurrying for cover.

No one was injured by the short, severe storm that struck unexpectedly.

— STEVE FRY, *Topeka* (Kansas)
Capital-Journal

The preceding example of a hard-news story tells readers what happened. The newspaper also printed this feature story focusing on people affected by the storm:

Becky Clark of Topeka was told the tornado sirens that sounded Friday afternoon were a false alarm.

Then she got home from work and saw her back yard at 2411 S.E. Gemini Ave. in the Aquarian Acres neighborhood.

"I couldn't believe it," she said.

A tornado had lifted up the family pontoon boat, which was parked in the back yard, and tossed it into the family swimming pool, crushing part of the boat.

"It just wanted to get in the water," said Joe Clark, Becky's husband.

"I guess it was tired of being in dry dock. . . . ."

— JOE TASCHLER, *Topeka* (Kansas) *Capital-Journal*

The hard-news story about the storm was the main story, called a "mainbar." Because the accompanying feature story was a different angle on the same topic, it was a sidebar packaged with the main story.

But many other features in a newspaper do not have a breaking news peg. They simply focus on interesting people or topics. For example, the *Boca Raton* (Florida) *News* printed a feature story on the growing popularity of waterbeds, a topic of interest to its readers.

THE IMPORTANCE OF VISUALS

The presentation of a story with photographs or graphics is crucial. Broadcast media depend on visuals for the majority of stories. Studies by The Poynter Institute in St. Petersburg, Florida, show an increased emphasis on graphic devices and color in print media.

Headgear to track readers' eye movements in the Poynter Eye Track study.

In one study, called "Eyes on the News," researchers measured eyetracking, the movements of people's eyes as they read the newspaper. The results of this study, also known as the Eye Track study, showed that readers are drawn to color photographs first, then headlines, cutlines (captions), briefs (stories abbreviated to one to three paragraphs) and a number of other graphic devices called "points of entry" — points where the reader enters a story. Some of those eye-catching points include subheadlines and quotations displayed in larger type within the story.

The study also concluded that most people only scan the newspaper, looking at headlines and graphics, and that they read very few stories all the way through. The average reader skims about 25 percent of the stories in the newspaper but thoroughly reads only half of those (about 12 percent), the study concluded.

Mario Garcia, who co-authored the Poynter study and is a world-renowned consultant on newspaper design, says the majority of readers today do not remember life without television, so visual elements are crucial in a newspaper. "The marriage of visual and words has to begin early — from the first time you learn reporting," he says. Garcia now says the iPad will have a dramatic effect on news.

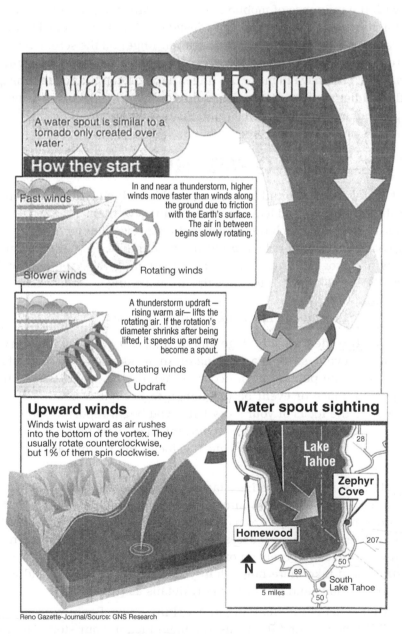

Graphic explaining how a waterspout is created.

The latest Eye Track study conducted by Poynter in 2012 on how people read on tablets revealed that people "tended to enter a screen through a dominant element, generally a photograph." Faces in photographs and videos, as well as maps and explanatory graphics, particularly graphics showing weather or traffic patterns, were viewed more on tablets than charts were in print and online media.

That finding contradicts an Eye Track study in 2007 of online readers that determined that graphics were less important in online news. The study found that online readers focused first on text in news websites rather than informational graphics.

But with the influence of mobile devices, the latest study on how people read on tablets is significant for writers and news designers. Another conclusion was that when people read on tablets, they tended to keep their finger on the screen and touched the screen frequently. This multitouch environment indicates a need for some interactivity, Garcia said. "You have to make the finger happy; keep the reader engaged."

All the studies confirm that in this multimedia world, planning visual elements is a crucial part of any news or public relations presentation.

THE COACHING METHOD

This book is developed around a coaching method, which is a way of helping writers discover their problems and learn techniques to solve them.

Just as a basketball coach trains players to improve their techniques on the court, a writing coach trains writers to improve their techniques in the craft. This book aims to serve as a surrogate writing coach by anticipating the problems writers might have and offering solutions. It features tips from leading writing coaches and award-winning journalists.

The coaching method in this book has four phases:

1. **Conceive the idea:** At this stage you develop the idea for the story. If you are covering an event, such as a meeting or an accident, you need to start with the idea — the main point of what occurred. Who, what, when, where and why will this person, place or event be of interest to become a news story? That main idea will be the focus of your story. Once you begin reporting, you may discover some information that is more important than your original focus. Therefore, you should be flexible and decide the focus for writing after you collect the material.

2. **Collect:** This is the reporting stage. Before you conduct your interview, you should look for background information: Check online sources and any available documents or clips from previous stories about your subject and your sources. Then interview sources, and gather as much information as you can about your topic. Don't rely on one source; seek several points of view. Ask more questions and take more notes than you plan to use. You should also jot down your observations and gather as many details as possible.

3. **Construct:** This is the planning and writing stage. Begin with a plan for your story developed around the focus, the main idea of your story. Then go through

your notes and mark only the information related to that focus. Like a carpenter building a house, you need a blueprint. Jot down a few key words to indicate how you will organize your story. Then write a first draft of your story. You may revise your original draft in the next step.

4. **Correct:** After you have written your story, read it and make any necessary changes. You may decide to add or delete information or to completely reorganize the story during this stage. You should also check the spelling of all names and the accuracy of facts, and you should correct grammar, style and typing errors.

These four steps constitute the basic process for all news stories. In the coming chapters you will learn many techniques for reporting and writing news.

EXERCISES

1 Visual awareness: Try this experiment to test your reading habits. Bring to class a copy of a newspaper you haven't read. Read the newspaper as you would for pleasure. Place a check on the first item you look at — a picture, graphic, headline or story. Mark the stories you read, and place an X at the point in the story where you decide to stop reading. Where did your eye go first? Why are visual elements so important? Now analyze which stories you read and how much of them you read. Where did you stop on most stories? Why? Keep in mind that because you are a journalism student, you may read more than the average reader. If you have an iPad or tablet computer, try the same experiment, and make notes of any differences in how you read.

2 Journal: Keep a journal of your reading or viewing habits of news for three days. Write a paragraph each day about the kinds of stories you read and didn't read, how many you read all the way through, and how many you read just through the headline or the first few paragraphs. Note how you accessed the stories — online, via a mobile phone

or tablet device or from a print publication or a TV newscast. Analyze your preferences. Then interview three other people — students, neighbors or strangers — and ask them what kinds of stories they do and don't read in print and online. Ask where they get the majority of their news — from print, broadcast, mobile or online media. Write a summary of your findings.

3 Online news ideas: Either in small groups or as a class, brainstorm topics and ideas that you would want to read in an online newspaper or magazine or on a digital device. Brainstorm at least three interactive features for an online college newspaper.

4 Qualities of news: Analyze your local or campus newspaper or website on the front page and/or local section. Identify the qualities of news of the main stories. Now do the same for a TV news broadcast. Jot down the stories in a 30-minute telecast, and identify the qualities of news in each segment.

 MindTap

FEATURED ONLINE ACTIVITIES: Log on to the MindTap for Rich's Writing and Reporting News to access a variety of robust additional material, including this chapter's learning objectives, activities, comprehension quizzes, and more!

CHAPTER 2

The Basic News Story

Too many stories fail to answer the reader's most challenging question: So what?

—ROY PETER CLARK, *Writing Coach and Author*

COACHING TIPS

State the focus, the main idea, of your story in one sentence.

To **find your lead,** ask yourself: What is most important or most interesting?

Write the story in a **conversational tone,** as though you were telling a friend.

Consider how your story will **affect readers.**

Consider what **photographs, graphics, audio or video** your story needs for print, broadcast or online delivery.

Consider how your story could be promoted or discussed on **Twitter or other social media.**

© kajakiki/Shutterstock.com

Roberts was a reporter at the *Goldsboro News-Argus* in North Carolina. His editor, Henry Belk, was blind. Many days Belk would call in Roberts to read his stories to him, and Belk would yell, "Make me see. You aren't making me see."

Advice from Roberts: "The best reporters, whatever their backgrounds or their personalities, share that consummate drive to get to the center of a story and then put the reader on the scene."

Much has changed in the media since Roberts was a reporter many years ago. But his advice is just as relevant today. Identify the center of the story, which is the focus; gather information to make the reader see; and write a compelling story to make the reader care.

ELEMENTS OF THE BASIC NEWS STORY

News stories in all media share some common elements. Every news story is based on one main idea — the focus. The basic news story structure includes a headline and three general parts: a beginning, called the "lead"; a middle, called the "body" and an ending.

Headline

The headline is the line on top of the story that identifies the main idea of the story so the reader can decide whether to access the full story. Online news sites and many newspapers today are using secondary headlines — called "deck heads," "summary lines" or "summary blurbs." The two headlines together give the reader a quick overview of the story's content.

Headline
Deck head/
summary
blurb

Salmon spawn a new crisis
Dwindling numbers and fading strength threaten to add the fish to the list of endangered species.

— *Los Angeles Times*

Salmon about to spawn.

National Oceanic and Atmospheric Administration (NOAA)

If you are having trouble identifying the main point of a story, think of a headline for it. Broadcast news scripts don't include headlines, but the concept will help you find focus.

Lead

At the beginning of the story, the hook that tells the reader what the story is about is called the "lead." A good lead entices the reader to continue reading. In a hard-news story, the lead usually is written in one sentence — the first sentence of the story — and gives the most important information about the event. But even a basic story can have a creative lead, called a "soft lead" or "feature lead."

Summary Leads The most common type of lead on a hard-news story is called a "summary lead" because it summarizes the main points about what happened. It answers the questions of who, what, when, where, why and how. The rest of the story elaborates about what, why and how.

Hard-News Leads These leads do not have to answer all those questions in the first sentence if doing so would make the lead too long and difficult to read.

Shorter leads of fewer than 35 words are preferable, but that number is only a guideline. With the increasing delivery of news for mobile media, brief writing is better for readers accessing information on their smartphones.

The writer has to decide which elements are most important to stress in the first sentence. The summary lead in the following example stresses who, what, where and when; the rest of the story gives more details, such as the names of the professor and the suspect:

A Northwestern University professor of hearing sciences was shot and seriously wounded in a university parking lot Thursday.

Feature Leads A lead that starts with a story or description about a person, place or incident, is called a "feature lead" or an "anecdotal lead." Many feature leads begin with a description of a person who is a key source in the story, and the focus of the story is explained in another paragraph.

Lead   When he was a little girl, Leo said he hated wearing dresses. Today the Ball State University graduate student is sitting in his office, clad in khakis and a button shirt.

At first encounter, Leo, who asked for his last name not to be used, looks like a typical thirty-something guy; sideburns, goatee, a little pudgy but nothing out of the ordinary. In a raspy tenor voice, he talks about the store he and his wife own, about their cats and about how he quit smoking three months ago and can't live without nicotine gum.

But Leo's demure appearance   *Focus* betrays his extraordinary past. In 1999 he began the process of physically transitioning from a woman named Lynette into a man named Leo.

— ADRIAN SHARP, *Ball State (Indiana) Daily News*

Nut Graph

The nut graph is a sentence or paragraph that states the focus — the main point — of the story. It should tell in a nutshell what the story is about and why it is newsworthy. The term was coined more than 50 years ago by *The Wall Street Journal* in a memo to its staff. The memo said a story must have one central theme that must be expressed in a "nutshell summary" high in the story. The concept of the nut graph has since become a standard formula for all news stories.

In a hard-news story with a direct summary lead, the lead contains the focus, so you don't need a separate nut graph. But the nut graph is crucial when a story starts with a feature lead because the reader has to wait for a few paragraphs to find out the reason for the story.

The nut graph should be placed high in the story, generally by the third to fifth paragraph. But if the lead is very compelling, the nut graph could come later. Rigid rules can ruin good writing.

Anecdotal lead

SANTA CRUZ — Until Hollywood calls, film major Wesley Adkins said he's OK with being a struggling artist. But by the time he graduates, the junior may wish he was a business major. Already his student loans total $25,000.

The cost of attending UC Santa Cruz, or for that matter most any university, has skyrocketed over the past three years. . . . More and more students are leaving school with huge financial burdens.

— *Santa Cruz* (California) *Sentinel*

Nut graph

Quotes or Sound Bites

After the lead, the body of the story should support the focus with information from sources, quotes or facts that explain the main idea. If you have a good quote or sound bite from a source, it should be placed high in the story after the lead or nut graph. The first quote that backs up the lead is called the "lead quote" or the "augmenting quote." It is usually the strongest quote you have, and it supports the concept in the lead without repeating the same information or wording. In broadcast news a good sound bite following the lead is equivalent to the lead quote.

A lead quote isn't required in all stories, but a strong quote or sound bite helps make the story more interesting. If the lead does not contain all the information about who, what, when, where, why and how, these questions should be answered in the body of the story. In this example, the lead quote is in the third paragraph, and the nut graph is in the fifth paragraph.

Lead quote

When he discusses drinking, tragedy and lawsuits with people nationwide, Dave Westol gets rapt attention by flashing a picture of grim young men in dark suits and ties — their hands folded. Their heads bowed.The picture shows the funeral of 19-year-old University of Kansas freshman Jason Wren, who was pronounced dead from alcohol poisoning on March 8, 2009, in his fraternity, Sigma Alpha Epsilon.

"I throw that slide up, and the audience inevitably becomes silent," said Westol, an official for the Fraternal Information and Programming Group, a non-profit that educates Greeks nationwide on risky behaviors and legal liabilities.

Before Jason Wren died, he was best known for his big heart and fun-loving nature. He was outgoing. He was athletic. He played for the KU lacrosse club.

Nut graph

But since his death, Wren is better known for how and where he died. His name has taken on a national and local role as an attention-grabber for experts like Westol and a wake-up call for universities. He is just one student among grim statistics that show significant alcohol abuse among college students — especially those at the University of Kansas — and even more abuse among fraternity members nationwide.

— GARTH SEARS, *University Daily Kansan*

Impact

Whenever possible, the writer should explain how the news affects readers. The "impact" sentence or paragraph should answer these questions: What is the significance of this story? What in the story makes the reader care? Sometimes the impact is explained in the lead or in the nut graph; sometimes it is lower in the story, in an explanatory paragraph.

Not all stories can show direct impact on readers, but they should all have a clear paragraph explaining the reason for the story. In some stories, such as police stories, the impact is that the news happened in the community and should be of interest to local residents.

Home users are now the top target for Internet attackers, who are launching increasingly sophisticated attacks.

That's the sobering warning from Symantec's latest Internet security threat report, released today.

— *The Vancouver Sun*

Online news sites provide impact in several interactive ways: Databases let readers search statistics about education, crime or property values in their communities; interactive calculators give readers a chance to figure what a tax increase might cost them; feedback questions, polls and blogs ask readers to comment on issues. Social media sites encourage readers and viewers to interact with the news.

Attribution

Where did you get the information? Who told you these facts? How can the reader be sure what you say is true? Attribution, which identifies the source of the information, can provide those answers. With the proliferation of social media (blogs, Twitter and other sites), it is even more difficult to determine the validity of information. Attribution adds credibility for the story.

You need to attribute all quotes — exact wording of statements that people made — and much information that you did not witness. If the information is common knowledge or indisputable, you do not have to attribute it. However, you need to attribute any statements that express opinions.

A driver distracted by her cellphone.

| *No attribution needed — common knowledge* | Millions of people in the U.S. and other countries use cell phones. | Drivers using cell phones are four times more likely to cause a crash than other drivers, according to a Harvard University study. | *Attribution needed — not common knowledge* |

The attribution should be in the lead for controversial or accusatory information, but in many other cases it can be delayed so it doesn't clutter the lead. Police stories often have attribution in the lead, especially if you get the information by telephone or if the information is accusatory:

| *Lead with attribution* | ST. PETERSBURG, Fla. — A 15-year-old boy was stabbed twice in the chest Thursday afternoon when he | apparently tried to break up a fight in a crowded parking lot at Northeast High School, authorities said. |

Backup   Police and school officials said the stabbing, believed to have occurred after one student took another's hat, was the first they could recall at Pinellas County schools.

— *Tampa Bay Times/St. Petersburg* (Florida) *Times*

In the next example, general attribution is in the lead, but the specific attribution is in the third paragraph. The sources for the study are too cumbersome to use in the lead.

Lead with general attribution   A smoky bar may be more harmful to your health than a city street filled with diesel truck fumes, according to a new study.
Smoky bars and casinos have up to 50 times more cancer-causing particles than air in highways and city streets clogged with diesel trucks, the study says.

Indoor air pollution virtually disappears when smoking is banned, according to the study published in the *Journal of Occupational and Environmental Medicine* and partially funded by the Robert Wood Johnson Foundation of New Jersey, a philanthropic organization devoted to health care.   *Backup with specific attribution*

Context/Background

Is there any history or background the reader needs in order to understand how a problem or action occurred? Put the story in perspective, or context. If the story is about a fire, accident or crime, how many other incidents of this type have occurred in the community recently? Most stories need some background to explain the action, as in this example:

Lead   Lock your doors. That's the advice of University of Iowa security chief Dan Hogan in light of recent reports of a prowler slipping into unlocked dormitory rooms at night.

Lead quote   "I can't stress that enough," he said. "It's a very serious situation."

Background   Since Aug. 24, there have been six reports of a man entering women's rooms between 3 a.m. and 5:30 a.m. Five incidents were in Burge Hall and one was in Currier Hall.

Two times the man touched the sleeping women, Hogan said. But there was no force or violence. In each instance the man ran when the woman discovered him.

More recently, a woman in Burge Hall heard someone at her door. She opened it and saw a man running down the hall, Hogan said.

— VALOREE ARMSTRONG, *Iowa City Press-Citizen*

Elaboration

Supporting points related to the main issue constitute "elaboration." These can be statements, quotes or more detail to explain what happened, how and why the problem or action occurred, and reactions to the event.

In this part of the story, seek other points of view to make sure you have balance and fairness. A story based on one source can be too biased. The preceding story about the University of Iowa continued with more explanation:

> George Droll, director of residence services, said main doors to the halls were locked from midnight to 6 a.m. But each resident has a key. Some floors have 24-hour visitation.
>
> Often students feel more secure than they should because the buildings are large and are home to many of their friends, he said.

Ending

The most common type of ending includes one of these elements: future action, a statement or quote that summarizes but does not repeat the previous information or more elaboration. If the future action is a key factor in the issue, it should be placed higher in the story. Avoid summary endings that repeat what you have already said. In a basic news story, end when you have no more new information to reveal.

The ending on the Iowa story follows the residence director's comments about why students feel secure in large buildings where they have friends:

> *Summary*   "That's a strength, but it can also
> *quote ending*   be a weakness in terms of people
>   securing their rooms," Droll said.

Fairness and Accuracy

If the story involves conflict, you should always get comments from both or all sides of an issue. Avoid one-source stories. Also, make sure you attribute your sources, including information you use from websites, other news organizations and quotes or statements from people you interview.

Visuals

Visual elements such as photographs, charts and other graphic illustrations are crucial to news presentation in print and online information. Video is also a major asset for digital media. Visuals also enhance news releases or media kits in public relations. Here are some other visual elements used to enhance news stories:

MULTIMEDIA COACH

FOCUS IS CRUCIAL in print, broadcast and online news. If the focus of the story is unclear to broadcast viewers, they will turn to another channel. If the focus in an online story is not clear in the headline or summary blurb, readers may not even click into your online story. Ask yourself these questions:

- What is the most important idea that will entice viewers to listen to your story or online readers to click into your story?

- Before you write your story for any medium, write a focus sentence in fewer than 35 words. This also can be the lead of your story for an online site or a broadcast story. Now convert the focus into a headline of no more than six words for an online site. Here's an example:

Headline: Campus booze arrests jump 24 percent

Summary blurb under the headline: Sex, drug, weapons violations also increase.

- Online stories often have comment boxes or polls seeking readers' feedback. If you were seeking feedback on the main idea of your story, what question would you ask? The question may give you a clue for finding your focus.

- Have you answered the questions of who, what, where, when, how and why, and explained the impact on the reader or viewer?

- If your story is about a conflict, have you contacted sources on both sides of the issue?

Summary Blurb

A paragraph or sentence summarizing the story is called a "summary blurb." It is placed below the headline.

In online news the summary and lead of the story may be the same because the blurb may be on an index page linking to stories inside the site. But in print stories when the blurb is published directly over the story, the lead does not have to repeat the summary. It can be more creative, as in this example:

Headline
Summary blurb

Papers a lesson in criminology
A USF professor follows a paper trail to a former student wanted on charges he sold term papers to criminology majors.

A. Engler Anderson's term papers weren't just bad. They were a crime, said one professor.

Anderson, 31, is wanted on charges that he sold term papers to two University of South Florida students.

Their major?

Criminology.

The charge — selling a term paper or dissertation to another person — is only a second-degree misdemeanor,

but if he is caught, Anderson
will be held without bail
because he failed to appear
for a court hearing this week.

— Tampa Bay Times/
St. Petersburg (Florida) *Times*

The story then explains how William Blount, chairman of the USF Criminology Department, received two papers that he thought were "awful" and then discovered they were written by Anderson, a former student.

Pull Quote

A good pull quote might be broken out of the story, placed in larger type and used as a point of entry to entice the reader. Although an editor may decide which quotes to pull for graphic display, when you write your story, consider which quotes could be used to entice readers. Then use your best quotes high in your story. In a story explaining sexual harassment, this "pull quote" from an employment lawyer was used for emphasis:

I think what the law says is that if you hit on me, and I say, "No way, Buster," I'm entitled to have you accept my rejection of you, and it shouldn't interfere with my work.

— JUDITH VLADECK, Employment Lawyer

Facts or Highlights Box

Information from a story is sometimes set off in a "facts box," also called a "highlights box," for reading at a glance or providing key points in the story. A facts or highlights box can include the dates in a chronology or the main points of a proposal or meeting. It is especially useful for breaking statistics out of a story. Although some information from a facts box may be crucial to include in the story, the writer should guard against too much repetition. Facts boxes are effective in newspaper and online stories as well as in magazine and public relations articles.

CNN uses highlights in a list at the top or on the side of major news stories on its website. The highlights are usually four to five bulleted facts from the story to give readers a quick summary of the main points as in this story about online dating:

STORY HIGHLIGHTS

- Some dating experts say online dating has sapped our social skills
- Approaching people and starting conversations can be hard if you're not used to it

- Users mistake social media for being social, says body language expert Blake Eastman
- Practice talking to others by striking up a conversation in the coffee line

— CNN

Here is an example of a facts box that accompanied a story from *The Kansas City Star* about the dangers of lightning. These statistics were not repeated in the story:

LIGHTNING DEATHS AND INJURIES

Figures below were compiled from 35 years of U.S. lightning statistics.

Location of incident
- Open fields, recreation areas: 27%
- Under trees (not golf): 14%
- Water-related (boating, fishing, swimming, etc.): 8%
- Golf/golf under trees: 5%

Month of most incidents
- July 30%

Deaths by state, top five
- Florida, Michigan, Texas, New York, Tennessee

Source: National Oceanic and Atmospheric Administration

Infographic

A chart, map, graph or other illustration meant to provide information is an "infographic." Examples of infographics are diagrams of plane crashes or major accidents and illustrations explaining how something works. The most common type of infographic, called a "location map," pinpoints the location of an accident, a crime or any other major news event.

It is the reporter's responsibility to supply the information for those maps. So when you report a story that may need a map, make sure you gather information about the exact location of the event by noting the streets, the number of feet or yards from a spot where an explosion or major crime occurred, or any other crucial information that would help readers visualize the location. Stories for online delivery might use Google maps or other programs to illustrate the location.

Many of the visual elements — such as headlines, boxes of information and summary sentences — are written by editors. However, reporters are expected to plan photos for their stories and to provide information for some of the graphics. When a chart, a graphic or a facts box will accompany your story, consider whether the story needlessly duplicates information that could be presented visually. So in the writing process, don't just think about information to put into your story; think also about information to pull out for visual devices.

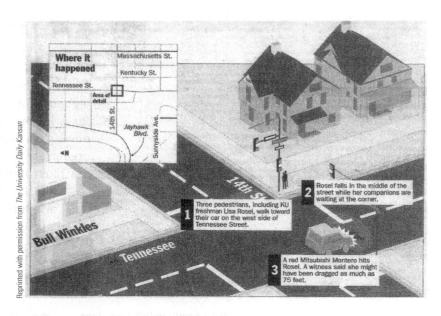

Reprinted with permission from The University Daily Kansan

Infographic by Andrew Rohrback, *The University Daily Kansan.*

Audio and Video for Online Delivery

Audio and video are crucial for television news stories, but if you are writing the story for a print publication, you still should think about sound and sight. Most news organizations have websites these days, so you should plan to record the interviews for posting on the organization's website. Also more news organizations — print and broadcast — are delivering information for mobile media in text and video forms.

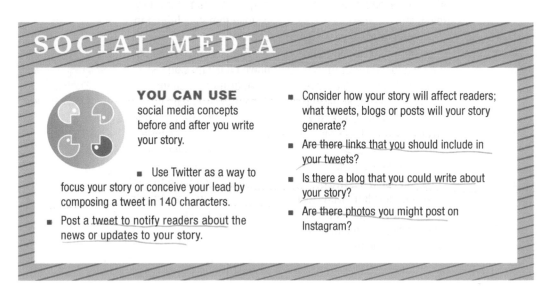

SOCIAL MEDIA

YOU CAN USE social media concepts before and after you write your story.

■ Use Twitter as a way to focus your story or conceive your lead by composing a tweet in 140 characters.

■ Post a tweet to notify readers about the news or updates to your story.

■ Consider how your story will affect readers; what tweets, blogs or posts will your story generate?

■ Are there links that you should include in your tweets?

■ Is there a blog that you could write about your story?

■ Are there photos you might post on Instagram?

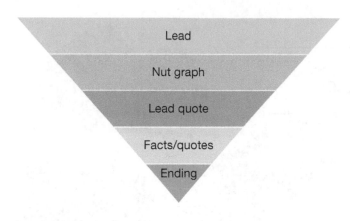

Lead

Nut graph

Lead quote

Facts/quotes

Ending

Inverted Pyramid.

EXAMPLE OF BASIC NEWS STORY

The following example will show you how elements of the basic news story fit together for print or online delivery. This is a standard news story with a summary lead. The story is organized in "inverted pyramid" form, giving the most important information first and the rest in descending order of importance.

This story contains most of the basic news elements described in this chapter.

Four families left homeless by Tacoma apartment blaze

Summary lead (who, what, where)

Four families were left homeless after fire raced through an apartment complex in this Tacoma suburb, officials said.

Backup

No one was injured, but a pet cat died in the two-alarm blaze, firefighters said Monday. About 12 people had to be relocated.

Background/ elaboration

The fire started yesterday in an upper corner unit at the Meadow Park Garden Court and spread to a two-bedroom apartment through a common attic, University Place Assistant Fire Chief Lynn Wilbur said.

The blaze destroyed two units and damaged two others.

Reaction

Rosemary Hurlburt, whose apartment was gutted, said she and her two daughters were at a convenience store when the fire started. The family lost a lot of new possessions, she said.

"We just got new stuff. My 5-year-old daughter just had a birthday party. We just got her a brand-new bunk bed set," Hurlburt said.

Investigators had not confirmed the cause of the fire, but Wilbur said the blaze may have been started by a stove that was left on in one unit.

"The pots were melted down on it," he said.

Ending: future action

Apartment manager Steve Edwards said he couldn't relocate the families in the apartment complex because it was filled to capacity. Some of the residents may have to seek shelter through the American Red Cross, he said.

— The Oregonian

ETHICAL DILEMMA: What do you do if a source tells you not to quote him at the end of an interview or after the interview but before you go to press or on the air?

Ethical values: Decency, fairness, accuracy, responsibility to readers and sources, credibility.

Ethical guidelines: The decision is more difficult when sources want to withdraw their quotes after you conduct an interview. Try to avoid this situation by making it clear at the start of your interview that you want your source to go "on the record." If you still encounter a source who wants to retract a quote, you can negotiate with the source, or you can insist that you have a right to use the information because you identified your purpose clearly. But that may not help you.

Here are some questions to consider when asked to withdraw a quote:

- Are you being fair to your source?
- Are you being fair to your readers?
- Are the quotes essential to your story?

These are tough decisions. You can read more about what constitutes "on the record" and "off the record" or "not for attribution" in the chapter on Interviewing Techniques.

QUOTES AND ATTRIBUTION

Readers come to the newspaper the way they come to a party. They want to talk to interesting people. Long quotes usually are not very interesting.

—SUSAN AGER, *Writing Coach*

Good quotes can back up your lead and substantiate information in your story. In addition, good quotes let the reader hear the speaker. But boring quotes can bog down stories. If they repeat what you have already said, it's better to paraphrase or eliminate them. In a broadcast story, sound bites take the place of quotes.

Susan Ager, a former columnist and writing coach for the *Detroit Free Press*, said reporters should consider quotes as the spice of the story, not the meat and potatoes.

Plagiarism

Copying the words of other writers is plagiarism, a cardinal sin in journalism. Even if you paraphrase information you receive from other publications, you are plagiarizing if you don't attribute it. Plagiarism is grounds for dismissal at most news organizations. If you take information from written or online resources, make sure you attribute it.

Plagiarism applies to blogs, tweets and other online sites as well. If you copy information from a source without needed attribution on your blog, you are still guilty of stealing information.

When to Use Direct Quotes

Here are some guidelines for deciding when to use direct quotes:

- Is the quote interesting and informative?
- Can the quote back up the lead, the nut graph or a supporting point in your story?
- Is the quote memorable without referring to your notes? If so, it's probably a good quote.
- Do your quotes repeat your transitions? In broadcast news avoid introducing a sound bite with a transition that repeats what the source will say. That is called "parroting," a technique that should be avoided.
- Can you state the information better in your own words? If so, paraphrase.
- Does the quote or sound bite advance the story by adding emotion, interest or new information?
- Are you including the quote or sound bite for your source or for your readers or viewers? That is the most important question of all. The readers' and viewers' interests always take priority.

Here are some types of quotes or sound bites to avoid:

- Avoid direct quotes when the source is boring or the information is factual and indisputable. For example, a city official who says, "We are going to have our regular monthly meeting Tuesday night" is not worth quoting directly.
- Avoid any direct quote or sound bite that isn't clearly worded. If a government official says something in bureaucratic language that you don't fully understand, ask for clarification and then paraphrase.
- Avoid accusatory quotes from politicians or witnesses of a crime. If you intend to include any accusations, get a response from the person accused. A direct quote or sound bite does not save you from libel. If police or other criminal justice officials make accusations in an official capacity, you may use direct or indirect quotes provided that you attribute them carefully.
- Avoid quotes that don't relate directly to the focus and supporting points in your story.

How to Write Quotes

On the surface, writing quotes may seem easy: You just write down what somebody else has said. The format for writing sound bites in a broadcast script differs from print style and will be explained in the broadcast chapter. For print and online delivery, observe the following guidelines if you want to use quotes correctly and effectively:

- Always put commas and periods inside the quotation marks:

  "There are no exceptions to that rule," the professor said.

- A question mark and other punctuation marks go within the quotation marks if the punctuation refers to the quoted material; otherwise, they go outside the quotation marks:

  He asked, "When does the semester end?"
  Who said, "I hope it ends soon"?

- Each new speaker must be quoted in a separate paragraph:

  "Never place quotes from two speakers in the same paragraph," Professor Les Polk said.
    "Even if it's short?" Janet Rojas asked.
    "Yes," Polk answered.

- Don't attribute a single quote more than once. If you have two quoted sentences from the same speaker in the same paragraph, you need only one attribution:

  "You must study your Associated Press Stylebook," the professor said. "You will have a test Tuesday on material in the first 30 pages."

- "When the quote is two or more sentences in the same paragraph, attribute it after the first sentence," Carol English said. "Don't make the reader wait until the end of the paragraph to discover who is speaking."
- Attribution in the middle of a quote is acceptable, but not preferable if it interrupts the thought:

  "It isn't the best way," he said, "to use a direct quote. But it is all right if the quote is very long. However, it's better to put it at the end of a complete sentence."

- Don't tack on long explanations for the quote. If the quote isn't clear by itself, paraphrase. For example, avoid the following:

> When asked how he learned about the fire at his apartment complex, he said, "I heard the news on the television."

- Just as bad:

> "I heard the news on the television," he said when asked how he learned about the fire at his apartment complex.

- Instead, introduce the quote with a transition:

> He was at a friend's house when the fire broke out at his apartment. "I heard the news on television," he said.

- Limit the use of partial quotes. They are acceptable when the whole quote would be cumbersome, but too many partial quotes make a story choppy. And the reader wonders what was left out. If you follow a partial quote with a full one, you must close the partial quote:

> McDonald says he sees the government as "weak and inept" and fraught with "major-league problems."
> "There's a crisis in our leadership," McDonald says.

- Limit the use of ellipses, which are sets of dots that indicate part of the quote is missing.

Use three dots for the middle of a sentence and four (one of which is the period) for an ellipsis at the end of the sentence. Use the ellipsis when you are condensing whole quotes or long passages from which you delete several sentences. It's useful for stories about speeches or excerpts from court rulings. Be careful not to leave out material that would change the speaker's meaning.

When to Use Attribution All quotes must be attributed to a speaker. In addition, you need to attribute information you paraphrase. In print and online writing, the attribution may follow the quote, but in broadcast writing, the attribution must come first. In many cases in broadcast news, the name and title of a speaker may be superimposed over the video on the bottom screen, so you don't always need to introduce the source in a sound bite.

Here are some guidelines for material you need and don't need to attribute:

■ You don't need to attribute facts that are on record or are general knowledge:

> The trial will resume tomorrow.
>
> A suspect has been arrested in connection with the slaying of a 16-year-old girl in Hometown last week.

■ You don't need to attribute information that you observed directly:

> The protesters, carrying signs and chanting songs, gathered in the park.

■ You don't need to attribute background information established in previous stories about the same subject:

> The defendant is accused of killing the three Overland Park women whose bodies have never been found.

■ You need to attribute information you receive from sources if it is accusatory, opinionated or not substantiated, and if you did not witness it — especially in crime and accident stories. However, you don't always have to attribute everything in the lead. The following statement is factual, so no attribution is needed:

> A 2-year-old girl escaped injury when a mattress she was sitting on caught fire and engulfed the studio apartment in flames at Wheatshocker Apartments.

■ Attribution is needed here, however, because the cause of fire is accusatory and the amount of damage is speculative:

> A 2-year-old girl playing with a lighter started the fire at the Wheatshocker Apartments near Wichita State University that caused about $400,000 in damages, fire authorities said Thursday.

"She was just kind of flicking it, and she caught the bedding on fire," said fire Capt. Ed Bricknell.

—The Wichita **(Kansas)** *Eagle*

Wording of Attribution For most hard-news stories, the word *said* is preferable. Although there are many synonyms for *said*, they make the reader pause. *Said* does not. Don't worry about overusing the word.

- Strictly speaking, *said*, the past tense, should be used if someone said something once. If someone always says the same thing, use *says,* the present tense. However, that rule is very restrictive. You could also just use *said* for most hard-news stories and use *says* for feature stories (if *says* seems appropriate to the context). In either case, keep the tense you choose throughout the story; if you start with *says*, continue using it for the rest of the story. In broadcast writing "says" gives more immediacy.

- Avoid substitutions for *said,* such as *giggled, laughed* or *choked*. It's almost impossible to giggle, laugh or choke at the same time you are speaking. If you want to convey the emotion, write it this way: "I'm going to try out for the circus," she said, laughing.

- Use *according to* when you are referring to inanimate objects: "*according to* a study." It is acceptable to say "*according to* police," but not preferable. People talk. Use *said* or *says* when you attribute to people; *according to* is vague.

- Normal speaking order is preferable. You should place *said* after the name or pronoun. If the person has a long title, *said* can be placed before the name and title.

Awkward: "Normal speaking order is preferred," said the professor.

Preferable: "Normal speaking order is preferred," the professor said.

Overview Attribution This is a technique that allows you to attribute information to one speaker for several paragraphs without attributing each statement or each paragraph. It is useful when you are giving a chronology of events, as in a police story. But if you change speakers, you need to use attribution for the new speaker. The overview attribution is a brief statement followed by a colon.

Police described the incident this way:

Witnesses said this is what happened:

Police gave this account:

Second References The second time you refer to a source in your story, use the last name only. If you have several sources — or two sources with the same last name, such as a husband and wife — use the full name again or an identifying phrase:

> James Jones, the director of public safety, was injured in a three-car crash yesterday. Jones was taken to Memorial Hospital, where he was treated for bruises and released.

If you have mentioned several other people and want to get back to Jones later in the story, remind the reader who Jones is by using his title:

> Public Safety Director Jones said he would return to work Monday.

Titles When a person's title is used before the name, capitalize it, as in the preceding example. When it is used after the name, use lowercase letters:

> Police Chief Ron Olin said the crime rate has gone down.
>
> Olin, police chief of Lawrence, said the crime rate has gone down.

Courtesy Titles Most newspapers and TV scripts no longer use courtesy titles — Mr., Miss, Mrs. or Ms. — before people's names. There are exceptions. *The New York Times* and *The Wall Street Journal* still use courtesy titles. Other newspapers use them in obituaries. For general purposes in this book, courtesy titles will be eliminated unless they are contained in examples from newspapers that still use them.

EXERCISES

1 Basic news story: Write a story based on the following information. Write a focus sentence before you start your story. For this story, your focus sentence should be the results of the study. If you want a lead that gets directly to the point, your focus sentence could also be your lead.

Once you have written a focus sentence, add a suggestion for visual presentation — a photograph, chart, facts box, video excerpt or other graphic illustration. Decide what facts, if any, should be duplicated in the story and the graphic. Then organize the story by placing facts, quotes and elaboration in an order, with the most important information near the top of the story and the least important material near the bottom; and perhaps end with a good quote. The following material is based on a story from *The* (San Bernardino, California) *Sun*.

Who/what: A study comparing the death and accident rates of left- and right-handed people.

When: Study was conducted last year and was reported in today's edition of the *New England Journal of Medicine.*

Where: Study was conducted by Diane Halpern, a psychology professor at California State University at San Bernardino, and Stanley Coren, a researcher at the University of British Columbia.

Why: To determine why fewer left-handed people are among the elderly population.

How: Researchers studied death certificates of 987 people in two Southern California counties. Relatives were queried by mail about the subjects' dominant hands.

Backup information: The following points are not necessarily in the order they should be used in your story.

The researchers found that the average age at death for right-handed people was 75 and for left-handed people, 66; left-handed people represent 10 percent of the U.S. population; right-handed females tend to live six years longer than left-handed females, and right-handed males live 11 years longer than left-handed males; left-handed people were four times more likely to die from injuries while driving than right-handers and six times more likely to die from accidents of all kinds.

Halpern said, "The results are striking in their magnitude." Halpern is right-handed.

She said her study should be interpreted cautiously. "It should not, of course, be used to predict the life span of any one individual. It does not take into account the fitness of any individual." Left-handed women die around age 72; right-handed women die around age 78. Left-handed men die about age 62; right-handed men die about age 73.

"Some of my best friends are left-handed," Halpern said. "It's important that mothers of left-handed children not be alarmed and not try to change which hand a child uses," she said. "There are many, many old left-handed people. We knew for years that there weren't as many old left-handers," Halpern said. "Researchers thought that was

because in the early years of the century, most people born left-handed were forced to change to their right hands. So we thought we were looking at old people who used to be left-handed, but we weren't. The truth was that there simply weren't many left-handers left alive, compared to right-handers."

"Almost all engineering is geared to the right hand and right foot," Halpern said. "There are many more car and other accidents among left-handers because of their environment."

2 Reaction story: Interview at least three students on campus who are left-handed. Ask them what problems they encounter because they are left-handed. Using the study in Exercise 1 as a focus for your story, write a reaction story with the students' comments. Make sure you get the full names of the students, their majors and year of study (freshman, sophomore and so on), so you can identify them properly in the story.

3 Find the focus: Using your local or campus newspaper or an online news site, find the focus paragraph (the nut graph) in three news stories on the front page or main screen of the online site.

4 Online focus exercise: Access an online news site for your community or for a national source, such as *www.cnn.com*, *www.msnbc.com* or *www .foxnews.com*, and discuss the following points:

- Do the headlines and/or summary blurbs clearly identify the main point of the story?

- Compare the headlines of major news stories in two online sites.

- Which headlines entice you to click into the story? Why?

- How long are the average online headlines?

- Do summary blurbs add or detract from your interest in reading the full story? How much information should the summary blurb reveal about the story? What type of summary blurbs do you prefer: a single sentence, a paragraph or a few paragraphs?

5 Quotes and attribution exercise: Check the appropriate column to indicate whether attribution is or is not needed:

**Not
Needed   Needed**

☐   ☐   **a**   Two leading figures in the growing national debate about political correctness on American college campuses will be at the University of South Florida in Tampa tonight.

☐   ☐   **b**   Dieting doesn't work for the vast majority of people.

☐   ☐   **c**   A 40-year-old woman went berserk in her ex-boyfriend's apartment early Monday, shooting him to death with seven shots from two guns.

☐   ☐   **d**   Members of a local gay rights group protested Thursday in support of a gay University of Tampa student's efforts to take an Army ROTC class.

☐   ☐   **e**   City council members voted unanimously Thursday to increase city fines for prostitution.

☐   ☐   **f**   A York College sophomore died early yesterday after drinking at a dormitory party.

☐   ☐   **g**   Alumni members of Skull and Bones, an all-male secret society at Yale University, have voted to admit women.

6 Enterprise: Attend an event on your campus, and write a basic news story about it. (Look in your campus newspaper or your university's website for a list of activities that will take place during the week, or check bulletin boards for notices of activities.) Talk to friends about other story possibilities. Here are some other possible topics for a news story at the start of the semester: a new course, problems that students are having enrolling in certain courses, a new club or organization on campus or a student support group.

7 Social media assignment: Search Twitter.com for tweets on topics of stories you have written or would like to write for a college publication (in print, broadcast or online). List at least three ideas for stories you could write that would be of interest to your audience.

 MindTap

FEATURED ONLINE ACTIVITIES: Log on to the MindTap for Rich's Writing and Reporting News to access a variety of robust additional material, including this chapter's learning objectives, activities, comprehension quizzes, and more. Be sure to check out the "Bank Robbery" NewsScene scenario for an interactive writing exercise that will help to reinforce many of the themes presented in this chapter.

CHAPTER 3
Social Media

SOCIAL
MEDIA

Our social tools are not an improvement to modern society; they are a challenge to it.

—**CLAY SHIRKY**, *Here Comes Everybody: The Power of Organizing Without Organizations*

© Michael D Brown/Shutterstock.com

COACHING TIPS

Provide links to related articles or sources.

Write a lead that gets to the **main point quickly.**

Write **short sentences.**

Use **strong verbs.**

Write in a **conversational tone,** the way you would tell your reader a story.

Keep your **blog short.**

Write a **clear headline** for your blog.

Plan **images or videos** for tweets and posts.

T

HE MORE YOU KNOW, THE LESS YOU MAY HAVE TO WRITE ABOUT IT.
"Short is in.

"Blogs are in.

"And.

"Tweets.

"R.

"In."

That is how Jodi Enda, a writer for *American Journalism Review*, summarized reporting and writing in this age of social media.

Social networking has changed the nature of journalism. Once a venue primarily for keeping up with friends, social networking sites are now essential journalism tools for finding sources and sharing information with the public.

New social media sites and applications are also proliferating. Twitter and Facebook lead the pack, but they've been joined by several other sites for posting images, videos and text.

DEFINING SOCIAL MEDIA

What is social media? Traditional media are print, broadcast or online forms of publication. Social media are Web-based technologies that provide ways people may connect, create and share content. With traditional media, people are receivers; with social media they are contributors.

Social media guru Clay Shirky, a New York University professor, says "user-generated" content revolutionizes communication by shifting power from the select few who have publishing capabilities to everyone. In his book *Here Comes Everybody: The Power of Organizing Without Organizations*, he writes:

The media landscape is transformed, because personal communication and publishing, previously separate functions, now shade into one another. Communications media was between one sender and one recipient. This is a one-to-one pattern — I talk and you listen, then you talk and I listen. Broadcast media was between one sender and many recipients, and the recipients couldn't talk

Robert Neff/Creative Common

Social media became a crucial part of the 2012 election in this Republican Party command center.

back. This is a one-to-many pattern — I talk, and talk, and talk, and all you can do is choose to listen or tune out. The pattern we *didn't* have until recently was many-to-many, where communications tools enabled group conversation. Everyone is a media outlet.

REPORTING WITH SOCIAL MEDIA

Social media have become vital resources for breaking news in major news events, especially during disasters. For the past few years, the Pulitzer Prize Board has recognized the importance of social media by awarding prizes to news organizations that have used these tools.

Here are some of the social media reporting techniques the award-winning news organizations used:

- *The Denver Post* won the Pulitzer Prize in 2013 for its coverage of a mass shooting at a movie theater in Aurora, Colorado. "The entire first day of the massacre was published on our digital platforms with updates virtually by the minute. Our social media team was aggressive and creative," the *Post* wrote in its Pulitzer entry. The social media coverage included tweets, photos, videos, interactive elements, and a live blog featuring conversations with reporters and community members on Facebook.

- *The Hartford* (Connecticut) *Courant*, a Pulitzer finalist for breaking news in 2013, explained how it used social media to cover a tragedy at Sandy Hook Elementary School in Newtown, Connecticut, where a gunman killed 20 children and six adults: "We aggressively updated our online story, sent out text messages and emails, posted powerful images, and engaged our readers on Facebook and through Twitter."

One of many homes destroyed by a tornado in Tuscaloosa.

Tim Burkitt/Federal Emergency Management Agency

- *The Tuscaloosa* (Alabama) *News*, winner for breaking news in 2012, was cited by the Pulitzer Prize Board "for its enterprising coverage of a deadly tornado, using social media as well as traditional reporting to provide real-time updates, help locate missing people and produce in-depth print accounts." The *News* also used social media to provide information on emergency resources.

Here are some other guidelines for reporting with social media:

- Research the topic by finding tweets or blogs.

- During the reporting process, post tweets to seek sources and update information.
- Connect with eyewitnesses, and post questions such as these on Twitter or Facebook: Did you witness the event? How do you know that?
- Ask permission before you use any photo or video submitted by users.

FACEBOOK

Those are just a few of the recent examples where social media played a critical role in reporting. But one of the defining moments of social media came with the use of Facebook in the aftermath of the shooting rampage at Virginia Polytechnic Institute in 2007, when 32 people were killed before the assailant shot himself. Telephone communication was limited that day, so students used Facebook to let friends and families know they were safe and to seek information about other students whose fate was not yet known. "To everyone I haven't talked to yet, I'm okay," one student wrote in a Facebook group called "I'm okay at VT." Journalists searched through profiles and blogs on that site and others to find sources and quotes for their stories about the massacre.

Facebook has since become the most popular social media site in the world, with more than 800 million users. If Facebook were a country, it would be the third most populated one in the world, exceeded only by China and India. Although Facebook began as a network to connect with friends, businesses, government agencies and all types of organizations now use it as a way to establish a presence, spread a message and communicate. It is also the largest social networking site among U.S. adults, and almost half of the users get their news from Facebook, according to a report from the Pew Research Center.

Eric Draper/U.S. White House

TWITTER

Twitter has become another crucial tool to report breaking news as it happens. With the limit of 140 characters (including punctuation and spaces) allowed for a message, it might not seem as though you could convey much information, but the brevity of a tweet can be deceptive. Many Twitter posts, called "tweets" are simply headlines that link to full stories — often posted on Facebook pages or websites. You can use abbreviations — a form of shorthand to squeeze in more information. Tweets also feature hashtags, represented by the # symbol, which are used to mark key words or phrases to related topics in other tweets.

The trial of Steven Hayes was an example. The courtroom was packed. Reporters had lined up at 5:30 a.m. to get a seat

Students comfort each other at a convocation at Virginia Tech University to honor the 33 people who died in a campus shooting.

in the small New Haven, Connecticut, courtroom where Hayes was on trial for a grisly crime. He had invaded a physician's home, killed the doctor's wife and two daughters and set the house on fire. The trial wasn't televised. Cameras weren't allowed in the courtroom. But thousands of people witnessed the trial as reporters tapped their smartphones or iPads to send minute-by-minute details of the trial to Twitter.

Consider these tweets with the hashtag #Hayes, which indicates a connection to other tweets about him:

We're in session; #**Hayes** enters glaring at front row of reporters as he moves to his seat.

Judge Blue: "Your fate is now in the hands of others. May God have mercy on your soul."

#**Hayes**: Words can never express what I feel for what I've done.

Twitter is also a way to get sources and eyewitness accounts quickly during a disaster, an accident or any local event. When a man jumped off an overpass on I-45 in Houston, traffic was stopped for three hours, but *Houston Chronicle* readers learned about it shortly after the incident occurred if they checked the Twitter feed at twitter.com/@HoustonChron. From trials to traffic, Twitter connects the community to the newsroom.

Here's how it works:

After you create a Twitter account, you can search for people whose tweets you want to read. To "follow" people or organizations, click the link under their names. That will take you to the Twitter member's home page, where you can see his or her recent tweets. When a username is preceded by the @ sign, it becomes a link to a Twitter page. When you follow certain Twitter users, you will receive their tweets on your Twitter home page. You can also "retweet" various user messages by adding them to your own tweet feed — much the same as you would forward email to a group of people.

Although Twitter is considered a social networking site, it is not limited to social connections. The network is used around the world by media, government agencies and corporations as a way to communicate a lot of information in a little amount of space. Twitter is considered a "microblogging" site, which is just a short form of blogging. For more information on how to use this program, go to Twitter help *support.twitter.com/groups/50-welcome-to-twitter#.*

Writing for Twitter

Twitter readers are scanners, so you need to write tweets like headlines that will grab attention. Tweets are limited to 140 characters, so be cautious of length (although Twitter will keep count and alert you when you try to post). Here are some writing tips:

- Read some Twitter posts before you begin to write.
- Find a focus. What are you trying to say and what is your point?
- Limit your tweet to one main point.

- Put the strongest words at the beginning of your tweet.
- Use strong verbs.
- Don't waste words — cut articles like "and," and "the."
- Use abbreviations only if they are clear. Some common ones are 2, b and u.
- Provide #hashtags, references to similar topics identified by the # symbol.
- Use a link shortening system such as bit.ly to abbreviate Web addresses.
- If tweeting photos, identify people with captions.
- Cite your sources; don't plagiarize.

Sree Sreenivasan, a social media expert who headed digital media for Columbia University, has created a success formula for tweets. "Make sure every one of your tweets has at least one of these qualities: helpful, useful, informative, relevant, practical, actionable, timely, generous, credible, brief, entertaining, fun, occasionally funny."

New social media sites continue to develop. As mobile media gain popularity, more social networking sites will emerge, including geolocation services, such as Foursquare, that can act like guidebooks on your smart phones. The future has no boundaries.

VERIFYING SOCIAL MEDIA

It is easy to find sources with social media, but it may be harder to verify the information they provide. Checking accuracy of tweets or posts during breaking news is more difficult, but just as essential as for any other news story. Try to contact the person who sends a tweet, or get an email address or phone number so you can confirm information.

Steve Buttry, a journalism trainer and digital media specialist, offers these tips for verifying information from tweets and other social media sites:

- Develop Twitter sources that you know are reliable.
- Check the profile of a contributor to Twitter.
- Check whom the person follows and who follows him, as well as who can vouch for this person; and check the person's previous tweets.
- Check the time of a tweet during breaking news to determine whether the person could be an eyewitness, and try to determine the person's location.
- Check for photos, especially during a breaking news event.
- Check whether you can corroborate this account with other users.

CURATION

Creation versus curation: Much of the information you send or receive on social media is what you create or share with others. But posts, pictures and video on social media sites also lend themselves to a way of sharing called "curation." When you gather information from various sources on the Web and organize it around a topic to present or share, you are curating it. And several social media sites have been created for just that purpose. Journalists can use these curation sites by collating photos, tweets, posts and items about a news story, and compiling a composite Web page.

Pinterest This site works like a bulletin board where you can "pin" information you have curated to create a composite page, or you can pin an image or video that will link back to the original website.

Storify Storify is a way to gather tweets, images and posts to create a story. Using the Storify site, you click "Create Story," enter a headline and drag posts from sites like Facebook, YouTube and Twitter into your own story to create a timeline or a story based on the events or information you gather.

Kelly Fincham, assistant professor of journalism at Hofstra University, says she uses Storify in the classroom to help students explore sources and understand context in news. "This is *not* cut-and-paste journalism. This is 21st century journalism which uses social media as dynamic wire postings and lets the reporter curate the content and provide context," she wrote in a guide to Storify. "I think it recreates that sense of discovery that we used to experience in research libraries. . . . We can explore news stories through several different social media streams. We can curate those stories and then show the finished project to the world."

MULTIMEDIA COACH

TECHNIQUES FOR incorporating blogs and comments in a news website are similar for print and broadcast news organizations. In a television newscast, the reporter or anchor will usually refer viewers to the website, where links, polls or surveys and comments are posted; print media organizations also promote additional material on their websites. To encourage reader and viewer interaction via blogs or just comments, consider using some of these techniques.

- Include a poll or quiz on the website.
- Promote added features to the news on the website, such as a photo gallery, full texts of speeches or documents.
- Add multimedia features — audio and video — of news on the website.
- Update your stories frequently, especially for breaking news.
- Offer links on your website to social media sites — Twitter, Facebook and others.

BLOGS

Blogs, short for Web logs, are online journals or columns in which the writer expresses opinions or describes personal experiences. Many media blogs are commentaries about news topics. Although many blogs began as personal journals produced for friends and other people with common interests, they have become valuable ways journalists can find sources. The other advantage of reading blogs for news tips is that they provide insight into what readers and viewers are concerned about, much like letters to the editor.

Blogs also provide sources for human-interest stories on news events. Beat reporters rely on blogs in their fields, and they can get additional help from the site *beatblogging.org*. Most corporate and government agencies also offer blogs where reporters can find valuable information.

With millions of blogs on every conceivable topic, how do you find them? In addition to popular search engines, such as Google and Yahoo!, which feature blog searches, these sites and programs can do the work for you:

- **Technorati:** A search engine that indexes millions of blogs and updates the references by tracking posts and links to them.
- **Permalink:** These are URLs (Web addresses) that link to comments or related sites. They are most often used in blogs.
- **RSS:** The letters stand for "Really Simple Syndication," which is a program that automatically sends information you requested to your computer or digital media player. The RSS online tool can track information that changes, whether it is in blogs or on websites, through an "aggregator," which is a program that compiles the information from the sites you have selected. It basically "feeds" the information to your computer or portable media device. It can be used for news summaries, blogs or podcasts, and audio or video digital files that can be downloaded to your computer or portable media device.
- **Trackbacks:** These links at the end of a blog, like footnotes or references you might put in a term paper, are similar to permalinks. Someone who posts a comment to your blog can insert a link back to his or her comment or related sites, provided that the software for both sites supports trackbacks.

Blogs in Public Relations and Marketing

Blogs are not limited to news and personal sites. Hill & Knowlton, one of the largest public relations/marketing firms in the world, supports blogs and calls them "collective communication." On its website, the company says,

Like many other companies, we believe that blogs have the potential to become powerful communications tools. We have created this community to optimize our consultants' participation in the blogosphere. They can listen to and learn from our audiences, while contributing their own insight and experience. All our bloggers are employees of Hill & Knowlton somewhere in the world and have signed up to a strict code of practice.

PRWeb, a wire service website that distributes news releases, also offers blogs in a blogroll, a list of links to blogs that the service recommends. The Public Relations Society of America offers a number of blogs, including prnewpros for new practitioners, a blog to foster diversity, and another for professionals to share ideas. The student chapter, PRSSA, also provides a blog and a social media toolkit.

Here's some advice from PRSSA on how to write better blogs:

- Decide who your audience is, and tailor the content to it.
- Consider the three C's: clear, concise, compelling.
- Connect with your readers. Comment on their blog posts, and encourage them to comment on yours.

"Blogs will make or break your business," according to Nora Ganim Barnes, author of the study "Behind the Scenes in the Blogosphere: Advice from Established Bloggers." She said that consumers want to talk about products, and if they can't talk to the vendor, they will talk to others online in blogs.

FTC Rules Affecting Bloggers and Advertisers

If you write a blog or post a tweet that endorses a product on a social media site, you have to disclose whether you received cash or gifts, or are employed by the company, according to new guidelines that the Federal Trade Commission imposed in 2009. The guidelines apply to bloggers and other users of social media. The FTC rulings require companies to disclose their relationship with celebrities or other people who endorse their products in advertisements in order to provide consumers with more knowledge about the claims that are being made. Although the FTC guidelines are not limited to social media, it was the first time in 30 years that the commission revised its guidelines regarding testimonials and endorsements for advertisements, a recognition of the impact of social media.

How to Write Blogs

A blog is an online conversation you are having with the reader. Consider it like a telephone conversation; it's a two-way communication where you say something and hope for a response. You may use the first-person voice (I or me) because you are expressing your thoughts, but you should not insert yourself into a news story. Some blogs may just be one or two paragraphs with links to related stories, especially on news items, whereas others can be a complete journal entry.

You don't have to have any technical knowledge to create or publish your own blog. Wordpress does that for you. *Wordpress.com* is free Web software you can use to create your own blogs or websites, but you do need an Internet provider where you can post your blog. Although it started as a blogging system, Wordpress now offers complete content management, and many college newspapers use the program for their websites. Blogger, a free program by Google, is another easy-to-learn site you can use to create and host blogs (*www.blogger.com*).

Here are some tips for writing your blog:

- Be brief. Blogs are not meant to be term papers.
- Write a clear headline that will hook the reader.
- Write a subhead or summary of key points.
- Use a strong lead. Consider a question, an anecdote or a dramatic factual lead such as an unusual statistic.
- Use the word "you" to hook readers.
- Be clear. Use simple sentences and short paragraphs.
- Be focused. A blog should center on one main topic.
- Be careful; check your spelling and grammar. Informal communication in email and blogs tends to be sloppy. Errors in spelling and grammar mar credibility.
- Be interesting. Provide something new or evocative if you are writing an opinion about news. Write about a topic that would be of interest to other people in your age group or community.
- Be accurate and fair. Don't spread rumors or information that may not be truthful. The basic guidelines of accuracy and fairness that apply to news stories apply to blogs as well.
- Target your audience. Consider the people you are trying to reach, and write about topics they would want to read, especially on social network blogs. If it is a personal blog, what do your friends and family want to know? If it is a blog intended for a public audience, ask yourself why anyone would want to read your comments.
- Be conversational. Write as though you are talking to a friend.
- Add links to related sites or other blogs if relevant.
- Add a question or thought at the end that would elicit readers to post their responses to your blog.
- Proofread.

PODCASTS

If you don't want to write a blog, you can hear it or see it by producing it as a podcast. Once a combination term for broadcast and iPod, podcast is now a legitimate word. It has been added to the New Oxford American Dictionary, which defines it as "a digital recording of a radio broadcast or similar program, made available on the Internet for downloading to a personal audio player."

Although the original definition was confined to audio files, definitions and uses of

Courtesy of the Federal Emergency Management Agency

Research and Writing Specialist Ernie Martz (left) and Social Media Specialist Steve Crider (right) record a podcast for the Federal Emergency Management multimedia site.

podcasts have expanded to include video. A video podcast is also called a "vidcast" or "vodcast," but whatever you call it, this form of media is now a common alternative format on news sites as well as social networking sites.

You don't need an iPod, a portable digital media player by Apple Inc., or an MP3 player, which also compresses audio files into digital form, to hear or view podcasts. You can click onto a podcast in your computer and listen to it with software for hearing audio or viewing video. You can also download a podcast to your computer and listen to it or view it with free software such as iTunes, Quicktime or Windows Media Player.

ETHICS

BE CAREFUL what you post on a blog, especially if you are seeking a job. Employers have been known to search popular sites such Twitter and Facebook when they are interviewing job candidates. In addition, posting personal information such as telephone numbers or addresses can make it easy for sexual predators or other undesirable people to contact you, despite attempts by social networking sites to protect privacy.

Here are some other ethical issues relating to social media:

■ **Plagiarism:** Don't take material from other people's blogs or websites and post the information on your blog without attributing it. Everything that is produced in a fixed form (print or online) is protected by U.S. copyright laws. That includes photos and videos — unless you have permission or you receive the information under a Creative Commons license, where the contributor has given permission for the material to be used. Check whether it is authorized for personal use or use with attribution, or whether it is fair use, generally from a government site.

■ **Neutrality:** Should staff reporters for TV news stations and newspapers write blogs that express their personal opinions when they are supposed to be impartial in covering the news? Several news organizations have created policies addressing this issue, such as this one from *The New York Times*: "If you have or are getting a Facebook page, leave blank the section that asks about your political views. . . . Be careful not to write anything on a blog or a personal Web page that you could not write in the Times. Anything you post online can and might be publicly disseminated."

■ Is the information on blogs accurate or based on rumors?

■ Should journalists use sources from social networking sites without contacting the person who posted the information?

■ Should blogs be edited or monitored for standards of taste?

■ How should editors deal with abusive posts on websites that seek comments from readers and viewers? This issue has become a problem as interaction with readers and viewers increases on websites that seek comments, but staff to supervise the websites is limited at most news organizations.

Because blogs and other forms of citizen journalism are evolving, media organizations are still wrestling with solutions to these concerns.

SOCIAL MEDIA

GLOSSARY

- **Apps:** Short for applications, apps are programs to download to phones or tablet computers to access media, music, games or other Web-based items.

- **Blog:** The U.S. dictionary publisher Merriam-Webster defines "blog," as "a website that contains an online personal journal with reflections, comments and often hyperlinks." Also known as "Web logs," or "weblogs," blogs have proliferated to such an extent that they have their own world called a "blogosphere," which is a social network of people who post blogs (bloggers). Other blogs are more like essays commenting on news or issues with links to related articles or sources.

- **Cloud computing:** A way to securely store and retrieve your computer information and software on a Web server; the cloud is a symbol for the Internet.

- **Creative Commons:** A copyright licensing system that allows content creators to specify whether and how they want their material to be shared. All work is automatically copyrighted once it is in fixed form, but under this licensing system the creator may decide whether the work may be used with or without attribution, shared, or used commercially, publicly or privately.

- **Crowdsourcing:** Using a large group of people to help gather or produce content with social media. The technique is often used by news organizations to get information about tragedies, accidents or breaking news stories.

- **Facebook:** The largest social network company based on technology that allows people who join the group to interact and share information. Facebook can include personal pages, group sites and fan pages that gather "friends," people with whom you want to keep in contact.

- **Flickr:** A photo-sharing repository.

- **Foursquare:** A mobile application with a built-in GPS (Global Positioning System). After you "check in" to a location, the application can broadcast your position to other people you choose.

- **Hashtag:** The # symbol used to mark keywords or other related topics in tweets or other social media. You can add a hashtag anywhere in the post to show similar topics such as #jobs for a tweet related to job searches.

- **iPad:** A tablet computer made by the Apple Corp. Other companies also produce tablet computers.

- **iPhone:** A phone, also made by Apple, that was the first to introduce a multitouch screen. This phone is considered a "smartphone" because with a simple touch you can access applications. Other companies also make these phones under different names.

- **LinkedIn:** A business-oriented network generally used for professional profiles and connections.

- **Skype:** A free videoconferencing program, a division of Microsoft, that allows people to communicate by voice and video calls.

- **Twitter:** A social network that limits messages, called "tweets," to 140 characters (including punctuation and spaces).

- **Wiki:** A type of software that allows people to add or edit information on a website.

- **YouTube:** A video-sharing site.

If you want to receive regularly updated information from podcasts of blogs or news, you can subscribe to a website that contains an RSS reader, the program that compiles sites you select and automatically delivers them to your computer or portable digital device.

EXERCISES

1 Word association exercise:
- Write five or 10 words that come to your mind associated with these words (one minute for each word association): snow, happy, sad, dreams, goals, pain.
- Now expand your thoughts to one paragraph (three minutes for each idea): I am afraid of . . . I hope to be . . . The best gift I received . . . My worst experience . . .

2 Blog: Write a blog on a personal topic that you think might be of interest to a campus audience.

You can expand some of the thoughts you just wrote in exercise 1 into a blog or write about a new topic. Add a question at the end to solicit responses to your blog.

3 Twitter following: Create a Twitter account and choose at least five people you want to follow. Study their tweets. Write a critique of the tweeters.

4 Tweets: Cover an event on campus (an athletic event, a lecture, a demonstration or any other event) and tweet about it in real time. If your instructor wishes, critique each other's tweets.

 MindTap

FEATURED ONLINE ACTIVITIES: Log on to the MindTap for Rich's Writing and Reporting News to access a variety of robust additional material, including this chapter's learning objectives, activities, comprehension quizzes, and more!

COACHING TIPS

Use the matchmaking technique: **Ask one source to recommend another** for your topic.

Check previous stories about the subject in your organization's databases.

Check any **records** or documents related to your story.

Check the Internet and social media.

Check the **credibility of websites** before you use information from them.

Attribute sources; **avoid anonymous sources.**

CHAPTER 4
Sources and Online Research

Anonymous sources challenge our credibility with readers.

—**PETER BHATIA**, Editor, *The* (Portland) *Oregonian*

MARK POTTER HAS COVERED STORIES FOR NBC, ABC AND CNN from all over the U.S. and other parts of the world. For many years wherever he went, he took his source book, a worn 7-by-9-inch address book held together by strips of packing tape. He called it his "bible" and said he couldn't function without it.

These days Potter uses Twitter and other social media for contacts, but he still uses a traditional method of cultivating sources for his stories on *NBC Nightly News* and *www. NBCNews.com*. He calls this technique "sponsorship." It is basically a referral system. He gets someone who knows him to sponsor, or recommend, him to the new source, or he introduces himself to a new source by referring to a contact that the source might know.

For example, when Potter was working on a story about the problems of Haitians in Miami, the Haitian refugees were illegal immigrants who were reluctant to talk to him. Potter said they thought he was an immigration officer who might report them to authorities for deportation. So Potter asked a community social worker who had gained the refugees' trust to recommend him to a Haitian who might speak with him. The social worker introduced him to a Haitian named Pierre, but Pierre didn't have the information Potter wanted. So Pierre introduced Potter to his brother-in-law, who then "sponsored" Potter by getting other Haitians to talk to him.

Potter cross-indexes his list of sources three ways — by name, occupation and location. If he wants to contact an FBI agent he previously interviewed in Detroit but whose name he may have forgotten, he looks up the agent's name under "FBI" or "Detroit." Under each listing he records the source's address and telephone numbers for work and home and email addresses.

It's not too early in your career for you to start a list of sources. The people you interview in college, such as professors who are experts on foreign policy or the economy, may be good sources for stories later in your career. Whether you keep your source list in your cell phone, computer or online, you should back it up on a storage device. And although it may seem old-fashioned in these days of digital devices, it's a good idea to have a printed copy of your source lists.

Social media like Twitter and Facebook make it easier to get sources today than in the past, but it isn't as easy to check their validity, especially on deadline.

"Social networks should never be used as a reporting shortcut when another method, like picking up a phone or knocking on a door, would yield more reliable or comprehensive information," according to social media guidelines in the Associated Press Stylebook.

Good reporters still cultivate sources several ways — in person, with records and online resources. You can even find ready-made source books for journalists online, such as an extensive list of qualified

Courtesy of Mark Potter

Mark Potter, NBC reporter (third from left).

experts in numerous fields collected by the Society of Professional Journalists (*www.spj.org/divsource-book .asp*). The National Scholastic Press Association and the Associated Collegiate Press have combined to provide a Student Media Sourcebook (*www.studentpress .org/sourcebook*). You'll find these and other resources on the website for this chapter.

Before you begin reporting for any assignment, check previous stories about the topic in databases and do online research. Most print and broadcast newsrooms maintain databases of stories the newspaper or television station has done, so it is easy to search for previous stories about the person or topic. If you are searching online for a source, check to make sure that the source is the person you want; many people have the same name, and the information you retrieve may not be for the correct source. For example, if you are checking a source in LinkedIn, a network often used by professional people, the profile might include a photo, which is helpful if you know the person. It will also list the person's job title and previous jobs.

When you are assigned to a breaking news event, such as a fire or accident, you may not have time to check previous stories before you leave the office. But you should check them before you begin writing. The building that burned may have had problems with sprinkler systems or previous fires.

Don't rely only on social media for sources. Check sources by telephone or in person when possible.

The same recommendation applies to crime stories. A suspect arrested on charges may have been arrested previously for the same or other charges. If you find a story about a suspect's previous arrest, make sure to find out if the charges were dropped or what happened in the case.

Use caution: Newsroom files and videotapes may not be up to date, and follow-up stories may not have been written or aired about crime suspects. Even more problematic is the Web, which can archive everything, but if the document is not dated, you may not be getting the most accurate information.

HUMAN SOURCES

News writing needs human sources to make the story credible and readable. Information from eyewitnesses and participants lends immediacy to a story, and direct quotes and sound bites make a story interesting. You can find human sources in a number of ways.

- **News releases:** All news releases list a contact person, usually a public information officer or public relations contact. Whenever possible, ask to speak to the people mentioned in the news release.

- **Up and down the ladder:** Who's in charge of the organization or department? You could start at the top by contacting the department head. On many other stories, you should also go down the ladder and try to contact the person closest to the incident. For example, if you are writing a police story, try to contact the officer who was at the scene. If you are writing about a study, contact the professor or researcher who did the study.

- **Names in the news:** If you read or view a news story from a newspaper, telecast, website or social media site, don't just quote the news story. Contact the primary source — the person involved.

- **Administrative assistants:** Get to know officials' administrative assistants, sometimes still called "secretaries."

- **Community and campus leaders:** Find out who are the leaders of groups in your community and campus.

- **Self-sponsorship:** If you have reported and written a previous news story about a subject of interest to the source you are trying to contact, you can sponsor yourself. When you contact the source, introduce yourself by referring to the relevant article or newscast you reported.

- **Matchmaking:** Once you have contacted a source and want to find others, use the matchmaking technique, which is related to the sponsorship method. Ask the source who else you might contact about the situation.

- **Fairness:** If you are writing a story involving conflict, find sources that have the opposing points of view. Do not report any accusations about a person without contacting the target of those comments.

- **Primary and secondary sources:** When you are conducting an interview, if your source says something about another person, particularly if it is derogatory or controversial, make sure that you check with that other person. The first source's statements not only could be wrong; they could also be libelous. You should even check out written information about sources, especially online information, to make sure it is accurate.

- **Blogs:** Postings on the Internet from people who have written blogs about an issue can be good sources for you to contact. Don't consider information from blogs as accurate news. Blogs are usually opinion columns and personal reflections, but they can be valuable for finding human sources.

DATA SOURCES

As more news organizations convert to digital delivery of their publications, data are becoming more common additions to news stories, especially on the Web. In the past databases were primarily used in investigative reporting, but these days data sources are readily available in publishable formats, including charts and infographics.

Data-driven journalism is the future. Journalists need to be data-savvy. It used to be that you would get stories by chatting to people in bars, and it still might be that you'll do it that way some times. But now it's also going to be about poring over data and equipping yourself with the tools to analyze it and picking out what's interesting. And keeping it in perspective, helping people out by really seeing where it all fits together, and what's going on in the country.

— TIM BERNERS-LEE, *Founder Of The World Wide Web. From The Data Journalism Handbook, a free resource at datajournalismhandbook.org*

Getting the data to accompany your story is now a standard part of the reporting process. And getting that data is easier than ever, especially from several government resources.

For example, if you are writing a story about a rape or some burglaries on your campus, you'll want data to answer these questions: How extensive is this problem? How many other crimes have been committed at your school? Your first step should be to check with your university's police department, which is required to keep a record of all crimes and report them to the U.S. Department of Education, where you can also get the information for your school or any others. Access the Campus Safety and Security Data Analysis tool at *ope.ed.gov/security*.

From finding the most popular baby names to block-by-block damage from Hurricane Sandy that devastated parts of New York and New Jersey, you can find the data and infographics at *data.gov*, a U.S. government data site.

And if you are writing about your community or any place you are considering for a job or a new home, you can research all the statistics about it with a few keystrokes at the U.S. Census American FactFinder website (*factfinder2 .census.gov/faces/nav/jsf/pages/index.xhtml*).

With all that information at your fingertips, you can easily add data to your stories. But learning to use data is not a separate skill; it's just part of good reporting.

U.S. Department of Education

Some Colleges and Universities will offer you a tool to help you find crimes on a campus.

data.gov/U.S. Government

From baby names to data about the number of parks in a city, the government data tool can provide databases at your fingertips.

SOCIAL MEDIA

WHEN A SUICIDAL pilot crashed a small plane into an office building in Austin, Texas, the local newspaper gained hundreds of sources in a matter of minutes. Robert Quigley, then social media editor for the *Austin* (Texas) *American–Statesman* newspaper, sent out a Twitter message asking the 20,000 people who follow the paper on its social media site if they had witnessed the incident. Photos and eyewitness accounts poured into the paper from its Twitter users. Social media sites have created opportunities for journalists to connect with the public on an unprecedented level, said Quigley, now senior lecturer at the University of Texas at Austin.

That's just one example of how social media can provide instant sources for journalists on a breaking news story. Twitter, Facebook, YouTube and other social media sites are commonly used sources for journalists. As sources multiply on social media sites, keeping track of them gets more difficult. But for every problem, a new site springs up to offer solutions. These are just two sites that will find or coordinate your sources.

- To search for people on all social network sites or blogs, a search engine called yoName will find them (*www.yoname.com*).

- To find the business or professional background of a source, check LinkedIn (*www.linkedin.com*).

This Census database provides information about population and most other statistics about communities.

U.S. Department of Commerce

ANONYMOUS SOURCES

Many people will be willing to talk to you if you promise not to use their names. An anonymous source is one who remains unnamed. (The terms "anonymous source" and "confidential source" are used interchangeably by most people.) But should you make this promise? Most editors today would say no, unless there is no other way to get the information. And even then, many editors would refuse to grant that immunity from identification. The more you rely on unnamed sources, the less credibility your story has.

The Associated Press policy on anonymous sources is as follows: "Reporters should proceed with interviews on the assumption they are on the record. If the source wants to set conditions, these should be negotiated at the start of the interview. At the end of the interview, the reporter should try once again to move some or all of the information back on the record."

In the past, reporters who promised their sources anonymity had a good chance of honoring their promise even if they were subpoenaed to reveal their sources. Most news organizations successfully fought any court attempts to reveal sources. But in the last few years, judges in several courts penalized reporters by sentencing them to jail for refusing to reveal their sources.

All states except Wyoming offer some protection to journalists from revealing their sources — either by shield laws or precedents from case law, but these state statutes do not apply to federal courts.

For several years bills have been introduced in Congress for a federal shield law that would prohibit federal courts from forcing reporters to reveal their confidential sources. The Free Flow of Information Act 2013, introduced in the Senate and a version in the House of Representatives, would provide some protections for reporters, with exceptions when the information is crucial to prevent terrorism or protect national security. But the issue has become more complicated with the increase in citizen journalism and social media. Who would be considered a journalist? Would everyone who publishes news on a website be protected by such a shield law? These are some of the issues that remain to be resolved.

Despite the problems with anonymous sources, it's unlikely that news organizations will eliminate them altogether. If you must use anonymous sources because you have no other alternative, you should check the information with other sources, preferably ones who will allow use of their names, and check documents. Many sources, named or unnamed, have their own agenda and want to manipulate reporters so the sources can promote their cause. For fairness and balance, it is crucial for reporters to check with other sources to confirm, deny or provide other points of view.

Janet Cooke didn't do that. And she touched off a furor in the newspaper industry that persists years after the incident. Cooke, then a reporter for *The Washington Post*, won the Pulitzer Prize in 1981 for a story called "Jimmy's World," about an 8-year-old heroin addict. There was only one problem: Jimmy didn't exist. When Cooke first discussed the story with her editors, she said she had located the child's mother, who was reluctant to talk. Her editors said she could grant the mother anonymity. Cooke turned in a compelling story about the child and his mother. But when Cooke won the Pulitzer and was profiled in newspapers, some discrepancies in her résumé were discovered. That led to questions about her story. She ultimately admitted that she had made up the story about Jimmy and his mother. The *Post* returned the Pulitzer, and Cooke resigned in disgrace.

Cooke's story wasn't based on an anonymous source; it was a fabricated source. The impact was a crisis of credibility for the press. Newspapers throughout the country began developing policies against using pseudonyms, and many editors banned the use of anonymous sources altogether.

Patricia Smith, a former columnist for *The Boston Globe*, had also been nominated for a Pulitzer Prize. She resigned after the *Globe* discovered that she had fabricated sources and quotes in her columns. In her last column she apologized and explained why she had attributed quotes to people who didn't exist.

"I could give them names, even occupations, but I couldn't give them what they needed most — a heartbeat," she wrote. "As anyone who's ever touched a newspaper knows, that's one of the cardinal sins of journalism: Thou shall not fabricate. No exceptions. No excuses."

Fabrication of sources and other information in news stories surfaced as a problem again in the 1990s and later in several high-profile scandals. Most notorious was the case of Jayson Blair, a reporter for *The New York Times*, who made up quotes, fictionalized scenes and plagiarized material in dozens of the stories he wrote during his four years at the newspaper. After the discovery of this and other stories that were fabricated or plagiarized, Blair resigned in disgrace, and the *Times* published an extensive front-page story about his deception. His scandal is also the subject of a movie, "A Fragile Trust."

Blair's trail of fabrication and plagiarism mirrored the pattern of Stephen Glass, a rising star at *The New Republic*, who was fired after his editor discovered that he had fabricated sources in many of his stories. His deception was discovered when a reporter for an online site questioned a story Glass had written about a convention of hackers. The convention didn't exist, nor did the software company cited in the story. Glass even created a phony website for the nonexistent software company. A complaint from an online magazine spurred the investigation, which revealed that the article was a hoax, and several others Glass had written were also fiction. A few years later, Glass published an autobiographical novel called *The Fabulist* about a reporter who fabricates stories. The Glass story also became the subject of a movie called "Shattered Glass."

ETHICS

ETHICAL DILEMMA: Should you show your story to a source before publication?

Discussion: Most journalists are opposed to prepublication review by a source because of fears that the source may recant statements or may wish to change the copy. Steve Weinberg, an author of several books and former director of the Investigative Reporters and Editors organization, strongly favors checking the story with a source because, he says, it will ensure accuracy. Other journalists have always favored reading parts of a story, especially technical or sensitive information, back to a source.

However, in 2012 *The New York Times* announced that it was banning a practice of

allowing a source to review, approve or edit quotes. A memo published by the paper's public editor said: "The practice risks giving readers a mistaken impression that we are ceding too much control over a story to our sources. In its most extreme form, it invites meddling by press aides and others that goes far beyond the traditional negotiations between reporter and source over the terms of an interview."

If your organization has no objection to such review, do you think it is OK for a source to review part or all of a story?

Ethical guidelines: Fairness, credibility, accuracy. The Society of Professional Journalists Code of Ethics says journalists should "test the accuracy of information from all sources and exercise care to avoid inadvertent error."

When using unnamed sources, you may identify the person with a vague reference, such as "according to one official." Or you might give the person a pseudonym, a false name. Although most editors discourage pseudonyms, they are sometimes allowed in feature stories about sensitive subjects such as rape. But they are rarely used in hard-news stories. It is preferable to use no name or a first name only. If you use a full-name pseudonym, which is not preferred, you should check your local telephone directories to make sure that you aren't using the name of someone in your community. And in all cases, to protect the identity of the source, you must tell the reader that this is a false name.

Despite these well-known cases and policies to prohibit plagiarism, every year more cases of it occur in all types of journalism publications — newspapers, campus publications and news sites, including social media networks. That is another reason journalists should avoid using information from unnamed sources on social media sites.

Promises of Confidentiality Dan Cohen made the issue of anonymous sources a legal matter that affects what journalists can promise sources. He was a public relations executive. In 1982 he gave reporters from the (Minneapolis) *Star Tribune* and the *St. Paul* (Minnesota) *Pioneer Press* damaging information about a candidate for lieutenant governor in Minnesota on the condition that they would not reveal him as the source. The reporters agreed to grant Cohen anonymity. But editors of the two newspapers overruled the reporters and insisted on printing Cohen's name in the story. The editors decided that since Cohen was working for the opposing political party, the readers had a right to know the source of the information.

Cohen sued on the grounds of breach of contract. He claimed that the newspapers had violated an oral contract of confidentiality and that, as a result, he had suffered harm by losing his job. A jury at the first trial level agreed that a reporter's promise of confidentiality is as legally binding as an oral contract. The newspaper appealed and lost. The case went all the way to the U.S. Supreme Court, which ruled in 1991 that the First Amendment does not protect journalists from being sued if they break promises of confidentiality. The high court sent the case back to the Minnesota Supreme Court for a ruling on damages, and Cohen was awarded $200,000.

Before you agree to grant anonymity to a source, you should check with your editors to determine the policies of your organization.

Even when sources agree to be identified, they often ask for anonymity for portions of the interview. They'll say, "This is off the record." Sometimes they aren't even aware of what the term means.

Here are some definitions of the terms used most often to establish ground rules in an interview:

On the Record The source agrees that all information can be used in a news story and that he can be identified as the source of it. The easiest way to establish this understanding is to identify yourself as a reporter immediately and state your purpose for the interview. If you are interviewing people who are not accustomed to dealing with the media, you may need to remind the source during the interview that you are quoting him about the material, especially if you are writing about controversial issues. Such a reminder may jeopardize your chances of using some of the material, but it is better to take that chance during the interview than later in a courtroom after you have been sued.

Off the Record The information from this source may not be used at all. If you can get the same information from another source, you may use it, but you may not attribute it to the source who told it to you off the record.

Not for Attribution You may use the information as background, but you may not identify the source.

Background This is similar to the term "not for attribution." Generally, it means that you may use the information but can't attribute it. Some reporters define background as the ability to use the information with a general attribution, such as "a city official said." If you are in doubt during the interview, ask the source how you can identify him, and give the specific wording you intend to use.

Deep Background This term is rarely used or understood by most sources except for officials in Washington, District of Columbia. It means you may use the material for your information only, but you may not attribute it at all, not even with a general term, such as "government official."

U.S. Census Bureau

Hispanic families are the fastest growing minorities in the U.S.

MULTICULTURAL SOURCES

One of every three people in the United States is a member of a minority racial or ethnic group, according to recent U.S. Census figures. Projections indicate that by 2050, minorities will make up nearly half of the country's population, which is expected to add another million people to its current 314 million. Hispanics made up 49 percent of the children born in the U.S. in the last decade, and Asians were the next fastest growing group. Do your local media reflect this diversity? Do your stories include sources from the minority members of your campus or community?

Members of minority journalism organizations have often complained that minorities are represented in the news media in stereotypical ways, especially in sports pages and crime stories, but not enough in the basic news stories. As this population increases, it is incumbent upon you to include diverse points of view in articles, photographs, video and other media.

In addition to racial and ethnic diversity, there are many other minority groups, such as members of the gay community and people with disabilities, who are often neglected by the news media until a controversy develops or they are subjects of a special feature story about their differences. Strive for inclusiveness in all media, including news and public relations materials. How can you develop multicultural sources?

- Identify leaders of minority groups, including religious organizations, and put them in your source list. But don't anoint them as the only spokespeople for their groups.

- Use the matchmaking technique when you are contacting these leaders, and ask them to connect you with other members in their community.

- Be sensitive. Ask people of diverse backgrounds how they would like to be described. Some Hispanics prefer to be called "Chicanos"; some blacks prefer the term "African-American"; and people with disabilities have several preferences about how they want to be referred to in stories. The Associated Press Stylebook recommends that you avoid describing anyone as "disabled" or "handicapped" unless it is pertinent to the story. Instead describe the disability and avoid euphemisms such as "mentally challenged."

- Use racial or ethnic labels only when they are relevant to the story.

- Rely on visuals. Photographs and videos can demonstrate inclusiveness.

WRITTEN SOURCES

You can find many additional clues for human sources and other information from a variety of written sources. Even though you may rely on Google or other Internet search engines and social media, don't overlook some traditional sources, which are available in print and in searchable online form.

Telephone Directories The white and yellow pages of telephone books are primary places to locate sources. Most local telephone books also contain information about city and county government agencies, utilities and other frequently used services.

Reverse Directories These directories, also called "city directories" or "cross directories," list residents of a community three ways: by name, address and telephone number. Imagine that you are on deadline and have the address of a woman whose house is on fire and that you want to reach her neighbors for comments. How can you do this if you don't know the neighbors' names? You can

Leif Skoogfors/Federal Emergency Management Agency

Telephone directories and government lists of voters or agency personnel are good sources of information.

Tulane Public Relations/Creative Commons

Howard-Tilton Memorial Library at Tulane University. Libraries today feature computers as well as bookshelves for online searches.

look in the cross directory under the address you have. The adjacent homes will be listed first by address, with names and telephone numbers of the occupants beside the address (unless they have unlisted telephone numbers). If you have a phone number, but not the name, check the section for phone numbers.

The reverse directory is one of the most useful ways of locating people for comment when you can't go to the scene. These directories are published by real estate firms in most major communities and are kept in most newsrooms and libraries. Some online search engines, such as *www.reversephonedirectory.com*, will provide the same information.

Libraries Your local public library and your college library contain a wealth of source material to help you find background about a story. Some of the most useful reference works are almanacs and other books of facts, population data and financial records of major corporations. Many of these resources are also online.

Most college and university libraries also have a section devoted to federal and state documents and publications. In this section you can find transcripts of congressional hearings, publications from federal and state agencies and reports from all sorts of government offices.

ONLINE SOURCES

You are writing a story about sexually transmitted diseases among college students. You check the Web for background by typing "sexually transmitted diseases" in a search engine such as Google. You get more than 11 million results. The first might be the U.S. Centers for Disease Control, which contains a wealth of information about these diseases. Which sites should you use? How do you know what information is credible?

Stephen C. Miller, assistant to the technology editor at *The New York Times*, offers his "trust-o-meter," a technique he uses to determine credibility of Web information. Miller says his first choice is government sources because the information is official and public. For background in the story about sexually transmitted diseases, the National Institutes of Health or the Centers for Disease Control would be considered a

U.S. Centers for Disease Control

The U.S. Centers for Disease Control offers credible information about sexually transmitted diseases.

MULTIMEDIA COACH

HERE IS A CHECKLIST to help you determine credibility of websites and search more effectively:

- **Who:** Is an author, site owner or name of sponsoring organization listed on the site? Avoid unnamed sites.

- **What:** Is the site affiliated with a government agency, an educational institution or a nationally credible organization? Check the site index for an "about us" page for further information.

- **When:** Is the site dated? This is crucial. Use the most current information you can find.

- **Where:** Does the site have any contact information — a phone number, address or names of individuals, not just "webmaster"?

- **Why:** Does the site have a bias or promotional agenda? If so, either avoid it or get other points of view, and check the accuracy.

- **How:** Narrow your search by typing specific key words instead of a broad topic.

- **Attribution:** Print the information you plan to use, so you can document it; sites frequently disappear. Copy the site name and URL (address) for a link or citation. Don't copy anything from a site without attributing it.

reliable government source. Next, Miller likes university studies because they are peer reviewed, but he says they should be linked to university sites or research journals. He finds personal sites the least trustworthy.

You might still check personal sites for ideas or contacts, but be wary of citing them without checking the information. Even if the information is trustworthy, you can still spend needless hours wading through it if you don't search effectively.

If you are writing a crime story or you just want to check a source's background to make sure that the person is not a sexual offender, all 50 states have sex offender registries with varying degrees of information available online. The U.S. Department of Justice hosts the Dru Sjodin National Sex Offender Public website (*www.nsopw.gov*), which features a search engine for each state. Another easy way to find these registries is to start with your state website. In one case a student doing a background check on a candidate for the campus student senate found the person on a local sex offender register.

U.S. Department of Justice

Use Journalism Directories Several journalists have created websites with links to all sorts of valuable resources for the media. From government agencies to businesses and public records, you can find useful sources without scouring the Web yourself. For example, the Investigative Reporters and Editors organization has a website with links to topics for numerous beats in its resource center (*www.ire.org*). Another thorough directory for finding people and other sources for journalists was created by Julian Sher, a Canadian investigative journalist (*www.peoplesearchpro.com/journalism*).

Find Experts An expert on almost every topic is willing to provide information to journalists. Profnet (*www.prnewswire.com/profnet*) is a site devoted to serving journalists with expert sources throughout the world. Designed for professional journalists by PRNewswire, this resource should be used for publications, not for term papers.

Find a Map If you are seeking directions to a location for an assignment or for personal use, use a map finder such *www.mapquest.com* or *maps.google.com* or any other maps linked to most search engines. If you have a smartphone, chances are you have a GPS app to guide you.

Find Press Releases and Wire Services Check *www.prnewswire.com*, *www .prweb.com* or *uwire.com* (for college wire stories) or *www.businesswire.com* (for business news).

PUBLIC RECORDS

Many government records, such as data from state and local agencies, may be obtained from databases consisting of public records. For example, if you want to find out who earns the highest salaries in each department at your university or college, you could spend days sifting through a printed version of the budget and trying to compare salaries. But if the budget is available on a database, you can use a computer program to analyze this information for you in minutes.

Or say an official at your university tells you that there are no serious fire safety violations on campus. But you want to be sure, so you decide to check the state fire marshal's report on the last fire safety inspection of campus buildings. The report may list many violations that the official might not have deemed serious. Records on paper or in computer form are valuable information sources.

Not only do such records as fire and police reports provide detail about investigations; they also give names of people to contact. When police officers investigate an accident or a crime, they fill out reports with details of the scene and crucial information about the people involved, including names, addresses, birth dates, physical descriptions and other material. Most of the records are public.

The following list mentions just a few of the public records that should be available to you locally or online.

Political Contributions To check campaign contributions to candidates for state offices, you can access a searchable database for each state at *www .followthemoney.org*.

Real Estate Records Mortgages, deeds (which record the property owners, purchase date and sale price in some states), the legal property description, indexes listing previous property owners and commercial property inventories (lists of everything the commercial property owner has, such as trucks, supplies and equipment) are available in the Register of Deeds office. This office also has maps showing all the property in the county and individual maps called "plats," which show the zoning of each piece of property. Records for tax rates and the assessed value of the property are located in the county assessor's office. If you don't have a property description or know what property your subject owns, the county clerk's office has a listing of who owns what. Some states post property records online; check your state assessor's office to see if you can access property records online.

Voter Registration Records These records, located in the county clerk's office, list people's political party if they are registered voters, as well as their addresses and dates of birth. They also list telephone numbers. In some cases, people who have unlisted telephone numbers may have listed their numbers on these records.

Fish and Game Licenses These are also recorded in the county clerk's office.

Salaries of County Employees The salaries are listed by position only (usually not by employees' names) in the county clerk's office. In some counties or cities, names may be included.

County Government Expenses These can also be found in the county clerk's office.

Corporate Records Articles of incorporation, which list the officers of the corporation and the date the company registered with the state, are very useful if you are trying to find out who the company officers are. Articles of incorporation are located in the Register of Deeds office or in the state office that regulates corporations.

Court Records Filings in all civil and criminal court cases, except juvenile cases, are open to the public. They are located in your county courthouse.

Military Records You can find out the details of individuals' military service in the Register of Deeds office in some municipalities, but only for people who registered for military service in that county. Otherwise, you have to file a request under the Freedom of Information Act to the individual branch of the service.

Personal Property Loans If a person has taken out a loan of more than $1,000 or has used credit to buy something worth more than $1,000, such as a stereo, the information could be on file under the Uniform Commercial Code listings kept in your county courthouse. Some states also have these listings online.

Tax Payments or Delinquent Tax Records These records are kept in the county treasurer's office.

Motor Vehicle Registrations These records and the personal property tax are on file in the county treasurer's office.

Building Inspection Records and Housing Permits These are available in the city's building inspection and housing department. Also available are all the complaints that have been filed against a property owner, which are useful for stories on substandard housing. This office also has records on all permits issued for construction or building improvements.

City Commission Meeting Records, Local Ordinances and Resolutions The city clerk's office keeps these records.

City Expenses Information about purchase orders, accounts payable, the inventory of city agencies, budgets, expenditures and the like are available in the city's finance department. Records of purchase orders and accounts payable are extremely useful if you are investigating the expenditures of any city department or the actions involving any contract the city has with a vendor or builder.

Public Works Records Plans for public works projects — such as sewers, traffic signals and traffic counts — should be available in the public works department of your municipality.

Fire Department Records These include records of all fire alarms, calls (including response times), fire inspections and firearms owners and registration (which may be in a different location in some cities). Also on file, but not available to the public, are personnel records, including pension records and other items of a personal nature. However, salaries are public record. These are in the fire department or in your city or county clerk's office.

Police Records Criminal offense reports, statistics of crime, accident reports and driving records are in the local police department and the sheriff's department. Records of ongoing investigations are generally not available to the public.

Utility Records Water records — such as bacterial counts, water production, chemical usage and other items pertaining to the city's water and sewage operations — are available in the city utilities department.

School District Records Almost all information pertaining to the expenditure of public school funds — including purchase orders, payroll records, audits, bids and contracts — is available from the school district. Personnel records of employees are also available in limited form. Names, addresses, home phone numbers, locations of employment, birth dates, dates hired and work records are available, but information about employee work performance and other personal information is not public. Information about students, other than confirmation that they are enrolled, is not public.

THE FREEDOM OF INFORMATION ACT

The Freedom of Information Act was established by Congress in 1966 to make federal records available to the public. It applies only to federal documents. In addition, the act allows for several exemptions that prohibit the release of documents. Records classified by the government because their release would endanger national defense or foreign policy are exempted. So are certain internal policies and personnel matters in federal agencies, as well as a number of records involving law enforcement investigations. If an agency refuses to release documents you have requested through the FOIA, you may appeal the decision.

In many cases, the document you request comes with information blacked out or cut out. Another drawback to using the FOIA is that it is time-consuming. Although an agency is required by law to respond to your request within 10 working days, delays are common.

FOIA.gov is one of several websites that provide guides to using the Freedom of Information Act *(www.foia.gov).*

However, many reporters have found the FOIA invaluable. The documents they have received have led to major investigative stories.

Before you file an FOIA request, try the direct approach: Ask the agency for the records. You might get them. If you must file a formal FOIA request, it is a good idea to check first and make sure that you are contacting the appropriate agency for your request.

You can also access a complete online guide to the FOIA through the Internet on these sites:

- National Freedom of Information Coalition: *www.nfoic.org.*
- FOI Resource Center: *www.spj.org/foi.asp.*
- The U.S. Department of Justice FOI site: *www.foia.gov.*
- The Federal Communications Commission: *www.fcc.gov/foia.*

When you file your request, be sure to write "Freedom of Information Request" on the envelope and on the letter. You do not have to explain your reason for the request. The agency may charge copying and processing fees, but if you are not using the material for commercial purposes and the material is likely to contribute to an understanding of government operations, you may be entitled to a fee waiver.

For questions or more advice, you can contact The Reporters Committee for Freedom of the Press at *www.rcfp.org/foia.* This site also offers a hotline that you can call for help and form letters to file FOIA requests.

EXERCISES

1 Reverse directory: Imagine that the mayor of your town, another city official or a university official has disappeared. You want to talk to members of his or her family and to the neighbors. Find the missing person's telephone number in the cross directory or an online search engine such as *www.reversephonedirectory.com.* Now find three neighbors you could interview by using the street address searches.

2 Databases: Select a topic for a feature story about an issue on your campus, such as date rape, racial tensions on college campuses, alcohol bans, political activism or a health issue such as sexually transmitted diseases among college students. Now check the Internet or go to your library and use a database to find stories about your topic. Make note of any national experts on the subject and any statistical material or reports you would find helpful in your story.

3 Primary sources: Get copies of a police report, a university study or any other report that has been released at your school or in your community. Make note of the primary sources (officers, investigators or researchers) you would contact.

4 Crime statistics: Access the website for the crime statistics on your campus. It should be on your college or university website, but if you can't find it there, go to the Security on Campus website (*ope.ed.gov/security*) and find the statistics. They may not be as recent as they should be on your university site. You might also compare the statistics for your campus with those from a neighboring or similar-size school. Look for patterns — increases and decreases. Write a news story. If possible, call your campus police department for comments.

5 Record search: Conduct a record search of a person, preferably a politician or other person in your community who owns property. Your task is to construct a paper-trail profile. Try to find out all you

can about the person without ever talking to him or her. However, you may drive by the person's home to observe the property and include that information in your report. Write the profile based only on records and observation. You may be surprised at how much you can write. Here are some suggestions for records that should be available to you:

- Land records, which should include a complete description of the person's house
- Court records of criminal and civil suits, possible marriage or divorce records, or even birth records
- Delinquent tax records
- Corporation records for ownership of personal property or corporation papers (if applicable)
- Records of voter registration, auto registration and tax liens
- Educational background, including curriculum vitae for university employees
- Financial disclosure (for politicians)
- Check the Internet by conducting a search for your source.

6 FOIA request: Write a Freedom of Information Act request for some information from a federal agency that funds a program in your school or community.

FEATURED ONLINE ACTIVITIES: Log on to the MindTap for Rich's Writing and Reporting News to access a variety of robust additional material, including this chapter's learning objectives, activities, comprehension quizzes, and

more. Be sure to check out the "Basketball Scandal" NewsScene scenario for an interactive writing exercise that will help to reinforce many of the themes presented in this chapter.

CHAPTER 5
Interviewing Techniques

COACHING TIPS

Write your observations in your notes; include specific details.

Mark or **highlight important quotes or facts** that you plan to use in the story.

When interviewing athletes or famous people, try to **find a question** they haven't been asked.

Research the background of your subject in social media and on websites.

Always **check the spelling** of the source's name and wording of job titles.

Ask **follow-up questions:** "why" and "how."

Gather **details for graphics, maps** or other illustrations.

Plan to **report with audio and video** for Web publication.

© withGod/Shutterstock.com

In interviewing, if you are sincere and the sources know that you have compassion, they're going to talk. A lot of the skill is just being open to what they have to say.

—**BARBARA WALSH**, *Pulitzer Prize–Winning reporter*

BARBARA WALSH SAID ONE OF THE "STUPIDEST" THINGS SHE ever did almost ruined the interview that led to a Pulitzer Prize.

Walsh had tried for months to get an interview with convicted murderer William R. Horton Jr. Finally, his lawyer gave her permission. She walked into the jail, met Horton and learned a painful lesson.

Horton was serving two life sentences plus 85 years in a Massachusetts prison for the murder of a gas station attendant and a subsequent crime he committed while out of prison on a weekend furlough (a brief stay in the community). He broke into the home of a Maryland man, slashed him repeatedly and raped his fiancée twice.

Walsh, then a reporter for the *Lawrence* (Massachusetts) *Eagle–Tribune*, faced Horton through the window that separated them. "The first question I asked was 'How the heck did you get out on furlough?' It was the stupidest thing I've ever done," she said.

Horton wanted to terminate the interview. Walsh salvaged the interview with Horton by switching to something he wanted to discuss.

"I asked him, 'What do you want to tell me?' And he said, 'I'm not a monster. You people (the press) have made me out to be a monster,'" Walsh said.

The interview then went on for two hours, and eventually Walsh returned to the tough questions she wanted to ask Horton.

The story was one of a series about the Massachusetts furlough program that earned Walsh the Pulitzer Prize. Walsh, who later worked at newspapers in Florida and Maine and now is a freelance writer, said she was lucky that Horton talked to her, but she learned a valuable lesson about interviewing techniques: "Save your tough questions for last."

She was just a rookie reporter when she was assigned to cover that story about the Massachusetts prison program in which many killers and rapists were getting furloughed without supervision on weekends. That program ended after her story was published. "The Horton story also taught me that journalists have tremendous power and responsibility to inform, to tell stories that need to be told," she wrote on her website (*barbarawalsh.net*).

But her journalism career almost ended before it began. Walsh said her journalism professor at the University of New Hampshire gave her an F for turning in a final paper late. "He wanted to prepare me for journalism and deadlines," she wrote. However, she persevered and for the next 25 years she worked at newspapers in Massachusetts, Maine, New Hampshire and Florida, winning prestigious prizes at all of them. She is also the author of two books and freelance articles.

She still asks tough questions — but at the end of the interview. "I've learned to be real slow and real patient," she said. "I'm more inclined to let people talk longer. You may not use all the information, but you can offend them if you rush. In interviewing, if you are sincere and the sources know that you have compassion, they're going to talk. A lot of the skill is just being open to what they have to say."

But when sources were reluctant to answer her questions, she rephrased the questions and asked them again — sometimes three or four times — as in the following story about women in a Florida prison. "I asked one of the female inmates on Death Row, 'What's it like to sit there and know the state wants to electrocute you?' She skirted the question the first time. I asked it three times during the interview." Eventually Walsh got the answer. "If you ask — not in a cold way, but sincerely ask what was it like for you — they'll answer." The result was this revealing portrait (also notice how Walsh weaves in her own observations):

Kaysie Dudley spent two years on Death Row meditating and learning more about how the state was going to kill her.

"I did a lot of research on what they were going to do to me," Dudley says. "It was very morbid, but I wanted to know."

Dudley, 28, was sent to Death Row at Broward Correctional Institution in 1987 after she was convicted with her boyfriend of strangling and slicing the throat of an elderly Clearwater woman.

"My boyfriend killed her," Dudley says. "I held the woman in my arms as she took her last breath. It was a terrible experience." As she talks, Dudley sits in the cafeteria of the women's prison, nervously rubbing her fingers together, her nails raw and bitten to the quick. From her neck hangs a small silver cross.

It is cool, and Dudley wears a black sweater over her state-issued aqua dress.

"I wasn't afraid of dying," Dudley says. "But I didn't like to think about electricity running through my body. . . ." After spending two years on Death Row, Dudley says, she feels she has suffered more than enough.

"I was 22 when they locked me up in there," she says. "I feel like in a way they've already killed me. It took me almost a year to get my facial expressions back, my emotions, my ability to laugh.

"I was a zombie when I came out of there," she says, absently twisting her hair with her constantly moving fingers.

— BARBARA WALSH, *South Florida Sun-Sentinel*

You can watch Barbara Walsh discussing her interview with Willie Horton and her thoughts about reporting on a C-SPAN video at *www.c-spanvideo.org/program /Horto*.

OBSERVATION

Observation is also a crucial reporting skill. Walsh videotapes some of her interviews and reviews them before she starts to write so that she can include details from her observations, as in this example from "Castaway Children: Maine's Most Vulnerable Kids," a three-part series about the lack of mental care for children in her state:

> Joey Tracy stares at the winter moon, looming beyond the razor wire, beyond the red-brick building where the door is locked and a guard keeps watch.
>
> The 16-year-old boy lies on his cot comforted by the thought of his mother staring at the same silver crescent illuminating the sky. He tucks his knees to his chest and whispers: "I love you, Mom." As he has done for four months, Joey cries himself to sleep, wondering if he'll ever go home.
>
> — BARBARA WALSH, *Portland* (Maine) *Press Herald/Maine Telegram*

These days it is even more essential to videotape interviews so you can produce audio and video that will enhance your stories for the Web and mobile media.

Observation for Breaking News

Although descriptive detail is more common in feature stories, you need the same observation techniques to gather information for hard-news stories. At a protest, use observation to report what signs the protesters carried and what they were chanting. At a trial, use observation to help the reader see how the defendant and other people in the courtroom reacted.

If you are reporting a news event for television, don't depend on video to record the observations. In any disaster, fire, or similar breaking news event, the reporter needs to describe the scene and answer questions the anchor might ask. In addition reporters may be expected to post blogs to describe breaking news events.

Such was the case when a tornado wiped out the small town of Greensburg, Kansas. In addition to reporting stories for print and video, the *Wichita* (Kansas) *Eagle* reporters posted their observations on blogs. Note the description based on observation in this newspaper version of the story.

Observe signs and sights at a protest, such as this one by people protesting the killing of seals in Canada.

This sun-baked High Plains town no longer has a grade school, a high school, a City Hall, a hospital, a water tower, a fire station, a business district or a main street.

It has people, but all 1,400 of them live elsewhere today. The homes they kept, the rooms where they were born, where they grew old together, now lie in millions of pieces, some of them as small as matchsticks. Tatters and shards of Greensburg flew for miles across the short grass and sage and yucca outside town on Friday night. Their branches now hold the shreds of housing insulation, pieces of tin, pieces of twisted roofing, crumpled family photographs, torn documents and bits and pieces of belongings.

— *Wichita* (Kansas) *Eagle*

Michael Raphael/Federal Emergency Management Agency

Greensburg tornado aftermath.

Here are two examples of a reporter's observations in blogs posted on the *Eagle's* news site:

HAVILAND — The street in front of Haviland High School looks like an insurance industry trade show. Major insurance companies have glitzy mobile trailers parked out front with satellite capability. High-tech toys help agents and adjusters access customer records. But the gadgets are also helping customers.

"Free Internet access" signs are posted along the sidewalk for people who want to check email messages.

Agents are everywhere, wearing business polos with their company logos.

— DEB GRUVER, *Wichita* (Kansas) *Eagle*

In a strange juxtaposition, a full set of white and blue china — including tea service — stands on display in a storefront on Haviland's main street, perfect, while Greensburg residents' dishes are strewn across their town.

People stop to hug in front of the hardware store, relieved to see one another.

— DEB GRUVER, *Wichita* (Kansas) *Eagle*

GATHERING DETAILS

Like Barbara Walsh, Edna Buchanan won a Pulitzer Prize — in her case, as a police reporter for *The Miami Herald*. Buchanan recounts one of her mistakes when she didn't ask the right question. Now an author, Buchanan offers this advice in her book *The Corpse Had a Familiar Face:*

What a reporter needs is detail, detail, detail.

If a man is shot for playing the same song on the jukebox too many times, I've got to name that tune. Questions unimportant to police add the color and detail that make a story human. What movie did they see? What color was their car? What did they have in their pockets? What were they doing the precise moment the bomb exploded or the tornado touched down?

Miami Homicide Lieutenant Mike Gonzalez, who has spent some thirty years solving murders, tells me that he now asks those questions and suggests to rookies that they do the same. The answers may not be relevant to an investigation, but he tells them, "Edna Buchanan will ask you, and you'll feel stupid if you don't know."

A question I always ask is "What was everybody wearing?" It has little to do with style. It has everything to do with the time I failed to ask. A man was shot and dumped into the street by a killer in a pickup truck. The case seemed somewhat routine — if one can ever call murder routine. But later, I learned that at the time the victim was shot, he was wearing a black taffeta cocktail dress and red high heels. I tracked down the detectives and asked, "Why didn't you tell me?"

"You didn't ask," they chorused. Now I always ask.

SENSITIVITY

The way you deal with sources can differ, depending on whether they are public or private individuals. Because public officials are accustomed to dealing with the media, you have a right to expect them to talk to you. Private individuals do not have to deal with the media, and you need to use more sensitivity when interviewing them.

All sources, public and private, want to be portrayed well in the media. Many sources, especially public officials, will manipulate reporters by revealing only information that furthers their cause. As a result, reporters need to be aware of the source's bias and ask probing questions that go beyond what the source wants to reveal. It is also crucial to check the information and seek alternative points of view.

A digital recorder is helpful, but don't rely on it without taking some notes.

PROS AND CONS OF DIGITAL RECORDERS/ VIDEOTAPE

In our multimedia world, electronic equipment is invaluable. When you conduct an interview, it helps to capture images with your cell phone or record audio and video that you can use on the Web or on TV. But electronic devices are not substitutes for good notes. Machines can fail you when you need them most. They can inhibit a source. They can also prevent you from taking good notes if you rely on them too much.

If you want to get the exact wording of quotes, or if you are interviewing a source about a controversial subject, a recorder is beneficial and even crucial in investigative reporting. But you shouldn't play back the entire recording and transcribe it before you write your story. That is too time-consuming. Scan the recording for the quotes you need.

Before you begin recording your interview, follow some etiquette. Start your interview with basic introductions — who you are and why you are there — and some opening conversation. To put the source at ease, you might even ask a few questions before you ask the source whether he would object to the recorder.

If you want to record a telephone interview, be aware of the laws in your state. Twelve states prohibit recorded conversations without the consent of the person being taped: California, Connecticut, Florida, Illinois, Maryland, Massachusetts, Michigan, Montana, Nevada, New Hampshire, Pennsylvania and Washington. Other states mandate that only one person must be aware of the taping, either the reporter or the person being interviewed. For a list of laws regarding taping in each state, check the Reporters Committee for Freedom of the Press at *www.rcfp.org/taping*.

You can't secretly record any conversation between two other people when you are not a part of the discourse. For example, if you are on an extension phone and neither party knows you are recording the conversation, you are violating a federal law against wiretapping. The Federal Wiretap Statute provides for penalties of up to $250,000 in fines and up to five years in prison.

The most ethical approach is to let your source know you are recording the interview, except in very few situations. For example, if you are conducting an undercover investigation in a state where the one-party rule applies, you could record a conversation without the source's knowledge. However, most editors consider the use of deception or other undercover techniques a last resort.

LISTENING TIPS

Before you write notes or record conversations, you should develop good listening skills. Here are some tips:

Focus on the 'Hear' and Now Concentrate on what the source is saying now, not on what you will ask next.

Practice Conversational Listening Base your next question on the last sentence or thought the source expressed, as though you were having a conversation with your friend.

Practice Critical Listening Evaluate what the source is saying as you hear it. Listen on one level for facts, on another for good quotes and on a third level for elaboration and substantiation. Is the source making a point clearly and supporting it? If not, ask the source to repeat, elaborate or define the meaning.

Be Quiet Whose interview is this anyway? Do not try to impress the source with what you know. You can't quote yourself. Let the source explain a point, even if you understand it, so you can get information in the source's words.

Be Responsive Make eye contact frequently, so your source knows you are listening. If you don't understand something, say so. "Why?" "How?" "I don't understand" and "Please explain."

Listen for What Isn't Said Is the source avoiding a topic? Who or what isn't the source talking about — a family member (in a personal profile), a close official, a crucial part of his background? Sometimes, what is omitted from a conversation is more revealing than what is included.

Listen With Your Eyes What kind of body language is the source displaying? Is the source smiling, frowning or exhibiting discomfort when you ask certain questions? Are these telltale signs that the source may be lying or withholding information? Observation can be a good listening tool.

Be Polite If the source starts to ramble or give you irrelevant information, don't interrupt. Wait for the source to pause briefly, and then change the subject.

Block Personal Intrusions You've had a bad day, your car broke down, you failed a test or you have some emotional concerns. Block personal thoughts that will affect your concentration. Your problems will still be there when the interview is over. The source will not.

Be Flexible Don't go to your interview with a rigid agenda of questions. Although you may start with prepared questions, if the interview goes in another direction, follow that course if it is interesting. Listen for what you want to know and what you didn't expect to know.

NOTE-TAKING TIPS

When the late Foster Davis was a writing coach at *The Charlotte* (North Carolina) *Observer,* he checked reporters' notes to determine whether problems in the stories originated in the reporting process. "The quality of stories

A reporter uses good eye contact with his source as he takes notes during an interview.

has something to do with the quality of notes," Davis said in an interview. "Writing is the least important part of it; everything that leads up to it is what matters."

Davis said he looked at notes to see if they were legible and if they included names and dates as well as reporters' observations. "When the notes said 'trees,' were they specific trees? Were the notebooks dated? Were exact titles spelled out? Detail is what makes the difference between good and bad notes," he said.

Detailed notes give you this advantage: When you begin writing your story, you may need more information than you anticipated during the reporting process. If you are dealing with people who are not accustomed to being interviewed, start your interview slowly by asking a few nonthreatening questions. After you have established some rapport with the source, take out your notebook.

Here are some tips to help you take good notes:

Be Prepared Do not rely solely on electronic equipment for note taking. Bring extra pens and pencils. You may run out of ink, or your pencils may break. If you do an interview in the rain, you'll want to have pencils handy.

Concentrate When you hear a good quote or the start of one, write rapidly and concentrate. Thinking of your next question while you are trying to write down a complete quote will interfere with your concentration.

Use Key Words Jot down key words to remind you of facts and statements from the source.

Develop a Shorthand System Abbreviate as many words as possible.

Slow the Pace When you are taking notes for a quote, slow the pace of the interview by pausing before your next question until you write the quote. If your source is speaking too fast, politely ask him to slow down.

Request Repetition Don't be afraid to ask your source to repeat a quote or fact you missed. Although the quote may not be worded exactly as before, it will be close enough. In fact, the repeated statement may be even better.

Make Eye Contact Look at your source while asking questions and taking notes.

Mark Your Margins or Notebook Covers When you hear something that prompts another question in your mind, jot it in the margin as soon as you think of it. Some reporters use the covers of their notebooks to write questions that come to mind during the interview, so they can find them easily without flipping through notebook pages.

Verify Vital Information Get the exact spelling of your source's name and his title during or at the end of the interview. Don't go by a nameplate on a door or desk. That could be a nickname. Ask the source for the name he prefers to use, and ask for the spelling even if you are sure of it. Even if you are reporting for television, you will need the spelling of the name, which may be superimposed on the screen during a sound bite.

Double-Check If your source says he has three main points or reasons for running for office, make sure that you get all three. Write "3 reasons" in the margin, number them as you hear them and check before you conclude the interview.

Be Open-Minded You may have one idea for the story when you begin taking notes. But don't limit your notes to one concept. Your story angle could change at any time during the interview.

Use a Symbol System To save time writing your story, mark your notes with a star or some symbol next to the information that you think will be important. Develop your own system.

Practice interviewing while standing.

Patsy Lynch/Federal Emergency Management Agency

Stand and Deliver Practice taking notes while you are standing. You will not have the luxury of sit-down reporting, especially at the scene of fires, accidents, disasters and most other breaking news stories.

Save Your Notes You should save your notes after the story is published or aired. How long you should save them is debatable. Lawyers disagree whether notes are helpful or harmful in court cases if you are sued for libel or any other reasons. But most editors advise saving the notes at least for a few weeks after the story appears, in case any questions about it arise. For this reason, it is helpful to date your notebooks.

SOCIAL MEDIA

 Twitter has become a useful interviewing tool for some reporters. It doesn't substitute for an in-depth interview, but a Twitter interview can serve several purposes. It can help you focus your questions and get essential information, especially for breaking news on radio, television or the Web. Some employers are even using "Twitterviews" for job interviews because they distill information so clearly.

You can also use Twitter for a pre-interview to get insight before a more in-depth one.

- Contact the subject initially to describe your purpose and explain how the interview will work. Make sure your subject is familiar with Twitter.

- Identify a clear purpose for the interview.

- Plan and limit the number of questions you want to ask — preferably about 10.

- Be responsive and adaptable to the answers, especially when during breaking news.

- Consider conducting an interview over several days instead of at one time.

- If you plan to make the interview public, use a hashtag and be selective about tracking the questions that come in.

- Check out interview tools such as tweeter-view (*www.tweeterview.com*) and TweetChat (*tweetchat.com*).

INTERVIEWING TIPS

First, consider your mission. You are a reporter, not a stenographer who just receives information and transcribes it. A reporter evaluates information for its accuracy, fairness, newsworthiness and potential to make a readable story. During the reporting process, look for facts, good quotes, substantiation and answers to the five W's — who, what, when, where, why — and also "how" and "so what." One question should lead to another until you have the information you need.

An interview with one source is just the beginning of reporting for most stories. For credibility and fairness, you need other sources — human and written — for differing points of view and accuracy checks.

Planning the Interview

The planning stages described here apply only to interviews that you need to set up in advance. Most of the other reporting techniques apply to both kinds of stories.

Identify Your Focus What is the purpose of your interview? The focus may change after you do the interview, but you need to start with a specific reason for your story so you know what kind of information you need to get and what sources you need.

Darby Duffin/Federal Emergency Management Agency

Reporters interview officials about a local flood.

Research the Background Check news clippings, TV footage, social media sites and written and online sources. Check with secondary sources — friends and opponents — before or after you interview the subject of a story.

Identify Your Goals What kind of information are you hoping to get from this source? Is the source going to be the central focus of the story, as in a profile, or just one of several people cited in the story? Get a general idea of why you need this source, so you can explain briefly when you call for an interview.

Plan Your Questions Prepare your list of questions in two ways: Write all the questions you want to ask, preferably in an abbreviated form. Then mark the questions you must ask to get the most crucial information for your story. If your source refuses to grant you the time you need, you can switch to the crucial list during your interview.

Request the Interview The most important point is to plan ahead. Officials and many other sources may not be able to see you on brief notice. When you make the call, state your name and purpose. Or try the sponsorship technique: "I'm working on a story about date rape on campus, and Officer John Brown suggested that I call you."

You can also try contacting a source by email to set up an appointment. State your name, affiliation and purpose. Save your questions until you find out whether you can get a telephone or face-to-face interview.

Dress Appropriately If you are interviewing a source on a farm, don't wear a business suit. However, if you are interviewing corporate officials or people in more formal business settings, you should dress as though you worked there.

Arrive on Time You could arrive 10 to 15 minutes early, but don't arrive too early because you could inconvenience people who are busy. And never come late.

Patsy Lynch/Federal Emergency Management Agency

Ask open-ended questions during an interview so you can get good quotes and sound bites.

Conducting the Interview

Interview questions can be classified as two types: closed-ended and open-ended. You need both types.

- **Closed-ended questions** are designed to elicit brief, specific answers that are factual. They are good for getting basic information, such as name and title; yes or no answers; and answers to some basic questions about who, where, when, such as: How long have you worked here? How many people were at the rally? When did the accident occur?

- **Open-ended questions** are designed to elicit quotes, elaboration or longer responses. Avoid being judgmental in the way you frame your initial questions and follow-up questions. The more neutral you are, the more responsive your source is likely to be.

The questions that will elicit the most quotes and anecdotes start with *what, why* and *how*:

- What (What happened? What is your reaction? What do you mean by that? Can you elaborate?)
- Why (Why did you do that? Why do you believe . . .?)
- How (How did something happen? How did you accomplish that?)
- Give me an example (a follow-up question to explain how the source felt, thought, acted in a specific situation)

Keep your questions brief. Ask questions in simple sentences — one question at a time. Don't combine two questions into one sentence.

Sit at an angle to make a source more comfortable in an interview.

The Dumb Factor Beginning reporters often worry that they will appear dumb to sources. Don't worry about what you don't know. You are there to listen and learn, not to be the expert. The whole point is to get information from the source. In fact, acting dumb can give you an advantage. Even if you know the answer to a question, you should ask it anyway so that you can get the information in the source's words. If the source gives you technical or confusing information, you might ask, "Could you explain that so I can write it clearly?" Most sources enjoy taking the teaching role or showing off what they know.

Here are some ways to conduct the interview and some types of questions to ask. Not all of these techniques and questions apply to every story.

Start Out by Using Icebreakers Introduce yourself and briefly state your purpose. Establish rapport with some general conversation. Don't pull out your notebook immediately. Try to sit at an angle to your source so you are not directly facing him in a confrontational manner.

Observe the surroundings. Do you notice something you can mention as an icebreaker, a way to establish rapport? If an official has a picture on his desk of his family, don't get overly familiar. Use good judgment. Then explain a little more about what you are seeking in your story.

Plan Your First Question Try to find a question or approach that would interest the source, especially if the person is a celebrity, an athlete or an official who has been interviewed often. These people often give standard answers to questions they consider boring because they have been asked the same questions so many times. If you research well, you will find some tidbit or angle to a story that might lead to an unusual question — and an interesting answer.

Ask follow-up questions using a conversational technique.

Put Your Questions in Nonthreatening Order In most cases you will want to follow Barbara Walsh's advice and start with nonthreatening questions. However, if you have only five minutes with a source, you may have to ask your toughest question first or whichever one will yield you the most crucial information for your story.

Ask the Basic Questions Who, what, when, where, why and how are the most basic. Then add the "so what" factor: Ask the significance. Who will be affected and how? This question will give you information for your impact paragraph.

Ask Follow-Up Questions These are the questions that will give you quotes and anecdotes. Use a conversational technique. When a source answers one question, follow the trend of thought by asking why and how, and asking the source to explain or give examples.

Here are some general follow-up questions to provide context and interesting material:

- What was your reaction?
- What do you mean by that?
- How did that happen?
- How did you do that?
- What is the significance?
- Who will be affected?

Keep Quiet Do not talk too much or try to impress your source with your knowledge. Let the source talk. You need to quote the source, not yourself.

Be Nonjudgmental Don't insert your comments or opinions into your questions. You should remain neutral and strive for fairness. If you have to ask a controversial question, use the "blame others" technique: Your opponent says that . . . How do you respond?

Control the Interview If your source rambles or prolongs an answer, and you want to move the interview in another direction, don't interrupt. Wait for a natural pause before asking your next question.

Repeat Questions What should you do if the source gives you an evasive or incomplete answer? The best tactic is to drop the question and continue the interview. After you have discussed a few other points, repeat the question you want answered, but state it in a slightly different way. Sometimes a source will recall or share more the second time the question is raised.

Ask Background Questions Get the history of the issue, if applicable. How and when did the problem or program start? Why?

Construct a Chronology When appropriate, ask questions to establish a sequence of events. You

Ed Edahl/Federal Emergency Management Agency

Get a chronology of events, and ask about future developments.

don't need to write the story in chronological order, but you need to understand the order in which events occurred.

Ask About Developments What are the current concerns and developments? How did the issue evolve? What is likely to happen in the future? The answer to the question about the future may provide you with a good ending for your story. In some cases, it may give you a lead and a new focus for your story. The next step in an action is often the most newsworthy angle. You will probably have to update your story anyway for TV, social media or the Web.

Role-Play If you were in the reader's place, how would you use the information? For example, if you needed to apply for a loan, what steps would you have to take, and where would you go? What does the reader or viewer need and want to know?

Ask About Pros and Cons Ask your source to discuss both sides of an issue, when relevant. Who agrees and disagrees with his point of view? What are his responses to the opposition?

Ask for Definitions Always get your source to define any bureaucratic or technical terms in language that you and your readers or viewers will understand. Don't accept or write any information that you can't explain. To clarify, you might restate the information in your own words and ask the source if you have the correct interpretation.

Verify Ask questions even if you know the answers. Always check the spelling of your source's name — first and last names as well as middle initial. Check the person's title and the dates of crucial events. Check the accuracy of information on a résumé or news release. You don't have to repeat everything, but you should ask the source whether the information released is correct. Then ask some questions that expand on the basic information.

Also, remember that if the source tells you something about another person, you must check it out with that person.

Use the 'Blame Others' Technique When you have to ask tough questions, blame someone else: "Your opponent says you cheated on your income taxes. How would you respond to that?"

Handle Emotional Questions With Tact Avoid insensitive questions. There's a saying in journalism that there are no stupid questions, only stupid answers. That's not exactly true. "How do you feel about the death of your three children?" is not only a stupid question; it's insensitive as well. Instead of asking such an emotionally loaded question, ask the person to recall specific memories about his children, or ask how the person is coping with the tragedy.

Ask Summary Questions Restate information, or ask the source to clarify the key points he is making — for example: "Of all the goals you have expressed, which would you say are the most important to you? What do you think are the three major issues you face?"

Use the 'Matchmaker' Technique Ask whether anyone else is involved in the issue or if there are other people the source would suggest you contact. Remember that you will want more than one source for your story so that you can strive for fairness and balance.

Ask Free-Choice Questions Ask the source whether there is anything he would like to add.

End on a Positive Note When you have finished the interview, thank your source. Ask whether you can call back if you have any further questions. At this point, you also could ask for another way to reach the source, such as an email address or cell phone number.

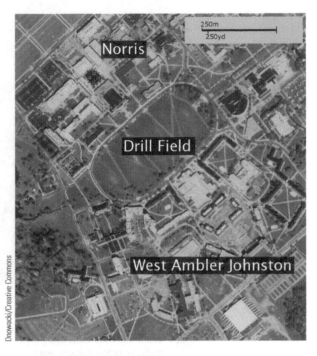

A location map of the shootings at Virginia Tech; Norris and West Ambler Johnson Hall.

Reporting for Visuals

Whenever you go on an assignment — especially a breaking news story involving an accident, a disaster such as a flood or explosion, or a crime — gather information for a graphic or map to pinpoint the location of the crime or disaster scene. Take photos with your cell phone or camera. With an application like Foursquare or GPS function, you can also use your cell phone to gather details about your location.

If you have video, don't describe the scene that viewers can see for themselves. But if you don't have video, gather details so you can describe the scene to viewers or the anchor, or use in a print story.

Locations Get the names of streets and major intersections nearest to the site of the incident. Even if you plan to use Google maps, ask details about specific measurements: yards, feet, number of city blocks or whatever else would help pinpoint locations. How many feet or yards away from the landfill is the nearest house? What buildings are in the area? When the gas pipe exploded, how many feet from the gas line was the nearest building? This information might be helpful for creating a graphic or describing the scene, especially if you are broadcasting on the scene.

Statistics Think of charts for print, broadcast or public relations materials. If your city council has raised taxes, what have taxes been during the past five years? How much has tuition increased during the past several years? Statistics like these can be boring to read. But they are easy to understand in chart form that can be posted in print or on the Web.

MULTIMEDIA COACH

Use the time to set up video for icebreakers and background information.

THE TECHNIQUES of interviewing are similar for print, broadcast or online reporting. You still need to decide the focus or main reason for the interview, research the background and prepare good questions. But much of broadcast and online reporting may be for spot news. In a convergent media world, you need video and audio for online delivery, even if you are a print reporter.

Setting up cameras for TV may make your source nervous, so use that time for icebreakers or for getting background information from the source. For broadcast and online audio and video, you need good quotes, so open-ended questions are preferable. Here are some tips especially geared to broadcast interviews:

- Ask open-ended questions to elicit quotes such as how, why, what was a person's reaction and what he was doing at the time of the incident. Avoid questions that can be answered "yes" or "no."

- Keep questions brief in simple sentences. Don't ask two questions at one time.

- Don't ask questions that express your opinion. Avoid leading questions such as "Don't you think that . . ." and similar ones that include preconceived suggestions.

- Ask questions that your audience would want answered.

- Ask free-choice questions: At the end of the interview, ask the source whether there is anything he would like to add.

Highlights Gather information for a facts box, such as important dates or highlights of someone's career. Suppose you are doing a profile. Instead of listing key dates and incidents in your story, could you place them more effectively in a box?

EMAIL INTERVIEWS

Although email is an effective tool for contacting sources, it is not the best method for interviewing people. However, in some cases, email may be the only way you can get comments from a source. Use it as a last resort if you can't interview a source in person or by telephone.

Advantages Email gives the source some time to think about responses to your questions. It also saves you from taking notes, and you can get accurate quotes when the source responds in writing.

Disadvantages Email interviews prohibit spontaneity and good follow-up questions. You also can't observe the source's reactions and body language, nor can you gather descriptive detail.

Several colleges are prohibiting email interviews because they give the source control over responses. The University of South Florida and Princeton University are two of them. The editor of *The Daily Princetonian* said email interviews result in stories with "stilted, manicured quotes . . . that make it extremely difficult for reporters to ask follow-up questions or build relationships with sources."

- **Limit the number of questions:** Sources will respond better to a few questions than to a long list. Strive for a maximum of five questions.

- **Clarify your purpose:** Make it clear that you intend to use the email message in a news story. Personal email messages are not intended for publication.

- **Verify the source's full name and title:** Email addresses do not always include the source's proper name.

- **Limit your follow-up email messages:** You may have to reply to the source's email with another question or a request for more information. But don't badger the source with several email messages.

- **Attribute to email:** Although not required, it is preferable to explain in your news story that the source made the comments in an email interview.

ETHICS

ETHICAL DILEMMA: Should you accept gifts from sources? Does the value of the gift make a difference?

The case: You are working on a feature story about a new music store in your community. After you finish the interview, the store owner offers you some gifts, such as a CD case, a baseball cap and a T-shirt with the store logo and a few CDs featuring your favorite musical artists. You do not plan to write reviews of the CDs. The total worth of the gifts is about $35. Should you accept some, all or none of these gifts? If you plan to review the CDs, should you keep them after you review them?

Ethical values: Credibility, conflict of interest

Ethical guidelines: The Society of Professional Journalists Code of Ethics says journalists "should refuse gifts, favors, fees, free travel and special treatment and shun secondary employment, political involvement, public office and service in community organizations if they compromise journalistic integrity."

David Fine/Federal Emergency Management Agency

Smartphones are useful tools for multimedia reporting.

TELEPHONE INTERVIEWING

The telephone is no longer just a tool for verbal conversations. Smartphones can be used in interviewing to capture audio, video and photos. If you can arrange it, you can conduct a video interview with your source on Skype, a free Internet-connected call. The network, operated by Microsoft, allows users to download a free application and send calls via audio, video, text messages and photos without charge to a recipient who has a Skype account or for a charge to people on landline and mobile phones who don't have accounts.

Although smartphones are more versatile than basic telephones, the techniques of conducting interviews by telephone still create more challenges than in-person interviews. You need to work harder at keeping the source's attention and focusing your questions. Researchers suggest that the average telephone interview should be limited to 20 minutes.

After that, the attention span of the person responding wanes. If you call a source at home, he or she may be further distracted by children or other family concerns. You also need to make sure that your mobile phone is fully charged.

Here are some guidelines for telephone interviewing:

Identification Immediately state your name and affiliation and the purpose for the call.

Icebreakers These may not be necessary. Get to the point quickly.

Length of Questions Keep questions very short. Limit the number of questions as well. Plan two lists: (1) all the questions you want to ask and (2) crucial questions. If you have time for only a few questions, switch to the crucial list. Don't wait too long to ask the crucial ones. You never can tell when the source will be interrupted and will terminate the interview.

Clarification It may be harder to understand information over the telephone, so clarify anything that is confusing. Repeat any confusing terms or information in your own words, and ask your source to verify your interpretation.

Specifics Ask for details and examples. If you want to describe the scene, ask your source to give you the descriptive details.

Chronology A chronology is especially important in police and fire stories you receive by telephone. After a source tells you the high points of what happened, you could ask him to explain the order in which events unfolded.

Control You need to control the interview by switching the subject so you get answers to the questions you need.

Verification Double-check the spelling of the name, title and other basic information. If you haven't heard it clearly, spell it back to the source, especially when dealing with police officers. They usually do not identify themselves by their full names when they answer the phone on duty, so make sure that you get first and last names and the proper rank, such as lieutenant, sergeant or captain.

COMMON INTERVIEWING PROBLEMS

- **What do you do if the source says something is "off the record" during an interview?** Ask the source why the information should be off the record (meaning you can't use it), and try to convince the source that the information is not harmful. Ask the question another way during the course of the interview to see whether you can get the information on the record.

- **What do you do if the source tells you not to use his name after the interview?** Try to prevent this by making sure you identify yourself and your purpose clearly at the start of the interview. If you suspect that this might happen, set ground rules at the beginning of the interview by explaining that you cannot use anonymous sources. Try to convince the source to be identified. If the source still refuses, ask if you can identify the source by a vague title or position such as "a source in the administration."

- **What do you do if the source terminates the interview abruptly before you have the information you need?** Ask if you may contact the source again for further questions.

- **What do you do if the source gives you information that is inaccurate or false?** Check your facts, and if you discover inaccuracies or falsehoods, contact the source again and confront him with the problems. Ask for an explanation.

EXERCISES

1 Interview a reporter from your local newspaper, radio station or television station about his reporting techniques. Or choose a reporter whose stories you like, and interview him about techniques.

2 **Icebreakers:** Make a list of questions you would use as icebreakers to interview a professor or a source whose office you have visited.

3 **Reporting scenarios:** Develop questions for the following situations:

- You learn that there is a fire in a residence hall on your campus. List at least 10 questions you would ask. List five sources you would contact. What kind of background information do you need?

- A professor on campus has received a $1 million grant to study plagiarism among college students. List at least five questions you would ask if you were interviewing the professor. What other sources would you use to make this a good story?

- A study at another university says college students are sleep deprived. Women students get less than six and a half hours of sleep, and men get seven to eight hours of sleep. You are writing this story for your campus newspaper. How will you localize this story? What sources (other than students) do you need to make this a credible story for your university audience? Where will you find them?

4 **Note taking:** The object of this exercise is to see how accurately you can quote sources. Tape an interview from any television news show. As you are watching the show, write down some direct quotes. If you use videotape, watch the screen periodically as though you were making eye contact with a source. Then play the tape and test your accuracy. If you do this in a classroom, you can compare your notes with classmates' notes. Analyze what caused you to be inaccurate — if you were — and how you can improve your note taking.

5 **Notes:** Submit your notes for the last story you wrote. Share your notes with another student, and critique each other's notes. Are your notes legible? Do they have names, dates, titles and details? Compare your rating of your notes with another student's evaluation of them. Discuss improvements in your note taking that might have helped your story.

6 **Social media research:** Choose a topic or person for an interview. Check social media sites to find out how much background information you can get. Write a blog about the most interesting information you found and which sites were the most useful.

FEATURED ONLINE ACTIVITIES: Log on to the MindTap for Rich's Writing and Reporting News to access a variety of robust additional material, including this chapter's learning objectives, activities, comprehension quizzes, and more. Be sure to check out the "Big Fire" NewsScene scenario for an interactive writing exercise that will help to reinforce many of the themes presented in this chapter.

COACHING TIPS

Stress immediacy — the latest developments in a story.

Plan to update your story continually for mobile and online delivery.

Write short versions for **mobile delivery.**

Read your story **out loud for broadcast.**

Plan audio and video elements for broadcast, the Web and mobile media.

Plan links to social media sites.

Consider **interactive features** for multimedia stories.

CHAPTER 6
Mobile and Multimedia Skills

© cyfrain/Shutterstock.com

It's mobile, immediate, visual, interactive, participatory and trusted. Make way for a generation of storytellers who totally get it.

—**THE FUTURE OF NEWS: MEDIA, TECHNOLOGY AND SOCIETY,**
report for the American Press Institute

M

OJOS ARE MAGIC CHARMS OR SPELLS, BUT IN MANY NEWS organizations, mojos are a new breed of journalists.

Mojos are mobile journalists equipped with notepads, cameras, recorders, cell phones and laptop computers so they can file community news stories for the Web at a moment's notice. They don't go to a newspaper office; their offices are in their cars. They don't wait for deadlines; their deadlines are whenever they get their information. Mojos can also be defined as journalists who only use mobile phones to report and produce stories with audio, video, text and social media.

The News Press/Fort Myers/Fla.

Graphic from *The* (Fort Myers, Florida) News Press for mobile news delivery.

Tom Morris/Creative Commons

More than 50 percent of U.S. adults own either a tablet or smartphone, and 66 percent of those get news on their device, according to Pew Research Center's Project for Excellence in Journalism.

"We believe that most reporters will soon be mojos, producing information seamlessly across platforms," said Kate Marymont, senior vice president of news at Gannett Co. "The most critical need is the ability to file material to online quickly and regularly."

The Gannett Co. started the mojo concept at its Fort Myers, Florida, newspaper in 2005 and has since expanded it to more than 100 of its news organizations. The company reorganized its newspapers and broadcast properties as "information centers," which develop local mobile sites for multiple platforms, including small screen and mobile devices.

Gannett is not the only company gravitating to the mobile market. Twelve major broadcast groups, including Fox, NBC and Hearst, formed a joint venture to develop a national mobile content service. The group allows member companies to share content for mobile devices, including video, local and national news from print and online sources and entertainment programming.

It is with good reason that mobile devices are generating so much attention by the media. "Half of all U.S. adults now have a mobile connection to the Web through either a smartphone or tablet . . . and this has major implications for how news will be consumed and paid for," according to a study, "The Future of Mobile News," by the Pew Research Center's Project for Excellence in Journalism in collaboration with The Economist Group.

"Rather than replacing old technology, the introduction of new devices and formats is creating a new kind of 'multi-platform' news consumer."

MULTI-PLATFORM CONSUMERS

These new consumers are not geared to one form of mobile media; they are attached to many mobile devices. Google describes the new media audience as a nation of multi-screeners. "Most of consumers' media time today is spent in front of a screen — computer, smartphone, tablet and TV. The device we choose to use is often driven by our context — where we are, what we want to accomplish and the amount of time needed," according to the report, "The New Multi-screen World."

Consumers use several mobile devices simultaneously most of the time, the report says. However, smartphones dominate as the most common starting point for activities across multiple screens.

As a result, Google adopted a "mobile first" strategy in which the company decided to focus more of its new products on smartphones rather than on desktops or other computer devices.

MOBILE REPORTING

Stephen Quinn, a mobile journalist and professor from Australia, calls the smartphone "the Swiss army knife" of journalism. "They're compact, light and discreet. Take a mobile phone and a broadcast quality microphone and the world is your storybook," he said at a World Journalism Education conference in South Africa. "Using cell phones forces journalists to think differently. This new notion of mobility changes the way you perceive and operate in the world. It's all about connection. Reporting involves thinking about how to find wifi; you have to be thinking about battery power. And our concept of news is broadening — if I can get there, it's news."

Although you may just be starting your journalism training, it's not too soon to develop that mobile media mindset.

One of the most important qualities of mobile journalism is immediacy. Mojos with smartphones can report wherever they are and instantly file tweets or posts on social media or text, audio and/or video to their news organization.

Students in a mobile reporting class at the Gaylord College of Journalism, University of Oklahoma, proved the importance of immediacy in 2012 when a tornado tore through their city of Norman. They put their smartphones to the test by filing reports from throughout the area to their website, OU StormCrowd, and beat all other media in the state.

Associate Professor Julie Jones said students were directed to emphasize immediacy over story and report every time they had new information. "This is a different mindset than working, under rolling deadlines, towards a complete story," she wrote in a post on the Mediashift website. "The question is not whether smartphones can be used for newsgathering, but rather when it is the best journalism tool and how that tool should be used to meet professional standards."

When immediacy is not the primary factor, many of the reporting principles that you use for traditional print or broadcast news apply to mobile media.

- Research the background of the story.
- Find sources online, in social media or on site.
- Plan your questions.
- Gather text, audio, video and photos (using personal interviews, email, social media or online sources).
- Produce the story in one or several methods: print, audio, video or a combination of them.
- Check and verify accuracy of your sources and information.

If you want to know what other equipment you can use, students at University of California Berkeley's Graduate of School of Journalism have created a free downloadable mobile reporting field guide, which reviews the best and worst of apps and gear (*multimediashooter.com/mobile/MobileGuide.pdf*).

ETHICS

ETHICS DILEMMA: You are a mojo and you hear on the radio that there is a five-car pileup on the interstate. You call police and confirm there is an accident, but you can't get to the scene for firsthand information because traffic is backed up for miles. However, you receive a photo and message on your cell phone from a trucker who claims he is at the scene. This is an important breaking news story, and you want to post it to your news organization's website as soon as possible. As a mobile journalist, it is part of your responsibilities to warn people about the traffic delays. Will you use the photo and description of the scene from this source? How do you know if the information is accurate?

Guidelines: The Radio Television Digital News Association says that citizens can provide valuable information, but some people try to fool news organizations with bad information or fake pictures. The association offers these ethical guidelines:

- Information gleaned online should be confirmed, just as you must confirm scanner traffic or phone tips before reporting them.
- If you cannot independently confirm critical information, reveal your sources; tell the public how you know what you know and what you cannot confirm. Don't stop there. Keep seeking confirmation.
- This guideline is the same for covering breaking news on station websites as on the air. You should not leave the public "hanging." Lead the public to completeness and understanding.

WRITING FOR MOBILE MEDIA

Access a news story on a website in your computer. Now access that story on a small-screen cell phone. Would you read more or less of the article on a small screen?

You would probably read much less. At least that's what researchers at the University of Colorado discovered when they surveyed how college students used media on their smartphones. Their findings:

- For text news stories, 56 percent of students in one group read less than the first three paragraphs, and 72 percent in another group read less than 25 percent of the article.

- For video news stories, 79 percent watched 59 seconds or less of each video.

- For audio news reports, 81 percent listened to 30 seconds or less.

How do those findings affect the ways you should write for mobile media? The easy answer is to keep your sentences and paragraphs short. But not all mobile phones are the same size, and one size does not fit all in writing styles either. If the content is compelling, readers may persevere. Good content providers offer versions of stories formatted for mobile devices to improve readability. However, writing techniques also need to be geared for readability on mobile devices. Here are some recommendations:

- Entice readers with clear, compelling headlines, preferably less than 25 words. Even better, write a Twitter-type headline limited to 140 characters.

- Write a summary lead that gives the most important information in a brief sentence.

- Use inverted pyramid structure. Put the most important information in the lead and first few paragraphs, and the rest of the story in descending order of importance. Make sure those first two or three paragraphs contain crucial information.

- Keep sentences short.

- Keep paragraphs short.

- Write for readers who scan text. Put key words at the beginning or end of the sentences.

- Spacing: Some news providers insert a space between paragraphs to aid readability, but that increases scrolling. Others

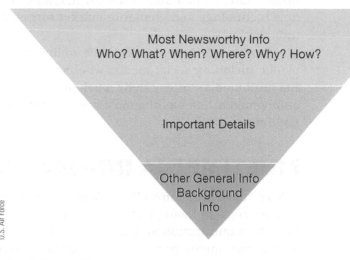

U.S. Air Force

Inverted pyramid.

Most Newsworthy Info
Who? What? When? Where? Why? How?

Important Details

Other General Info
Background
Info

eliminate spaces or paragraph indentations so more text can be viewed in less space. Decide how you prefer to read; then write that way.

- Use lists to itemize information if you want to make several points in your story.
- Be concise. Edit your text carefully. Eliminate repetition. Cut extra words. Study Twitter for concise writing (but avoid the abbreviations).
- Add photos or video only if they relate to or enhance your text. Don't add to the downloading time if you aren't adding worthwhile content.
- Provide links, but choose them carefully. Once you take readers to a new site, don't expect them to return to your story.
- Offer interaction. After all, this is a phone or mobile device designed for communication.
- Test how your story will look on a mobile phone or iPad. If you don't have one, use a mobile phone simulator: iPhone 4 Simulator (*iphone4simulator.com*), iPhoney (*www.marketcircle.com/iphoney*) or iPad Peek (*ipadpeek.com*).

MULTIMEDIA AND CONVERGENCE

Multimedia is defined as a combination of media — usually print, audio, video, photos, graphics and the Web. It can also be called "convergence," which often refers to a story or project that merges a combination of media. The terms can be interchangeable.

The Radio Television Digital News Association explains convergence this way: "Communications and electronic journalism have changed dramatically in recent years and promise to change even more in years to come. The familiar lines that once marked the boundaries between radio, television, print, computers, telephones and other media are blurring. News in the future will be a fully digital broadband mix of audio, video, print, graphics and databases. In the coming years, new technology and changing market forces will completely transform the news industry."

That future has arrived. Most online information contains a combination of media, including social media, whether accessed on computers or mobile devices. But multimedia stories can be much more than just a mixture of print, broadcast and online media. Some of the most innovative forms of storytelling can be offered with multimedia tools.

MULTIMEDIA INNOVATION

"We're redefining journalism." That's the motto of students in News21, an innovative program headquartered at the Walter Cronkite School of Journalism and Mass Communication at Arizona State University, where the goal is to produce in-depth, multimedia projects. The program is a consortium of students from several universities who collaborate on projects to explore creative multimedia ways of storytelling.

Using print, graphics, photos, video and interactive features such as games, questionnaires and searchable maps, students have produced multimedia projects revealing dangers of our transportation system, failures of our food inspection system and battles that veterans face after they return home.

But what makes these projects special is the in-depth reporting, compelling writing and interactive features in which you can personalize graphics for your state, trace the path of salmonella in chicken production or take a quiz to see if you can spot mislabeled seafood.

SOCIAL MEDIA

SOCIAL MEDIA APPLICATIONS have become standard features in most news, government and public relations websites. The U.S. Centers for Disease Control is an example of an extensive newsroom that features multimedia and social media. Glen Nowak, Ph.D., former director of the centers' news and electronic media, said the addition of social media allows the agency to reach more audiences with more varied formats.

Nowak said that in some ways social media have made it harder to reach audiences because there are so many choices and so many places where they can go for information. "Now you have to use a lot more media to reach the same number of people."

His advice for students: Learn how to use different media. "They should also have good communication and writing skills. They should know what makes good messages. So it's not just a matter of knowing the technical elements of creating a Facebook page, but also knowing what makes a good one versus a bad one." *www.cdc.gov/socialmedia/tools/guidelines /socialmediatoolkit.html*

Here are some of the ways the CDC offers social media and multimedia:

- Audio/video resources: Online videos, podcasts and public service announcements and B-Roll for productions. Videos on YouTube and CDC-TV online.

- RSS feeds of formatted articles and newsroom releases. (RSS, Really Simple Syndication, is a Web feed that automatically updates information.)

- Newsroom library with images in low to high resolution for downloading.

- Mobile website.

- Facebook and Twitter pages.

- Blogs.

- Flickr, Instagram and YouTube.

Filthy seafood infected with bacteria or tainted with drugs and antibiotics banned in the U.S. is finding its way onto the plates of health-conscious Americans, according to state and federal officials, consumer advocates, academics and food safety experts.

> The U.S. imported more than 17.6 million tons of seafood in the last decade, according to a News21 analysis of import data from the U.S. Food and Drug Administration and the U.S. Department of Agriculture.
>
> Only about 1 percent is inspected, and only 0.1 percent is tested for banned drug residues, according to the U.S. Government Accountability Office, the investigative arm of Congress. More than 51 percent of the seafood that was inspected and turned away from ports was filthy, meaning it was spoiled or contained physical abnormalities, or it was contaminated with a foodborne pathogen. About 20 percent of those cases involved salmonella, according to the News21 analysis of FDA import refusal data.
>
> — NICOLE GILBERT, *Carnegie-Knight News21*

You can read more about this project in Chapter 12 and access the series in News21 at *foodsafety.news21.com/index.html*.

MULTIMEDIA PLANNING

Writing news for print, broadcast and the Web requires careful planning and reporting for more than one story. Here are some things to keep in mind:

- Immediacy: Plan to file breaking news immediately on the Web.
- Follow-up: While you are reporting, plan for the next cycle of the story. Always consider what will happen next. You will need a fresh angle for the next broadcast or the next day's newspaper.
- Evaluate story content: Consider what type of media the story needs: audio, video, maps, graphics and text — one or a combination of these forms. Just because you can use multimedia doesn't mean you should. What does the reader need to understand and want to read in your story?

WRITING FOR MULTIMEDIA

Here are some principles that apply to writing for cross-media platforms:

Immediacy

Just as immediacy is crucial for mobile media, it is also a major factor for news organizations that publish websites. Even if you are reporting a breaking news story for a newspaper, plan to report it first on the Web. The days of waiting until the next publication cycle for a breaking news story in a newspaper are over. What is happening now? What are the latest developments? How can you update the story, giving it a "forward spin" to tell what will happen next?

MULTIMEDIA COACH

IF YOU WANT TO produce good multimedia websites, you need more than just a smartphone. You also need some tools and skills to create good photos, video and audio — lessons that are beyond the purview of this basic journalism textbook. However, you can access many of these applications and instructions online, most without charge. Here are some helpful sites for multimedia development:

- *www.lynda.com*: This site offers video courses in all areas of multimedia development, but it is not free. However, the site, created by Lynda Weinman, is often recommended by Web developers for skill development.

- *wordpress..com*: This is free Web publishing software, which you can use to create a website or a blog. Although there are many other free website tools, this one is used by many schools and bloggers for its simplicity.

- *vimeo.com*: Vimeo is a free video-sharing website where you can post your videos (with a membership) for noncommercial use.

- *www.youtube.com*: You may be more familiar with YouTube, probably the most popular free video-sharing website.

- *www.pinterest.com*: Pinterest is a free program where you can create and post a collection of photos in a collage or "bulletin board" of information you want to share with people.

- *www.slideshare.net/slideshare*: SlideShare is the site where you can post and share presentations such as slides you have created on PowerPoint or other programs.

- *audacity.sourceforge.net*: Audacity is a free software program for recording and editing audio.

- *maps.google.com*: You can use Google maps to embed maps into your site, and Google has made them interactive. Clicking anywhere focuses the map on that location and shows you related places and the best ways to get there.

This is how print and broadcast style differ:

- **Print:** What happened or who did what? Past tense. Fire destroyed a duplex in midtown yesterday morning, leaving two families homeless.

- **Broadcast and the Web:** What is happening *now* or who is doing what *now*. Present tense is preferable. For example: Two families are homeless today after a fire destroyed their midtown duplex.

Conversational Style

Writing simple sentences in a conversational style — the way you talk — is preferable for all media, but essential for broadcast. Stories on the Web resemble print style.

- **Print:** Write to be read. Sentences may be longer, and the story may include more detail.

■ **Broadcast:** Write for the ear and the eye. Write in conversational style. You are talking to the viewer. Read your story aloud. Writing for the eye means you should plan your story around the images. In most cases, broadcast stories are shorter than their print counterparts. The average TV news story is 1:30, meaning one minute and 30 seconds. Keep the sentences short and simple, structured as subject–verb–object, meaning who did what or what is happening.

Here is the print lead on a story:

> Talking on a cell phone while driving is as dangerous as driving while drunk, new federally funded research shows, and it doesn't matter whether you use a hands-free model or hold the phone up to your ear during the conversation.
>
> — *South Florida Sun-Sentinel*

Here is a conversational approach to the cell phone story for broadcast:

> How many times have you been cut off or otherwise annoyed on the road, only to find the other driver is talking on a cell phone?
>   A new scientific study says it now proves that talking and driving is as dangerous as drinking and driving!
>
> — *KXAN-TV* (Austin, Texas)

Active Voice

The structure in active voice is subject–verb–object: who is doing the action. Passive voice explains what action is being done to whom. Active voice is preferable for all media but more essential for broadcast because it conveys more immediacy. In some cases the passive voice is more appropriate. For example:

Active: Police rescued the woman. (Who did what.)

Passive: The woman was rescued by police. (What was done to whom.)

Passive: The defendant was sentenced to 10 years in prison. In this case the emphasis on the defendant may be preferable.

Active: The judge sentenced the defendant to 10 years in prison. The emphasis here is on the judge, who may not be as important to stress as the defendant.

Impact

When possible, lead with the effect a story will have on viewers. In breaking news this isn't always appropriate, but explaining the impact on the audience is a good way to grab the viewers' attention. This technique also works well for print. The following example from broadcast news would work as well in print or online stories:

> Anchorage residents will able to breathe air that's a little cleaner this weekend. A new, tougher version of the citywide smoking ban goes into effect July 1.
>
> The new smoking ban effectively updates the previous ban by adding daycare centers, outdoor stadiums and bars to the list of places where smoking is against the law.
>
> — *KTUU-TV* (Anchorage, Alaska)

Attribution

Put the attribution at the beginning of the sentence in broadcast writing. In print and Web writing, the attribution may come at the end of the sentence. When you put the attribution last in a broadcast story, it sounds as though the reporter is the source of the information or opinion, which can be dangerous, especially if the statement is an accusation.

Print: The blaze started in the basement, fire officials say.

Broadcast: Fire officials say the blaze started in the basement.

Consider how dangerous the following sentence would sound if the attribution is not clear at the beginning of this sentence: The suspect abused the animals, police say. A better way to say it is: Police say the suspect abused the animals.

If the information is on public records, a statement without attribution is OK, as in this sentence: The suspect is charged with three counts of animal abuse.

'Said' Versus 'Says'

When you attribute information in broadcast writing, "says" gives more immediacy than "said." However, if it is awkward to use the present tense, use "said." If a source said something a week ago, using "says" would be improper. In print, "said" is used more often except in features because generally the source said the quote in the past.

Print: The first firefighters arrived on the scene about three minutes later, at 7:43 a.m., the Fire Department spokesman **said**.

Broadcast: The Fire Department **says** the blaze broke out about 8 a.m., in a child's bedroom at 800 Northview Ave.

Visuals

In print publications, photos and graphics enhance a story. In television news the visual elements are crucial. In this age of convergence, many news organizations publish stories in multiple media. As a result, if you are writing for a print publication, you should still plan photos, audio and video to post on the organization's website.

Interactivity

Try to get readers and viewers involved in all media, but particularly in broadcast and online. In print and broadcast you might add a question or poll and refer your readers to the organization's website. On the Web, there are several ways to interact with the reader through questions, polls, chats, blogs or requests for readers' photos and stories. You can also encourage readers and viewers to comment on a Twitter or Facebook site.

EXERCISES

1 Convert from print to broadcast: Take any story in today's newspaper and convert it for mobile media by updating the lead and condensing the story.

2 Police story — print and broadcast: Write a brief story for print and another version for broadcast, based on the information in the following news release. Use your city's name for the police department and attribute information to Police Spokesman John Coptalker:

At about 2:54 a.m. on Thursday — March 22nd (use this year) Police Mid Shift Patrol Officers responded to reports of a shooting at an apartment located at the 7000 block of Walker Road.

Responding officers located two persons who had been shot. One victim, a male adult in his mid-40s was dead of the apparent gunshot wounds. Another victim, identified as Mary Pothead — age 36 — was transported to a local hospital for emergency treatment. Pothead is listed in serious condition.

Details about the incident are sketchy. Detectives believe that this incident is possibly related to illegal drug activity. Detectives are seeking a possible suspect in this case, described

only as an unknown male. No other information is available at this time.

Detectives are actively seeking information from any persons who may have been in the area of or have knowledge of this shooting incident. Persons with information are asked to call the (use your city) Police at 123-4567.

Persons who wish to remain anonymous may call the city's Crime Stoppers at 123-STOP or on the Web at *www.crimetips.com*. Callers whose tip leads to an arrest of a felony suspect are eligible for a reward of up to $1,000.

3 Mobile media: Using the mobile media writing guidelines, rewrite the previous story or another story from a newspaper or website, for readability on a cell phone.

4 Interactivity:

- Using the example about cell phones cited in this chapter, write a poll question for online readers.

- Write a poll question or comment to elicit responses from readers on your website, Twitter or Facebook site about some controversial issue on your campus or in your community.

5 Multimedia site evaluation: Go to the News21 website (*news21.com*) and access one of the projects. Write an evaluation of the project you chose for its interactivity, innovation and multimedia elements. Give a brief synopsis of the project, and then list the multimedia qualities, critiquing them for their effectiveness.

 MindTap·

FEATURED ONLINE ACTIVITIES: Log on to the MindTap for Rich's Writing and Reporting News to access a variety of robust additional material, including this chapter's learning objectives, activities, comprehension quizzes, and more!

CHAPTER 7
Leads and Nut Graphs

© iQoncept/Shutterstock.com

The best day is the one when I can write a lead that will cause the reader at his breakfast the next morning to spit up his coffee, clutch at his heart and shout, "My God! Martha, did you read this?"

—EDNA BUCHANAN, *Former Police Reporter, The Miami Herald*

COACHING TIPS

Keep leads short — preferably **fewer than 35 words.**

Write your nut graph as a tweet to **identify your focus in 140 characters.**

To find your lead, ask yourself: "What struck me as **most important or interesting?"**

Write a headline for your story; that could be a clue for your lead.

Points of emphasis: Place the **key words at the beginning or the end** of the sentence for emphasis.

Avoid suffering: If you can't devise your lead, **start with your nut graph,** and write your lead later.

Don't invent your lead. **Base it on the backup** in your notes.

THE LEAD IS THE BEGINNING OF THE STORY THAT ENTICES THE reader, so why does renowned writing coach Don Fry write his leads last? Most writers agonize over their leads, but Fry almost never worries about what he is going to say first.

Fry says he begins the writing process long before he sits down at his computer. "I'm imagining the story while I'm reporting it," he says. Fry concentrates on what he calls the "point statement," also known as a "focus graph" or "nut graph." He asks himself what is the story about and what is the point of the story. Any information that doesn't relate to the point statement doesn't get included in the story.

And then he starts writing. Not at the beginning, but at the paragraph containing the point statement. He continues writing until he gets to his ending, which he calls the "kicker." Then he writes his lead. After that he revises.

Mervin Block, a leading writing coach for broadcast journalism, has similar advice. "Think. Don't write yet. Just think," he says in his book *Writing Broadcast News.* "Think about what you want to say and how best to say it: clearly, concisely, conversationally… Start strong. Well begun is half done."

Don Fry, Writing Coach

The lead is crucial in any medium, especially these days when readers and viewers are bombarded with so much information from social media, print, broadcast and online sources. Studies show that most online readers are scanners who just read headlines. How can your leads entice the readers, listeners or viewers to continue? Take a clue from television teasers: Does the anchor tease you about a story that makes you stay tuned after the break? Leads should entice the reader to stay tuned into the rest of the story.

TYPES OF LEADS

The lead (originally spelled "lede" to differentiate it from lead type) tells the reader what the story is about. Think of the lead as a teaser or foreshadowing of what will come in the story. No matter what type of lead you write, you must back it up with information that substantiates it. If you haven't got material to support your lead, you have the wrong lead.

First determine the focus of the story. Ask yourself: What is the story about? What is the most important information? What is the point of this story? Those are the questions you need to ask yourself to write a lead or a focus graph, also called a "nut graph."

Summary Leads

Also called "hard-news leads," or "direct leads," these types of lead summarize what the story is about in the first sentence, getting directly to the point.

With the increasing use of cell phones, tablet computers and other small-screen devices for news reading, the summary lead is an ideal form. Summary leads also are useful in any type of media. Public relations practitioners use summary leads in news releases, which need to be brief and newsworthy.

In these examples, note that the broadcast version uses present tense and a more current angle:

- **Print version:** A 20-year-old Franklin and Marshall College student was shot a block from campus early this morning during an attempted robbery, police said.

- **Broadcast or Web version:** A 20-year-old Franklin and Marshall College student is in critical condition today after he was shot early this morning during an attempted robbery a block from campus.

Soft Leads

Also called "feature leads," "delayed leads" or "indirect leads" soft leads delay telling the reader what the story is about by teasing the reader with a description or a storytelling approach before the focus is stated in a separate paragraph called the "nut graph." In these days of impatient readers and small-screen delivery, the nut graph should be early in the story — usually by the third to fifth paragraph. In this example, the lead is purposely vague to entice readers to continue, and the nut graph is in the third paragraph:

The Alpha Gamma Rho fraternity president says it was a practical joke that got blown out of proportion.

Police say it was a hazing incident that involved new AGR members preparing to have sex with a goat.

Nut graph stating the focus

And Western officials are still trying to determine if AGR members violated university policy by having a goat in their house that may have been used to intimidate new members.

— COREY PAUL, *College Heights Herald*, Western Kentucky University

HARD-NEWS LEADS

How do you decide whether to use a direct or indirect lead? The choice depends on several factors: the significance of the news, the timing, proximity (interest to your local readers or viewers) or subject matter. If the subject is serious — death, disaster, a major change in the law — consider a summary-lead approach. Breaking news that happened yesterday or today also lends itself to a hard-news lead.

Elements of Summary Leads

A summary lead should answer several, but not all, of the basic questions: *who, what, when, where* and *why*, plus *how* and *so what*. If you cram all of them into the lead, it could be cumbersome.

Choose the most important factors for the lead. Save the others for the second or third paragraph.

Subject–Verb–Object Order Summary leads are most effective when they follow subject–verb–object order (who did what or what happened). This order is also favored for broadcast writing. The following lead, which works for print, broadcast and online media, starts with who, what, when and why:

> A 20-year-old Anchorage woman was charged today with offering an undercover police officer $1,000 to kill a woman who appeared on her boyfriend's Facebook page.

Order of Information When you write a summary lead, how do you decide which basics to include and in what order? The points of emphasis should be the first or last words in the lead. Decide which elements are the most important — who, what, where, when, why, how or so what. Usually it is safe to use a subject–verb–object format: who did the action, what happened, to whom. But sometimes the how or why is most important.

Here are some facts presented in a story:

> **Who:** Three boaters
> **What happened:** Two killed, the third injured when the boat capsized
> **When:** Sunday
> **Where:** Lake Harney near the Volusia-Seminole county line in Florida
> **Why:** High winds and waves
> **How:** Explained later in the story

The lead that appeared in the newspaper stresses who first, followed by what:

> Two boaters were killed and a third was injured Sunday when their small boat capsized in high winds and waves on Lake Harney near the Volusia-Seminole county line.
>
> — *The Orlando* (**Florida**) *Sentinel*

Christopher Enoksen/U.S. Coast Guard

Decide which lead is best on this story about a boat capsizing.

Now look at the way the lead would read with different elements placed first:

What	A small boat that capsized in high winds and waves on Lake Harney near the Volusia-Seminole county line caused the death of two boaters and injuries to a third Sunday.	On Lake Harney near the Volusia-Seminole county line, a small boat capsized Sunday in high winds and waves, causing the death of two boaters and injuries to a third.	*Where*
When	On Sunday two boaters were killed and a third was injured when their small boat capsized in high winds and waves on Lake Harney near the Volusia-Seminole county line.	High winds and waves on Lake Harney near the Volusia-Seminole county line caused a small boat to capsize Sunday, killing two boaters and injuring a third.	*Why*

The actual lead from the newspaper seems the most logical because the point of emphasis — the important news (boaters died) — is first. The last lead, focusing on why, is the next best option; the point of emphasis (boaters died) is at the end.

If you were writing that story for broadcast news, you would update the information and use present tense:

Two boaters are dead and a third is suffering from injuries caused when their small boat capsized today on Lake Harney near the Volusia-Seminole county line.

Point of Emphasis Most of the time when you write a hard-news lead, you put the most important information first.

Interest rates on federal student loans will double if Congress fails to reach an agreement on a deal.

Or you might want the point of emphasis at the end of the sentence:

If Congress fails to reach an agreement on a deal, interest rates on federal student loans will double.

Active Versus Passive Voice Active voice is generally preferable to passive in print and always preferred in broadcast writing. Active voice stresses who is doing the action; passive voice stresses those to whom the action is done. But you may need to use passive voice when the emphasis is on what happened instead of who caused it to happen, especially in police or court stories.

Active voice is stronger for the following example because it emphasizes the iguana as the subject; for broadcast put the attribution first.

Active	A pet iguana started a fire in a split-level house in Hillsmere Shores by knocking over a heat lamp with its tail, fire officials said.	over a heat lamp with its tail, fire officials said. Fire officials say a pet iguana started a fire in a split-level house in Hillsmere Shores by knocking over a heat lamp with its tail.
Passive	A fire in a split-level house in Hillsmere Shores was started by a pet iguana that knocked	*Broadcast version with attribution first — active voice*

A pet iguana.

University of Pennsylvania Van Pelt Library.

In the next example, however, passive voice is preferable because it gets to the point faster:

Passive	A former employee of the University of Pennsylvania's Van Pelt Library was sentenced to seven years of psychiatric probation yesterday for the theft	of $1,798,310 worth of rare books and documents. — *The Philadelphia Inquirer*

The sentence was imposed by Philadelphia Common Pleas Court Judge Russell M. Nigro, as the story later explains. The emphasis in the lead is on the employee who was sentenced. Here is how the lead would sound in active voice:

| *Active* | Philadelphia Common Pleas Court Judge Russell M. Nigro yesterday sentenced a former employee of the University of Pennsylvania's Van Pelt Library | to seven years of psychiatric probation for the theft of $1,798,310 worth of rare books and documents. |

In the active version, it takes longer to get to the point of the story, and the emphasis is on the judge, not the employee.

Where to Say When The time element can be confusing in a lead. In breaking news, when something happened yesterday, the time element usually does not come first in the sentence. But you need to place it where it is accurate, even if it sounds awkward.

Here is an example of a confusing time element:

University officials agreed to raise tuition by $100 Monday.

As written, the lead indicates the tuition will increase on Monday. Wrong. Tuition won't go up until next fall. Here's what really happened:

University officials agreed Monday to raise tuition by $100.

Delayed Identification When the *who* in your lead is not a well-known person in your community or in the nation, you can identify the person by age, location, occupation or another modifier in the first paragraph. Then identify the person by name in the second paragraph. When you use delayed identification, even if your story involves several people, the first name you use should be the one you referred to in your lead.

All states have laws restricting the release of juvenile offenders' names, and several states prohibit the release of names of rape victims. In addition, many newspapers and television news organizations have policies to withhold names of criminal suspects until they are formally charged with crimes. Therefore, you need to use alternative forms of identification in these situations as well.

The following examples show different ways to delay identification:

| *Age* | A 104-year-old Michigan grandmother claims she was forced to lie about her age on Facebook. |

Marguerite Joseph says when she entered her real birth year on the social networking site, Facebook automatically changed it to 1928 because the site doesn't list years before that date. A Facebook spokesman said the site discovered the error and apologized.

Occupation   Two Minneapolis meter monitors have been charged with stealing an estimated $35,000 worth of nickels, dimes and quarters from parking meters.

Dale Timinskis, 42, and Leroy Siner, 40, both of Minneapolis, were arrested Tuesday after police watched their activities.

— *Minneapolis Star Tribune*

Location   A Sacramento woman was sentenced to seven years in prison Monday after being convicted of identity theft.

Mary Stealer used indentifying information of more than 10 victims to pay bills and buy luxuries such as a fur coat, computers and other items, with licenses she obtained from wallets and purses stolen in a series of car burglaries.

Other identifier   A former Duke University student who posed as a wealthy French baron was sentenced to three years in prison for fraud.

Maurice Jeffrey Locke Rothschild, 38, was sentenced in Greensboro, North Carolina, for bilking two banks by posing as a nobleman from France's wealthy Rothschild family.

If you are writing a story about a person who has been in the news frequently, such as a suspect in a trial, you may use the name, but add a phrase or clause to identify the person, as in this example about a woman on trial for the murder of her former fiancé.

Prosecutors in the trial of former stripper Michele Linehan want the jury to watch a movie called "The Last Seduction," about a woman who tried to manipulate her lover into killing her husband for $1 million.

Updated Leads

The summary lead usually stresses basic facts about the news in the immediate past, and it is usually written in past tense. This type of breaking news lead is often referred to as a "first-day lead," as if readers were hearing the news for the first time. Because television and online news sites require immediacy, leads are usually updated by advancing the story to the next step.

Here is an example of how you might update a lead, especially for broadcast or online media, even if you have no new information:

Original version	Princeton University officials have placed a cap on the number of A's that professors can award, in an effort to crack down on grade inflation.	Students at Princeton University won't be receiving as many A's this year. School officials are cracking down on grade inflation by placing a cap on the number of A's professors can award.	*Updated version*

Impact Leads

The "impact lead" explains how the readers and viewers will be affected by an issue. This type of lead is also good for broadcast stories. It is an excellent tool to make a story seem fresh and relevant. The impact lead is especially helpful on bureaucratic stories. It answers the questions "So what? What does this news mean to a reader?"

Impact leads can be written in a hard-news summary form or in a soft lead. The information you give must be factual, not your interpretation. If you use a soft lead, you must write a clear nut graph early in the story.

The previous updated lead is also an example of an impact lead because it starts with how students at Princeton University will be affected by the new grade restrictions.

This impact lead uses a direct summary approach:

Summary lead with impact	San Francisco has become the first city in the nation to require cell phone companies to disclose how much radiation their phones emit.

The Centers for Disease Control

This story about dieting lends itself to an impact lead.

Here is an impact lead that directly addresses readers and viewers; this lead would work equally well in print, broadcast or on the Web:

Are your jeans a little too tight? Do you wake up tired from only a few hours of sleep?

If the answer is "yes," you probably could lose a few pounds. But you may not have to diet. What you might not know is that a little extra sleep could be the answer.

Studies show that people who sleep too little are actually more likely to gain weight.

Attribution in Leads

Attribution tells the reader where you got your information. Too much attribution can clutter a lead. Too little attribution can get you in trouble. For print and online stories, you may put the attribution at the beginning or the end of the sentence; for broadcast, attribution must come first. Here are some guidelines:

- If you know the information is factual and you witnessed it or have firsthand knowledge that it is true, you may eliminate the attribution. If you received the information by telephone, as in police or fire stories, attribute it to your source.

- Whenever you are saying anything accusatory, as in police or political stories, you must attribute the information.

- You also must attribute the quotes or partial quotes you use in a lead.

To keep attribution clutter to a minimum, you may give a general reference to some sources — such as "police said" or "experts say" — if their titles are long. Then, as in delayed identification, give the specific name and title in the second reference.

In broadcast news, if the source is shown on videotape, the name and title may be superimposed under the video, so you may not need to attribute by name and title. If you do use attribution, put the source's title before the name:

Right: Police Chief John Law says the suspect is in custody.

Wrong: John Law, police chief, says the suspect is in custody.

Fact Versus Opinion: Here are some examples that demonstrate when to use attribution:

SOCIAL MEDIA

USE TWITTER as a way to write a succinct summary lead in 140 characters, but don't use abbreviations. Search for tweets on a subject of interest to you. Then click the links and read the leads on the full post. Notice how many of the leads are summary leads, which are ideal for tweets and mobile media, as in these examples.

Child care costs more than food, rent and college in some metros

Pell grant and scholarship funds pay college tuition costs and fees

You can also tweet your nut graph, which will help you identify the focus of your story. You don't have to post your tweets; just use the Twitter concepts to improve your skills in writing leads and nut graphs.

Fact: No attribution is needed.

An 88-year-old man died Monday afternoon when fire spread through his second-floor apartment at the Wellington Arms Apartments in north St. Louis County.

Opinion: Speculation about the cause needs to be attributed.

An 88-year-old man died in north St. Louis County Monday afternoon, apparently after he started a fire while smoking in bed, authorities said.

The body of a man who had been fatally stabbed was discovered Monday morning in a city trash bin in the Lewis Place neighborhood, police said.

— *St. Louis* **(Missouri)** *Post-Dispatch*

Attributed fact: Attribution for fact is needed because the reporter got the information secondhand (by telephone).

Accusations A person is innocent until proved guilty in court. In crime stories, attribute any accusatory statements to police or other authorities, especially when you are using a suspect's name. If the person has been charged with a crime, you may state that fact without attribution. The word allegedly can be used when the charges have not been proved, but direct attribution to the police is preferable. Here are some examples:

No attribution is needed.

A 25-year-old Fairbanks woman was charged with misdemeanor assault for allegedly biting her husband's ribcage and pinky Saturday night at their home.

Attribution is needed for an accusatory statement.

David Roger Flint killed 16-month-old Brittany K. Boyer on Monday by dangling her by the arms, swinging her side to side and beating her head against the floor and wooden furniture, police say. The 23-year-old Flint was arrested about 10:30 p.m. Tuesday and accused of murder.

— **JANE MEINHARDT,** *Tampa Bay Times/St. Petersburg* (Florida) *Times*

The word "allegedly" is used because it has not yet been proved that the kidnap and rape occurred.

A 38-year-old paroled murderer has been arrested in St. Croix County, Wisconsin, for allegedly kidnapping and raping two 16-year-old girls in Minneapolis last month. . . .

Later, the lead is backed up this way.

He was charged with two counts of first-degree criminal sexual conduct and two counts of kidnapping.

— *St. Paul* (**Minnesota**) *Pioneer Press*

This lead would be a safer alternative.

A 38-year-old paroled murderer has been charged with kidnapping and raping two 16-year-old girls in Minneapolis last month.

Quotes Whenever you quote someone directly, indirectly or partially, you need to attribute the statement.

Full quotes are difficult in leads and can be awkward. Reading a story that starts with a full quote is like coming into the middle of a conversation; it's hard to tell the context and meaning of the quote. Full quotes are also ineffective for broadcast writing.

A more effective technique is the use of partial quotes, especially when the speaker says something controversial or dramatic. Leads may also contain reference quotes, a few words referring to something controversial. Both partial and reference quotes should be backed up later in the story with the full quote or with the context in which the statement was made.

A full quote is used in this lead because it is dramatic, but it is still confusing.

"I've done everything out there," 31-year-old Gilbert Franco told his wife Thursday. "All that's left to do is learn the Bible and to die."

The next day, San Jose police say, Franco entered the C&S Market at East Julian and 26th streets and shot to death Katherine Young Suk Choe, 40, whose family owns the store.

Seconds later, 50 yards away, Franco fatally shot himself in the head.

— *San Jose* (**California**) *Mercury News*

In this example a partial quote is used and backed up later with the full quote, a technique used more often in stories about speeches, politics and court stories:

A reference quote is used in the lead.

The University of Pennsylvania announced yesterday that it was penalizing a senior scientist for "lapses of judgment" in an experiment last April in which more than 120 people may have been exposed to a virus that can cause a fatal form of leukemia. . . .

The backup puts the partial quote in context.

The committee concluded that the professor was not guilty of research misconduct as defined in a school policy. However, the committee concluded that there were "lapses of judgment and failures of communication" in the experiment.

— *The Philadelphia Inquirer*

Attribution First or Last The general rule in the lead is to put the most important information first. If the attribution is cumbersome and will slow the lead, put it at the end. If it is brief, you can put it first. In broadcast writing, however, you need to put the attribution first. If the attribution is cumbersome, refer to the source broadly as in "a new study" or "a state official," and state the full attribution in the next paragraph.

Attribution last

Casual drug use has dropped sharply during the last five years, but the number of addicts using cocaine daily has not changed significantly, the federal government reported yesterday.

— *The Philadelphia Inquirer*

Attribution first (acceptable, and preferable for broadcast writing)

The federal government reports that casual drug use has dropped sharply during the last five years, but the number of addicts using cocaine daily has not changed significantly.

Attribution last (because name is cumbersome and not as important as conclusions)

America's newspaper journalists want a faster transition of print to digital delivery of the news, according to "Life Beyond Print," a study of nearly 3,800 journalists by researchers at the Media Management Center of Northwestern University.

Cluttered Attribution In the example that follows, note how a long attribution at the start of the sentence clutters the lead:

Cluttered

Karen Davisson, child protection worker with the Kansas Department of Social Rehabilitation Services district office in

Emporia, said Tuesday that only rarely are neglected or abused children removed from their parents' care and placed in foster homes or put up for adoption.

Uncluttered   Neglected or abused children are rarely removed from their parents' care and placed in foster homes or put up for adoption, a state social worker said Tuesday.

Karen Davisson, who made the comment, is a child protection worker with the Kansas Department of Social Rehabilitation Services district office in Emporia.

One of the most common causes of clutter in leads is too much information about where and when something was said. Put some of this material in the second paragraph. Put the location of the meeting much farther down in the story, or eliminate it altogether unless it is important to the reader.

Cluttered   Fort Riley is being considered as a possible host for the proposed joint landfill for Geary and Riley counties, Riley County Director of Public Works Dan Harden said during an informational meeting Tuesday night at the Geary County 4-H Senior Citizens Center.

Uncluttered   Fort Riley is being considered as a possible site for a landfill, a Riley County official said Tuesday. Dan Harden, director of public works said . . .

SOFT LEADS

- Try writing many different leads instead of struggling to find the perfect one.
- Make sure that your lead is related to your focus and can be backed up in your story.
- Do not strain to "create" a lead from your head. Pull from the story, not from your head, for inspiration.

Soft leads can be fun to write and fun to read. They can also be painful. If you don't get to the point quickly, they can also be tedious. They can be as effective in broadcast writing as in print.

MULTIMEDIA COACH

THE TECHNIQUES of writing leads apply to all media, but broadcast leads should stress the most current information. If you are posting the information first on the Web, you need to update the lead for the next print edition as well as the next broadcast.

Online writing is similar to print, but summary leads are often preferred because readers are impatient to discover the main point of the story, especially for news that is delivered to cell phones or other small-screen devices. Summary leads are also preferred for public relations writing in news releases. If you use a descriptive or anecdotal lead, make sure that the nut graph is high in the story.

Here are some guidelines for broadcast and online writing:

- Use the active voice, with an emphasis on short, uncomplicated sentences. State who is doing the action rather than to whom the action was done.
- Use simple sentences, preferably in subject–verb–object order (who did what). Avoid long sentences that begin with clauses.
- Put the most important information first in the sentence.
- Use a conversational tone. Addressing the reader as "you" works well in broadcast and on the Web.
- For broadcast, place the attribution first, not at the end of the sentence; either order works for the Web. If the attribution is cumbersome, put it in another paragraph.

Although soft leads are also called "delayed leads," the lead is still first. Only the nut graph is delayed. It is preferable to place the nut graph high in the story, by the third to fifth paragraph.

There are many types of soft leads. They can be used on both news and feature stories. Most of them follow a simple concept: specific to general. Use a specific example at the beginning to illustrate the main point of the story.

ETHICS

ETHICAL DILEMMA: You want to write an anecdotal lead focusing on a person for your story, but you don't have a real source. Should you use a hypothetical person without telling the reader? Should you use a hypothetical situation at all?

Ethical values: Credibility, accuracy, truthfulness.

Ethical guidelines: The Society of Professional Journalists Code of Ethics says, "Seek the truth and report it. Avoid misleading re-enactments or staged news events."

People like to read about other people. As a result, many soft leads start with something about a person who is one of many people sharing the same problem. The idea behind these soft leads — called "anecdotal leads" — is that readers can relate better to one person's problem than to a general statement of a problem.

Other common types of soft leads are descriptive and narrative. "Descriptive leads" describe a person or a scene. "Narrative leads" are storytelling leads that recount the event in a dramatic way to put the reader on the scene as the action occurs.

And then there are leads that are just clever or catchy.

It's not what you call soft leads that matters; it's how you write them. The important point is to tell a good story. When writers struggle with soft leads, it is often because they think they must create something clever. All too often, the result is a cliché. It is best to look at your notes and build a lead based on something interesting in the story.

The sections that follow show a variety of ways to structure a soft lead. The basic techniques are descriptive, anecdotal and narrative.

Descriptive Leads

This type of lead describes a person, place or event. It is like the descriptive focus-on-a-person lead, but it doesn't have to focus on a person who is one of many. It can be used for news or feature stories.

In this example, the story focuses on the man who is causing the problem:

Skippack farmer John W. Hasson stood ankle-deep in mud, pumping milk into a wooden trough as his pigs, squealing and grunting, snouts quivering, climbed over each other to get to their feed.

Hasson inhaled deeply.

"Does that smell sour to you?

That's what they call noxious fumes," he said with a sniff toward his new neighbors, Ironbridge Estates, a subdivision of two-story colonial houses costing $200,000 plus.

Ironbridge's developers say Hasson's farm smells. And his 250 pigs squeal too much.

So they have filed suit in Montgomery County to force him to clean up his act. The case is scheduled to be heard May 8.

— ERIN KENNEDY, *The Philadelphia Inquirer*

U.S. Department of Agriculture

Little pigs could cause big problems, as in the opposite example.

Anecdotal Leads

This type of lead starts with a story about a person or an event. In a sense, all soft leads are anecdotal because they are all storytelling approaches. Many combine descriptive and anecdotal techniques.

This lead is an anecdote — the story behind a woman's court case:

> Late one spring night, after drinks at a bar and a bit of protest, Elaine Hollis agreed to her boyfriend's desire to capture their passion on videotape.
>
> Inside Edward Bayliss' apartment, the video camera rolled at the foot of his bed.
>
> He promised to erase the tape.
>
> Seven years later, Hollis, who has a son with Bayliss, was in Delaware County Court accusing him of contriving to bring her into disrepute by exhibiting the tape. Bayliss, president of Philadelphia Suburban Electrical Service in Upper Darby, admitted showing the tape to one of his friends.
>
> Hollis contended he showed and distributed the tape in Delaware County and surrounding areas, as well as gave copies of it to two bar owners in Darby, who played it for customers.
>
> Last week, after three years of litigation, a county judge upheld an Oct. 15 Common Pleas Court order that mandated Bayliss pay Hollis $125,000 to settle her lawsuit.
>
> — PATRICK SCOTT, *The Philadelphia Inquirer*

This lead uses both anecdotal and descriptive techniques:

> Dawn Clark's cat walked carefully across the lawn, then stopped suddenly, looking bewildered.
>
> The cat sniffed tentatively, then bolted off the grass and spent the next few minutes licking its paws — trying to clean the paint flecks from them.
>
> The lawn had recently been mowed and was green as a billiard table, because it had just been painted with a vegetable dye.
>
> Santa Barbara residents have devised innovative ways to keep their yards green since the city, faced with an expected water shortfall of nearly 50 percent for the year, declared a "drought emergency" in late February and banned lawn watering.   *Nut graph*
>
> Clark's cat had just experienced one: Several landscape companies now offer painting and local nurseries are stocking their shelves with green paint and pump sprayers.   *Extension of nut graph*
>
> — MILES CORWIN, *Los Angeles Times*

RabidsquirrellDK/Creative Commons

This story starts with an anecdote about a woman's cat, to personalize the story about the city's drought problems.

Narrative Leads

Like an anecdotal lead, a narrative lead tells a story with enough dramatic action for readers to feel as if they are witnessing the event. Narrative writing uses all the techniques of fiction, including dialogue, scene setting and foreshadowing, giving the reader clues to what will happen. It takes longer to set up the nut graph for this kind of lead, but if the story is dramatic enough, the narrative approach may work.

A California Big Spin lottery ticket.

The case has all the elements of a 1950s film noir mystery.

The characters: the scheming husband, the trusting wife, the other woman.

The story: The husband, Ray Valois, buys a lottery ticket, scratches it and finds three "Spin, Spin, Spin" symbols. That makes him eligible to win up to $2 million in the California "Big Spin" lottery, but he does not want to tell his wife, Monica, according to his statement in San Luis Obispo County Superior Court records. So he gives the ticket to another woman, waitress Stephanie Martin. She agrees to cash in the ticket, according to court records, and secretly give him half.

The inevitable plot twist: Valois and Martin turn on each other. He claims that he owns the ticket. She claims that she owns the ticket.

The conclusion: Martin spins and wins $100,000. But the wife finds out and sues both of them for fraud.

Nut graph

Now neither Martin nor Valois has the $100,000. His wife's attorney, Gary Dunlap, obtained a temporary restraining order, restricting lottery officials from awarding the winnings until a court hearing today.

— MILES CORWIN, *Los Angeles Times*

Other Soft Leads

Soft leads can be written in many other ways. The following techniques are variations on the three main types of soft leads, combining features of descriptive, anecdotal and narrative leads.

Focus-on-a-Person Leads You can focus on a person in two ways: Use an anecdotal approach, telling a little story about the person, or use a descriptive approach that describes the person or shows the person in action. This type of lead can be used in profile stories about the person or in news stories about issues, where the person is one of many affected by the point of your story.

This example uses the descriptive approach:

Nita walked slowly down the narrow hall, deftly guiding her tottering 11-month-old son around the abandoned baby walkers, strollers and toys.

Inside her tiny bedroom, the 17-year-old mother pointed to photographs of her son's father and some of her friends. Cards congratulating her on her recent high school graduation were nearby. The baby's crib was crammed into an area near the door.

Nita, one of 85 residents at Florence Crittenton Services in Fullerton, is one of a growing number of teenagers having babies in Orange County — a figure that has increased 36 percent in five years.

— JANINE ANDERSON, *The Orange County* (California)*Register*

Nut graph: points out that this person is one of many

The focus-on-a-person lead is an effective technique for broadcast news as well, especially when the person or people used in the lead exemplify a problem shared by many other people in your community.

Residents in this flood-damaged community share problems described in the next example.

Judy and Jose Westbrook spent the morning cleaning up the furniture in their front yard. The Blue River had overflowed its banks and forced its way into their Independence home.

More than 25 families share their predicament. Late this afternoon, all of those families were awaiting word about their flood insurance claims.

Nut graph: points out that these people are like many others

Contrast Leads This type of lead can be used to set up stories about conflicts or unusual circumstances. The two most common ways to write contrast leads emphasize circumstances and time:

But-Guess-What Contrast: Contrast leads that revolve around circumstances can be used to explain something unusual:

William Pearce, known to his patients as Dr. William J. Rick, was charming and slick, say his former associates and police detectives.

He came to town with medical degrees, numerous national board certificates and myriad other qualifications.

But the real Dr. Rick died in 1986, police say. And now William John Pearce, 57, is in jail on charges of impersonating a doctor.

— SHARON MCBREEN, *The Orlando* (Florida) *Sentinel*

Nut graph

Then-and-Now Contrast: Time contrasts — then and now — are useful ways to show change. This type of lead also can be used when the background is interesting or important and is relevant to the focus.

It was March 1964 when Lewis "Hackie" Wilson, the 7-year-old son of a St. Petersburg firefighter, disappeared after stopping to pick up flowers on his way home from school.

His case received national attention a month later when a sheriff's posse on horseback, flushing out rattlesnakes ahead of a line of 80 searchers, found the child's bones in a field south of Venice.

Now the case may be revived. Prosecutors in Sarasota County have realized that Joseph Francis Bryan, a convicted child kidnapper indicted for Hackie's murder in 1965, has never been brought to trial.

— KAREN DATKO, *Tampa Bay Times/St. Petersburg* (Florida) *Times*

Nut graph

Teaser Leads These leads use the element of surprise to tease the reader into the story. The nut graph may also be a contrast, but the first sentence sets it up as a tease into something unusual. Broadcast news uses the concept of teasers before commercials to convince the audience to stay tuned after the break, but teasers are also effective in leads on broadcast stories.

BURLINGTON, Vermont — This is no ordinary public library.

For one thing, there are only four books on the shelves. For another, you won't find any of these works, or the many that are expected to join them soon, at other libraries or bookstores.

You probably never will.

That's because the Brautigan Library, which opened here last weekend, has a unique policy — it only accepts books that have never been published.   *Nut graph*

— STEVE STECKLOW, *The Philadelphia Inquirer*

Mystery Leads Like teasers, mystery leads promise the reader a surprise or a treat for reading on. They set up the story like a mystery novel. They're fun to write and fun to read, but they won't work unless the subject matter lends itself to this approach. They are effective for print and broadcast writing.

One technique for writing mystery leads is to start with a vague pronoun, *it* or *they,* and to delay naming the noun to which the pronoun refers: "It began at midnight." Later you specify what "it" was. Here is an example of a mystery lead:

They know who you are, what you eat, how you procreate — and where to find you.

Been turned down for a MasterCard or Visa? List Brokerage and Management, a New York list marketer, may have your name. It rents a list of 1.6 million people rejected for bank cards — obtained, the company says, from the very banks that turned you down. . . .

Computer companies are   *Nut graph* hooking up with credit bureaus and massive data banks to allow people with only a desktop computer to single you out by income, age, neighborhood, car model or waist size.

— STEPHEN KOFF, *Tampa Bay Times/St. Petersburg* (Florida) *Times*

Build-on-a-Quote Leads If you have a great quote, build your lead around the quote that will back up your first sentence. But be careful not to repeat too much of the quote in your lead; that's boring and repetitious. Building on a quote is an easy and effective way to find a lead, provided the quote is related to the focus of the story. This technique works equally well for hard-news leads. For broadcast news, however, you would not read a quote. Instead, you might start with a video of a person speaking, called a "sound on tape" (SOT).

ANDOVER, Kan. — Melinda Easterbrook knows exactly how long it took for a tornado to blast apart her comfortable home while she and her husband huddled in the basement.

"It lasted five Hail Marys and two Our Fathers, but you have to say them quickly," she said yesterday.

While she was praying, the concrete basement rumbled and shook. When she and her husband, Bryan, came upstairs, they were hardly prepared for the scope of the destruction that had swept through this small town about five miles east of Wichita.

Nut graph

— LARRY FISH, *The Philadelphia Inquirer*

The next example is the kind of build-on-a-quote lead to avoid. The backup quote says the same thing as the lead, and it's right after the lead, so it's boring. In broadcast writing this is called "parroting," when the reporter introduces a sound bite that repeats what the source says on tape. It should be avoided as well.

Linda Winkler/Federal Emergency Management Agency

Residents search for treasured memorabilia in the debris from a tornado that damaged homes in Kansas.

A commitment to high-tech learning and small classes taught by professors has made Fort Hays State University the fastest-growing university in the state Board of Regents system, FHSU's president said today.

FHSU had the largest spring semester enrollment increase among the six regents' universities — 2.4 percent compared with the previous spring.

"We've been the fastest growing of the regents' institutions over the last five years," FHSU President Edward Hammond said.

List Leads If you have a few brief examples to lead into your focus, you may list them in parallel sentences — making sure that your sentences have the same construction, such as subject–verb–object order. A list of three items or sentences provides good rhythm.

David Hodges isn't in prison. He's not in jail. He didn't sit through a trial, and he didn't plead his case before a judge or jury.

Six years ago, police charged the then-Coralville resident with viewing child pornography on a University of Iowa computer. His trial was set, then reset, then reset again. A judge denied a motion to throw out the case. In

January 2007, Hodges, who had been convicted of the same crime in 2003, failed to appear for his pretrial conference.

Law enforcement officials haven't seen him since — and that's not unusual. State data and interviews with law-enforcement officials reveal a system lacking the budget and manpower to adequately deal with fugitives.

— REGINA ZIBERMINTS, *The Daily Iowan,* University of Iowa

Question Leads These can be effective if the reader is interested in finding the answer to the question you pose. If not, you could lose the reader. One way to test question leads is to determine whether the answer would be yes or no. Those are the dangerous ones. A question that raises a more thoughtful, and more interesting, answer is preferable.

What are the odds of finding your true love by placing an ad with a telephone dating service?

About one in 40, according to Terry Ehlbert.

On April 13, Ehlbert is planning to marry Scott Anderson, who was the last of 40 guys she agreed to meet after placing a voicemail ad with the dating service she saw advertised on TV. . . .

— RICK SHEFCHIK, *St. Paul* (Minnesota) *Pioneer Press*

The next example is a little dangerous. What if you don't want to buy cigarettes at all? Will you read on?

Want to buy cigarettes while at the gas station? Or while sipping a cocktail at your favorite bar?

Not in Lower Merion, if township officials have their way.

Nut graph   Officials there, concerned about the availability of cigarettes to minors, have proposed a municipal law prohibiting cigarette vending machines in the township. The law would be the first of its kind in Pennsylvania.

— *The Philadelphia Inquirer*

Cliché Leads In general, avoid clichés. But occasionally, a play on words will work as a clever lead. Consider this:

Nick Agid's workshop is just a stone's throw from the Torrance post office. Good thing, too. When Agid drops a post card into the mail, it lands with a five-pound thud.

Agid is a sculptor who   *Nut graph* carves messages on leftover chunks of marble and granite. They become postcards when he adds scratched-on addresses and slaps stamps on the slabs.

— BOB POOL, *Los Angeles Times*

Leads to Avoid

The leads described in this section are strained, obtuse, rambling or just plain awful. They don't work for a variety of reasons.

Cluttered Leads Keep your leads simple, especially for broadcast. Don't try to cram all the major facts of the story in one sentence. This lead is too complex and contains the cliché "killed two birds with one stone."

Rolling up their sleeves, 20 students from Voznesenka School, near the head of Kachemak Bay, killed two birds with one stone Saturday: they washed away the grit and grime and put a shine on more than 25 local vehicles, and they raised more than $300 to help pay for next spring's graduation expenses.

Good News/Bad News Leads The bad news is this type of lead. They're clichés, and they're used so often that they're boring. They're also judgmental.

Some good news for city workers: The county administration says it might not have to give out any pink slips, at least for now.

Some bad news for city taxpayers: The county administration has shown no signs of scaling back its proposal to raise taxes for the next several years.

Crystal-Ball Leads These are dream-sequence leads that foretell the future. If you were writing about psychics, perhaps you could write this kind of lead. But most people can't predict the future. "John Jones never imagined when he boarded the plane that it was going to crash." Would he have been stupid enough to board it if he had known? Leads that emphasize "if only they had known" are far-fetched. Consider the following. It's unlikely that a child who is choking is thinking about the future — much less about what he can do for someone else.

When 10-year-old Jason Finser of Clermont was saved from choking to death at a family dinner two years ago, he never dreamed he would be able to return the favor.

Nut graph   But luckily for his classmate, 9-year-old Abby Muick, Jason knew exactly what to do when she choked on a chocolate-and-Rice Krispies treat in the lunchroom at Minneola Elementary School.

— *The Orlando* (Florida) *Sentinel*

Nightmare Leads These are also dream leads, usually relating to a past experience. The nightmare analogy is overused: "The past three days were like a nightmare for John Jones." For the reader too: Every bad experience someone has does not have to be compared to a nightmare.

The nightmare became reality for local police yesterday when a drug dealer was arrested at the Phoenix Sky Harbor International Airport.

Hidden in his baggage were $50,000 worth of heroin, some PCP and 500 grams of crack cocaine, with an estimated street value of at least $15,000.

Plop-a-Person Leads This type of lead is a misuse of the focus-on-a-person lead. When the writer just tops the story with a sketch of a person and does not back it up in the text, that's plopping. It's also misleading. The reader starts the story thinking that the person has something to say or do in the story. But after the lead, the person disappears.

This is the last time we hear about Nelson, despite that he was a good example.

Tuesday was a good day for psychology professor Carnot Nelson.

He spent most of it helping an honors student work on her thesis. He read another student's doctoral dissertation and two master's thesis proposals. Then he went to a meeting, which he left after an hour and a half so he could do some reading of his own.

Nelson, a senior professor at the University of South Florida, who also teaches large undergraduate classes and small graduate seminars, is a good example of the range of activity involved in teaching Florida university students.

"Education is a one-at-a-time, hand-made business," said state university spokesman Pat Riordan. "You can't mechanize it, you can't computerize it and you can't put it on an assembly line."

But college professors in Florida are under increasing pressure to do exactly that. Recurring state budget cuts have made some classes larger and eliminated many others. And a political climate that says there can be no new taxes until a state government becomes "more productive" has fueled a drive to force professors to spend more time in the classroom.

Nut graphs

— *Tampa Bay Times/St. Petersburg* (Florida) *Times*

Weather-Report Leads These leads set the scene by describing the weather: "It was a dark and stormy night." Avoid using the weather as a lead when it isn't related to the story.

> It was hot and humid the day the city council decided to ban smoking from all public buildings.
> The ordinance, passed unanimously, will go into effect immediately.

Stereotype Leads These are most common in features about older people, women and groups with special interests. The writer tries hard to be complimentary but instead only reinforces stereotypes. This is the lead for a story about Senior Olympics, games for people over age 60:

U.S. Army Sgt. 1st Class Michael J. Cardin/U.S. Army

> At the age when most of their contemporaries are in rocking chairs, these athletes will be competing in swimming, archery, badminton, bicycle racing — just about every imaginable sport, through the long jump and shot put.
>
> — *The Baltimore Sun*

These seniors are participating in the National Golden Age Games in Birmingham, Alabama.

If you look around your college campus, you're likely to see many professors in their 60s, and most of them don't spend much time in rocking chairs.

Soft leads can be enticing and creative, but they must be accurate.

REMINDERS: TIPS FOR FINDING YOUR LEAD

To find a lead that will work for you in your story, first find your nut graph. Ask yourself what the main point of the story is. Then ask some of these questions to find your lead:

- *Reader Interest:* What did you or would the reader find most interesting about this subject?
- *Memorable Item:* What was the most memorable impression or fact?
- *Focus on a Person:* Is there someone who exemplifies the problem or issue? If you tell a story about this person or show the person in action, will it lead to the point in the nut graph?

- *Descriptive Approach:* Will a description of the scene relate to the focus?

- *Mystery Approach:* Can you tease the reader with a surprise that leads to the nut graph?

- *Build on a Quote:* Is there a great quote to back up the lead? If so, write the lead so it refers to the quote without repeating it.

- *Contrast:* Would a then-and-now approach work?

- *Problem/Solution:* Can you set up a problem so the reader wants to discover the solution?

- *Narrative Storytelling:* If you were just telling a good story, how would you start? Can you reconstruct the events to put the reader on the scene?

EXERCISES

1 Hard-news leads: Write summary leads from the following information. For the time element, use the day of the week instead of "yesterday" or "today."

- Write this lead for a print publication: A study was released yesterday by the University of Colorado. The study was funded by the Alfred P. Sloan Foundation. The study said that 60 percent of college students who begin studying science, mathematics or engineering switch to another major. The study cited poor teaching and an aloof faculty as the cause.

- There was a fire yesterday at a pizza restaurant. It is located at 2035 Main St. Two firefighters were injured when the roof fell in. They were treated at St. Luke's Medical Center for minor injuries. The fire started in the basement of the building. The cause is under investigation. The roof collapsed, and the inside of the restaurant was destroyed. Damages are estimated at $100,000. The information comes from fire officials in your community.

- The Centers for Disease Control today released the results of a survey of nutritional supplements. Nutritional supplements include vitamins, protein supplements and products promising muscle growth. Only supplements in powder, capsule or tablet form were surveyed. "It turned out that at least half of the ingredients have no documented medical effect," said Rossane Philen, a medical epidemiologist at the National Center for

Environmental Health and Injury Control. She was part of the surveying team. The survey said many nutritional supplements have no medical support for their advertised claims.

2 Broadcast versions: Convert the leads you wrote in Exercise 1 to broadcast leads.

3 Active/passive voice: Change this lead to active voice:

A 29-year-old Phoenix man was killed Tuesday when his motorcycle was struck by a car on East Ina Road.

Write a lead in passive voice from this information:

Jones County Circuit Court Judge Billy Landrum yesterday sentenced a 17-year-old high school sophomore to two consecutive life terms for the murder of two men in a convenience store.

4 Delayed identification: From the following information, write a lead using delayed identification.

Background provided by the police: Michael Jones, who lives in the 3700 block of North Camino Street in Tucson, was driving a flatbed truck in central Tucson early yesterday morning. He lost control of his truck, and it overturned on East 15th Street near South Kino Parkway. He died of head injuries at the scene of the accident at 2:30 a.m. He was 44 years old.

5 Updated lead: From this information, give the lead a forward spin for the next edition of your print, broadcast or online publication.

Background: Vandals broke into the Midtown Magnet Middle School at 300 Fifth Ave. just before 7 p.m. on Sunday. They broke windows and damaged 11 classrooms and an office area. They damaged computers and other equipment. The cost of the damages has not yet been estimated. Classes are scheduled to resume today. School was closed Monday while school district employees spent the day cleaning up damage to the school.

6 **Impact leads:** Write impact leads from this information:

- The Board of Regents (or the governing body of universities in your state) has approved an increase in rates for campus housing at your university. The biggest increase will be in residence halls, where rates will increase 14.8 percent for double-room occupancy. The current rate is $2,684, and it will increase to $3,080 next fall.

- The Rockville Centre City Council will meet at 7 p.m. Tuesday. The council will consider adopting an ordinance that would impose penalties for false alarms that are sent to the police department from faulty or improperly operated electronic security systems. Under the proposed ordinance, an alarm system owner would be allowed six free false alarms. The owner would have to pay a $30 penalty for each additional false alarm.

7 **Attribution:** Write a summary lead from the following information. Decide whether you need to include attribution.

Capt. J. Randall Ogden, a spokesman for the Tucson Fire Department (or use your local fire department spokesperson): A fire destroyed a home on East 17th Street. It was started by a cigarette that was discarded in a sofa. The fire left the husband, his wife and their four children homeless. The fire started at 1 a.m. and caused $30,000 in damages.

8 **Anecdotal, focus-on-a-person lead:** Write an anecdotal lead with a person focus from the following information; include a nut graph. Your focus is about the frustrations that students experience trying to park on campus because the parking department has sold too many permits.

Background: Nancy Pauw is a graduate student. One morning, she circled the parking lot east of the computer center three times before she found a parking space. Last year, there were 7,565 student parking permits sold for 3,930 spaces. "I have to get here an hour early so I can get to class on time," Pauw says. She is one of many students (on your campus) who experience the daily frustration of not finding a parking space even though they have purchased $30 and $50 permits.

9 **Specific to general with nut graph:** Write a soft lead, including a nut graph, that uses the specific-to-general technique to convey the following information:

Background: The General Accounting Office, the investigative arm for Congress, issued a report yesterday that said record keeping at the National Park Service is defective. The report said information in the Park Service's financial statements is inaccurate and filled with accounting errors. Property owned by the Park Service is overstated by more than $90 million, the report stated. Examples of inaccurate data in the Park Service records include a vacuum cleaner that is really worth $150 but is listed in records as worth $800,000, a dishwasher worth $350 but valued at over $700,000, and a fire truck worth $133,000 but undervalued at 1 cent.

10 **Descriptive:** Write a descriptive lead for a story about apartments that violate city codes and are considered hazardous but that are often rented to students anyway.

Background: You interviewed a student who lives in an attic apartment. His story is similar to the stories of many other students in this neighborhood, known as the Oread neighborhood. As you climbed the steps to his apartment, you noticed that duct tape keeps the banister in place on the stairs. You saw that the kitchen is infested with mice and roaches. The student, Ted Flis, took you to the bathroom and said it has no electricity. "It's a dump," said Flis, a senior majoring in architecture. "But it was the cheapest thing I could find." This apartment is located at 1032 Main St.

11 Narrative: Change this lead into a narrative lead:

A man threatening suicide kept police at bay for more than nine hours Sunday before he was pulled back from the ledge of a parking garage rooftop.

The man, a 36-year-old Topeka State Hospital patient and Wichita resident whose name wasn't released, threatened to jump from the south ledge of St. Francis Hospital and Medical Center's three-story parking garage at S.W. 6th St. and Mulvane.

Louis Cortez, St. Francis public safety officer, spotted the patient walking toward the ledge on the roof of the garage about 8:40 a.m. Sunday. Cortez stopped his vehicle and told the man to move away from the ledge.

The patient shook his head, "No."

"I stepped out and asked him, 'Can I help you, sir?' and he said, 'I'm going to jump,'" Cortez said.

Shortly before 6 p.m. several teenagers in front of St. Francis House, 701 S.W. Mulvane, began shouting, "Don't jump!" and "It's not worth it." The patient shouted back, "You want to see me jump?"

But the teens distracted the patient just long enough for Cortez to grab him around his waist and pull him from the ledge.

12 Leads analysis: Use two or three different newspapers or online news sites. Find leads as directed, and attach copies of the leads to your report.

- Find an example of a descriptive lead, an anecdotal lead and a narrative lead. Label each type. Analyze whether your examples are effective, and explain why or why not.
- Find three feature news leads you like. Explain what techniques the writers used and why you like them.
- Find three feature leads you do not like, and explain why.

13 Print to broadcast: Using your local or campus newspaper, change the leads on three newspaper stories to broadcast form.

 MindTap

FEATURED ONLINE ACTIVITIES: Log on to the MindTap for Rich's Writing and Reporting News to access a variety of robust additional material, including this chapter's learning objectives, activities, comprehension quizzes, and more. Be sure to check out the "Big Fire" NewsScene scenario for an interactive writing exercise that will help to reinforce many of the themes presented in this chapter.

COACHING TIPS

Write a first draft. Don't perfect every line during the drafting process; **fix it later during the revision process.**

Plan an order for your story: Write a **highlights box listing key points.**

Try **free-writing.** If you are stuck organizing your story, put away your notes and just write what you remember. Then plug in the facts and quotes from your notes.

Read your story aloud when you finish. You will catch errors and hear the pacing.

Plan how **social media might enhance** your story.

CHAPTER 8
STORY ORGANIZATION

© Helder Almeida/Shutterstock.com

The scariest moment is always just before you start.

—**STEPHEN KING,** *On Writing*

WRITING NEWS THESE DAYS IS LIKE SPEED DATING; YOU ONLY have a few minutes to make decisions about the story before you post parts of it on Twitter or the Web. You don't have the luxury of time to agonize over the lead or organization of a story. So how can you develop a writing process that works in this age of digital delivery?

Before you turn on your computer, you need to turn on your mind. You still need to develop a writing process, but the most important steps may be before and after you write the story.

STAGES OF THE WRITING PROCESS

Here are four coaching method steps in the writing process:

- Conceive
- Collect
- Construct
- Correct

Conceive the Idea

The idea for a story may start with information from blogs, an assignment from an editor, a breaking news event or a topic you proposed. Although you may have an initial focus, that can change after you gather the information. These questions will help you determine a focus before, during and after the reporting and writing process.

- What struck you as most interesting or important?
- What is most newsworthy?
- What is the main point of the story that readers or viewers need to know or would want to know?

Collect the Information

Consider the focus as you do the reporting. That is especially important when you have to post information quickly on mobile or other online media. What stands out in your mind as the most important or newsworthy idea?

- Get the basics: who, what, when, where, why and how.
- Take notes on your observations as well as quotes, facts and comments from your sources.

- Tape interviews for audio and video to include on the Web, but don't rely on technology to substitute for note taking.

- Note the information and background you will need to get after your interviews.

- Highlight or underline your notes for important points and good quotes to include in your story.

- Gather anecdotes — brief stories from sources about their experiences.

- Think ahead. Gather information for the next step in the action or an updated version for the next broadcast, online or print publication.

- Collect documents or complete information for the Web.

- Verify names and spelling.

Construct the Story

Write a focus sentence on top of your story as a tool to help you select pertinent information. Here are some other ways to determine your focus:

- Write a headline for your story in fewer than 10 words.

- Express your focus as a tweet (Twitter post).

- Determine the most newsworthy, important or current information.

- Decide what main point would elicit responses if you were asking readers or viewers to comment on a blog, Twitter or other interactive site.

Plan an Order

Highlight or underline your notes for important points, good quotes or sound bites. Then jot down a preliminary order in your notes or at the top of your story document. Here are some ways to organize your story:

- **Topics:** List all the main points you want to cover. Decide which are the most important and which point naturally follows another. Arrange information from the most important to the least important points. Then insert the quotes and other information related to those topics when you write the story.

- **Highlights:** If you were writing a highlights box, what would your main points be? Use the highlights as a guide to organize your story.

- **Time Sequence:** Does the story have distinct time elements? Can it be arranged in a chronology? For example, start with the present (what is happening now); go to the past (background or how the situation developed); return to the present; and end with the future.

- **Block Sources:** If you have several sources, you might organize the story with a blocking technique. Place all the comments from one source in one part of the story, and then place the next source's comments in another block, and so on, instead of going back and forth among sources.

- *Question-and-Answer:* What question does one topic or paragraph raise that needs to be answered in the next paragraph?

- *Images and Sound Bites:* For broadcast writing, arrange your story around your images and sound bites. Let the video images tell the story.

- *Free-writing:* If you can't figure out an order, put away your notes and just write what you remember. Then review your draft, and arrange it in an order that seems logical. Plug in quotes and facts later.

- *Ending:* Decide how you want to end the story. Do you have a strong quote for an ending or information about a future action? What lasting impression do you want to leave?

Correct the Story

Before you turn in your story, revise and correct your work. Even if you are writing on deadline or posting to the Web, don't skip this step. These tips apply to all types of media.

- **Read your story aloud:** If you are writing for broadcast, reading the copy aloud is essential. This is also one of the best self-editing steps you can use for print or online publication.

- **Basics:** Have you covered the basics — who, what, when, where, why, how and so what (impact)?

- **Context:** Have you included background or context to help the readers and viewers understand the significance of the story?

- **Check accuracy:** Double-check the spelling and titles of names and accuracy of facts.

- **Avoid adjectives:** Show, don't tell. Let your video tell the story if you are writing for broadcast. Use observation and details to describe actions and feelings.

- **Use vigorous verbs:** Have you used strong, active verbs? Can you rearrange sentences that start with "There is" or "There are" and substitute active verbs?

- **Purge any parroting:** If your transitions repeat a quote or sound bite, rewrite or cut them. Let the quotes and sound bites move the story naturally.

- **Cut useless or excess words:** If you had to cut your story, what words, sentences or paragraphs could you eliminate?

- **Edit the pace:** Do you have a good mix of short and long sentences — most of them short? Does your story flow?

- **Check grammar:** Do your subjects, verbs and pronouns agree? Is your grammar correct?

- **Cut jargon:** Eliminate bureaucratic language and jargon (such as "hot topic") or other clichés.

SOCIAL MEDIA

WHEN PLANNING your story, think how social media could be used.

Conceive: Start with the conception stage. What is most newsworthy that you could promote on Twitter or Facebook?

Collect: Use social media sites and blogs to gather information and sources. Ask your followers in a social media site for input.

Construct: Identify your focus by writing it as a tweet or a headline you might use for a blog or post on other social media sites. Add related links at the end of your story or post a question.

Correct: Check the accuracy of your social media sources, and check your links. Check your share boxes or icons.

ETHICS

ETHICAL DILEMMA: You belong to a campus group that is sponsoring a charity event. You think the event will be a good story. Should you write the story? Is it a conflict of interest to write about an organization to which you belong?

Ethical guidelines: The Society of Professional Journalists Code of Ethics says journalists should be free of any interest other than the public's right to know. Journalists should avoid conflicts of interest, real or perceived, and should disclose unavoidable conflicts.

ORGANIZATIONAL TECHNIQUES

The two most common problems of professional writers are writing the lead and organizing the story. Here are some techniques to help you write well from start to finish:

Leads

Many writers insist that they can't write the rest of the story until they find their lead. That is a luxury you can't afford when you need to file the story quickly for online delivery. To find your lead, ask yourself these questions:

- What will hook the reader's or viewer's attention?
- What does the reader or viewer need to know first or most to understand the story?
- What is the story about?

Write a lead that will follow with your strongest quote. Start with the focus graph, and write the lead later.

Transition Techniques

How do you get from one point to another smoothly? The best transition is no transition — a story so well organized that one thought follows another naturally. But if you are changing speakers or topics, you may need some of these transition techniques:

- Use cause and effect: If one paragraph raises a question, answer it in the next paragraph, or elaborate with an example or quote. Try to anticipate questions the reader might have.
- To make a transition from one source to another, introduce the new source. Don't string several quotes from different sources together. For example:

Statement introducing speaker

A controversial proposal that would require all Temple University undergraduates to take a course related to racism drew strong support yesterday from a racially mixed group of students and faculty members who testified at a campus hearing.

Anika Trahan, a junior, said the proposed requirement would encourage more dialogue among students who come to the university from largely segregated neighborhoods.

"They (white students) come from communities where they are never able to interact with black people," she said.

But opinion was sharply divided on whether the course should focus on black–white relations in America or include racism against Asian-Americans and other groups.

Transition to new speaker

Molefi K. Asante, chairman of Temple's African-American studies department, contended that the requirement should focus on the white racism toward African-Americans because that has been "the fundamental pattern of racism" in the United States.

Transition to new speaker

A white student, sophomore Amy Dixon, agreed. "Our predominant problem on campus is black–white relations," she said.

— HUNTLY COLLINS, *The Philadelphia Inquirer*

Several universities offer courses on racism and diversity.

Repetition of Key Words

This is a technique that provides smooth transitions during the writing process. A word or phrase from one paragraph can be repeated in the next paragraph. The technique is also known as "stitching" because it helps stitch one paragraph to the other. In broadcast news, anchors often use repetition of key words to segue from one story to another.

As you write, look at the last sentence in each paragraph, and find a key word that will trigger a question you can answer in the next paragraph or that will serve as a bridge for the next thought. You may either repeat the word in the next sentence as a transitional device or just use the concept of the word as a bridge to the idea in your next paragraph. Don't overuse this technique, because your writing could become boring.

In the following example, the underlined key words serve as transitions to the next thought. In some cases the writer repeats the key word, and in others he uses it as a thought bridge.

What we need are some mandatory classes that you would attend before you attempted to move your household. These would be much more useful than those classes you go to before you have a baby.

When you have a baby, you are surrounded by skilled professionals, who, if things get really bad, give you drugs, whereas nobody performs any such service when you move. This is wrong.

Key word baby is repeated for initial transition and key word drugs serves

as a bridge to the next thought

The first thing the burly men should do when they get off the moving van is seize you and forcibly inject you with a <u>two-week supply of sedatives,</u> because moving, to judge from its effect on my wife, is far more stressful than childbirth.

— DAVE BARRY, *Syndicated Columnist*

Here is another example of this technique:

With a relentless sun beating on him as he cut through fields, swamps and shaggy forests, Earl Davis always looked ahead to the next <u>leg</u> of the project.

The <u>legs</u> were long and stretched interminably. The crews made slow progress. Mosquitoes whined about their heads, and snakes thrashed away when the right-of-way crews stumbled across them. . . .

Davis, who had lived in Pinellas County for almost 50 years, sympathized and <u>suffered</u> with them (the road builders).

The <u>suffering</u> wouldn't be over for a long time.

— MARK DAVIS, *The Tampa* (Florida) *Tribune*

Road builders face hot and difficult conditions.

Susie Shapira/Federal Emergency Management Agency

Transitions for Background

To insert background, you can use words and phrases, such as "Previously" or "In the past," or specific time elements, such as "Two months ago." If you are going to recount part of the story chronologically, you can set it up with a phrase like "The incident began this way."

To get from one point to another, especially in stories about meetings where several issues are discussed, you can use transitional phrases: "In another matter," "On a related issue," or "Other items discussed included."

Blocking Sources

Do you get annoyed when you encounter a second reference to a person's last name in a story, but you have forgotten who the person is? After a person is identified by full name once, newspapers and online sites use only the last name if the person is mentioned again in the story. If only one or two people are mentioned in a story, this device isn't confusing. But the reader will have trouble remembering sources by their last names if the story refers to several of them.

The blocking technique helps eliminate such confusion. It is a way of organizing information by using sources in blocks instead of placing them sporadically throughout a story. The problem of last names on second reference is even more confusing for online readers when a story spans several screens or Web pages.

Here is how the blocking technique works to avoid this problem: When you have three or more sources in a story, use each source once or in consecutive paragraphs, blocking all his or her comments in one part of the story. If you must use a source again in another part of the story, reintroduce the person by title or some reference to remind the reader of the person's identity. The exception is a well-known source, such as the mayor, the governor, the president, a celebrity or the central character in a story. The name of such a source may be placed anywhere in the story without confusing the reader.

In this example, which contains several sources, notice how each source is blocked in one or more consecutive paragraphs.

First source

Beneath the shock and the tears lies the anger.

It smoldered in Patrick Thomas' eyes as he sat holding his 15-month-old daughter, Lisa, in a Red Cross evacuation shelter set up at the Job Corps Center on Kerry Street.

Thomas was among the refugees from the neighborhood where a gas pipeline exploded Thursday morning, sending balls of fire racing through their homes. Like other residents living near the side of the May 12 train derailment on Duffy Street, he thought the worst was over.

A gas pipeline explosion created a disaster.

Photo by Yuisa Rios/Courtesy of Federal Emergency Management Agency

His home at 2313 Adams St. survived the train wreck unscathed. It was situated five houses from another Adams Street house that blew up.

"I am mad," he said. "I am mad as hell — at the railroad, at whoever put that fuel line in, at whoever built those houses over a fuel line, at the city for not doing something."

Transition to new sources

Other residents focused their anger on the company that operates the pipeline, Calnev Pipeline Co.

Second source

"It makes me sick that this fire happened — especially if somebody knew it needed to be repaired. Somebody ought to be hung out to dry," said Mark Kingston.

Transition to another source

Another Duffy Street resident's fury knew no bounds.

Third source

"They had no damn business trying to patch no pipe up anyway," said Vincent Hemphill. "They should have discontinued that until they fixed it."

Hemphill, 25, grew up in the house at 2604 Duffy St. Even if his home survived, he said he won't go back.

Many of the residents believe they were betrayed.

Transition to more sources

"If it wasn't safe for us to live, why'd they tell us it's OK to move back there?" wondered Georgia Mitchell.

Fourth source

Mitchell's house was destroyed and her daughter, a son-in-law and two grandchildren were injured.

Bonita Campbell walked around in the nightgown, robe and slippers she wore when the explosion occurred.

Fifth source

Her family got out of their San Carlo Avenue home safely; her two dogs waited in her car.

"Right now I don't know what to think. I don't know what to do. I know I can't continue to live like this not knowing what's going to happen."

—THERESA WALKER AND CARLA WHEELER, *The* (San Bernardino, California) *Sun*

The blocking technique is only a guideline and should not be adhered to strictly when the story order would be more logical if sources were used in different places throughout the story.

MULTIMEDIA COACH

 IN A MULTIMEDIA environment where immediacy is required for posting news online or on TV before print, you may not think you have time for the correction step in the writing process. But you can actually save time writing because you can write your copy quickly if you know that you can revise it. The writing process tips in this chapter apply to all media, but here are some suggestions targeted to broadcast copy in the correction step:

- Read your copy aloud.
- Check your copy to see if the text corresponds to your video. Does the text lead smoothly to sound bites? Does the video enhance your story?

- Now read your text aloud without viewing the video. Is the text clear?
- Remove adjectives that express your opinion, such as descriptive terms — tragic, frightening, beautiful, etc.
- Do your transitions flow smoothly from the videotape to the text?
- Remove and revise any transitions that repeat sound bites.
- Rewrite any bureaucratic terms such as police lingo (perpetrator) or government jargon (infrastructure) and others.
- Check spelling and grammar and make sure names are spelled and pronounced correctly.
- Check your facts for accuracy.

MAKING MIDDLES MOVE

How do you maintain interest in the middle of the story? Transitions are one method, but these other writing techniques will help keep the middles moving:

Vary the Pace Follow long sentences with short ones. Pacing is even more important in broadcast writing when you are writing for the ear. If you use complex sentences, follow them with short, punchy ones:

> Pamela Lewiston thought she was leading a normal life as the daughter of Dr. Normal Lewiston, a respected Stanford University physician, and his wife, Diana.
>
> She thought wrong. Her father had been married to — and lived with — two women besides her mother, all at the same time. His carefully managed deception ended in a cascading series of revelations after his death from a heart attack in August.
>
> — S. L. WYKES, *The San Jose* (California) *Mercury News*

Another example of following a long sentence with a short, punchy one follows:

> On New Year's Eve Lisa Botzum visited the emergency room of the Hospital of the University of Pennsylvania, complaining of nausea and vomiting. She was given a pregnancy test. She was elated by the result.
>
> Few others were.
>
> — LORETTA TOFANI, *The Philadelphia Inquirer*

Use Parallel Construction Parallel sentences help the reader move quickly through the story. Parallel construction means the sentences are worded in the same grammatical order. Some of the words can be repeated for effect, especially those at the beginning of sentences. In this example, the writer uses parallelism at the beginning of the story, but you can use it anywhere:

> Rudolph Almaraz kept his battle with AIDS his personal business, even though his professional business was surgery.
>
> He didn't tell his patients. He didn't tell officials at Baltimore Johns Hopkins Hospital, where he was a cancer surgeon. He didn't tell the doctor who bought his medical practice earlier this year.
>
> But now the case of Dr. Almaraz, who died of AIDS on Nov. 16 at the age of 41, has frightened his patients.
>
> — MATTHEW PURDY, *The Philadelphia Inquirer*

Use Dialogue When possible and appropriate, use dialogue in your story. It works well in feature stories and especially in stories about court cases. For broadcast stories, sound bites and video constitute dialogue. In this print feature story, "13: Life at the Edge of Everything," reporters spent several months reporting about the lives of middle school students. Then they wrote a series in dramatic storytelling form, making extensive use of dialogue to put the reader on the scene. In this section, Joanne, the mother of a teenage girl, Danielle, is worried about her daughter, who is starting to date:

A few months ago, when Danielle started to show more interest in boys, Joanne cornered her.

"You're not doing anything, are you?"

Danielle looked at her. "What do you mean?"

"You're not doing anything with that boy that calls up?"

Meaning Nelson.

"No," said Danielle. "We're just friends."

— THOMAS FRENCH, MONIQUE FIELDS, DONG-PHUONG NGUYEN, *Tampa Bay Times/St. Petersburg* (Florida) *Times*

BBI: Boring but Important Stuff Many stories, especially government stories, need explanation or background that could be boring. Don't put all the boring information in a long block. Break it into small paragraphs, and place it where it will fit. Also consider graphics as a way to present statistics and other information that could clog a story.

Simple Sentences for Complex Information The more difficult the information is, the simpler your sentences should be. Use short sentences with simple construction, especially for bureaucratic information that would be hard for the reader to comprehend. This excerpt is from a story explaining how the judiciary committee of the Connecticut legislature works:

Connecticut State Capitol.

The judiciary is one of the legislature's busiest. By the end of the five-month session in June, the committee will have drafted, amended, approved or killed about 500 bills — about 14 percent of the 3,649 bills filed with the Senate and House clerks.

Judiciary's 14 percent will touch nearly everyone. The committee considers matters of life and death, marriage and divorce, freedom and imprisonment.

This year's issues include surrogate parenting, birth certificates and adoption. The death penalty and letting the terminally ill die. Longer prison sentences and home release. Committing the mentally ill to hospitals.

— MARK PAZNIOKAS, *The Hartford* (Connecticut) *Courant*

Lists Itemizing information is an excellent way to keep the flow going through the middle of your story. Lists work well in summarizing studies, statistical information or the main points in government actions. They also work well on the Web, where readers tend to scan stories. You may use lists in a couple of ways:

- To itemize a group of statistics or any other cumbersome information
- To highlight key points within a story

Lists are usually preceded by a dot called a "bullet" or by some other graphic device as in this example:

Courtesy of the U.S. Census Bureau

More women than men hold advanced degrees, according to the U.S. Census Bureau.

The U.S. Census Bureau reported today that more women than men are expected to occupy professions such as doctors, lawyers and college professors. They represent approximately 58 percent of young adults, age 25 to 29, who hold an advanced degree. In addition, among all adults 25 and older, more women than men had high school diplomas and bachelor's degrees.

The data from the 2010 census also demonstrate the extent to which having such a degree pays off: Average earnings totaled $83,144 for those with an advanced degree, compared with $58,613 for those with a bachelor's degree only. People whose highest level of attainment was a high school diploma had average earnings of $31,283.

Other highlights:

- Overall, 87 percent of adults 25 and older had a high school diploma, with 30 percent holding at least a bachelor's degree.
- The number of U.S. residents with bachelor's degrees or more climbed 34 percent, from 43.8 million to 58.6 million.
- More than half (53 percent) of Asians 25 and older had a bachelor's degree or more, much higher than the rate for non-Hispanic whites (33 percent), blacks (19 percent) and Hispanics (13 percent).

Use Active Voice Whenever Possible Here's an example of active voice:

She will always remember her first story.

Here is the same sentence in passive voice:

Her first story will always be remembered by her.

The active voice has more impact.

Write Short Sentences On average, your sentences should have fewer than 25 words.

Write Simple Sentences Keep the subject and verb close together. This example shows what happens when you don't. It is from a story about school board approval of remodeling and construction projects at the city's two schools.

Those two projects — calling for construction of classrooms, office area and media center at Wakefield and construction of a new district-wide kitchen and computer lab plus remodeling projects at the high school — will be paid for by using approximately $800,000 of the district's special capital outlay fund.

Whew! That's a long sentence. The subject is *projects*, and the verb is *will be paid*. They are separated by too many words. Split it into three sentences:

One project will involve construction of classrooms, an office area and a media center at Wakefield. The other includes building a new district-wide kitchen and a computer lab as well as remodeling projects at the high school. The $800,000 approximate cost of the projects will be paid from the district's special capital outlay fund.

Avoid Jargon Translate bureaucratic terms into simple ones; define technical terms. Here's advice from writer George Orwell:

Never use a metaphor, simile or other figure of speech which you are used to seeing in print. Never use a long word when a short one will do. If it is possible to cut a word out, always cut it out. Never use the passive when you can use the active. Never use a foreign phrase, a scientific word or a jargon word if you can think of an everyday English equivalent. Break any of these rules sooner than say anything outright barbarous.

Here's an example of garbled writing from the U.S. federal budget:

Funds obligated for military assistance as of September 30 may, if deobligated, be reobligated.

ENDINGS

Call them lasting impressions. To many writers, the ending is as important as the beginning of the story. Unfortunately, many readers don't get that far. But if they do, you should reward them with a memorable ending.

The ending also is called the "kicker." Think of it as a clincher. It should give a summary feeling to your story without repeating any information you have stated previously.

For columnists, the ending is more important than the beginning. The twist or main point the writer is trying to make is at the end of the column. In many cases the lead could be an ending. And returning to your lead as a way to find your ending is an excellent technique.

Don't use the ending to summarize information as you might in a term paper. Instead of repeating information, cut the story to the last important point or last good quote.

The following sections describe some ways to form your endings.

Quote Kickers The most common type of ending is the quote kicker. Look for a quote that sums up the mood or main idea of the story. When you end with a quote, put the attribution before the quote or, in a two-quote ending, after the first sentence. Do not let the last words the reader remembers be "he said."

You might not know your sweetie is about to break up with you, but Facebook knows.

That's due to an analysis of Facebook postings compiled by David McCandless, a British journalist and graphic designer. He and a colleague scraped 10,000 Facebook status updates for the phrases "break-up" and "broken up."

The most hazardous times for romantic relationships are after Valentine's Day and before Spring Break, according to their research.

What's the day you are least likely to get dumped?

"Christmas Day," McCandless said. "Who would do that?"

Quote kicker

Circle Kickers When you return to your lead for an idea to end your story in a full circle, you are using a circle kicker. In this example from a story about how families cope with Alzheimer's disease, the writer repeats phrases from the lead — but ends with a twist:

Circle kicker, which ties together the lead and the ending.

"*Mother, mother, mother, other, other, other . . .*"

The sound comes in short, grating bursts, like a children's record played at too high a speed.

Every day, relentlessly, another small slice of the person that once was Betty Jennings disappears. The brand of hell called Alzheimer's disease has reduced the 58-year-old woman to a stoop-shouldered, hand-wringing blabber of meaningless words and phrases.

She must be fed, bathed and diapered. Some mornings, after a particularly brutal night, Gordon Hanchett will look in the living room and see that his sister has attacked her plastic diaper, ripping it apart with her fingers and leaving small pieces littering the floor.

"It looks like a miniature snowstorm," he says.

The limits of devotion are stretched thinnest in the homes of Alzheimer's victims. Often operating on little or no sleep and frequently ruining their own physical health, family members witness the disintegration of a loved one's mind with the understanding that no matter what they do today, tomorrow will be worse.

Birds rescued from the Exxon tanker oil spill in Alaska.

The story continues with more about the family in particular and the disease in general. Here's how it ends:

"Mother, this mother, this other . . . Daddy, daddy, daddy."

The chatter is loud, constant and haunting. His sister's voice fills the house.

"Oh that," says Hanchett, waving his hand. "I don't even hear that anymore."

— KEN FUSON, *The Des Moines* (Iowa) *Register*

Future-Action Kickers Many stories end with the next step in the development of an issue. But this technique only works if the story lends itself to a future element. If the next step is crucial to the story, it should be higher in the body. But if it works as a natural conclusion, then it can be the ending. It can be in the form of a statement or a quote.

HERRING BAY, Alaska — World attention focused Friday on the attempt to rescue birds and animals from the oil spilled in Prince William Sound.

Cameras in Valdez focused on the few animals saved — fewer than 20 birds and four sea otters by evening Friday. The birds on the evening news were expensive symbols for Exxon, costing more than $1,000 apiece to rescue.

But on the water, the rescue efforts getting all the attention stumbled along with the air of a Sunday outing. In this bay at the north end of Knight Island, a diverse and committed group of people tried to learn to perform a futile task.

The story continues with detail about the rescue operation. Here is the ending:

By Friday afternoon, about two miles of the shore of Herring Bay had been thoroughly searched.

Only a few thousand left to go.

— CHARLES WOHLFORTH, *Anchorage Daily News*

Climaxes This type of ending works on stories written like fiction, where the reader is kept in suspense until the end. It is more suited to features in narrative style or short news stories that tease the reader in the beginning and compel the reader to find out what happens.

Scott T. Grabowski sat Tuesday in the courtroom where a federal judge would determine his future, hoping that when the words were pronounced he would hear probation and not prison.

But Grabowski, 27, of Greenfield, is an admitted drug dealer. Early last summer, he pleaded guilty to a charge of possessing 3 ounces of cocaine that he intended to sell on behalf of an international drug network.

The story continues with the arguments from Grabowski's defense lawyer and the prosecutor. But what sentence did he receive? The reader doesn't find out until the end.

Finally, after a 2½ hour hearing, Curran (the judge) sentenced Grabowski to 30 months in prison, to be followed by three years of parole.

And with a nod to the parents, Curran told Grabowski: "I'm sure their hearts are aching as they sit here today."

— JILL ZUCKMAN, *The Milwaukee Journal*

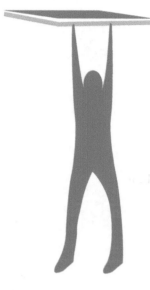

Cliffhangers Every day millions of people watch soap operas. The concept is a simple one: Give the readers or viewers a mystery, and make them want to find out what happens next. In writing, this kind of suspense ending is called a "cliffhanger." It is usually reserved for the endings of stories arranged in sections or series that will continue on another day. But it also can be used in the middle of stories to compel the reader to continue.

Cliffhangers are excellent devices for stories on the Web. At the end of a cliffhanger in the middle of a story, you could place a hyperlink to entice readers to click to the next section.

Not all stories lend themselves to cliffhangers. But many could be structured that way by putting the key points of the story on the front page and stopping with a question or suspenseful point in the last sentence before the story continues or "jumps" to another page.

This method is much more conducive to narrative storytelling, especially in a long feature, but it can be applied to hard news if the story stops at a crucial point.

Cliffhanger or suspense ending.

IN FORT MYERS: MONEY, MERCY AND MURDER

Patricia Rosier's death was supposed to be peaceful and dignified.

She had made all the arrangements. Ordered food for the wake. Said a final goodbye to friends and family. Put the children to sleep.

On the nightstand rested a bottle of Seconals, powerful sedatives prescribed by her husband, Dr. Peter Rosier. Suicide would finally free Pat, 43, from the pain of invading cancer.

When the time came, she downed Seconals like "jellybeans," one witness recalled.

Cliffhanger

But something went wrong in the Rosier's stylish Fort Myers home that January night in 1985.

Pat wouldn't die.

Peter frantically began injecting doses of morphine to finish the job.

Pat's breathing slowed to a rasp.

But after 12 hours of the grim ritual, Pat would not die.

Finally, Pat's stepfather, Vincent Delman, decided something had to be done. Pat, he would later tell prosecutors, was suffering too much.

He took Pat's two half brothers into the bedroom and closed the door.

Twenty minutes later, the door opened. The Delmans walked out, their faces sullen. Peter was waiting in the living room, calming his ravaged nerves with a beer.

"Patty is dead," Vincent said.

After the funeral, the Delmans left Fort Myers. They carried with them the dark secret of what happened behind the bedroom door.

On Monday, Peter Rosier, 47, is scheduled to go on trial for the first-degree murder of his wife of 22 years.

Another cliffhanger

| *And another cliffhanger* | The Rosier story has it all — sex, love, wealth, murder and a major mystery: Who really killed Pat Rosier? | — MARK STEPHENS AND WILLIAM SABO, *Fort Myers* (Florida) *News-Press* |

This is only the beginning of a story that uses cliffhangers. Would you want to turn the page to continue reading?

On the jump page you would find out why Peter is on trial and what kind of evidence exists to try him. You also would find out why this is an unusual case: There's no body and no autopsy report. Pat's body was cremated. There are no morphine syringes; they were thrown away when she died. And there is one other unusual twist: Peter wasn't even in the room when Pat was killed.

Court stories lend themselves to this kind of dramatic structure. But so do many others.

Out-of-Gas Endings You can always just end when you have no more to say. This method is appropriate for hard-news stories, particularly those structured with a summary lead and arranged with supporting points in descending order of importance. You can end on a quote, future action or another fact in the story.

EXERCISES

1 Pacing exercise: Listen to classical music or other music of your choice. With your eyes closed, draw lines on a piece of paper to express the rhythm or movements of the music. Then find a story that you think has good pacing and analyze it for the mixture of short and long sentences and paragraphs.

2 Read aloud: Read aloud any story you have written, and note any errors you have made. Analyze how the story sounds for pacing.

3 Endings: Take any story you have written and try different endings, using a circle kicker, quote kicker or factual kicker.

4 Analyze endings: Using any local news story from your campus or community newspaper or website, analyze which stories have quote endings, circle kickers or factual endings. Watch your local TV news station and note how the reporters end their stories.

5 Correction process: Take any story you have written and check it for accuracy, grammar, spelling and other factors in the correction process.

 MindTap

FEATURED ONLINE ACTIVITIES: Log on to the MindTap for Rich's Writing and Reporting News to access a variety of robust additional material, including this chapter's learning objectives, activities, comprehension quizzes, and more. Be sure to check out the "Basketball Scandal" NewsScene scenario for an interactive writing exercise that will help to reinforce many of the themes presented in this chapter.

CHAPTER 9
Story Forms

© Alberto Zornetta/Shutterstock.com

COACHING TIPS

Gather information during the reporting process for **several versions of a story:** broadcast, print and online delivery.

Consider the **form of your story for social media.**

Consider the form of your story for **delivery on mobile media.**

Good structure keeps a writer's material from being like a bag of meal cut and then spilled all over the floor.

—**JOHN MCPHEE**, *Author*

THE NEWSROOM AT THE *DENVER POST* WAS ALMOST EMPTY AFTER midnight on July 20, when the night producer heard the call on the police radio for units to head to a movie theater where shots had been fired. Just before 1 a.m. a second dispatch on the police radio said that one person had been shot and hundreds of other people were running from the theater, which had a midnight showing of the movie "The Dark Knight Rises."

Within minutes the reporters, photographers and video producers of the *Post* were on the scene and in the newsroom. By 2:42 a.m. the staff published its first story online about the tragedy. The story would be updated 36 times in the next 18 hours, according to the account that *Post* editors submitted in their entry that won the Pulitzer Prize.

Along with social media and Twitter posts, the *Post* also published videos, blogs, interactive timelines and maps in the first 24 hours, with 48 pages of Facebook and Twitter updates. The initial stories were written in one of the most basic forms of news writing — the inverted pyramid — in which the most important information is in the lead, as in this first post:

> An unknown number of people were injured early Friday when shots rang out at an Aurora movie theater during a premiere showing of the new Batman movie.

By 12:34 p.m. the following day, the 19th update of the news would still follow this inverted pyramid format.

> A guman burst into the emergency exit door of a theater and shot 71 people, killing at least 12 of them, at a midnight premiere of a new Batman movie Friday, creating a chaotic, smoke-filled scene that had bloody moviegoers dragging each other outside.

The inverted pyramid form is one of the most common writing forms for breaking news. But it is only one of several ways to write news.

When *The Philadelphia Inquirer* published a series about school violence, the reporters chose a different form to tell the story of how teachers are targets of terror. The reporters wrote this story in *The Wall Street Journal* structure, a form that starts with an anecdotal lead focusing on one person who exemplifies the problems of many others:

> Veteran Philadelphia school teacher Lou Austin endured 40 minutes of terror as the 15-year-old ninth grader jabbed his index finger into Austin's temple and threatened to kill him while swinging a pair of scissors menacingly.

Austin didn't even know the youth, who ransacked his classroom — flipping desks and attempting to set fire to books — at Lincoln High School in Mayfair on Valentine's Day. He'd merely asked him to step away from his classroom door and go to his own class when the youth exploded.

Austin's experience illustrates the dangers and frustration that teachers in Philadelphia public schools face daily.

— The Philadelphia Inquirer

Summary lead

Backup (quotes or facts)

Supporting points

Ending

Inverted pyramid structure

Different stories lend themselves to different writing forms. The most common story structures were created for print media, but smartphones, tablets and multimedia storytelling are fostering new ways of telling stories. Good content and good writing are still the most important factors for any platform.

STORY STRUCTURES

Here are some basic story forms that work in print and online media and may be adapted for mobile media.

INVERTED PYRAMID

The inverted pyramid is the most common form used for print, broadcast and online news as well as news releases in public relations. The story is structured with the most important information at the top of the story, followed by supporting points in descending order of importance. It usually starts with a summary lead that gives some of the basics: who, what, when, where, why.

If you were watching a mystery TV show or movie, you would have to wait until the end to find out who was guilty. But with a story using the inverted pyramid, you tell the outcome in the lead.

The advantage of this form is that the reader gets the crucial information quickly. The disadvantage is that the reader may not read past the crucial information. This form is the primary structure for breaking news, and it is an important form for online news, where readers have unlimited choices. It is a way to let readers determine immediately whether they are interested in the story. It is also an ideal form for distribution on mobile phones and other small-screen devices. To adapt this form for social media, add "share" tools — links to Facebook, Twitter, Digg and other sites.

Spc. Cassandra Monroe/Courtesy of the U.S. Army

In fire stories include fatalities, injuries or whether people were left homeless.

How do you decide what information should be arranged from most to least importance? Use your judgment. Some questions to ask:

- What will affect the reader most?
- What questions does the lead raise that need to be answered immediately?
- What supporting quotes are strongest?
- How does the story affect readers?

HEADLINE: FISH FRY DESTROYS 6 APARTMENTS

Summary lead: who, what, when, why, where

A woman frying fish in her apartment kitchen started a fire that destroyed six units in the complex last night and left 18 people homeless, Anchorage fire officials said.

Backup: who, how, where, when

Sheila Flister said she was just frying halibut in about an inch of oil when the whole stove was suddenly covered in flames.

Lead quote

"I don't know if it was the stove or the oil that caught fire," she said. "All of a sudden it just blew up."

Supporting facts

The fire started about 7:30 p.m. in the basement-level apartment and promptly spread through the three-story building at 5000 Lake Otis Parkway. All the residents got out safely.

Anchorage Fire Department spokesman Tom Kempton said no one appeared to be hurt, but two cats were found dead. He said six units appeared to be a total loss while another six may have been damaged by smoke. The apartment building includes 24 units.

Supporting quote

"Even though the fire department arrived within four minutes, it didn't take long for the flames to spread," Kempton said.

More explanation

Kempton said it's not a good idea to use a fire extinguisher on a pan full of hot grease.

"In some cases people take a dry chem extinguisher that's under high pressure, and they try to hit that pan of flaming oil, and it spreads all over the kitchen," he said. "What happens is that people panic and try to carry the flaming pan outside. It's best to cover it with another pan, turn the heat off and call 911."

Factual ending

Red Cross volunteer John Jones said the building was evacuated and the organization will house the displaced families. Any others who lost their apartment and need help can contact the Red Cross at 646-5400.

— Adapted from an online story by KTUU (Anchorage) Channel 2 News

---

THE WALL STREET JOURNAL FORMULA

The Wall Street Journal format starts with a soft lead, focusing on a person, scene or event. The idea is to go from the specific to the general, starting with a paragraph or two about a person, place or event that illustrates the main point of the story.

Soft lead

Nut graph

Backup for lead and nut graph

Supporting points: quotes, facts, anecdotes

Developments: cause/effect, explanations, points of view

Circle kicker: anecdote, description, future action related to lead

The Wall Street Journal formula

The lead can be anecdotal, descriptive or narrative. It is followed by a focus graph — nut graph — that gives the main point of the story. This paragraph should explain what the story is about and why it is important (the "so what" factor).

The story then presents backup for the lead and supporting points. The body of the story is arranged topically, with one point leading to another. The ending usually comes full circle by using a quote or anecdote from the person in the lead or a future development of something mentioned in the beginning of the story.

This structure is useful for stories about trends, major issues, features, news sidebars and news events that lend themselves to a feature approach. This technique is also effective for broadcast news because viewers relate to people, so starting the story by focusing on a person affected by a problem is a good way to hook viewers.

Although it is used in newspapers throughout the country for many news and feature stories, it is named after *The Wall Street Journal* because that newspaper originated the term "nut graph" and recommended this form to its reporters many years ago as a way to humanize business stories and make them readable for all types of readers.

This is a very versatile formula that can be applied to many news and feature stories. It is useful for brightening bureaucratic stories. While you are reporting, seek out a person who is one of many exemplifying your point, or try to find an anecdote that illustrates the main point of your story.

In this example, the reporter uses an anecdotal lead that focuses on a person who exemplifies the problem in the nut graph — joblessness.

A volunteer for Americorps helps a student learn reading and writing skills.

Anecdotal lead

When he graduated from Northwestern University, Marty Siewart did not anticipate that he would spend seven months unemployed, pondering the real-world value of his college degree.

Discouraged and "just about to get panicky" over his job search, Siewart finally landed a job with a federal poverty-fighting program in Hollywood where he tries to help others find employment.

Lead quote

"I've always been interested in social service, so this is a good opportunity to get a better feel for it, said Siewart, sitting in the small office from which he finds temporary jobs for teenage runaways and homeless youths.

"Plus with the economy the way it is, I feel lucky to be working here."

Emblematic of the rise in volunteerism among college-age individuals that blends idealism with economic realities, Siewart recently began a one-year enlistment in Americorps Vista, the federal agency dedicated to alleviating domestic poverty.

A stagnant economy, changing attitudes toward volunteer work and heightened interest in world affairs have given organizations like the Peace Corps, VISTA and Teach for America a higher profile on college campuses, generating applications at an unparalleled rate.

Nut graph

The story continues with comments from Teach for America founder and volunteers. It ends with a quote kicker from another student contemplating volunteer service.

William Baldwin, a University of Southern California senior contemplating several volunteer options, said that many students are "learning there's more to being satisfied than making $50,000 to $60,000 a year."

"Those values may be satisfying in the short run," he said. "These programs have a lasting value that isn't going to disappear."

Quote kicker

— *Los Angeles Times*

A version of *The Wall Street Journal* formula also works well for some broadcast stories, especially when you want the lead to focus on a person in order to explain a larger issue, a program, a trend or a study. The structure would look like this:

- Anchor lead-in setting up the problem.
- Lead focusing on a person who exemplifies the problem.
- Nut graph explaining the problem.

- Supporting information in sound bites, facts and other sources.
- Circular ending returning to the person in the lead or main point.

The following story, produced by students in a convergent media class at the University of Kansas, is a version of *The Wall Street Journal* structure. It would work in print or online as well by using quotes instead of sound bites and starting with the reporter's lead.

Tom howell/creative commons

A hookah, a waterpipe used for smoking a form of tobacco.

Anchor lead-in

A fast-growing trend in tobacco products may be causing more harm than first believed. KUJH-TV's Dylan Schoonover reports that college students who use hookah tobacco may be causing greater damage to their lungs than those who smoke cigarettes.

Reporter — lead focusing on a person

Smoking hookah is generally described as a social event that draws in experimental and young crowds for a so-called healthier and more arousing way of smoking tobacco. Many college students across the nation have caught on to this Middle Eastern tradition, including KU junior Pat Sullivan, who owns a hookah and uses it regularly.

Sound bite — Sullivan identifier superimposed on screen

"I've read some stuff on it (hookah) and it's not a healthy alternative to smoking cigarettes, but I don't know. I think it's a lot cooler than smoking cigarettes and it's more relaxing."

Reporter — nut graph

Smoking hookah can actually be more dangerous to the lungs than cigarettes. A recent report issued by the World Health Organization claims that one 45-minute smoking session of smoking hookah exposes the user to as much as 200 times the volume of smoke inhaled in one cigarette.

Hazem Chahine, owner of the Hookah House, said customers smoking hookah generally do it for the company and relaxation of a session.

Supporting information introducing next source

"People don't smoke it all the time. It's not like a cigarette and you just pick it up and smoke it, you know? Customers come in one time a week; three times a week is the maximum people you've got coming in here. I see them regularly."

Sound bite with identifier of Chahine superimposed on screen

According to the American Cancer Society, nearly one third of all cancerous deaths result from tobacco use. Despite the risk, hookah smoking is becoming more and more popular. Eighty-six percent of colleges and universities have at least one hookah lounge within close proximity of the school.

Reporter — more supporting information

"Saudis, Egyptians, Americans, Japanese, Italians, Germans, French people; all of them have a great time. We offer them drums. Basically we give them a drum so they can loosen up a little and hit it hard."

Sound bite with Chahine

Despite the health risks, Chahine is confident that students like Sullivan will continue to frequent his Hookah House.

Reporter — circular ending

— DYLAN SCHOONOVER, *KUJH-TV News*, University of Kansas

MULTIMEDIA COACH

BASIC STORY STRUCTURES FOR BROADCAST
When you are writing a story for print, broadcast and online publication, you will probably rely on the two most common formats: the inverted pyramid and a version of *The Wall Street Journal* formula. Basic news stories for the Web resemble print formats, but broadcast news stories must be developed around sound and images. The broadcast story structure may be interpreted as sequences developed around a chronology:

- Lead-in tells who or what happened
- Current situation
- Background
- Ending with current or future developments

Another version of the inverted pyramid format for broadcast is chronological storytelling. After the hard-news lead, the story may be told from beginning to end. If the story starts with a soft lead, such as a focus on a person, the structure resembles *The Wall Street Journal* formula. As with a print story, the story is organized from the specific to the general information. It still follows a sequence developed around a basic chronology:

- Lead-in focuses on a person who exemplifies the problem
- General idea: statement of the problem or situation (equivalent to the nut graph in print writing)

- Background or past issues that led to the current situation
- Return to current or future developments

This storytelling model may be preferable for broadcast, according to Annie Lang and Deborah Potter in their article "The Seven Habits of Highly Effective Storytellers," written for Newslab, a training center for broadcasters. As they explain,

To engage your viewers, tell stories on television the way you tell them in person. Use strong, chronological narratives whenever possible. Studies have found that narrative stories are remembered substantially better than stories told in the old "inverted pyramid" style. Whatever structure you choose, don't make viewers search their memories in order to understand your story. Give them the information they need when they need it, so they can follow each part of the story. Use words which connect the pieces of the story to each other, and which make the chronology of events clear.

HOURGLASS STRUCTURE

The hourglass form can start like the inverted pyramid, giving the most important hard-news information in the top of the story. Then it contains chronological storytelling for a part or for the rest of the story. This approach also works for broadcast news.

Summary lead

Backup

Overview attribution

Chronological
storytelling

Hourglass structure

Use the hourglass structure when the story has dramatic action that lends itself to chronological order for part of the story. The technique is useful in crime or disaster stories to recount the event.

To set up the chronological narrative, you can use an overview attribution such as "Police gave the following account" or "Witnesses described the accident this way," followed by a colon. However, this type of attribution should be used only for a few paragraphs, so the reader does not forget who is speaking. All quotes still need attribution. If the speaker changes, you must attribute the new source.

Advantage: Narrative storytelling in the chronological portion adds drama to the story.

Disadvantage: The chronological portion of the story may repeat some of the key information in the top of the story, making it longer than a basic inverted pyramid.

BOY, 3, SHOOTS 16-MONTH-OLD

Summary lead
Attribution
TAMPA, Fla. — A 3-year-old boy shot and seriously wounded his 16-month-old half brother Thursday after he found a .32-caliber pistol under a chair cushion in the family's apartment, Hillsborough sheriff's deputies said.

Backup for lead
Melvin Hamilton, shot once in the chest about 9:30 a.m., was flown by helicopter to Tampa General Hospital, where he was in serious but stable condition late Thursday after surgery, hospital officials said.

Attribution
Otis Neal, who pulled the trigger, did it accidentally, authorities said.

Basic inverted pyramid structure with attribution for each point
Sheriff's officials said they did not know who owned the handgun but were still investigating. Under state law, the gun's owner could be criminally liable for leaving the gun in a place where a child could get it. . . .

Facts
Otis and Melvin live with their mother, Dina Varnes, in the Terrace Oaks Apartment complex at 6611 50th St.

Overview attribution: chronological narrative begins and continues to the end
Relatives and sheriff's officials gave this account: The two youngsters were downstairs in the living room playing Thursday morning, while a 15-year-old friend of the family slept on the couch. Ms. Varnes was upstairs.

Melvin was walking around the living room when Otis found the gun under the seat cushion. He pulled the gun out and fired one shot.

Arabell Ricks, Ms. Varnes' aunt and neighbor, said she was walking to the store when her niece ran out of the apartment screaming.

"She said, 'Melvin is shot.' She said the oldest shot Melvin," Ms. Ricks said. "I went in and looked at him, and then I just ran out of the house and started praying." She said she flagged down a sheriff's deputy who was patrolling the area.

Ending reaction quote
"I said, 'Lord, please don't let him die,'" Ms. Ricks said.

— HEDDY MURPHY, *Tampa Bay Times/St. Petersburg* (Florida) *Times*

SOCIAL MEDIA

THE FORM MOST used for writing on social media sites is the inverted pyramid, but it does not have to be the only one. This form has a definite advantage for mobile media because you get to the point quickly, which is especially helpful for small screens. But some of the other forms discussed in this chapter can work very well on social media sites: the question/answer form and the list technique are also adaptable for social media sites, especially if they are geared to mobile media and small tablet screens. If you have a compelling story that will entice readers to click to another page, you could also try the sections technique, especially if each section is relatively brief. The most important factor, however, is to tell a good story.

LIST TECHNIQUE

Lists can be useful in stories when you have several important points to stress. Think of a list as a highlights box within the story or at the end of the story. This technique works well for stories about studies, government stories such as meetings and even features about people or programs, if there are several key points to list. This structure is useful for online stories and for mobile media delivery because readers often scan the text. It is also an effective technique for news releases, which should be brief.

When using a list for the body and ending of a story, you can start with a summary lead or a soft lead followed by a nut graph. Give some backup for the lead with quotes, facts or both. Then itemize the main points until the ending. Investigative reporters often use the list high in the story to itemize the findings of their investigation.

Limit lists in the beginnings and middles of stories to five items or fewer; lists at the end can be longer. Parallel sentence structure is most effective, but not essential, for lists. Each item should be in a separate paragraph. Lists are often used in stories about meetings to itemize actions not related to the lead. The list is preceded by "In other business" or a similar transition or sentence ending with a colon, as in this example:

> Finally, some facts to justify cursing at people with car phones.
>
> A recent study of car phoning showed that drivers involved in car-phone conversations were 30 percent more likely to overlook potential hazards, such as your rear bumper.
>
> "They were so engrossed in the phone call that they were oblivious to what was going on," said James McKnight, whose experiments with 51 drivers were the basis for the findings.

Summary lead and backup

Key points
- •
- •
- •

Summary lead and backup

Key points
- •
- •
- •

Elaboration

Ending

List technique

Amanda Mills/Centers for Disease Control and Prevention

Drivers distracted by talking or texting with cell phones have high rates of accidents.

What McKnight found through controlled tests on driving simulators was this:

- Even casual chitchat or just dialing a car phone distracted drivers enough so that they failed to respond to hazards nearly 7 percent more often.
- When talk turned to solving simple math problems — designed to simulate business conversations — drivers failed to respond to hazards nearly 30 percent more often.
- When engaged in casual or businesslike conversations, drivers 50 or older failed to respond to hazards 38 percent more often than younger drivers.
- Drivers who had experience with car phones were as easily distracted as drivers who were using the phones for the first time.

— MARK VOSBURGH, *The Orlando Sentinel*

QUESTION/ANSWER FORMAT

Organizing a story by questions and answers is an effective technique for print and Web stories, and it can also be effective in some news releases. It is also a useful form for mobile media stories.

The Q and A, as it is commonly called, is often used for profiles, and it can be a helpful way to explain issues such as a budget increase or any controversial proposal. Even though the answer part of the story is verbatim quotes, the writer still has to be selective about which questions and answers to include from a lengthy interview. The

ETHICS

ETHICAL DILEMMA: You are covering an automobile accident in your community. When you arrive on the scene, the bodies of two victims are still on the ground. A third person, covered in blood, is weeping beside one of the victims. Police tell you that the accident was caused by a drunken driver, who has been taken into custody. You want to convey the deadly consequences of drunken driving in your story. Should you use the graphic images of the bodies and the blood-soaked survivor? How do you know when to use disturbing images?

The Radio Television Digital News Association suggests that before you air graphic content, consider the following questions:

- What is the journalistic purpose behind broadcasting the graphic content? Does the display of such material clarify and help the audience understand the story better? Is there an issue of great public importance involved, such as public policy, community benefit or social significance?

- Is the use of graphic material the only way to tell the story? What are your alternatives?

- If asked to defend the decision to your audience or the stakeholders in the story, such as a family member, how will you justify your decision? Are you prepared to broadcast your rationale to your audience? If not, why?

following investigative story by the nonprofit website ProPublica uses a question/answer format (and combines the list format) by putting the questions in boldface type. The full story and entire series about internship pay is at *www.propublica.org /article/when-interns-should-be-paid-explained.*

WHEN IS IT OK TO NOT PAY AN INTERN?

Is your unpaid summer internship illegal? A breakdown of the laws on working for free.
Blair Hickman and Christie Thompson, ProPublica

WHAT LAWS DETERMINE WHEN AN INTERN SHOULD OR SHOULD NOT BE PAID?

The Fair Labor Standards Act, or FLSA, regulates minimum wage and overtime for U.S. workers, including interns. The Department of Labor's Wage and Hour Division is responsible for enforcing the law, and has a six-factor test to determine whether interns at private sector employers must be paid minimum wage.

According to the Department of Labor, an unpaid internship must meet all these criteria:

- The internship is similar to training, which would be given in an educational environment.

- It's for the benefit of the intern.
- The intern doesn't displace paid employees.
- The employer doesn't benefit from work the intern is doing, "and on occasion its operations may actually be impeded."
- The intern isn't promised a job at the end (unpaid "tryouts" aren't allowed).
- Both the intern and their boss understand it's an unpaid position.

SO, ARE UNPAID INTERNSHIPS EVER OK?

Very rarely, for work done at for-profit companies. According to the Department of Labor's test, companies can't derive an "immediate advantage" from an intern's work. And in the private sector, work that doesn't benefit the company is rare.

"It's fair to say most private-sector employers who employ volunteers are violating the law," said David Yamada, a professor of law at Suffolk University in Boston.

WHAT ABOUT INTERNSHIPS AT NONPROFITS?

According to the Department of Labor, nonprofits have an additional exception for unpaid interns who "volunteer their time." The government's guidelines state that "unpaid internships in the public sector and for non-profit charitable organizations ... are generally permissible."

WHAT ABOUT GIGS WITH THE GOVERNMENT?

For most interns on Capitol Hill, it's perfectly legal for them to be working for free. Congress conveniently exempted itself from the Fair Labor Standards Act, meaning they don't have to pay their interns. (It's just one of many workplace laws that Congress doesn't have to follow.) Most federal-level internships including the White House's program, are also unpaid.

DOES GETTING COLLEGE CREDIT MEAN IT'S OK TO NOT GET PAID?

Not really. Many companies attempt to use academic credit as legal justification for an unpaid internship. (The story continues with a judge's ruling on a New York labor law case.)

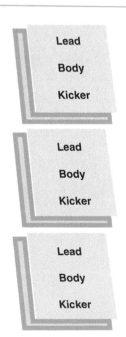

Sections technique

SECTIONS TECHNIQUE

This technique involves dividing a story into sections, like book chapters, and separating them by a graphic device such as a large dot or a large capital letter. It works best for in-depth stories such as investigations or long features. It is also useful for the Web because the story can be divided into several Web pages — one section with audio and video per page. It may also work for small-screen mobile media devices if the story is compelling enough to entice readers to click into the next section.

The most effective section stories have good leads and good endings for each section. This form lends itself to cliffhanger endings for each section or for each day's installment if the story is presented as a series. Think of the sections as separate chapters, complete in themselves but tied together by the overall focus and story plot. This technique is used often in nonfiction storytelling called "narrative writing."

One common way to organize section stories is by points of view. For example, in a story about a controversial government issue, such as a new landfill, you could arrange the story in sections for each group affected by the proposal.

The other way frequently used to organize section stories is by time frames — starting with the present, moving to the past for background, then back to present developments and ending with the future. Although the order can be flexible, the opening section must contain a nut graph explaining why you are telling the reader this story now. This technique is very effective for stories written in narrative style.

To determine whether your story is suitable for sections, envision subheads for it. Then decide whether you have enough information in each subhead group to warrant a separate section.

The following story uses a combination of points of view and time sequences to organize the sections. This is written in dramatic narrative form, using storytelling that reconstructs the event. Notice how the sections are structured as separate chapters with kicker endings.

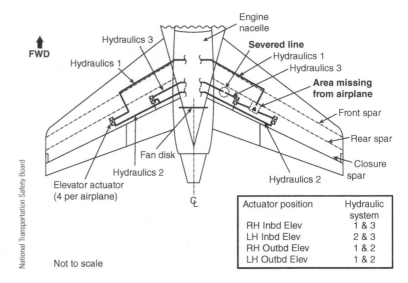

A graphic of the damage to United Airlines Flight 232, which took off in Denver and crashed in Sioux City, Iowa.

Actuator position	Hydraulic system
RH Inbd Elev	1 & 3
LH Inbd Elev	2 & 3
RH Outbd Elev	1 & 2
LH Outbd Elev	1 & 2

National Transportation Safety Board

THEY GOT OUT ALIVE, BUT NO ONE WAS SPARED

BOULDER, Colo. — For weeks after the crash, David Hooker found the love notes his fiancée had hidden around the house.

In the medicine cabinet: "David, I love you this much."

In the sock drawer: "Poo — Here's a hug for you! Susan."

In the silverware tray: "I'll miss you! Take care."

Five months have passed since Susan Fyler boarded United Airlines Flight 282. Hooker carefully stacks the yellow slips of paper into a neat pile on the corner of his dresser, next to the framed photographs of Fyler and the mahogany box that holds her ashes.

Less than a half-hour away in Denver, Garry Priest can't sleep.

He watched a movie — he doesn't even remember what it was about — and one scene stuck. A woman is thrown from a car and the pavement scrapes her skin raw.

This paragraph tells why you are reading this story now.

Suddenly it was July 19 again and Priest was back in Sioux City, Ia., escaping from the plane, racing along the runway, seeing the debris, the charred metal, the boy's body.

Then he thinks of Christmas. And his eyes will not close.

* * *

This section gives the crucial information that ties the story together.

Five months ago, they were strangers, bound only by an airplane flight.

Susan Fyler was headed to Ohio to surprise her parents with news of her engagement. Garry Priest was going to Chicago on business.

Both boarded Flight 232 in Denver. She sat in seat 31K, he in seat 15G. Fyler was one of 112 people killed in the crash. She was 32. Priest was one of 184 survivors. He is 23.

For those most directly affected — the family and friends of the victims, the survivors and their families — the holidays are proving that time has not healed all wounds. ...

Five months later, they are strangers, but David Hooker and Garry Priest share a common grief.

* * *

This section is about David Hooker and how he is dealing with the loss of his fiancée.

Every night, David Hooker walks into his bedroom, lights a candle and shares his day with Susan Fyler. Shortly after the crash, a friend admonished Hooker to stop feeling sorry for himself and to ask Fyler for guidance.

"I asked Susan to come live with me inside my body and to stay alive inside my body," he says, "and right after I did that, I felt a very dramatic change going on in me. I just felt all this energy coming over me."

After he lights the candle, Hooker may read the Lord's Prayer or flip through the love notes Fyler left him or look at the five photographs on his dresser.

* * *

It didn't make sense. Why, Garry Priest wondered, were people acting this way? He had survived one of the worst airplane disasters in U.S. history. He had seen horrible things, scenes that made his legs shake, pictures he will remember the rest of his life.

So why was everyone calling him lucky?

"People want to pinch you," he says. "They say, 'Let's play bingo,' or 'Let's buy a lottery ticket.' They pat your head.

"I don't feel lucky at all. If I was lucky, I wouldn't have been on that plane. Nobody would have been on the plane."

* * *

This section gives the story from Garry Priest's point of view.

They are strangers, but Garry Priest would like David Hooker to know that he, too, mourns Susan Fyler.

"Could you do me a favor?" Priest asks. "Could you tell all the people who lost loved ones and all the people who survived that I wish them a merry Christmas and that my thoughts and prayers and love are with them?"

— KEN FUSON, *The Des Moines (Iowa) Register*

Two more sections follow before this ending section.

EXERCISES

1 Inverted pyramid exercise: Organize the information for this story in the inverted pyramid order for print or broadcast. Here are your notes:

Who: Connecticut State Police

What: Ordered ban of handheld radar guns

When: Yesterday

Where: Meriden, Conn.

Why: Because of concerns that troopers could develop cancer from long-term exposure to the radiation waves emitted by the devices. The ban was ordered as a precaution while researchers study the possible links between cancer and use of the devices.

How: The ban affects 70 radar guns, which will be withdrawn from service. State troopers will continue to use radar units with transmitters mounted on the outside of their cruisers.

Source: Adam Berluti, a state police spokesman

Backup information: "The feeling here is to err on the side of caution until more is known about the issue," Berluti said. "The whole situation is under review." The move is considered to be the first of its kind by a state police agency. It comes two months after three municipal police officers in Connecticut filed workers' compensation claims, saying they developed cancer from using handheld radar guns.

2 *The Wall Street Journal* formula exercise: Here are some excerpts from a story that was originally written according to *The Wall Street Journal* formula by Matt Gowen of the *Lawrence* (Kansas) *Journal-World*. Rearrange the paragraphs to conform to *The Wall Street Journal* style. Use an anecdotal lead followed by a nut graph and a circular ending.

College students are most susceptible to online obsession, experts say

Jonathan Kandell, assistant director of the counseling center at the University of Maryland, has found that college students — especially those in the 18 to 22 age range — are quite susceptible to an Internet obsession. Kandell, an assistant professor of psychology at Maryland, recently published his theories in the journal *Cyber Psychology and Behavior.*

A few years ago, Stacie Kawaguchi started tinkering with the Internet. She clicked her mouse, surfed around and delved into an international pen-pal site. At the time a Kansas University graduate student in botany, Kawaguchi "met" folks from Canada, France, Japan and Brazil. Through the Internet, she even met her eventual fiancé, a Ph.D. candidate in engineering at Virginia Tech University. "When you first start, you get really into it," said Kawaguchi, 26. "You get stuck on it for long periods of time."

The search for identity, the need for intimate relationships and the need for control often play a significant role in this potentially unhealthy behavior, Kandell said. Logging on, whether in chat rooms or through websites, can help students ranging academically from the inept to the astute cope with life's hardships. "If it's fulfilling a need, it's hard to give it up," Kandell said.

Simply put, Kawaguchi was online and overwhelmed. "You stay up late instead of going to sleep," she said. "It sucked up a lot of time." In a few months, the novelty began to wear off. "After a while, it was like, geez, this is enough," she said, adding that many of her chatmates were there night after night, even when she was gone for weeks at a time. "Basically, their whole world revolved around being there."

Studies on college campuses have shown between 6 percent and 12 percent of students may be spending too much time online, thanks in part to the ease of campus Internet access.

Kawaguchi saw the obsessive side of the Internet and managed to escape it. Others aren't as lucky.

Kandell was quick to note, however, that "addiction" was probably not the most accurate term in these cases. He compared overuse of the Internet to compulsive behaviors such as pathological gambling.

"I do see it as a psychological dependency," Kandell said. Kandell's evidence is mostly anecdotal, culled from student clients and classrooms filled with students who say they're downloading to the point of distraction.

In one class he visited, between 70 percent and 80 percent of the students raised their hands when asked whether the Internet was their chief obstacle to concentrating on projects and papers. "People are staying up all night, not going to class, not doing their homework — ultimately flunking out of school," Kandell said. "It's more pervasive than people think. There's something inherently tempting about the Internet."

Kawaguchi sees both good and bad in the Internet. The native of Oahu, Hawaii, considers it an effective communication tool but not a surrogate for human relationships. She calls it "luck" that she met her Iowa-born husband-to-be online. They traded photos and talked on the phone for a long time before taking the big step of meeting in person. The couple plan to wed in June in Lawrence. "Personally, I wouldn't recommend someone going out to look for someone on the Internet," she said. "I completely lucked out."

In addition to academic problems, jobs and relationships can be affected as social isolation grows. The Internet can provide an arena for people to simulate personal contact without actually having to meet face to face.

---

3 Hourglass structure exercise: Arrange these facts in hourglass order, placing attribution where it is needed. (This story is taken from the *St. Louis Post-Dispatch* of Missouri.) Attribute information to Capt. Ed Kemp of the Jefferson County Sheriff's Department unless otherwise noted.

Who: Two bank couriers

What: Helped police capture three suspects in a robbery

When: Last night

Where: At the Boatman's Bank of Pevely, Missouri

How: One courier, Dennis Boushie, who lives near Festus, chased a suspect on foot. The other courier, Willie Moore of St. Louis, drove a bank van, chasing a getaway car.

Police have booked three people on suspicion of drug possession. The three, who were found in the getaway car, are being held in the jail at Pevely.

Backup information: "This is beyond the call of duty. They acted more like police officers than private citizens or bank couriers," said Capt. Ed Kemp.

Boushie said he had asked the teller who was robbed if the robber had a weapon, and she said he did not. He said his pursuit of the robber had been "just common sense."

A man entered the bank shortly after it opened Tuesday morning and shouted, "Give me the money or else!" The teller gave the man an envelope containing the money, and the man ran out the front door.

Boushie chased the man on foot, and when the suspect jumped into a car, Boushie pointed the car out to Moore, who pursued it in a bank van. A few minutes later, Boushie got in a police patrol car and helped police track the getaway car.

Police broadcast a description of the getaway car, which had continued north on I-55 carrying two men and a woman. Police spotted the car, stopped it and arrested three suspects.

Police said they had found several thousand dollars in the car. The female suspect had stuffed money down her pants, police said.

Police were seeking federal warrants for bank robbery.

4 List technique exercise: Write a brief news story in list format based on this information:

Who: Stephen J. Blumberg, health scientist and lead author of study for the U.S. Centers for Disease Control and Prevention Health Statistics

What: Report on households using only wireless phones; "Wireless substitution: State-level estimates from the National Health Interview Survey"

When: Results of a study released today (use current date)

Why: To determine how telephone surveys for the CDC will be affected by wireless-only households

Elaboration: Oklahoma leads the nation in the percentage of households that only use cell phones.

More than a quarter of households (26.2 percent) in Oklahoma had only wireless and no landline phones. At the other end of the spectrum, only 5.1 percent of households in Vermont used only wireless phones. "These findings are important to CDC because many of our largest surveys are done on calls to landline phone numbers. All of those adults with only cell phones are being missed in these surveys," Blumberg said.

In addition to Oklahoma, states with the highest percentage of wireless–only households are Utah (25.5 percent), Nebraska (23.2 percent), Arkansas (22.6 percent) and Idaho (22.1 percent). States with the lowest percentages, following Vermont, are Connecticut (5.6 percent), Delaware (5.7 percent), South Dakota (6.4 percent) and Rhode Island (7.9 percent). Results from previous CDC reports on wireless substitution show wireless–only phone use continues to grow on a national level.

FEATURED ONLINE ACTIVITIES: Log on to the MindTap for Rich's Writing and Reporting News to access a variety of robust additional material, including this chapter's learning objectives, activities, comprehension quizzes, and more!

CHAPTER 10
Storytelling and Feature Techniques

We're supposed to be tellers of tales as well as purveyors of facts. When we don't live up to that responsibility, we don't get read.

—**BILL BLUNDELL**, *The Art and Craft of Feature Writing*

© marekuliasz/Shutterstock.com

COACHING TIPS

Gather details and **take notes of your observations.**

Use **show-in-action** techniques. Describe what people are doing.

Use vivid **action verbs.**

For narrative writing, get a chronology to **reconstruct events** as they occurred.

Think of your story as a plot with a **beginning, a middle and a climax.**

Think of your sources as characters in a book; **make your reader see, hear and care** about them.

To write well, **read well.** Read as much fiction and nonfiction as you can, and study the writing styles.

TOM FRENCH WAS FASCINATED BY KAREN GREGORY'S CASE. HE wrote a 10-part series, called "A Cry in the Night," about her murder and the man on trial for it.

Something very unusual happened when the series began. Readers ran out to greet the newspaper delivery trucks each day to get the next chapter in the series. Why were they so eager to read these stories? You decide.

....

> The victim wasn't rich. She wasn't the daughter of anyone powerful. She was simply a 36-year-old woman trying to make a life for herself. Her name was Karen Gregory. The night she died, Karen became part of a numbing statistic. . . . It was what people sometimes casually refer to as "a little murder."
>
> — TOM FRENCH, *Tampa Bay Times/St. Petersburg* (Florida) *Times*

....

This passage was the introduction to the series. The first story began with a description of the trial of George Lewis, a firefighter who lived across the street from Karen Gregory and the person who was charged with her murder:

....

> His lawyer called out his name. He stood up, put his hand on a Bible and swore to tell the truth and nothing but. He sat down in the witness box and looked toward the jurors so they could see his face and study it and decide for themselves what kind of man he was.
>
> "Did you rape Karen Gregory?" asked his lawyer.
>
> "No sir, I did not." "Did you murder Karen Gregory?"
>
> "No sir."
>
> He heard a scream that night, he said. He heard it, and he went out to the street to look around. He saw a man he did not know, standing over in Karen's yard. The man said to go away, to not tell anyone what he'd seen. He waited for the man to leave — watched him walk away into the darkness — and then he went up to Karen's house. There was broken glass on the front walk. He knocked on the front door. There was no answer. He found an open window. He called out to ask whether anyone needed help. There was still no answer. He looked through the window and saw someone lying on the floor. He decided he had to go in. He climbed inside, and there was Karen. Blood was everywhere.
>
> He was afraid. He ran to the bathroom and threw up. He knew no one would believe how he had ended up standing inside that house with her body. He had to get out of there. He was running toward the window to climb out when he saw something moving in the dark. He thought someone was jumping toward him. Then he realized he was looking at a mirror, and

the only person moving was him. It was his own reflection that had startled him. It was George.

— TOM FRENCH, *Tampa Bay Times/St. Petersburg* (Florida) *Times*

The entire series was written like a mystery novel. But it was all true, based on interviews with more than 50 people and 6,000 pages of court documents. The writing style, called narrative writing, is a form of dramatic storytelling that reconstructs the events as though the reader were witnessing them as they happened. French later turned the series into a book called *Unanswered Cries*.

French said he never believed his series would be so popular. "The way the readers responded was so gratifying," he said.

French relied heavily on dialogue throughout the series, even from the dead woman. Although most of the dialogue and description are based on interviews and his observations, Karen's dialogue was secondhand information, based on recollections about her.

James Brosher/Indiana University

Tom French

"After I wrote it, I spent three weeks checking everything with all the participants," French said. "I read it to them word for word to make sure it was accurate."

In 1998 French won the Pulitzer Prize for another narrative series about murder. This time he researched 4,000 pages of police reports and court documents and conducted scores of interviews to reconstruct the chilling story of an Ohio woman and her two daughters. They were on vacation in Florida when they were raped, killed and dumped into Tampa Bay. Once again, French wrote a gripping account of their murders, the three-year search for their killer and his trial. The killer was convicted and sentenced to death.

These days French teaches narrative writing to journalism students at his alma mater, Indiana University. He worked with several of the students who won honors in the writing categories of the prestigious Hearst Journalism Awards, often considered equivalent to the Pulitzer Prizes for college journalism students.

NARRATIVE WRITING

"Narrative writing" is a dramatic account of a fiction or nonfiction story. Writing in this style requires thorough reporting and descriptive detail. Dialogue also enhances the storytelling. Narrative writing for news often reconstructs events to put the reader on the scene. The sources are like characters who relive the events as they happened. But the story must include the basic factual elements of news.

Jeff Klinkenberg, a *Tampa Bay Times/St. Petersburg* (Florida) *Times* writer, views the five W's this way: *Who* is character, *what* is plot, *when* is chronology, *why* is motive and *where* is place.

French uses all these elements in his stories by weaving facts with description and dramatic tension. In this section from his Pulitzer Prize–winning series, "Angels and Demons," French uses descriptive detail to reveal how the bodies of the women were found.

> It was a female, floating face down, with her hands tied behind her back and her feet bound and a thin yellow rope around her neck. She was naked from the waist down.
>
> A man from the *Amber Waves* (sailboat) radioed the Coast Guard, and a rescue boat was dispatched from the station at Bayboro Harbor in St. Petersburg. The Coast Guard crew quickly found the body, but recovering it from the water was difficult. The rope around the neck was attached to something heavy below the surface that could not be lifted. Noting the coordinates where the body had been found, the Coast Guard crew cut the line, placed the female in a body bag, pulled the bag onto the boat and headed back toward the station. The crew members had not yet reached the shore when they received another radio message: A second female body had just been sighted by two people on a sailboat.
>
> This one was floating to the north of where the first body had been sighted. It was 2 miles off The Pier in St. Petersburg. Like the first, this body was face down, bound, with a rope around the neck and naked below the waist. The same Coast Guard crew was sent to recover it, and while the crew was doing so, a call came in of yet a third female, seen floating only a couple of hundred yards to the east.
>
> — TOM FRENCH, *Tampa Bay Times/St. Petersburg* (Florida) *Times*

In the following section, French uses dialogue to reconstruct the scene when Hal Rogers, the husband and father of the dead women, tells the boyfriend of his daughter Michelle that his wife and daughters won't be coming home:

> That day, Jeff Feasby phoned the Rogers house again, hoping Michelle would be back.
>
> Hal picked up. His voice was strange. He sounded furious.
>
> "Who is this?" he demanded.
>
> Jeff told him who it was and asked if he'd heard anything. With that, Hal broke down.
>
> "They're not coming home," he said, his voice trembling.
>
> Jeff paused for a second. He didn't understand.
>
> So Hal told him. They were gone, he said. All of them.
>
> — TOM FRENCH, *Tampa Bay Times/St. Petersburg* (Florida) *Times*

READING TO WRITE

Good writers are good readers, and French said he was inspired to do narrative writing after he read a book by the Latin American writer Gabriel García Márquez. *The Story of a Shipwrecked Sailor* is a riveting story about a man who survived 10 days at sea without food and water.

French was also influenced by the literary journalists, a group of writers who, in the 1960s and 1970s, used the storytelling techniques of fiction for nonfiction newspaper and magazine stories. These journalists — Joan Didion, John McPhee, Tracy Kidder and Tom Wolfe — were influenced by Truman Capote's nonfiction book *In Cold Blood*. The literary journalists immersed themselves in a subject and wrote their stories with characters, scene, dialogue and plot. These were factual stories written like fiction.

Journalists often think storytelling techniques are limited to feature stories, but as you will see, you can apply this kind of writing to news about crime and courts and many other news stories.

REPORTING TOOLS

Good storytelling requires using observation and gathering details.

Other people see flies; a writer sees how they move.

— WILLIAM RUEHLMANN, *Author*

William Ruehlmann, author of *Stalking the Feature Story*, says writers must concentrate when they observe and then analyze what they observe. He gives this example: "Flies take off backward. So in order to swat one, you must strike slightly behind him. An interesting detail, and certainly one a writer would be able to pick up on. Other people see flies; a writer sees how they move."

During the reporting process, you don't always know what details you will need when you write your story. Ask what were people thinking, saying, hearing, smelling, wearing and feeling. Be precise. Take notes when you hear dialogue that could enhance your story.

To help you gather specific details, envision a ladder with rungs leading from general to specific. Start with the broadest noun, and take it to the most specific level, as in the adjacent diagram. Then use those details to write. For example:

Lhasa apso named for Joe DiMaggio

Lhasa apso named Joe

Tan and white Lhasa apso

Lhasa apso

Dog

Ladder of details

A tan and white Lhasa Apso named Joe ran onto the baseball field and interrupted the game when he stole the ball. It was only natural. After all, his namesake was Joe DiMaggio.

WRITING TOOLS

Once you have gathered all those details, what do you do with them? The better you are as a reporter, the more you will struggle as a writer deciding what information to use. The three basic tools of storytelling are theme, descriptive writing techniques and narrative writing techniques.

Theme

Before you begin writing a feature story, develop a theme — a concept that gives the story meaning.

David Maraniss, a Pulitzer Prize winner from *The Washington Post*, describes it this way:

> The theme is why readers want to read the story, not the nut graph required by many editors. To write something universal . . . death, life, fear, joy . . . that every person can connect to in some way is what I look for in every story.

Descriptive Techniques

Too much description will clutter a story. Too little will leave the reader blank. How much is enough? First decide whether the story lends itself to description of the scene or person. Then take the advice of Bruce DeSilva, a writing coach who teaches at Columbia University.

> Description, like every element in either fiction or nonfiction, should advance the meaning of your story. It would be a good idea to describe the brown house in more detail only if those details are important. Description never should be there for decoration. It never should be there because you are showing off. And when you do describe, you should never use more words than you need to trigger that mental image readers already have in their minds.

Techniques for good descriptive writing include the following:

Avoid Adjectives Write specific detail with vivid nouns and verbs, but avoid modifiers. When you use adjectives, you run the risk of inserting your opinions into the story. The late author Norman Mailer put it this way:

> The adjective is the author's opinion of what is going on, no more. If I write, "A strong man came into the room," that only means he is strong in relation to me. Unless I've established myself for the reader, I might be the only fellow in the bar who is impressed by the guy who just came in.

It is better to say: "A man entered. He was holding a walking stick, and for some reason, he now broke it in two like a twig." Of course, this takes more time to narrate. So adjectives bring on quick tell-you-how-to-live writing. Advertising thrives on it. "A super-efficient, silent, sensuous, five-speed shift." Put 20 adjectives before a noun and no one will know you are describing a turd.

Use Analogies A good analogy compares a vague concept to something familiar to readers. For example, what is a "fat" man? David Finkel leaves no doubt in his story about a circus performer. How do you visualize the "World's Biggest Man" at 891 pounds? Finkel uses familiar items to help the reader see.

Now: 891 and climbing. That's more than twice as much as Sears' best refrigerator-freezer — a 26-cubic-footer with automatic ice and water dispensers on side-by-side doors. That's almost as much as a Steinway grand piano.

— DAVID FINKEL, *Tampa Bay Times/St. Petersburg* (Florida) *Times*

Limit Physical Descriptions Use physical descriptions only when they are relevant to the content. They work well in profiles; in stories about crime, courts and disasters; and whenever they fit with the context. They don't work when they are tacked onto impersonal quotes.

Avoid stage directions — descriptions of people's gestures, facial expressions and physical characteristics inserted artificially as though you were directing a play. You don't need to describe what city commissioners are wearing at a meeting or how they gesture unless their clothing and movements enhance what they are saying and doing.

Advice from the famous mystery writer, Stephen King:

I'm not particularly keen on writing which exhaustively describes the physical characteristics of the people in the story and what they're wearing . . . I can always get a J. Crew catalogue. . . . So spare me, if you please, the hero's "sharply intelligent blue eyes" and "outthrust determined chin."

But there are times when such description enhances a story.

Effective The 50-year-old airline pilot — who prosecutors say killed his wife by unknown means, cut up her body with a chain saw, and disposed of it with a wood chipper — testified with a voice and

manner that was so calm
it bordered at times on
nonchalance.

— LYNNE TUOHY, *The
Hartford* (Connecticut) *Courant*

Ineffective   The study shows college students are becoming more conservative,
the researcher said, blinking her blue eyes and clasping her carefully
manicured hands.

Avoid Sexist/Racist Descriptions When you decide to include descriptions of
people, beware of sexism, racism or other biased writing. Writers often describe men
with action verbs, showing what they are doing, and women with adjectives showing
what they are wearing and how they look. One way to avoid bias is to ask yourself if
you would use a similar description for both men and women or equal treatment for
all racial and ethnic groups.

Consider this example:

Ineffective   Even Chandra Smith, busy being adorable in her perky non-runner's running outfit, actually looked at the track. A minute later, she was jumping around and yelling, along with most of the other 41,600 people on the old wooden benches at Franklin Field.

— *The Philadelphia Inquirer*

The story about the Penn Relay Carnival, a track meet in Philadelphia, also mentions
a few men among those 41,600 people, including some volunteers who wear gray
trousers and red caps. But they aren't "adorable" or "perky" or even "macho."

Show People in Action One of the most effective ways to describe people or
places is to show action. For example, Tom French doesn't write only about murder.
In a series about life in a Florida high school, he used the show-in-action technique
extensively, as in this passage about a history teacher's first day on the job. The
teacher, Mr. Samsel, has given his homeroom students some forms to fill out:

The future leaders of America sit silently, some of them slumped forward,
staring into space through half-closed eyes. Over to the side sits a boy. He

is wearing a crucifix, blue jeans and a T-shirt. On the front of the shirt is a big smiley face. In the center of the face's forehead is a bullet hole, dripping blood. . . .

Around the room, students begin writing.

"Isn't this great?" says Samsel. "Just like real life — forms and everything."

Smiley Face looks at one of the sheets in front of him. He reads aloud as he fills it out.

"Please list medical problems."

He stops.

"Brain dead," he says.

— TOM FRENCH, *Tampa Bay Times/St. Petersburg* (Florida) *Times*

Use Lively Verbs News is action, says Jack Hart, *The* (Portland) *Oregonian's* former writing coach. But writers often "squeeze the life out of an action-filled world," he says. "We write that thousands of bullet holes were in the hotel, instead of noting that the holes pocked the hotel. We report that a jumper died Monday when his parachute failed, instead of turning to action verbs such as *plummeted* or *plunged* or *streamed*."

Set the Scene You need to set the scene by establishing where and when. Although it is common to establish the time and weather, often in a lead, beware of using that technique unless time and weather factors are relevant to your story. "It was 2 a.m. and the wind was blowing" is akin to the cliché "It was a dark and stormy night." In this story from a California State University student newspaper, the time and weather conditions are relevant to the story:

TIJUANA, Mexico — Shivering in the mud under a 2-foot-high chaparral, Jose carefully lifts his head into the cold night mist to monitor the movements of the U.S. Border Patrol.

On a ridge above a small ravine, patrol trucks scurry back and forth while a helicopter above provides the only light, turning spots of the nighttime terrain into day. In the distance, guard dogs growl, bark and yelp.

At one point a patrol truck speeds toward Jose and his group of six Mexican farm laborers. Squatting in the brush, they quickly slide flat into the mud like reptiles seeking shelter.

Within seconds the helicopter hovers above them as its searchlight passes nearby, then at once directly over them. All their faces are turned downward to avoid detection by the brightness of the light that illuminates every detail of the soil, roots and insects that lie inches under them.

Soon, the truck and helicopter make a slow retreat. Jose

James Tourtellotte/Courtesy of U.S. Customs and Border Protection

The U.S. Border Patrol seeking people attempting to enter the U.S. illegally.

and his group, safe for the moment, will remain motionless in that same muddy spot for the next three hours as the mist turns to rain and the rain turns back to mist.

Nut graphs

To those who have never passed this way before, the sights and sounds are of another world. But to the expert scouts called "coyotes," this alien land between Mexico and the United States is home.

Every weekday evening, approximately 2,000 people attempt to illegally cross the border from Mexico to the United States. On weekends the numbers can climb to between 5,000 and 10,000, said Victor Clark, director of the Binational Center for Human Rights in Tijuana, Mexico.

— BRETT C. SPORICH, (Long Beach, California) *Daily 49er*

In the next example, the story is about a reading program. Although the lead about the weather is backed up by a quote, the weather has nothing to do with the focus or the rest of the story.

It was a beautiful spring-like Sunday, and the heat on the first floor of the Kansas City Public Library Downtown was on full-blast. But that didn't stop about 400 people from crowding inside to read and hear their favorite selections from African-American authors.

The crowd, people of all ages and races, was there to take part in the national Read-In sponsored by the Black Caucus of the National Teachers of English.

"That is true commitment," said Mamie Isler, program director for Genesis School, which helped coordinate the event in Kansas City.

The second annual Kansas City Read-In opened with a performance by 30 students from the Genesis School choir.

— *The Kansas City* (Missouri) *Star*

Narrative Techniques

Narrative writing combines show-in-action description, dialogue, plot and reconstruction of an event as it occurred. This type of writing requires a bond of faith with the reader because attribution is limited. You need to make it clear where you got the information, but you don't need to attribute repeatedly. You can also use an overview attribution for portions of the story and then attribute periodically, especially when you are quoting sources.

Before you can do narrative writing, you need to do thorough reporting. It takes a different kind of questioning to gather the information you will need to reconstruct a scene with dialogue and detail. Narrative writing is not fiction. You must stick to the facts even though the story may read like a novel. You need to ask questions like these: What were you thinking at the time? What were you feeling? What did you say? What were you wearing? What were you doing? You need to get details about colors, sounds, sights, smells, sizes, shapes, times and places.

If you were witnessing the event, you would see, hear, smell and feel — perhaps even taste — the experiences of your subject. Because you are reconstructing the event, you need to ask the questions that will evoke all those images.

Those are the kinds of questions Jane Schorer Meisner asked when she wrote this Pulitzer Prize–winning story about a woman who had been raped. The woman had agreed to use her name. In this opening part of her series, the reporter sets the scene (with relevant weather and time references) and reconstructs the woman's experience, so the reader is a witness to the event:

She would have to allow extra driving time because of the fog.

A heavy gray veil had enveloped Grinnell overnight, and Nancy Ziegenmeyer — always methodical, always in control — decided to leave home early for her 7:30 a.m. appointment at Grand View College in Des Moines.

It was Nov. 19, a day Ziegenmeyer had awaited eagerly, because she knew that whatever happened during those morning hours in Des Moines would determine her future. If she passed the state real-estate licensing exam that Saturday morning, she would begin a new career. If she failed the test, she would continue the child-care service she provided in her home.

At 6 a.m. Ziegenmeyer unlocked the door of her Pontiac Grand Am and tossed her long denim jacket in the back seat. The weather was mild for mid-November, and her Gloria Vanderbilt denim jumper, red turtleneck sweater and red wool tights would keep her warm enough without a coat.

The fog lifted as Ziegenmeyer drove west on Interstate Highway 80 and she made good time after all. The digital clock on the dashboard read 7:05 as she pulled into a parking lot near Grand View's Science Building. She had 25 minutes to sit in the car and review her notes before test time.

Suddenly the driver's door opened. She turned to see a man, probably in his late 20s, wearing a navy pin-striped suit. He smelled of alcohol.

"Move over," the man ordered, grabbing her neck. She instinctively reached up to scratch him, but he was stronger than she was. He pushed a white dish towel into her face and shoved her into the front passenger seat, reclining it to a nearly horizontal position. Then he took her denim jacket from the back seat and covered her head.

He wasn't going to hurt her, the man said; he wanted money. She reached toward the console for the only cash she had with her — $3 or $4 — and gave it to him. He slid the driver's seat back to make room for his long legs, started the car and drove out of the parking lot.

"Is this guy going to kill me?" Ziegenmeyer wondered. "Is he going to rape me? Does he just want my money? Does he want my car?" She thought about her three children — ages 4, 5 and 7 — and realized she might never see them again.

— JANE SCHORER MEISNER, *The Des Moines* (Iowa) *Register*

Create Tone Hard-news stories often have an objective, factual tone, mostly an absence of mood. But in storytelling, you should create a tone, or mood, such as happiness, sadness, mystery, excitement or some other emotion.

You don't need to tell the reader that the mood of the place was festive or mournful. You can show it by the images, quotes and style that you select for your story. In this example, the writer tries to recreate the somber tone of the story by using a narrative lead.

A 9-year-old boy watches in horror as his grandparents contemplate suicide. He cannot cry out to them or he will make certain of their death as well as his own. At such a tender age, he learns that he must keep quiet and keep everything inside in order to live to see another day.

That was the lesson that Zev Kedem learned as a young Jewish boy in Nazi Germany during World War II.

Kedem, a survivor of the Holocaust because of Oskar Schindler's list, gave a talk to nearly 800 students at the University of Kansas ballroom

Monday night. The audience listened silently as he recounted the horrifying story of his childhood during the second World War.

As a young boy, Kedem remembers traveling with his mother and sister to his grandparents' apartment in the dark of night.

"That darkness would continue for five or six years until I was liberated," he said. "The rats were just as hungry as we were."

Since work permits were only given to Jewish males between the ages of 13 and 45, Kedem's mother feared for his life because he was only 9. Children who were not old enough to work were shot, Kedem said. In desperation his mother hid him in a loot wagon, which was taken into a concentration camp. She thought his chances of survival were better in the concentration camp than in the ghetto.

"She didn't know if I would be found and shot, but she knew that sooner or later I would be shot in the ghetto."

For two years in the camp, Kedem worked among brush piles. He surrounded himself with the piles in an attempt to hide his age and small size from the German guards.

— JOY PETERS, *Journalism Student*

Conversely, in this example, the writer creates a lighthearted tone by mirroring the subject matter — a profile of a hypnotist:

You will read this story.

You will hang on its every word, and you will not get sleepy.

As you proceed, you will learn about hypnosis and a Clive hypnotherapist whose work has led her to the International Hypnosis Hall of Fame.

You are ready to begin. Shari Patton is sitting on the couch in her home, telling you that she first went for hypnosis "like a doubting Thomas." She was a student at the University of Minnesota when a friend was going to be hypnotized and wanted Patton to come along. Listen, now what she has to say:

"My friend had said, 'Go with me.' And I had said no, and after several requests begging me, I said 'All right. I'll go.' And I went to stop smoking, not believing it would work, but very much wanting to stop smoking, and I was so amazed and delighted that it worked for me that I went back and started using hypnosis for weight control and lost 90 pounds."

— MARY ANN LICKTEIG, *The Des Moines* (Iowa) *Register*

Seek Unusual Stories The next example is the type of human-interest story that Charles Kuralt would have enjoyed reporting. It is also the type of story you might do if you work in a small community for a newspaper or TV station. Chances are, you will seek stories about people who are doing interesting or unusual things in your community.

MULTIMEDIA COACH

CHARLES KURALT was a consummate storyteller who wrote human-interest features for "On the Road," a series for CBS-TV's "Sunday Morning" show. Long before "convergence" became a buzzword for a type of journalism merging print, broadcast and the Web, Kuralt epitomized a multimedia journalist. He began his career as a print reporter for the *Charlotte News* in North Carolina, where he won the Ernie Pyle Memorial Award in 1956 for his offbeat human-interest columns. When he joined CBS in 1957, he continued producing human-interest features and later wrote several books about his adventures on the road and the people he met. He loved storytelling about people in newspapers, television and books, but he was a bit baffled by the Web.

"For most of my career I didn't do stories about things that go wrong," he once said. "I did stories about unexpected encounters, back roads, small towns and ordinary folk, sometimes doing something a little extraordinary. I would not argue that it was important to society at large; it was

just fun," according to the website Annenberg /CPB learner.org (*www.learner.org/catalog/extras /interviews/ckuralt/ck02.html*).

Kuralt always found something extraordinary in the people and places he visited. "I don't know what makes a good feature story," he said. "I've always assumed that if it was a story that interested or amused me, that it would have the same impact on other people."

Kuralt learned early in his career at CBS that a good feature story for television was dependent on visuals. He said a CBS writer told him that "you must never write a sentence that fights the picture."

Whether you are writing feature stories for print, broadcast or the Web, take Kuralt's advice and find a story that interests you. Seek universal qualities of human interest such as people's hopes, fears, dreams, love, hate, the ability to triumph over adversity or the ability to achieve something special.

To read the entire interview with Kuralt, access the Academy of Achievement website at *www.achievement.org/autodoc/page/kur0int-1.*

COOPER LANDING MAN REVELS IN CLOVER COLLECTION

KENAI, Alaska — Some people believe the Kenai Peninsula is the luckiest place on Earth. Cooper Landing resident Ed Martin Sr. said he believes it is time somebody proved it.

Martin has been finding four-leaf clovers since his childhood and started to save them only two years ago. Since then he has rounded up more than 76,000 clovers.

Some people likely would ask why a person would be so concentrated on how many mutated clovers they found, especially a collection well into five figures. The answer is it has to do with a little competition and a little bit of pride.

Martin has surpassed the previously largest known four-leaf clover collection held by George J. Kaminski, who collected 72,927 clovers within

An Alaska man has the world's largest collection of four-leaf clovers.

prison grounds in Pennsylvania (Guinness World Records). Kaminski has held the record since April of 1995.

Although Martin's world record-breaking application still is being completed, he is confident it will stand officially. The city of Soldotna, where many of the clovers were found, is handling the paperwork.

Actually finding a handful of four-leaf clovers, let alone 76,000, is a difficult task, so Martin shared his secret:

"I look for mutated clovers, ones with four clovers and above. Now, you're not going to believe this, but once I found 880 in one day. I found 90 percent in the Soldotna-Kenai Borough area."

It's a knack, Martin said. "People just don't see what I see," he said.

Martin expects to break a world record, but he says the accomplishment goes beyond that.

"I'm interested in the good that will come out of this," he said. "We have a wonderful country, a wonderful state and community. We are all lucky to be living here. It's just a fact of life. I really think this is the luckiest place in the world, and this will prove it."

— LAYTON EHMKE, *The Peninsula* (Alaska) *Clarion*

SOCIAL MEDIA

PEOPLE ARE eager to share stories. That's why social media sites like Facebook are so successful. You can use social media to enhance your reporting and writing, especially when you are trying to gather details and eyewitness accounts for storytelling.

- Use Twitter to post messages about the story you are writing, and ask followers to tweet any information they have about the incident, if that is the basis for your story. You can also ask people to send you any photos or videos they have on the subject.

- Use Facebook to search for sources related to your topic.

- Read blogs related to the topic. Ask sources if they have firsthand observations of your topic or a chronology if you are trying to reconstruct events of an incident for narrative writing.

- Use polls or questions with your story to encourage interactive feedback and post share icons.

STORYTELLING STRUCTURE

Up to this point in the book, even though you have had many story structures from which to choose, you probably have been organizing your stories by focus and supporting topics or in chronological order. Even with a storytelling approach, you still need to get the focus first. A narrative story can then be arranged topically or chronologically, or it can follow a literary plot form — with a beginning, a middle and an ending called a "climax."

"Most news stories are endings without beginnings attached," says Jon Franklin, a Pulitzer Prize–winning writer and author of *Writing for Story*. Reporters miss the dramatic point of view when they concentrate only on the result instead of on the actions leading up to the event. Franklin says stories should be built around a complication and a resolution. In the middle is the development, how the central character gets from the problem to the solution.

If you have a story that lends itself to this kind of plot, your focus would be the complication that the main character has to overcome. The organization could be chronological, starting with the inception of the problem. The middle would be how the character wrestles with the problem, and the climax would be the resolution of the problem.

Writing coach Bruce DeSilva says the writer must determine a resolution to do narrative writing. "That's one of the most important things for people to understand about narrative storytelling: picking the problem," DeSilva said at a Neiman Conference on narrative writing.

"So many people write the lead first," DeSilva says. "They slave away at the lead and spend lots of time on it before they write the rest of the story. Don't do that. It's almost always a bad idea. . . . When you write the ending first, then when you go back to the top of the story and start to write it, you know what your destination is. You know where you're going."

The technique of developing the story in sections, perhaps arranged by points of view, can also work in a narrative story. You can start the story in the middle of the action as long as you explain to the reader why you are telling this story now (the "so what" factor). This approach is somewhat like using the time frame organization — starting with the present, going to the past, back to the present and on to the future. Regardless of the technique you choose, you should plan your order before you write.

William Blundell, who spent years writing features and profiles for *The Wall Street Journal,* suggests in his book *The Art and Craft of Feature Writing* that features should be organized around "The Laws of Progressive Reader Involvement":

Stage one: Tease me, you devil. (Give the reader a reason to continue reading.)

Stage two: Tell me what you're up to. What is the story really about?

Stage three: Oh yeah? Prove what you said. (Include the evidence to support your theme.)

Stage four: Help me remember it. (Make it clear and forceful, and give it a memorable ending.)

Blundell says features should include the following elements, but not necessarily in this order:

- **Focus:** What is the central theme?
- **Lead and nut graph:** What is the point of the story? (Often, it is introduced anecdotally or descriptively.)
- **History:** How did the problem develop?
- **Scope:** How widespread is the development?
- **Reasons:** Why is this problem or conflict happening now?
- **Impacts:** Who is affected and how?
- **Moves and countermoves:** Who is acting to promote or oppose the development, and what are they doing?
- **Future:** What could happen as a result of the situation and developments?

Blundell also suggests blocking material from any one source in one place in the story, especially if the story has many sources. The organization is not as rigid as the list implies. If the material lends itself to narrative storytelling, it can be told in chronological order or natural story order: beginning, middle, climax and ending.

Here are some reminders of good storytelling techniques:

- Use concrete details rather than vague adjectives.
- Use dialogue when possible and appropriate.
- Set a scene.
- Use action verbs.
- Observe or ask questions involving all your senses.

ETHICS

ETHICAL DILEMMA: Is it OK to make up quotes? Is it OK to reconstruct scenes in feature stories?

Tom French reconstructed scenes, quotes and dialogue in his story about the murdered woman in one story and the other women in "Angels and Demons" based on court documents and interviews with sources who knew the women. How does that differ from cases of Jayson Blair, a former reporter for *The New York Times*, and Stephen Glass, a former reporter for *The New Republic*, who were both fired in disgrace for fabricating information in their stories?

Ethical values: Credibility, truth, accuracy, fairness

- Use show-in-action description.

- Tell a story like a plot, with a beginning, middle and climax. Get a chronology or sequence of events. You may want to use the chronology in all or part of your story. Even if you don't use chronological order, you need to understand the sequence of events.

- Follow Mark Twain's advice: "Don't say the old lady screamed — bring her on and let her scream."

Narrative Storytelling

Martha Miller interviewed Vietnam veteran Dan Vickroy several times before she wrote this story about his injuries in the war. Each time he remembered more. She asked him to recall what he was thinking, feeling, saying and experiencing when he was injured 25 years earlier.

Miller also reconstructed dialogue, based on Vickroy's recollections as he related them to her. The technique is acceptable if you are basing your information on documents and sources, but it is not preferable. If you can't confirm the dialogue with the original source, you can attribute it to the source who related it. If it is not controversial and you are sure it is accurate, you can reconstruct it as Miller has done.

After she finished all her interviews and filled several notebooks, Miller sat down to write the story. She was overwhelmed. She planned the story and organized it by different periods of Vickroy's life. Then she tried free-writing, just writing what she remembered to get it out of her head. After that she began refining the story, and before she revised her final draft, she read the story aloud.

The part of the story included here, the second section, contains almost no direct attribution. It is all based on Vickroy's recollections. Do you think the story needs attribution in this part? Is the story believable without it?

A SOLDIER'S STORY

BY MARTHA MILLER

Iowa City Press-Citizen

Descriptive beginning for section: sets scene

Two hands lifted the sheet that covered what was left of Dan Vickroy's body.

Reconstructed dialogue

"You're one tough son of a bitch," the surgeon said from behind a green mask.

"I'm a Vickroy," Dan said. "Take me in and sew me up." They did.

Narrative chronological storytelling through Vickroy

Vickroy regained consciousness. He figured he was in the base hospital at Cam Ranh Bay. He could see nothing through the bandages over his eyes, but he could hear the squeaks of rubber soles in the hallway and hushed conversations between doctors as they hurried from bed to bed. It sounded like a busy place.

He was scared, scared to death he was blind.

His ears wanted to believe what he heard, but his eyes would believe what they saw.

The nurses told him they were bandages and that he was strapped down. They told him he had been in bed for almost two weeks. And they told him he had a 104-degree temperature. He knew that. He couldn't stop shivering.

Clues of attribution without direct attribution (he remembered)

As he lay there, his memory returned. He knew the mine had exploded and that he was badly hurt. He remembered waking up twice in surgery. The last time, he felt a surge of pain. He saw a surgeon cutting off his leg with a bone saw.

The days and nights came and went. All the same. Dark.

This time, it was night. Someone shut off all the lights in his hospital room. The doctors were back. Slowly, they unraveled the gauze around his eyes.

Scene

Vickroy held his breath. He opened his eyes and saw a faint light. It burned, but this time it was a good sign. Doctors had worked through the night cleaning his eyes. What he saw made him want to put the bandages back on.

There were wire stitches in his stomach and his right hip. There were tubes in his nose and left arm. Instead of legs, he saw blood-soaked gauze wrapped around two stumps.

The doctors told him what happened: His right leg was blown away by the explosion and his left leg was amputated in surgery; his right arm was amputated below the elbow; and he had lost part of his stomach. Being so close to the mine saved his life; the blast threw him up and out of the way.

His face was intact, saved by that last glance back to camp. Vickroy took the news better than most.

"Psychologically, I was pretty positive." He had no legs, but he did have a wife and new baby. He had married Sharon Kay in 1968 in Tulsa. She was 8½ months pregnant when he left for Vietnam. Danny Ray was born March 28, 1969.

Direct quote with no attribution: speaker understood

Short sentences and pacing

Baby pictures were taped, one under the other, on the side of his bed so Vickroy could look at Danny Ray while lying on his back.

Those pictures and thoughts of heading back to the U.S. kept Vickroy's hopes up. But back home, his family wasn't so positive.

Dan's mother, Louise, was waiting tables in a Cedar Rapids restaurant when an Army officer handed her a telegram. She cried.

Louise had never wanted her youngest to join the service. She wouldn't sign his enlistment papers and couldn't see him off.

Vickroy had started to believe he could live without legs until the day a nurse read him a letter. It had arrived at Cam Ranh Bay several days earlier, but nobody wanted to read it to him.

It was from his wife. She wanted a divorce.

"She told me she didn't want half a man."

Punch ending to this section: short sentences

Reporting Techniques Establishing chronology, gathering detail, asking questions to get source to reconstruct specific events using all senses.

Writing Techniques Organized by sections technique in time sequences; although most of the story takes place in the past, each section deals with a different part of the character's life. The story primarily follows chronological order, with cliffhanger endings for each section. Other techniques used: short sentences, pacing, dialogue, definitions, description, narration.

SERIAL NARRATIVES

Stories written like novels in chapter form are called "serial narratives." The form is related to the sections technique, but each part is a separate story in a continuing saga.

This style of storytelling has become very popular for long stories presented in a series, with each part published on a separate day. Cliffhangers at the end of each chapter entice the reader to seek the next part of the serial. If the story is compelling enough, readers will come back for the next part. The format is well suited for the Web, where each chapter can be presented on separate Web pages. It also could work well for reading on small screen mobile media and tablet devices.

A serial narrative needs a compelling plot with these elements:

- A character coping with a problem
- Development of the situation
- Resolution

To write a story in this form, you need to start with a good plot. Organize the story by dividing it into parts with logical breaks, just as in the sections technique. One organization technique is time frames:

- Past and present — what led to the situation and the current status to explain why you are telling the reader this story now
- Past — development of the situation
- Present — return to present
- Future — what lies ahead

Web Storytelling

The Web is an ideal medium for storytelling in many forms. Short segments are preferable to long stories that span several screens. But the Web is a perfect place to experiment with new forms of storytelling, especially nonlinear treatment with links to elements of the story, audio and video to enhance the storytelling.

Storytelling on the Web can be in multimedia format, photo essays, short chunks or serial narratives. Most of all, storytelling can be interactive on the Web. Stories can involve readers by asking them to participate in polls, blogs, answer questions, write their own endings or opinions or submit their own experiences. For examples of innovative storytelling, access Musarium (*www.musarium.com*), a site that offers stories in several creative forms. The Online News Association (*journalists.org*) also features examples of innovative multimedia journalism.

EXERCISES

1 Scene: Go to a busy place on campus or to the cafeteria, and listen to people talking. Gather information about the scene. Then write a few paragraphs, setting the scene and weaving in dialogue.

2 Analogies: Study some objects on your campus. Write similes and metaphors to describe the objects.

3 Narrative writing exercise: Interview a classmate about any experience he has had, preferably a traumatic or emotional one. If your subject can't think of one, ask him to describe the morning routine from today or yesterday. Imagine that the nut graph is "And then (your subject) disappeared and hasn't been seen since." You will need to ask specific questions, such as what was the person wearing, what color and kind of car was he driving (if a car is involved), what time of day the events occurred, what he was thinking, feeling, doing, saying. Get the person to reconstruct the event exactly as it happened by asking questions about the sequence of events and details. Then write the information in narrative style in a few paragraphs or a brief story.

4 Timed free-writing: This exercise, borrowed from Lucille deView, a former writing coach for *The Orange County* (California) *Register*, requires you to write very quickly — in 10 to 15 minutes. Write a story about a personal experience and let your mind ramble, or write your thoughts about a topic. Remember that you are just getting your thoughts on paper. You can take any words that trigger thoughts — "soup," "pizza," "cars" — or a topic the instructor gives the class. Some topic suggestions from deView:

- The happiest day of my childhood
- My favorite assignment
- My worst assignment
- The most interesting person I interviewed (or know)
- A turning point in my life

 MindTap

FEATURED ONLINE ACTIVITIES: Log on to the MindTap for Rich's Writing and Reporting News to access a variety of robust additional material, including this chapter's learning objectives, activities, comprehension quizzes, and more. Be sure to check out the "Sports Story" and/or "Theatre Feature" NewsScene scenarios for an interactive writing exercise that will help to reinforce many of the themes presented in this chapter.

CHAPTER 11

Broadcast News Writing

© Mauricio Ricaldi/Shutterstock.com

Good writing counts for more than anything else.
. . . I don't care how pretty you are; I don't care
how good looking you are or how well you can
chat on the air. The fundamental value around
here is breaking news and reporting it well.
Everything goes back to writing well.

—**ED BENNETT,** *Assignment Editor, KTUU-TV, Channel 2,
Anchorage, Alaska*

COACHING TIPS

Update leads: Tell **what is
happening now.**

Use a **conversational style**
of writing.

Read your copy out loud
before recording it or
going on the air.

Use the **active voice.**

Use **short sentences** — one
idea per sentence.

Use the **present tense** when
possible.

Use subject–verb–object
order: **Who did what.**

Give **attribution first;** tell
who said what before
telling what was said.

T'S 9:15 ON A MONDAY MORNING, AND STAFF MEMBERS OF KTUU-TV Channel 2 in Anchorage are discussing story ideas at their daily planning meeting. It's going to be a busy day. A press conference is scheduled for 10 a.m. about a major donation for the library, and more than a dozen American bald eagles covered with slime are being cleaned at the bird rescue center in Anchorage. That's going to be a very visual story.

Reporter Jennifer Zilko is assigned to the eagle story. She heads to the bird rescue center with a photographer. Workers at the Bird Treatment and Learning Center are in a turmoil. They have 18 birds that were flown in by airplane from Kodiak Island, 252 miles south of Anchorage. The eagles usually nest outside a fish processing plant in Kodiak, but when a dump truck left the plant with fish guts, about 50 eagles dove into the uncovered rear of the truck in search of an easy meal. Twenty of the eagles were crushed or drowned in the mucky guts. The others were covered with the sticky fish slime, which glued their feathers and prevented them from retaining body heat. Volunteers at the bird rescue center are trying to save the big raptors from certain death by washing them off with Dawn detergent.

Photographer Mike Nederbrock enters the small washing area to videotape the volunteers as they wash an eagle. A press conference follows. At the end of the conference, Zilko asks the director if there is anything else she would like to add.

"If I could give any advice to students, that would be the question to ask: 'Is there anything else you want to share?' And ask them (the sources) to spell their first and last name," Zilko says.

Zilko began working at the station while she was a student at the University of Alaska Anchorage. Her first assignment was to convert broadcast scripts into print-style stories for the station's website. "The AP Stylebook was my bible for two years." She says students really need to know AP style even if they are going into broadcast and especially if they are planning to work in public relations.

Photographer Mike Nederbrock and reporter Jennifer Zilko watch workers wash an eagle.

PRODUCING A NEWSCAST

Zilko's story is only one of 14 news stories to be squeezed into a 30-minute broadcast that also includes weather, sports and commercial breaks. The process of producing a newscast is complex. It involves several editors and producers who must plan every second of the broadcast and adapt to constant changes throughout the day as news breaks.

Logging the Tape

When Zilko returns from the eagle assignment, Nederbrock hands her his videotape, and she inserts it into a machine so she can watch the video and choose the sound bites she wants to use. This process is called "logging" the tape. She types the complete sound bite with the time listed on the tape. Some TV stations require scripts that just use the first few words and last few words of a sound bite, but at KTUU reporters type the entire sound bite so it can be read on the screen as closed captions for hearing-impaired viewers. This also helps the Web editor so he doesn't have to listen to the tape when he converts her script into an online story, Zilko says.

She types quickly as she listens to the tape. "Grammar is not my best part when I'm logging, so I fix it later," she says. "The goal is not to go over 15 seconds on your bites. If they can say it in a shorter bite, that's better." Sometimes Zilko will ask the photographer to recommend his best shot to open the story, but today he has been called away to another assignment.

Jennifer Zilko logs the tape to listen to sound bites.

Planning a Rundown

The photographer shot 32 minutes of tape, but Zilko will have only one minute and 30 seconds (1:30) for her story for the 30-minute newscast at 5 p.m. and 2 minutes (2:00) for the hour-long 6 p.m. newscast. "It may not seem like very much time, but I write short, so it's fine," she says.

The introduction to her story, which she writes for the anchor, will run 15 seconds before the story, and there will be 20 seconds for a question-and-answer session with the anchor at the end of the story. "I sometimes come in under the time they [the producers] give me, which they like because they're always over."

The producers determine how much time each story can run. Everything is timed to the second in a television newscast. KTUU has two producers: one for the 5 p.m. newscast and one for the 6 p.m. show, but they work together throughout the day.

As soon as the morning planning meeting ends, Aniela Whah starts drafting a schedule called a "rundown" for the 5 p.m. newscast, in which she allocates minutes and seconds for every story. Then she begins writing promotional briefs called "teasers," news briefs of about 20 to 25 seconds that will air a few times a day to encourage viewers to tune into the evening newscast. That's not always easy. A story might fall through, or breaking news may force a story to be canceled. Writing teasers is an art.

Producers Aniela Whah and Tracy Holenport

"You have to keep it really short and not give too much away," says Tracy Holenport, the producer for the 6 p.m. newscast.

Scheduling the stories isn't easy either. Every story has to be timed to the second. "I would say that's the hardest part," Holenport says. If a story runs over the allotted time, she has to subtract time from another report such as weather or sports. The time allocated to news is especially limited. The 30-minute news-cast at 5 p.m. has only 14 minutes and 9 seconds for news, and the hour-long

Page	Story Slug	Segment	Story Writer	Source Tape	Source	Key	Graphic
A16		A	JM		INTV		
A17	ANADARKO GAS DRILLING	BTS	JM		INTV		
A18		QA	JM		INTV		
A19		INTRO	JZ		ROOF	TREATING THE EAGLES	
A20		A	JZ		ROOF		
A21	EAGLE CLEAN UP	B+	JZ		ROOF		
A22		C	JZ		ROOF		
A23		QA	JZ		ROOF		
A24	5P TEASE 2	FOSTER TRIAL SETTLEMENT	AW			in court today	
A25		MYSPACE RULES	AW			myspace	
B0	COM BREAK 1						
B1	REOPEN	((BLUE))					
B2	MYSPACE RULES	A	LT			SAFETY RULES	
B3		B	LT				
B4		A	AB			CASE SETTLED	
B5	FOSTER TRIAL SETTLEMENT	BTS	AB				
B6		GFX	AB				
B7	JUNEAU SESSION ADVANCE	INTRO	WM		FIBR	LEGISLATIVE SESSION	

KTUU-News Channel2/Anchorage, Alaska

This is page 2 of the rundown sheet for the 5 p.m. newscast. The story slug is Eagle Cleanup; the intro to the story is on p. A19 of the script; the writer is JZ, for Jennifer Zilko, and the source is where she will report the story — on the roof of the KTUU building so that the background is outside when she is talking.

newscast at 6 p.m. has 22 minutes for news. Weather runs eight minutes and sports runs six minutes. The rest of the time is allotted to teasers before the breaks and advertisements.

In addition to scheduling the rundowns and writing teasers, the producers write most of the anchor's material and some of the smaller stories, including rewrites of national stories. "I probably end up writing about 10 stories per newscast; it depends on the day," Holenport says. "If we are short of reporters, those days are tough on producers."

Before a show, the producers check all the graphics and names flashed on the screen to make sure they are accurate. The producers work closely with assignment editor Ed Bennett, whose desk is a few feet away from theirs.

Assigning the Stories

Bennett starts his day by checking his email, wire stories, websites and other news media. Then he reviews the 30-day file of story ideas that he keeps in his desk. He creates an assignment sheet as a starting point for discussion at the morning planning meeting. Then he adds or changes the story list, depending on the discussion and story suggestions from the reporters, who are expected to come to the meeting with some story ideas based on their beats.

"I try to have one or two stories every day set up and ready to shoot or in certain cases ready in the can for the air," Bennett says. He can count on some stories every week because the station airs regular features each day, and he listens to the police scanner for breaking news.

"Some days it's completely slow; other days are just running and gunning from dawn to dusk, so it varies a lot," he says.

He also assigns the photographers to pair with the reporters. "This is TV; the pictures often come first. The availability of a photographer determines when we go on a story or if we go on a story," Bennett says.

He says the Web doesn't affect his job too much, but if a big story breaks, he makes sure the Web editor is aware of it. "The way you cover TV news is to go quickly, go now. It's a very nice marriage with the Web because the Web is also aimed at getting information out there as soon as it comes."

But immediacy can pose problems. The Web editor might hear about a story on the police radio and want to post it, Bennett says. "Sometimes you have to wait for official confirmation. Standard journalism rules do apply to the Web and must be enforced," he says.

In addition to planning the news, Bennett edits scripts along with other newsroom managers. He looks for spelling, accuracy and completeness. He speaks emphatically when he talks about writing:

"This is the thing that people don't understand: Good writing counts for more than anything else, at least in this television newsroom — period. I don't care how pretty you are; I don't care how good looking you are or how well you can chat on

Carole Rich

Assignment editor Ed Bennett discusses a story with a reporter.

the air. The fundamental value around here is breaking news and reporting it well. Everything goes back to writing it well."

Here are his recommendations for writing well:

- Write for clarity and brevity.
- Use plain English.
- Avoid repetition, especially between the reporter's writing and the sound bite.
- Pick sound bites that have emotion. "A reporter can give you the facts," Bennett says. "I don't need people telling you what the facts are. A reporter can do that better and faster."

It's Showtime

It's time for the 5 p.m. show. News director John Tracy heads for the studio where he anchors the 5 p.m. show. Tracy reads from the teleprompter, a machine that contains the scripts, which scroll as he reads.

Tracy introduces the stories before the reporters deliver them, and at the end of the story Tracy asks the reporters some questions to provide additional information, called a "tag." Reporters often write the questions the anchor will ask. The show ends promptly at 5:30, to be followed by "NBC Nightly News."

MULTIMEDIA COACH

ERIC ADAMS, Web editor for KTUU, spends much of his day checking for breaking news to post on the station's website. If a major story breaks, Adams sends email to the 8,000 people who signed up to receive the station's news alerts. "I want to make sure it's something that 8,000 people want in their email," he says. After the reporters write their scripts for the evening newscasts, he checks them to prepare them for the Web. A style editor will rewrite them later in print format with AP style for the Web.

Adams is convinced that the future of journalism is on the Web. "I would say the biggest obstacles that broadcasters need to overcome and be aware of when they are writing stories and reporting for air is that they also need to be cognizant of online elements," Adams says. "They need to think of how they can present their story in an interactive way on a website, which is where people might see it first or might follow up for information as opposed to just writing for broadcast."

Here are some tips to help you prepare for the Web:

- Gather more information than you need for your TV story, so you can offer additional material for the Web. Consider the viewer. What information related to your story would the reader or viewer find helpful?

- When you log in your tape, consider the sound bites and video that will look good on the Web.

- Gather full text of speeches, budgets or other material that would not be in your broadcast story but could go on the Web.

- Consider an interactive question or poll that might work with your story on the Web.

Carole Rich

Eric Adams, Web editor for KTUU-TV.

KTUU is an NBC affiliate and one of three network-affiliated television news stations in Anchorage, but it has the largest audience in Alaska. Nationally it is ranked 155 out of 210 markets for television stations.

WRITING TIPS

Here are excerpts from a booklet of writing and reporting guidelines that Tracy wrote for his reporters:

- **Why should I care?** In every story you write, think about the viewers. Why should they care about your story?

- **What's it all about?** You should be able to state your focus with a simple sentence containing a subject, verb and object. Who is doing what to whom?

- **So what?** Does your story meet the "so what" test? Does it address a larger issue? Did I learn anything new by watching the story?
- **Attribution:** Who said what? If you are going to state anything but the most obvious fact, back it up with attribution. We don't use unnamed sources without the permission of the news director.
- **A good lead:**
  - Captures the viewer's attention
  - Is conversational
  - Uses active voice
  - Moves the story forward
- **Guillotine the Gimmes:** In the body of your story, get rid of the information that people already know. Focus on what they don't know. What's new?
- **Write to the corners:** It still amazes me when reporters describe the video to me. "The suspect was visibly upset." No kidding. I can see the picture. Your words should complement the video, not describe it.
- **Bounce the babble:** Don't write like a police report. People are caught, not apprehended.
- **Sound:** Use it whenever you can. It takes the viewers out of the studio and puts them at the story.
- **Sound bites:** Write to them. They shouldn't come out of nowhere, and they should not repeat what you said leading up to the bite.
- **The end:** All good stories build to a strong finish. You can only finish strong if you know how you are going to finish in the field. Your story should leave the viewer feeling something. A successful story evokes an emotional response. Does your story close the circle? Sometimes you can end your story by returning to the start of the story, having answered the question you posed.

BROADCAST WRITING STYLE

Good writing is crucial in every area of the media, including public relations, which involves writing for print, broadcast and the Web. Here are a few major differences between print and broadcast writing:

Attribution

> **Always first in broadcast:** The bird rescue center's director says one of the eagles died.

> **First or last for print and the Web:** One of the eagles died last night, said the director of the bird rescue center.

Active Voice Who is doing what, not what was done to whom. Active voice is preferable for print but even more necessary for broadcast.

Active: Volunteers at the center washed the eagles with Dawn detergent.

Passive: The eagles were washed with Dawn detergent by the volunteers at the center.

Present Tense Use when possible for broadcast; past tense is more common in print and the Web.

Present: One eagle remains in critical condition.

Past: One eagle remained in critical condition.

Update Leads Use the latest information. This technique is recommended for all media, but especially for broadcast and the Web.

Old news: Eighteen eagles were flown to the bird rescue center Saturday.

Updated: Eighteen eagles are recovering at the bird rescue center, where they were flown Saturday.

Broadcast Script Format

Broadcast scripts are written in two columns, with directions for the technical crew on the left and the story text on the right. Most newsrooms use a computer program that automatically formats the scripts. The reporter's text is usually in capital letters, and the sound bites are in uppercase and lowercase letters. Sources for sound bites are identified by a machine called a "character generator," which produces titles that are superimposed under the video, to identify the speaker.

TV stations have different methods of writing directions. Some stations identify sound bites as SOT, meaning "sound on tape." At KTUU each sound bite is on a different tape, so the bites are identified as "A roll" on one tape, "B roll" on another tape, and so on.

Many of the terms previously used in scripts are changing. The script should contain a slug (a one- or two-word title), which is usually assigned by the producers. The reporter's copy is usually written in capital letters, and the sound bites are typed in uppercase and lowercase letters. Although you no longer have to be concerned about typing directions in columns, you should not split or hyphenate words at the end of a sentence. Remember that the script will be read on a teleprompter, and the anchor or reporter needs to see the whole word. A reporter's story that includes the video, reporter's narration and sound bites is called a "package."

Here is Jennifer Zilko's script about the eagle story:

EAGLE CLEANUP-PKG

SHOW EAGLES IN SOAP
TREATING THE EAGLES
Reporter Jennifer Zilko
Anchor — John

Readrate 13:75

{***JOHN***}

THE BIRD TREATMENT AND LEARNING CENTER IS TRYING TO SAVE THE LIVES OF MORE THAN A DOZEN EAGLES.

SINCE LAST NIGHT 18 BALD EAGLES HAVE BEEN BROUGHT TO THE CENTER AFTER DIVING INTO THE BACK OF A TRUCK FULL OF FISH SLIME IN KODIAK ... AND MORE ARE ON THE WAY.

TAKE: TAKE SPLIT

{***TAKE SPLIT***}

AND AS CHANNEL 2'S JENNIFER ZILKO TELLS US — WASHING AMERICA'S CHERISHED BIRDS IS A LENGTHY PROCESS.

JENNIFER?

TAKE: A ROLL (Jennifer speaking)
(also called SOT — sound on tape)

(**A ROLL)

FIRST EACH BIRD IS DUNKED INTO A WARM BATH OF SOAPY WATER.

THE SECRET WEAPON?

DAWN DISH SOAP.

AFTER BEING METICULOUSLY SCRUBBED, THEY'RE THEN RINSED.

VOLUNTEERS GO THROUGH EVERY FEATHER ON THE EAGLE TO MAKE SURE ALL THE SOAP IS WASHED OUT.

BUT EVEN AFTER THE WASH — SOME OF THE EAGLES AREN'T DONE YET.

TAKE: B ROLL (also called SOT)
AT: 12:53
TO: 13:03
DURATION: 0:10
(This is the sound bite and the time on the tape plus the CG) Cindy Palmatier, director of Avian care, Bird Treatment Center

{***B ROLL***}

<12:53 We have to wait until they're dry, and then we go through a sniff test. If they smell like a wet eagle, you're good.

TAKE: AUDIO CUE

{***AUDIO:CUE***}

IF THE EAGLE SMELLS LIKE FISH, IT IS SPOT WASHED AGAIN.

THE REASON IT'S SO CRITICAL TO GET ALL THE OIL OFF IS THAT EAGLES REGULATE THEIR TEMPERATURE WITH THEIR FEATHERS, AND THE OIL INHIBITS THAT ABILITY — MAKING THEM SUSCEPTIBLE TO HYPOTHERMIA.

	BUT EVEN THOUGH IT'S GOOD FOR THEM SOME, OF THESE EAGLES DON'T EXACTLY LIKE HAVING A BATH. ONE VOLUNTEER GOT NIPPED TWICE TODAY.
TAKE: C ROLL (third sound bite) AT: 27:31 TO: 27:38 DURATION: 0:07 CG — Gina Hollomon, volunteer, Bird Treatment Center	{***C ROLL***} <27:31 No hard feelings, none whatsoever. If I were being manhandled, I might nip myself.
TAKE: LOSE IT	{***LOSE IT***} THE CENTER SAYS EACH OF THESE EAGLES EATS ABOUT 400 GRAMS OF SALMON A DAY, SO THEY'RE ASKING FOR PEOPLE TO DONATE IF YOU HAVE SOME EXTRA SALMON IN YOUR FREEZER.
Anchor: JOHN Readrate 13.75	{***QUESTION***}
TAKE: QUESTION	JENNIFER — WHAT CONDITION ARE THE EAGLES IN AT THE CENTER?
TAKE: ANSWER	{***ANSWER***} ACCORDING TO CINDY PALMATIER, THEY'RE ALL DOING WELL EXCEPT FOR ONE OF THE BIRDS. THE CENTER DEEMS THAT EAGLE IS IN CRITICAL CONDITION BECAUSE IT'S HAVING A LOT OF PROBLEMS WITH TEMPERATURE REGULATION. THE CENTER WAS EXPECTING TO GET 13 MORE EAGLES IN TODAY, BUT THE WEATHER IN KODIAK WAS TOO BAD TO FLY THEM TO ANCHORAGE.

Web Versions

The story posted on KTUU's website, shown on the next page, was offered in video, not text.

TEASERS AND LEAD-INS

A teaser, also called a "tease," is a short blurb to entice viewers to tune in or stay tuned to a newscast. It is broadcast during the day before the newscast or during

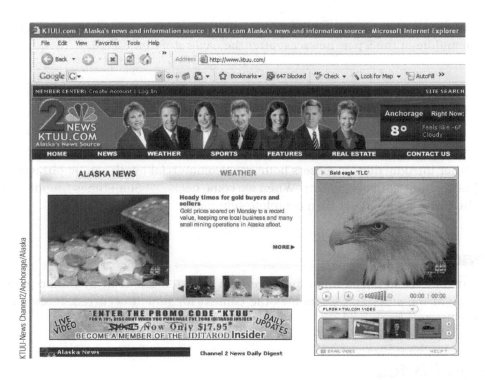

KTUU–News Channel2/Anchorage/Alaska

ETHICS

ETHICAL DILEMMA: The Radio Television Digital News Association (RTDNA) is the largest group for electronic journalists. Although many television stations have their own codes of ethics, the RTDNA code of ethics serves as a guide for the broadcast industry. Here are a few of the main principles:

- Professional electronic journalists should pursue truth aggressively and present the news accurately, in context and as completely as possible.

- Professional electronic journalists should present the news fairly and impartially, placing primary value on significance and relevance.

- Professional electronic journalists should present the news with integrity and decency, avoiding real or perceived conflicts of interest, and respect the dignity and intelligence of the audience as well as the subjects of news.

- Professional electronic journalists should defend the independence of all journalists from those seeking influence or control over news content.

the newscast before a commercial break. Don't tease the regular segments in general terms like weather and sports; tease something interesting or unique in your program that will affect the viewers. Write a tease as though you were telling a friend, "Guess what?" or "You won't want to miss this!" Teasers can include audio and video.

Here is a tease that the news anchor read before the commercial break that came in the middle of the 5 p.m. newscast after the eagle story on KTUU.

COMING UP ON THE 5 O'CLOCK REPORT . . . TWO FOSTER CARE TEENS SUED THE STATE SAYING IT DID NOT KEEP THEM SAFE. NOW BOTH SIDES AGREE TO A SETTLEMENT.

Other introductions to teasers before the commercial break can be phrases such as "Just ahead," "Still to come" or "When we come back . . . " Sometimes fragments can get the point across better than complete sentences.

Lead-ins

The anchor reads a lead into a package by a reporter. The lead-in should give the essence of the story and sometimes the context for how it occurred. It should not repeat the reporter's lead.

Sound Bites

Sound bites, also called SOTs — sound on tape — are the equivalents of quotes in print and Web stories. The best ones are usually short — less than 10 seconds — and reflect emotion or information that is better coming from the source than from the reporter. Is it memorable? If you didn't have your notebook and you weren't listening to your tape, what comment do you remember the source saying? That's a clue for a good sound bite. Avoid quotes that repeat what the reporter explained, called "echo" quotes.

Robert Papper, author of *Broadcast News & Writing Stylebook*, lists four qualities for good sound bites:

- Personal account — people telling what they saw, heard, felt, smelled or tasted
- Witness account
- Personal opinion
- Expert opinion

Natural Sound

Background sound that is intended to play while the reporter or anchor is speaking is called "natural" or "ambient" sound. It should enhance the story by giving the viewer a sense of being on the scene without distracting from the words the anchor or reporter is speaking. It could be the sound of wind, traffic noise, sizzling meat on a grill for a barbecue story, sirens or other sounds to enhance the story.

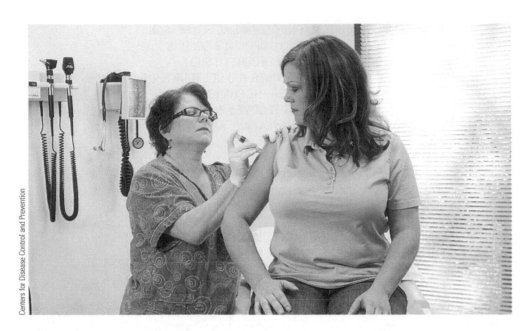

A nurse injects a flu shot into a patient.

VOs and VOSOTs

A VO is a voice-over, a story that the anchor reads over pictures but without any audio sound bites. A VOSOT (pronounced "VOH-SOT") is voice-over the anchor reads plus a sound bite — also called sound on tape. Both formats are usually brief — from 0:20 (20 seconds) to 0:45 (45 seconds). These two formats often comprise a majority of the stories on a broadcast. Because TV depends on images, both VOs and VOSOTs feature images while the anchor is reading the story. However, it is not always possible to time the visuals exactly to the text the anchor is reading, so it is best not to say "as on your screen" or to use other direct reference to the video.

The VO and VO-SOT differ from a "package," which is a story that includes an introduction by the anchor to the story that a reporter narrates with sound bites and pictures and sometimes a "stand-up," which features the reporter on camera. It usually ends with a "standard outcue," which is the reporter sign-off, such as "This is Jennifer Zilko for KTUU."

Some VOs begin with the image, whereas others insert the images after the anchor starts to read. Here is a sample script for a VO-SOT:

Writer (your name)   {***CAM/ANCHOR FIRST NAME***}
Anchor — Name —
Date

TAKE VO   ***VO/ANCHOR FIRST NAME***

(This is where you start to see video while anchor reads.)	IT MAY NOT SEEM LIKE FLU SEASON, BUT HEALTH OFFICIALS SAY IT IS TIME TO GET YOUR FLU SHOT. 　　THE SOONER YOU GET YOUR SHOT, THE BETTER THE CHANCE IT HAS OF WORKING. IT COMES IN TWO FORMS: A NASAL SPRAY AND AN INJECTION.
TAKE SOT 0:10 CG: BRUCE GELLIN, director, National Vaccine Office	It's important to note that neither of these vaccines cause the flu. That is just a dangerous myth.
TAKE VO TRT (total running time — 25 seconds)	HEALTH OFFICIALS RECOMMEND THE VACCINE FOR EVERYONE SIX MONTHS AND OLDER.

SOCIAL MEDIA

THE ETHICS GUIDELINES OF the Radio Television Digital News Association have been expanded to include social media. Although social media sites pose some unique dilemmas, the association recommends that journalists should "uphold the same professional and ethical standards for fairness, accuracy, truthfulness and independence as they do on air and on all digital platforms."

　　Here are some of the RTDNA guidelines that refer to social media:

- "Remember that what's posted online is open to the public (even if you consider it to be private). Personal and professional lives merge online.

- "Consider whom you 'friend' on sites like Facebook or follow on Twitter. You may believe that online 'friends' are different from other 'friends' in your life, but the public may not see it that way.

- "Be especially careful when registering for social network sites. Pay attention to how the public may interpret Facebook information that describes your relationship status, age, sexual preference and political or religious views.

- "Avoid posting photos or any other content on any website, blog, social network or video/photo sharing website that might embarrass you or undermine your journalistic credibility."

WRITING FOR RADIO

Radio news writing follows many of the same principles as writing for television news, but the copy is shorter. Stories can be more like the TV teasers in length. A radio newscast may total about 90 seconds, with six or seven stories, unless it is NPR, which offers longer stories. A typical story might contain fewer than 100 words. And because you can't show video, you should create word pictures by describing the scene.

Peter King, CBS News Radio correspondent, covers complicated stories in a clear, concise way. In an interview with the Poynter Institute, King offers this advice for writing radio news:

> You have to be able to pick out the most important information and not get caught up in the minutiae. And you have to keep it simple. It's a big mistake to try to cram too much information into too little time, which is why you have to prioritize and do it quickly.

King says most of his sentences last only five to six seconds on the radio.

> My rule of thumb is, "If it seems awkward and long when you say it aloud, it probably sounds that way to the listener." I try to keep each sentence focused on a single thought, and keep it simple. And keep in mind: You have to keep asking what the listener will and won't be able to digest.

Scripts for radio can be written in uppercase and lowercase letters instead of all capital letters, depending on the preference of the radio station. The following terms are used in radio:

Reader: A script that a newscaster reads without any background noise or comments from sources.

Actuality: The equivalent of a sound bite.

Natural sound: Also called "ambient" sound. This is background sound, the same term that's used in television news.

Wrap: A story from a reporter that may include actualities.

Voicer: A story a reporter reads; it may contain natural sound but does not include actualities.

Here are examples of public service announcements written for radio:

30-Second Script

> Soon, all over-the-counter medicines will have one thing in common: simplicity. That's because all over-the-counter medicines will feature new, easier-to-read labels that clearly show their ingredients, uses, warnings and directions. Because if there's one symptom we all want to relieve, it's confusion. For more information, call the Food and Drug Administration at 1-888-INFO-FDA. The new label — It's clearly better.
>
> *— Food and Drug Administration*

15-Second Script

Tired of being confused when comparing over-the-counter medicines?
Soon, all over-the-counter medicines will feature new, easier-to-read labels.
For more information, call the Food and Drug Administration at 1-888-INFO-FDA. The new label — It's clearly better.

— Food and Drug Administration

BROADCAST STYLE

Broadcast scripts are meant to be read from a teleprompter. As a result, style rules are designed to make scripts easy for a reporter or announcer to read out loud and for a listener to understand.

Punctuation

Avoid quotation marks. Generally, sound bites take the place of quotations. But if you want to quote someone, write out the word "quote" in this way: "She said . . . quote . . . this situation is impossible" or "and these are her exact words . . . . " Don't end the quote by saying "unquote." The reader's emphasis should make the end of the quote clear.

Limit punctuation to the comma, period, question mark and dash.

Numbers

Round off numbers when possible. Write out the numbers one through nine; use numerals for numbers over 10. Write out hundred, thousand, million, billion and trillion.

Write numbers to be read as follows: 13-hundred, two-thousand, 14-thousand, one-million, 17-million. More complicated numbers would be written this way: 320-thousand, not 320,000; 15-million-230-thousand, not 15,230,000.

Spell out fractions: one-half, three-quarters.

For decimals, write out the word "point": "It comes to 17-point-two-million dollars." Write out the word "dollars" also, instead of using the symbol.

There are some exceptions. Addresses, telephone numbers and time of day are written in numerals, even if the figures are lower than 10: "She lives at 5 Westbrooke Avenue"; "The accident occurred at 10:30 this morning" (avoid "a.m." and "p.m."); "The telephone number to call for information is 5-5-5-1-2-3-4" (separate the numerals with dashes so they are easier to read).

Limit the Use of Numbers They can be numbing, especially to the ear. Use percentages to give comparisons when possible. If you must use numbers, round them off and reinforce them with a graphic. Say "320-million dollars," not "320-million-122-thousand-three-hundred-44 dollars." Whenever possible, use an analogy to help viewers visualize numbers, for example, "The world's largest oil tanker is 15-hundred feet, equivalent to five football fields."

Names and Titles

Spell difficult pronunciations of names and locations phonetically. Some anchors prefer only the phonetic spelling instead of the real name followed by the phonetic pronunciation. John Blum would be written as it is pronounced — John Bloom. Identify a person's title before the name: "State Attorney General John Lawmaker is pleased with the results of a crackdown on fraudulent coal dust testing," not "John Lawmaker, state attorney general, is pleased with the results …"

Other Style Considerations

Use Contractions With Caution Write them out. Let the anchors contract them if they want to. Avoid "can't." It may sound too much like "can."

Omit Needless Words Words like "that" and "which" aren't always needed.

Timing of Copy Broadcast scripts use 1:30 for 1 minute and 30 seconds; 2:00 for 2 minutes; and so on.

STORY STRUCTURE

Like a newspaper story, a broadcast story needs a clear focus, a lead, a body and an ending. Unlike newspaper writing, however, broadcast writing should be geared to audio and video.

Bob Dotson, an award-winning NBC correspondent, calls the focus sentence a "commitment" statement. It is still a one-sentence summary of the story, but it is centered more on visual impact — what you want the audience to take away from the report. Provide the commitment visually. In his book *Make It Memorable*, Dotson says, "You aren't ready to write a story until you can state in one sentence what you want the audience to learn from your report."

In speeches he makes to journalism groups, Dotson offers these tips:

Beginning Write to your pictures first. Build your lead around a visual that foreshadows the story to come.

Middle

- Use, in most cases, no more than three to five points, which you prove visually.
- Use strong natural sound to let the viewer experience what happened.
- Use people engaged in compelling action that is visual.

- Use surprises to keep viewers involved and lure uninterested viewers.
- Use short sound bites.

Ending Build to a strong ending throughout the story, and make it visual. Make your viewers care about the story and the people.

Here are some ways to structure each part of a package, a story that contains video and sound bites.

Leads

An anchor will introduce your story, but every story in a package needs its own lead. Max Utsler, a broadcast journalism professor at the University of Kansas, said the main consideration for a lead is that it must fit the pictures the viewer sees. "Good television writing is not the craftsmanship of words; it is the presentation of the words and pictures fitting together," he said.

Once you have decided which images to use at the beginning of your package, you can decide whether the story needs a hard or soft lead. Feature stories may take softer leads; a breaking news story calls for a direct approach. In all cases, you must get to the focus — the nut graph — very quickly, generally by the second or third sentence.

	IRIS DUNCAN WOKE UP ONE MORNING AND SAID SHE THOUGHT SOMEONE HAD PUT WAXED PAPER OVER HER EYES.	I HAD NO IDEA WHAT WAS WRONG.
Sound bite	IT WAS ALL FUZZY AND CLOUDY AND I COULDN'T SEE.	SHE WENT TO HER DOCTOR THAT AFTERNOON. SHE LEARNED SHE HAD GLAUCOMA. THE DISEASE STRIKES ONE OF EVERY 200-THOUSAND PEOPLE.

Put a Human Face on the on the Story Whenever Possible Try to find someone personally affected by the issue. You can start with the specific, using a person first, and then go to the nut graph:

Starting with a general statement and going to a specific person is less effective:

GLAUCOMA STRIKES ONE OF EVERY 200-THOUSAND PEOPLE.
IRIS DUNCAN IS ONE OF THEM. SHE WOKE UP ONE MORNING AND SAID SHE THOUGHT SOMEONE HAD PUT WAXED PAPER OVER HER EYES.

Use the 'You' Voice Not all stories directly affect viewers' lives. But when possible, try to stress the impact within the first few sentences. Use an element that will make viewers care or understand why this story is important, unusual or of human interest. Don't be afraid to use the pronoun "you," especially in consumer stories, to heighten impact. Instead of writing a story about a drought in California that will cause lettuce prices to increase, try this approach:

> YOU'RE ABOUT TO PAY MORE FOR YOUR SALAD. A DROUGHT IN CALIFORNIA
> IS RAISING THE PRICE OF LETTUCE.

Use Impact Leads Lead with the effect on viewers as in the previous lead. An impact lead often uses the "you" voice.

> IF YOU TOOK YOUR CAR TO SEARS FOR REPAIRS IN THE PAST TWO YEARS,
> YOU MAY GET A REFUND.
>   THE COMPANY AGREED TO SETTLE CHARGES THAT IT CHEATED
> CUSTOMERS BY DOING SHODDY OR UNNECESSARY CAR REPAIR WORK.
>   AN ESTIMATED 12-THOUSAND-500 MISSOURIANS WILL BE
> ELIGIBLE TO RECEIVE 50-DOLLAR CREDIT COUPONS FOR ANY SEARS
> MERCHANDISE.

Advance the Lead When you can, advance the lead by stressing the next step to gain immediacy:

Immediacy	TWO PEOPLE REMAIN IN SERIOUS CONDITION FOLLOWING A CAR ACCIDENT THIS AFTERNOON.	TWO PEOPLE WERE INJURED IN A CAR ACCIDENT TODAY.	*No immediacy*

Focus on a Person The focus-on-a-person lead works as well in broadcast as in print, especially for a feature or a news story that the anchor introduces with a hard-news lead-in. Like *The Wall Street Journal* formula, this type of lead goes from the specific to the general. The person is one of many affected by the problem.

> JUDY AND JOE WESTBROOK SPENT THE MORNING CLEANING UP THE
> FURNITURE IN THEIR FRONT YARD. THE BLUE RIVER HAD OVERFLOWED ITS
> BANKS AND FORCED ITS WAY INTO THEIR INDEPENDENCE HOME.
>   MORE THAN 25 FAMILIES SHARE THEIR PREDICAMENT. LATE THIS
> AFTERNOON ALL OF THOSE FAMILIES WERE AWAITING WORD ABOUT THEIR
> FLOOD INSURANCE CLAIMS.

Mystery-Teaser Lead The mystery-teaser lead is another effective soft-lead technique, as long as you don't keep the viewer wondering what the story is about for too long. You must get to the point within the first few sentences.

IN SOME WAYS IT LOOKS
LIKE AN ORDINARY CAMP.
IT HAS HIKING TRAILS,
A SWIMMING POOL AND
TENNIS COURTS.
  BUT YOU DON'T HAVE
TO WORRY ABOUT WHAT
CLOTHES TO WEAR. IN
FACT, THIS IS ONE OF
THE FEW PLACES WHERE
YOU'LL FEEL OUT OF PLACE
WEARING CLOTHES.

AT THIS CAMP NEAR
DENVER, MEN AND WOMEN
OF ALL AGES FROLIC IN THE
NUDE.
  NUDISM IS ABOUT
THE ONLY RECREATION
THAT ANYBODY CAN DO
WHETHER THEY'RE RICH
OR POOR. WE ALL SHARE IN
THE SAME SATISFACTION,
SO IT'S A VERY GREAT
EQUALIZER.

*Sound
bite*

Body of the Story

As with all story structures, you must identify your focus first. Then jot down the order of your supporting points — facts or quotes from sources in sound bites.

One point should follow another one naturally. You have little time for wasted words or redundant transitions that parrot what the source will say in a sound bite. If you need transitions from the present to the past in your story, you can start the sentence with the time element — "yesterday" or "earlier today," for example.

Most of the basic news elements — who, what, when, where, how and so what — must be included in the story, but not all in the same paragraph. In broadcast writing, placement of points of emphasis for these elements differs from print.

Where Because most radio and television stations reach such a broad audience, the location of a story is even more important in broadcast than in print. Broadcast reports can superimpose the name of the location on the screen, but you also need to say it in the story. If the story follows a series of other stories from different regions, you might start this way:

IN PAWTUCKET, RHODE ISLAND, POLICE ARE LOOKING INTO THE
SUSPICIOUS DEATH OF A 15-MONTH-OLD BABY.

When Almost all broadcast stories have a "today" element. Avoid using "a.m." or "p.m." If the specific time element is important, say something like "An earthquake struck Southern California at 7:15 this morning"; or "earlier today" is sufficient. Place your time element after the verb, which is a more natural, conversational order.

Awkward   AT LEAST FIVE PEOPLE TODAY   ANTI-ABORTION PROTEST
WERE ARRESTED IN AN   OUTSIDE A MILWAUKEE CLINIC.

Preferred	AT LEAST FIVE PEOPLE WERE ARRESTED TODAY IN AN	ANTI-ABORTION PROTEST OUTSIDE A MILWAUKEE CLINIC.

Who Avoid using unfamiliar names in a lead and too many names in a story. When you have video sound bites, you may not even need the name in the story. The person can be identified by a superimposed title under his image in the taped segment. For delayed identification, follow the same guidelines as for print journalism. Identify the person by age, location, occupation or some other generic identifier. Then follow with the person's name. If you do have to identify a speaker, use his title before the name:

Say	BROWARD COUNTY SHERIFF JOHN LAW SAID TODAY HE WOULD NOT SEEK RE-ELECTION WHEN HIS TERM ENDS NEXT YEAR.	JOHN LAW, SHERIFF OF BROWARD COUNTY, SAID TODAY . . .	*Do not say*

Organizing Broadcast Stories

Here are some ways of organizing broadcast stories:

Problem/Solution The most common structure starts with a statement of the problem, provides support in sound bites and facts, offers background and discusses the solutions if any exist. It often ends with the next step in the action.

Time Sequence A story may lend itself to order by time. Because broadcast stories need immediacy, the time sequence is usually a reverse chronology that starts with the present action, goes to the past (background) and ends with a future element. Here is an example of reverse chronology:

Present	ANIMAL-RIGHTS ACTIVISTS ARE PROTESTING THIS MORNING OUTSIDE THE PITTSBURGH HOSPITAL WHERE DOCTORS TRANSPLANTED A LIVER FROM A BABOON TO SAVE A MAN'S LIFE.	ONE MEMBER OF THE PITTSBURGH ANIMAL ACTIVISTS SAYS THEY DON'T BELIEVE ONE SPECIES SHOULD BE SACRIFICED FOR ANOTHER.	
Past (background)	ABOUT 15 PROTESTERS CARRIED SIGNS AND CHANTED AT THE ENTRANCE TO THE UNIVERSITY OF PITTSBURGH MEDICAL CENTER.	DOCTORS SAY IF THEIR PATIENT CONTINUES TO RECOVER FOR THE NEXT MONTH OR MORE, THEY'LL DO THREE MORE OF THE SAME TRANSPLANTS.	*Future*

Hourglass This structure is a type of time sequence. However, you start with a hard-news summary lead and then rebuild the story chronologically.

Summary lead

A TOXIC CHEMICAL SPILL NEAR SUPERIOR, WISCONSIN, FORCED HUNDREDS OF RESIDENTS FROM TWO CITIES TO FLEE THEIR HOMES. AT LEAST TWO CHILDREN RECEIVED HOSPITAL TREATMENT. A HOSPITAL OFFICIAL SAYS MORE PEOPLE WILL NEED TREATMENT.

Beginning of chronology

THE PROBLEMS BEGAN THIS MORNING WHEN 13 FREIGHT CARS DERAILED JUST OUTSIDE SUPERIOR. ONE BURLINGTON NORTHERN CAR FELL INTO THE NEMADJI (NEH-MA´-JEE) RIVER, SPILLING SOME OF ITS CARGO OF BENZENE. BENZENE IS A FLAMMABLE SOLVENT, AND ITS FUMES CAN CAUSE HALLUCINATIONS, DIZZINESS AND COUGHING.

IN SUPERIOR AND NEIGHBORING DULUTH, MINNESOTA, OFFICIALS ORDERED THE EVACUATION OF HUNDREDS OF HOMES WITHIN A MILE OF THE RIVER. AND THE COAST GUARD SAYS IT'S PLACED A BOOM ACROSS SUPERIOR BAY TO PREVENT THE BENZENE FROM SPREADING.

Circle Envision your story as a circle. The main point is the lead. All supporting points should relate to the focus in the lead. Unlike an inverted pyramid, where points are placed in descending order of importance, in a circular construction, each part of the story is equally important. Your ending can refer back to a point in the lead, as in this example about a water problem in a Kansas community:

Lead

IF YOU LIVE NEAR BALDWIN CITY, YOU MAY WANT TO AVOID DRINKING THE WATER TONIGHT.

Supporting points

THE KANSAS DEPARTMENT OF HEALTH AND ENVIRONMENT IS WARNING FOLKS IN WATER DISTRICT NO. 2 IN DOUGLAS COUNTY ABOUT THE WATER. OFFICIALS FOUND BACTERIA IN THE WATER THAT MAY BE HARMFUL.

SOUND BITE (from Greg

These are indicator bacteria, which may indicate the presence of more serious bacteria. These can cause a number of gastrointestinal problems, and we would like people to boil their water or use bottled water or treat their water with Clorox.

CRAWFORD SAYS BACTERIA COME FROM DEAD ANIMALS. UNTIL OFFICIALS CAN CLEAR UP THE PROBLEMS, PEOPLE IN THE AREA SHOULD TAKE PRECAUTIONS.

Crawford, an official with the Kansas Department of Health and Environment)

Ending referring to lead

— *KSNT-TV*

Endings

In broadcast writing, endings are called "tags" or "wrap-ups." Newspaper stories often end with a quote from a source, but in broadcast writing, the reporter has the last word in a package, followed by his name and the station identification. Often the only time the viewer sees the reporter is at the end of the story. However, many news directors now prefer using reporter stand-ups within the story rather than at the end.

The most common endings:

- **Summary:** A fact that reinforces the main idea without repeating previous points.
- **Future:** The next step in some action.
- **Factual:** A background statement or just another fact.
- **Consumer:** Helpful items, such as where to call or go for additional information. If this information is important to the viewer, avoid giving it only one time. Warn the viewer that you will be repeating telephone numbers or locations later in the program. Plan to have phone numbers posted on the screen. You can also refer to your station's website for additional information.

REVISING STORIES

When you write the ending for your story, you are not at the end of the writing process. Revision is an important part of writing your story.

- Read your story aloud. Rewrite any sentences that sound strained.
- Check all your sources' names and titles for spelling, accuracy and pronunciation.
- Eliminate any bureaucratic language and replace it with simple, clear terms.
- Delete adjectives. Let the video show the viewers the scene.
- Make sure your transitions don't repeat the sound bites.
- Look at the video without the sound; then listen to your story without the video.

GLOSSARY

Here are some basic terms used in broadcast news:

Actuality: A radio term for recorded comments from a news source. Same as a sound bite, the term used in television.

Anchor: The person who reads the news on the set in the studio.

Backtiming: Exact time in the newscast that a segment will air. For example, a story that will air 12 minutes and 15 seconds into the newscast will be labeled 12:15. If the last segment in a 30-minute newscast is one minute, the backtiming will be 29, alerting the anchor that the segment must start at precisely that time or it will have to be cut.

Brief: Abbreviated news story, from 10 to 20 seconds long.

Character generator: Computer-type machine that produces the letters, numbers or words superimposed on the screen to label a visual image, such as a person or place. Also called a "Chyron," the brand name of the machine that generates these titles.

IN: Indicates the first few words of the source's quote to start a sound bite and the time on the tape, used at stations that don't include the entire sound bite in the script.

News director: Oversees all news operations at the station.

One-man-band: Based on the definition of a musician who plays a number of instruments, in television a one-man-band refers to a reporter who shoots, tapes and writes the story — a person who does it all.

OUT: Indicates the last few words of the source's quote, ending the sound bite.

Package: Reporter's story that includes narration, visual images and sound bites from sources.

Producer: Plans the newscast and often writes teasers and some copy for the anchors.

PSA: Abbreviation for a public service announcement.

Reader: Story the anchor or radio announcer reads without visuals or sound bites.

Rip-and-read: Copy from the wire services that is read exactly as it was written instead of being rewritten.

Seg time: Length of time for a news segment. A brief may be 0:10, or 10 seconds; a reporter's package, including the lead-in by an anchor, may be 1:45 — one minute and 45 seconds.

SOC (standard out cue): Reporter's sign-off comments at the end of the story. For example, "This is Jennifer Zilko for KTUU Anchorage."

SOT (sound on tape): Similar to a sound bite; indicated in copy along with the amount of time the taped comments will take. For example, SOT 0:15 means the comments on the tape will take 15 seconds.

Sound bite: Video segment showing the source speaking.

Stand-up: A part of the story in which the reporter talks on camera at the scene; sometimes at the end of a story.

Super: Letters, numbers or words produced by the character generator and superimposed over visual images; often used to identify the person appearing on the tape. At some stations, the letters CG — for character generator — are used to indicate the super.

Tag: The closing sentence for a TV or radio story or package.

Teaser: Introduction to a story on the next newscast, to tease viewers to tune in.

Teleprompter: Video terminal that displays the script for the anchor to read. This term was previously a trademark, but AP style now considers it generic.

VO (voice over): Anchor's voice over video images. Words and images should coincide.

VOB (voice over bite): Anchor's voice over video images with a sound bite from a source.

VO-SOT (voice over sound on tape): Anchor's voice over video and sound bite; same as VOB but more commonly used.

EXERCISES

1 Write a broadcast brief, about 15 seconds, based on this information from an NBC News Channel story:

Who: A consumer group, the Florida Consumer's Federation.

What: Filed a suit charging the Publix Grocery Store chain with discrimination.

Why: Group claims that the grocery chain failed to put enough women, blacks and Hispanics in management jobs and that the company doesn't have enough stores in minority neighborhoods.

When: Today.

Backup information: Publix management agrees with some of the complaints but says it is working to overcome them, according to Publix president Mark Hollis.

2 Write a broadcast story based on this press release from the police department:

Two vehicles have been reported to the (your town) Police Department as stolen at two Anchorage churches over the last two Sundays, in thefts that bear a remarkable resemblance to one another.

On last Sunday (insert date) at 09:30 hours, a woman was attending services at a church located on 8th Avenue. She left her coat with her car keys in the pocket, hanging on the coat rack of the church. When services were concluded, she discovered that her coat was missing from the rack, as was her silver 2009 Toyota Yaris from the parking lot. Her vehicle was recovered by police just after noon on that same day. The suspect was not located.

On this past Sunday, (insert date), a man and his wife attended church services at 09:30 hours on Parkside Road. The man left his vehicle keys in his jacket pocket and hung his jacket in a coat closet during the service. At 10:45, when he and his wife left church, he discovered that his jacket was missing from the closet, and his blue 2006 Chevy 1500 pickup was missing from the parking lot. It has not yet been recovered.

The Police Department would like to remind residents not to leave their keys or other valuables in coat pockets, where they may be easily located and stolen by thieves. Also, as cold weather approaches, thieves often steal vehicles that are left running while warming up.

3 Write a teaser for the previous story.

4 Convert the following newspaper story into a TV story.

A 16-year-old boy, driving without a license, led Louisville police on a 13-minute chase yesterday afternoon, driving at up to 80 mph on streets in the Highlands sections where the sidewalks were crowded with pedestrians.

The pursuit ended at 5:05 p.m., when the boy — whose name police did not release because of his age — rammed his father's 1991 Honda Accord into the rear of Officer Bob Arnold's patrol car on Trevilian Way, just east of Valley Vista.

No one was injured, and the police car suffered only a minor scrape on the rear bumper. The Honda Accord was damaged more extensively.

Officer John Butts said the chase started near Cherokee Park, when he tried to stop the boy for running a stop sign, and the boy refused to pull over. Butts radioed for help, and Arnold joined the chase.

"I was concerned because he came close to hitting several pedestrians who were out walking because of the nice weather," Butts said last night.

"Anxiety sets in when a chase continues for this amount of time," he added. "It's longer than any officer would prefer to be in a high-speed vehicle pursuit."

Butts said the boy forced several cars off the road during the chase, which came to an end when Arnold managed to get in front of the boy and slowed down. He said the boy will be charged with numerous felonies and traffic violations;

among the charges are wanton endangerment and resisting arrest. The boy was taken to the Jefferson County Youth Center.

Butts said he did not know why the boy refused to stop, but added, "He has no license, and he was not supposed to be driving his father's car."

— *The* (Louisville, Kentucky)
Courier-Journal

5 Write a VO-SOT from information in the previous story.

FEATURED ONLINE ACTIVITIES: Log on to the MindTap for Rich's Writing and Reporting News to access a variety of robust additional material, including this chapter's learning objectives, activities, comprehension quizzes, and more. Be sure to check out the "Bank Robbery" NewsScene scenario for an interactive writing exercise that will help to reinforce many of the themes presented in this chapter.

COACHING TIPS

Write **short, simple** sentences.

Write **clear headlines.**

Plan **photos, audio and video** elements.

Provide blogs and **social media links.**

Consider **summaries** or highlights for the story.

Plan **interactive elements** such as polls, quizzes, discussion questions or searchable graphics.

CHAPTER 12
Online Journalism

© jocic/Shutterstock.com

The experience of consuming news on the Web today fails to take full advantage of the power of technology. It doesn't understand what users want in order to give them what they need. Of course, the greatest user experience is pretty useless if there's nothing good to read.

—JONATHAN ROSENBERG, *Senior Vice President, Product Management, Google*

HOW SAFE IS THE FOOD YOU EAT? YOU MAY BE RELUCTANT TO eat a hamburger again after you read this innovative Web project by students in the News21 team, a collaborative university project based at Arizona State University. Switching to seafood isn't a much safer alternative. And becoming a vegetarian isn't a sure solution either.

Federal agencies entrusted with the safety of the nation's food supply routinely fail to prevent bacteria-infected food from reaching grocery stores and restaurants, putting millions of Americans at risk. A News21 investigation found that food safety in the U.S. depends on ineffective regulations and underfunded government agencies that lack the authority to protect consumers. Each year, one in six Americans — 48 million people — gets sick, 128,000 are hospitalized and 3,000 die from foodborne diseases, according to estimates from the Centers for Disease Control and Prevention. See more at: *foodsafety.news21.com/index.html*

— MAX LEVY AND MATTEA KRAMER, *Carnegie-Knight News21*

On the one hand the U.S. Department of Agriculture recommends that Americans eat 8 ounces or at least two servings of seafood a week. But seafood isn't a healthy alternative if it is imported and infected with bacteria or tainted with drugs and antibiotics banned in the U.S.

You're looking at fresh and frozen seafood that's being turned away at the border by FDA because it's decomposed and infected with salmonella," said Zach Corrigan of the Washington, D.C.-based Food & Water Watch, a consumer advocacy organization. "Filthy fish products may contain dirt, insect fragments and rodent hair," Corrigan said, adding, "I don't think people realize when they're eating their dinners every night . . . so much of that is getting through without any sort of inspection."

— NICOLE GILBERT, *Carnegie-Knight News21*

Carnegie-Knight News21

Food safety Web project by News21, a collaborative university project at the Walter Cronkite School of Journalism and Mass Communication, Arizona State University.

Do you even know what kind of fish you are eating? Only 1 percent of imported fish is inspected, and from 25 to 75 percent of fish sold in the U.S. is mislabeled, according to the study. Take the quiz and find out if you can identify mislabeled fish (*foodsafety.news21 .com/2011/imports/seafood/index.html*).

Although News21 has produced some award-winning innovative projects, it is not the only university group creating innovative Web projects that inspire creativity and ideas you could emulate in your own community.

The Red Line Project, an online journalism project by students of DePaul University College of Communication in Chicago, is an example. Named after the Chicago Red Lion El train, which goes through 34 stations traversing Chicago communities, "students report, write and edit stories, photos, multimedia maps, social media and other cutting-edge, cross-platform storytelling tools to capture what's happening in these communities," according to the website.

For example, a website you might create in almost any community in the country can mirror "The Chicago Stumbler," a blog on Tumblr that features photos, video, anecdotes and quotes from residents about cracked sidewalks in Chicago neighborhoods. It also includes a map locating each sidewalk mentioned and an interactive feature asking users to tweet their photos to the project.

The Red Line Project is an award-winning website created by students at DePaul University College of Communication (*www.redlineproject.org*).

This Chicago Stumbler blog project about cracked sidewalks, by the DePaul University students, features maps, photos and requests for tweets about other bad sidewalks.

Another Web project that can be done anywhere is one that students at the Medill School of Journalism created to show that journalism on the Internet should be about connectivity. "So, to test our idea, we decided to focus on something simple, something to which everyone can relate. We went with love. We all have stories about our first loves. Whether it was a boy at camp, a wife, a favorite old teddy bear or a life-long love of fishing, the experience of falling head-over-heels for the first time is something everyone shares."

The result was "Our First Loves," multimedia vignettes ranging from a first love with the boy next door to love of spaghetti. One of the features that make this website interactive is a chance to vote on how the story made you feel: smile, cringe, giggle, gasp or ponder life, among other choices (*www.ourfirstloves.com*).

Those are just a few examples of excellence in online journalism produced by university students who are the new generation of digital journalists.

DIGITAL FIRST MEDIA

Digital journalism, which is synonymous with online journalism, is the new norm. More newspapers and other printed or broadcast media are now publishing first on the Web, in some cases eliminating print products altogether. A movement for this trend is called "Digital First," generally defined as publishing first online in any form of digital media such as websites, blogs, social media or on mobile media devices.

Digital has become the buzzword for almost everything in media and products these days. What does it mean? A digit is a number from zero to nine. But computer information involves just two digits — ones and zeros, called a binary system. They can be arranged in billions of combinations to create words, images, sound and motion. When computers first began to transmit digital information, they sent it in codes consisting of "bits" and "bytes." A bit was a single unit of data, either a one or a zero, and a byte was a string of eight ones and zeros. For example, a byte to make the letter A requires eight digits: 01000001. Now data can be in gigabytes, billions of patterns of ones and zeroes, and computer coding has become more complex, but it is still just combinations of digits.

However, data on the Web, an abbreviation for the World Wide Web, is not coded in all those ones and zeroes. Tim Berners Lee, a computer scientist, invented the Web as a global information sharing system in 1989 and created HTML, HyperText Markup Language, a way of formatting documents to be viewed on the Internet, a system of networks connecting computers. Since then, many forms of computer coding have been created to produce the myriad of multimedia information now available on the Web.

You don't have to write codes to do great digital journalism. Many free programs such as WordPress (*wordpress.org*) and blog software (*www.blogger.com*) automatically create websites for you, but you need to understand qualities of online journalism and how to write well for the Web.

QUALITIES OF ONLINE NEWS

The basic concepts for breaking news on the Web are short, fast and frequent.

Immediacy As soon as news breaks, it should be posted on the Web. News must be updated throughout the day. It can be delivered to cell phones, email, tablets such as iPads, websites via automatic updates called RSS (Really Simple Syndication), feeds or applications you choose to download. Twitter has become one of the main venues for breaking and updating news.

Interactivity Interactivity is a key element that makes online news distinctive from traditional print or broadcast media. Journalists aren't the only providers of news anymore. Websites feature blogs and messages posted by subscribers to the site. Interactive graphics and databases allow readers to click on a map or illustration to find the cheapest gas prices or check crime rates in their neighborhoods. And most websites offer links to share information via social media.

Innovation Storytelling on the Web can take many forms. The inverted pyramid is still preferable for breaking news stories, but you can also tell stories in many other ways.

Multimedia In the past, multimedia projects were limited to major projects. Now multimedia is standard on many print and broadcast websites. A multimedia story uses a variety of media such as text with photographs, video, audio and graphics.

A multimedia online newspaper by students at the University of Arizona School of Journalism about issues relating to the U.S.-Mexico border.

ONLINE READERS

Many Web stories are versions of a print or broadcast story. But online users don't read the same way on the Web as they do in print publications.

Eye Track Studies

Several studies about how people read in print and online have concluded that online readers tend to scan rather than read an article completely. These studies, called "eye track studies," tested readers by using specially fitted glasses to track their eye movements. They showed that users looked first at headlines, blurbs and photos or images. An eye track study by the Poynter Institute in 2012, which tested how users read on iPads, showed that they tend to enter a screen through a dominant element, usually a photograph.

Some of the conclusions from an earlier Poynter study comparing print and online reading habits revealed the following:

- People will read a story online thoroughly if they are interested in it. This is a major change from past thinking, that Web readers only scanned stories.

ETHICS

THE CODE OF ETHICS by the Society of Professional Journalists, referred to throughout this book, is considered a standard for most media professionals (*www.spj.org /ethicscode.asp*). Although the basic principles apply to online journalism, some journalists believe that online journalism and social media require a different code of ethics. Kelly McBride, author of a blog called "The New Ethics of Journalism" for the Poynter Institute recommends three overriding guiding principles for journalists: "1. Seek truth and report it as fully as possible. 2. Be transparent. 3. Engage the community as an end, rather than as a means." Under transparency she explains that journalists should "show how the reporting was done and why people should believe it. Explain your sources, evidence and the choices you made."

The AP Stylebook says that you should never lift quotes, photos or video from social networking sites and attribute them to the name on the profile or feed without contacting the user who created them.

And the ethics handbook for NPR lists social media guidelines including this one: "Take care in using images that have been posted online." The handbook recommends asking these questions before using online images and video from multimedia and social media sites:

- "When was it posted?
- Do the images or video match what has been distributed by professionals (wire services, news networks, etc.)?
- Is it original work or copies of what others have done?
- Does the person have the legal right to distribute the work and has he made the materials available for others to use?"

- Both print and online readers rarely read stories to the end, but online readers read more of a story on the Web than print readers.
- Alternative story forms such as question/answer, timelines, lists and fact boxes help readers remember facts.

Jakob Nielsen, a leading expert on Web usability, has concluded for many years that Web readers are primarily scanners, not in-depth readers. They generally only take time to read about 28 percent of the words on a page. Thus, the first two words of headlines and links are critical.

However one of his studies in 2013 concluded that sometimes users will switch from scanning to reading if they are interested in the content and if the page design is easy to navigate, with good headings and subheads. "Good Web content isn't just about excellent prose," he said in a column about his findings. "Quality digital content that goes beyond print needs to include clear headlines and other elements that help users save time by focusing their scanning eyes on information that they actually want to read."

In general online readers don't spend much time on a Web page after scanning headlines, key words and links. Readers will only take three seconds to decide whether to continue reading, according to a Yahoo! digital style guide.

Linear vs. Nonlinear

The interactive nature of the Web makes it nonlinear, meaning users may access information in any order they choose. Conversely, print and broadcast stories are written in linear order from beginning to end, as in a straight line, offering readers no choice except to stop reading. Although many Web stories are still written in linear order, Web readers have nonlinear choices of accessing related elements linked to the story or the site.

A Web package created in nonlinear order might be divided into smaller chunks spanning several pages, or it might contain links to timelines, related stories, polls, photo essays, searchable maps and other interactive elements.

Embedded or External Links

Should you include links within the text (embedded) of your story or at the end (external)? In the past, most Web designers and usability experts recommended that links be placed on the side or at the end of a story because a reader who clicked on an embedded link might not return to the article. However, the current thinking is that online readers have become so sophisticated that they will return to articles they want to read even if they access a link on another page, so embedded links are used regularly in news stories.

STORY PLANNING

Whether readers scan or thoroughly read Web stories, the hyperlink nature of the Web changes the way writers need to plan their stories. You should plan the story *before* the reporting process so you know what information to gather. Most news organizations use formatted programs for Web stories, so you don't have to worry about designing the Web page for your story. If you plan to create a multimedia package or website, you should plan for photos, audio, video and graphic elements.

Web designers plan sites by drawing a "storyboard," which is similar to an organizational chart, to show the main parts and related pieces. A storyboard can be used to plan news stories as well. You could also draft a simple outline to plan elements of the story.

First decide the best way to tell the story. Not all stories need to be written in linear text format. A story or some of its parts may be presented in alternative forms. Writing for the Web requires envisioning a story in layers. Will your story be one page of text, or will you write it in chunks? Will you use photos, audio and/or video? Will you have sidebars, maps and/or interactive elements? These are some elements to consider:

Plan elements of your website by creating a storyboard.

Bill Branson/National Cancer Institute

The ProPublica project investigating internship practices includes such features as interactive requests for sharing information from people who have had internships. One of the stories, in question/answer format, is in Chapter 9.

Timelines Does the story lend itself to background created as a timeline?

Frequently Asked Questions Would a question/answer format or FAQ (Frequently Asked Questions) be a good way to present the story or accompany it?

Interactivity Will the story feature a discussion question, poll, quiz, searchable databases, maps, social media or other information the reporter may need to gather for reader involvement?

Lists or Data for Full Coverage Will the story be accompanied by a complete list of contest winners, school test scores or other information?

Multimedia Will the story include audio or video? Do you need to tape an interview for sound bites?

Related Links Plan relevant links.

Email Addresses of Reporters Not all news sites include these addresses, but it's a good idea to add your email address to your byline.

Social Media Links Will you include social media links or related blogs?

REPORTING FOR THE WEB

Good reporting is similar in any medium, but you need some additional tools and reporting steps for the Web.

Plan for Full Coverage Be prepared to report your story for text delivery and for audio or video elements. Plan to get the full text of a speech, a city budget, lists of contest winners or other additional information to post on the Web.

Equipment For basic reporting, in addition to a notebook and pens or pencils, take a tape recorder to get audio sound bites and some form of digital storage media such as a jump drive for the extended information mentioned in the previous point. Other necessities include a cell phone to call in your story, a digital camera with extra batteries and a notebook computer or mobile media if you are going to transmit a story from your location. You can also record and take photos with your smartphones. If you are using it to shoot video, take lens wipes to make sure your smartphone camera lens is clean.

Timelines When you are covering a major disaster or crime event, mark your notes with time periods for a timeline that might be posted on the Web.

Email Reporting Don't depend on it for deadline. Email is a good way to reach people and get limited information, but face-to-face or telephone interviewing is still preferable.

Check Accuracy and Timeliness If you are using information from the Web or from social media, check the date of the information and the reliability of the website for accuracy. Is the information from a site by a government agency, a university or a respected media organization, or is it from a personal site? Is the social media information reliable, checked for accuracy and legal to use? This is especially important if you are using photos.

Updates and Follow-Up Stories Plan to file your story in a brief form as soon as the news breaks. Then plan an updated version for your next print or broadcast edition. If you are covering a major breaking news story, plan to file for the Web every time you receive new information. Think ahead. Plan to write a follow-up story for the next edition of your broadcast or print publication.

ANATOMY OF A NEWS STORY ON THE WEB

It was a major news story for *The News-Press* in Fort Myers, Florida. A 2-year-old child had discovered the bodies of his parents, both 25, who had been murdered in their home in the Gateway section of the city. It was also a chance for the newspaper to demonstrate its commitment to breaking news online. "We don't hold back anything," said Kate Marymont, then executive editor of the paper. "As soon as we know and it is verified, it goes online. It doesn't have to be the complete print story."

Marymont, now senior vice president of news at Gannett Co., explained how the paper handled this story:

- Announce the news as soon as possible. In this case, *The News-Press* posted the breaking news at 4:47 p.m. and mentioned an upcoming news conference.

Lower off-peak Sanibel toll possible

BREAKING NEWS: POSTED 4:47 P.M.
Suspect arrested in Gateway homicides
Lee County sheriff's officials are holding a news conference at 5:30 p.m. to announce an arrest in the Dec. 27 slaying of a young Gateway couple, news-press.com has learned.
• Gateway homicide investigation
| Readers' forum: What do you think? | Photo gallery: Images from the investigation

LATEST NEWS - POSTED 1:55 P.M.
• State ends cutting of canker-exposed trees (1:52 p.m.)
⇒ Readers' forum: Should program have been stopped earlier?
• Jury sees bloody knives in Cape teen murder trial (1:55 p.m.)

Courtesy of Gannett Co. Inc.

- Update in increments. Tell when there is more to come. The next information was posted on the Web at 5:30 p.m., alerting viewers that *The News-Press* would soon be posting tapes of the police interviews shortly.

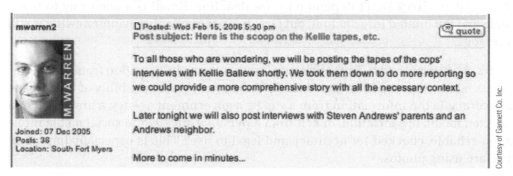

- Promote within the site. In this case, the promotion said the tapes mentioned before are live online now.

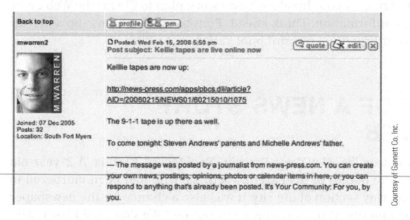

- Post multimedia — in this case, exclusive audio and video.

WRITING TECHNIQUES

There is no single way to write for the Web. Choose the form that best fits the story or purpose. Is your purpose to inform, entertain or do both? If you are writing for a corporate or public relations site, determine the best way to convey information quickly and clearly. If you are writing news, consider the inverted pyramid for breaking or serious news. If you want to tell a good story, perhaps a narrative form is suitable.

Jakob Nielsen, often considered the world's leading expert on Web usability, originally set the standards for online writing. He influenced a generation of Web designers and writers with his biweekly columns about Web usability (*www.nngroup.com /articles*). Nielsen's early recommendations about how to write for the Web were based on studies he conducted in the late 1990s about how people read Web content. Many of his writing guidelines are still valid, but he admits that "because people read differently, you have to write differently."

MULTIMEDIA COACH

MOST OF THESE tips apply to online writing for print, broadcast or public relations sites.

- Enlist "crowdsourcing," contributions from readers and viewers in blogs, messages, Twitter, Facebook or other social media.

- Use photos, graphics, audio and video that complement your story; don't just add multimedia for its own sake. Choose the form that best fits or enhances the content.

- Gather more information than you need for a single story. Always plan follow-up stories, full text of documents and other materials for the reader who wants in-depth material on your website.

- Check the date of information from the Web.

- Add contact information to your website. Provide a name, email address, phone number and physical address, especially on corporate sites or public relations materials.

- Add information such as "About Us," especially for corporate information or multimedia projects. Explain who created the project and other pertinent information for viewers.

- Plan social media blogs and links to posts on Twitter, Facebook, YouTube or other popular sites.

Some of his early writing guidelines that he still espouses include:

- Write short.
- Write for readers who scan websites instead of reading thoroughly.
- Write to the point; avoid "fluffy marketese."
- Use common language, not made-up terms.
- State the most important information in the first two paragraphs.

"But the very best content strategy is one that mirrors the users' mixed diet," Nielsen said in one of his recent columns. "There's no reason to limit yourself to only one content type. It's possible to have short overviews for the majority of users and to supplement them with in-depth coverage and white papers for those few users who need to know more."

In a recent eye track study Nielsen conducted, he reaffirmed his conclusion that the most important information in a Web page should be "above the fold," meaning information that can be viewed without scrolling. However, he said scrolling is preferable to clicking to different pages in a story. Mobile users may be forced to scroll or click to new pages if their viewing screens don't accommodate much text.

Here are some other writing tips that apply to most Web stories:

- Write a clear headline and subhead summarizing the main idea of the story. This is especially critical for stories distributed to mobile

Courtesy of Jakob Nielsen

Jakob Nielsen.

media. Twitter is a good way to practice writing good headlines and key words because you are limited to 140 characters.

- Summarize key points (a highlights box or list) under or alongside of the story.

- Write a clear focus statement or nut graph high in the story, especially if you use an anecdotal lead.

- Write boldface subheadings for paragraphs, especially in a long story.

- Write short, simple sentences. Avoid sentences with long clauses and complex sentences. Be concise.

- Use bulleted lists to help readers scan text when the story lends itself to itemized information.

- Limit each paragraph to one idea. Keep paragraphs short. This is even more important for small screens of mobile media.

- Write in the active, not the passive, voice: who did what rather than what was done to whom; "The student won an award," not "An award was won by the student."

- Avoid the last name only on second reference in subsequent screens or Web pages, unless the source is well known or is the main person in the story. Apply the blocking technique of restricting each source's comments to one block in the story so the reader doesn't have to scroll up and down a page or refer to a previous page to remember someone's name.

- Use conversational style. Write as though you were talking to a single reader. Borrow from broadcast writing. The "you" voice works well online. Try to let readers know what the story means for them.

SOCIAL MEDIA

USE SOCIAL MEDIA *before* you report or write your story. Tell readers about your topic and ask them to submit related information on Twitter, Facebook or message boards on your website.

Almost all websites these days include share buttons linking directly to social network sites. But limit the number of buttons to sites you think your users want the most. One designer called the overuse of these icons "the swamp" of share buttons.

Although college students are social media savvy, they don't want social networking on all the websites they visit, according to one study by Nielsen. He concluded that students are multitaskers who keep many browsers open at the same time, but when a site slows them down, they switch to another tab. "Student users' high inclination to multitask and low patience reinforce the need for quick, responsive and easy Web design," Nielsen reported. "Don't give students even the smallest excuse to check Facebook instead of staying with your site."

HEADLINES, SUMMARY BLURBS AND BRIEFS

Headlines, summary blurbs and briefs are called "microcontent," the smaller elements of a story. But they are the biggest factor in determining whether someone will click into the story. Clarity is crucial. The headline and a summary blurb of one or two sentences should accurately summarize the story. Readers in a rush want to know exactly what they're getting when they link into a story. And smartphones and small screen devices make this even more critical.

Most Web experts advise against writing catchy, teaser headlines because they could be misleading. A teaser headline may work if it is accompanied by a clear summary blurb. But Web pages with many headlines may not contain summary blurbs, so the headline must tell the story by itself.

Although headlines are often written *after* the story is submitted, one of the best ways of focusing your story is to write a headline and summary blurb *before* you write the full story. Writing a brief first or a tweet is another good way to identify the essential information for a fuller story.

Here are some guidelines for Web headlines that link to the main story:

Write Brief Headlines Fewer than six to 10 words create better links than headlines that span two or three lines as this one from the ProPublica project about interns:

How Unpaid Interns Aren't Protected Against Sexual Harassment

Use strong verbs: Some headlines may be written without verbs.

Lose 10 pounds in five weeks

(No verb) Top 10 diet tips

Put the Most Important Words First

Tainted Seafood Reaching U.S., Food Safety Experts Say

Avoid Articles Don't use "the," "a," or "an" at the start of a headline:

Web makes cheating easy

(not) The Web makes cheating easy

Use Question Headlines If the Subject is Interesting Enough to Entice Readers

How safe is your food?

Make Headlines Clear by Themselves (for search engines)

Ground Turkey Linked to Drug-Resistant Bacteria

Write Subheads and Blurbs

Many news sites just repeat the story lead for the subhead or blurb under the headline. But with small screens, redundancy is a waste of space. If the lead doesn't give the main point of the story, write a clear summary or use the nut graph as the blurb. Here is the subhead for this headline from the News21 food series:

Headline	Laws Haven't Kept Deadly Pathogens Out of Meat, Poultry	meat and poultry largely in the hands of private companies.
Subhead	A complex system of self-regulation leaves the safety of	

Avoid Writing Summaries That Repeat the Headline The first sentence in this blurb is too repetitive:

Headline	Is work a pain in the neck . . . or hands?	manager of the Physical Therapy department at Fairbanks Memorial Hospital, says proper ergonomics is essential to preventing problems.
Blurb	Has work become a real pain? If so, the problem might not be your job but your workstation. Judy Gibson,	

Address the Reader When Appropriate Use the "you" voice:

Headline	Get free cash for college	You can collect thousands of dollars in scholarship money just by filling out a form. *Blurb*

Summary Highlights

Another tool that serves as a quick summary for Web readers who are scanners is the highlights box on top or alongside of the story. For example, CNN tops its Web stories with a bulleted list of the main points in a story or places them on the side, as in this example about new caps on Tylenol:

STORY HIGHLIGHTS

- New caps will say: "Contains acetaminophen. Always read the label."
- Company hopes to reduce number of accidental acetaminophen overdoses.
- FDA sets daily limit for adults at 4,000 milligrams of acetaminophen.

STORY STRUCTURE

Get to the point of the story quickly — within the first 50 words. If you picture a news website with a title image and possibly a banner advertisement at the top of the page plus the story headline, this doesn't leave you much room. In addition, text on most news sites is enclosed in tables about 4 inches wide, to facilitate reading. That translates to about 100 to 150 words per screen.

Inverted Pyramid

The inverted pyramid is a favored form for Web stories because the main idea is in the lead or the first few paragraphs. The inverted pyramid form places the main point at the top of the story, with the rest of the information in descending order of importance. This form is good for basic news stories, but it is too restrictive for features and other types of storytelling. As long as the nut graph expressing the main point is high in the story, writers may have as much flexibility for Web stories as for print.

The main food safety story discussed in this chapter begins with the traditional inverted pyramid structure, which supports the headline and subhead:

Headline	Federal Agencies Falling Short in Protecting U.S. Food Supply	food supply routinely fail to prevent bacteria-infected food
Subhead	FDA-regulated goods are up 200 percent in a decade, but the agency inspects only about 2 percent of all imported food.	from reaching grocery stores and restaurants, putting millions of Americans at risk.
Inverted pyramid lead	Federal agencies entrusted with the safety of the nation's	— MAX LEVY AND MATTEA KRAMER, *Carnegie-Knight News21*

List Format

Lists within stories break up the text and help readers scan Web stories quickly. In this excerpt from one of the food safety stories, the writers used the list format for most of the story:

Headline   Rising Chinese Imports Draw Safety Activists' Concerns

Subhead   The market for imported food from China has exploded in recent years, creating worries stateside.

China didn't become a powerhouse food trader until 2001 when it joined the World Trade Organization. Since then, it has nearly tripled its food exports to the U.S., providing 78 percent of the tilapia we eat, 70 percent of the apple juice concentrate we consume and about 90 percent of the Vitamin C we take.

Food safety activists say that the increasing use of cheaper Chinese ingredients poses a risk to Americans' health because of China's history of lax health regulations and food safety cover-ups.

Among the concerns:

- China ranks third among U.S. trade partners — after India and Mexico — in food shipments rejected at our borders, according to the Food and Drug Administration.
- Internal scandals have rocked the country. Six babies died and hundreds of thousands were sickened in China in 2008 when manufacturers added melamine, a chemical used in plastics and fertilizer, to infant formula.
- Some of China's contaminants have already made it into American products. Pets here died in 2007 after eating food that contained an ingredient from China that had been adulterated with melamine. The chemical is still showing up: FDA data shows that 363 Chinese food shipments have been turned away since 2008 for suspicion of containing the melamine. Cocoa is the most common ingredient on the list. . . .

— KERRY DAVIS, *Carnegie-Knight News21*

Check out the story at *foodsafety.news21.com/2011/imports/seafood/china*.

Question/Answer Format

The question/answer format is a good structure for Web stories and for mobile media. It's a quick way of providing a lot of information in an easily scannable form. The ProPublica story, "When Is It OK to Not Pay an Intern," is a good example. You can find it in Chapter 9, Story Forms, and at *www.propublica.org/article/when-interns -should-be-paid-explained*.

Storytelling Format

Web stories can use feature leads and storytelling format, such as *The Wall Street Journal* formula focusing on a person, but the nut graph needs to be high in the story. That's especially important for online stories that will be read on small screens such as smartphones or iPads, so readers know the main point of the story without scrolling or linking to another screen.

In this example from the ProPublica series about unpaid internships, the writers began with a focus-on-a-person lead, but the nut graph is in the third paragraph:

Headline **HOW UNPAID INTERNS AREN'T PROTECTED AGAINST SEXUAL HARASSMENT**

In 1994, Bridget O'Connor began an internship at Rockland Psychiatric Center, where one of the doctors allegedly began to refer to her as Miss Sexual Harassment, told her that she should participate in an orgy, and suggested that she remove her clothing before meeting with him. Other women in the office made similar claims.

Yet when O'Connor filed a lawsuit, her sexual harassment claims were dismissed because she was an unpaid intern. A federal appeals court affirmed the decision to throw out the claim.

Unpaid interns miss out on wages and employment benefits, but they can also find themselves in "legal limbo" when it comes to civil rights, according to law professor and intern labor rights advocate David Yamada. The O'Connor decision (the leading ruling on the matter, according to Yamada) held that because they don't get a paycheck, unpaid interns are not "employees" under the Civil Rights Act — and thus, they're not protected.

Federal policies echo court rulings. The laws enforced by the U.S. Equal Employment Opportunity Commission, including the Civil Rights Act, don't cover interns unless they receive "significant remuneration," according to commission spokesperson Joseph Olivares.

— BLAIR HICKMAN AND
CHRISTIE THOMPSON,
ProPublica

PERSONAL STORYTELLING

Human beings have been telling stories since prehistoric man drew pictures on caves and recited stories around a fire. The Web is simply a new cave blending old and new techniques. People still want to hear, read and share stories. And that's how the Web can exceed any other medium in history. Personal storytelling thrives on the Web, especially in blogs, and it is increasing on news sites.

Some of the best personal storytelling sites are not traditional broadcast or newspaper sites. Musarium (*www.musarium.com*), a site devoted to photography and storytelling, is an example. "Just when you think that television has mind-numbed the brains of most people, these presentations celebrate and enforce the power of still photographs to affect people and tell great stories," the site says. The site features innovative multimedia packages with personal stories in several formats. Some of the storytelling is told in photo essays.

One of the most chilling is "Without Sanctuary," a multimedia photo essay of lynchings documented in old postcards. This story has since moved to its own site (*www.withoutsanctuary.org*).

Another unusual website for storytelling is Pete Berg's website, Six Word Stories, *www.sixwordstories.net*. It is a creative and often poignant variation of Twitter that you can check for inspiration.

REVISE

Don't eliminate this crucial process. Be concise. Cut every word or paragraph that does not advance the story. Short sentences, short paragraphs and active verbs make Web writing more readable. The same principles that William Strunk Jr. offered for print writing in E.B. White's *The Elements of Style* apply to the Web:

> Vigorous writing is concise. A sentence should contain no unnecessary words, a paragraph no unnecessary sentences . . . This requires not that the writer make all sentences short, or that he avoid all detail and treat his subjects only in outline, but that every word tell.

EXERCISES

1 Headlines and blurbs: Using your local or campus newspaper, write Web headlines and summary blurbs for news and feature stories.

2 Personal essay: Write a personal essay using a compelling headline and subheads on a topic of interest to you.

3 Convert a story to the Web: Using any news or feature story you have written for this course, convert it to Web style as suggested in this chapter. Add a discussion question, poll or quiz.

4 Web story: Write a story for the Web based on this information. Include a headline and summary blurb. Use a bulleted list, add a discussion question to the end of your story and consider creating a poll.

New data on marriage, divorce and remarriage in the United States show that 43 percent of first marriages end in separation or divorce within 15 years, according to a report released today by the Centers for Disease Control and Prevention (CDC). The report, "First Marriage Dissolution, Divorce, and Remarriage: United States," also shows that one in three first marriages end within 10 years, and one in five end within five years.

The findings are based on data from the National Survey of Family Growth, a study of 10,847 women 15–44 years of age.

"Separation and divorce can have adverse effects on the health and well-being of children and adults," said CDC Director Jeffrey Koplan. "Past research has shown that divorce is associated with higher rates of mortality, more health problems, and more risky behaviors such as increased alcohol use."

The study also showed that duration of marriage is linked to a woman's age at first marriage; the older a woman is at first marriage, the longer that marriage is likely to last. For example, 59 percent of marriages to brides under 18 end in separation or divorce within 15 years, compared with 36 percent of those married at age 20 or over.

About 97 percent of separated non-Hispanic white women are divorced within five years of separation, compared with 77 percent of separated Hispanic women and only 67 percent of non-Hispanic black women. Younger women who divorce are more likely to remarry: 81 percent of those divorced before age 25 remarry within 10 years, compared with 68 percent of those divorced at age 25 or over. Non-Hispanic black women are less likely than other women to remain in a first marriage, to make the transition from separation to divorce, to remarry, and to remain in a remarriage.

"These data offer an important glimpse into the social fabric of this country," said Dr. Edward Sondik, director of CDC's National Center for Health Statistics, which conducted the study. "The implications of divorce cut across a number of societal issues — socioeconomics, health and the welfare of our children."

FEATURED ONLINE ACTIVITIES: Log on to the MindTap for Rich's Writing and Reporting News to access a variety of robust addtional material, including this chapter's learning objectives, activities, comprehension quizzes, and more!

CHAPTER 13
Public Relations Writing

The overall role of public relations is to motivate a person or a group to take a specific action. No new invention or methodology can ever change the basic human characteristic of communicating ideas with the basic purpose of influencing agreement or support or otherwise.

—**HAROLD BURSON,** *Founder of Burson-Marsteller Public Relations and Communications Firm*

COACHING TIPS

Study your audience. Find out **what kind of information they need** and how they prefer to receive it.

Plan visuals — charts, illustrations, photographs, diagrams and video — to make your package more appealing.

Plan video opportunities for **broadcast and online media.**

Offer press releases via email, **Web, podcasts, mobile or social media.**

Always **include contact information:** name, company address, telephone numbers (including cell phone and fax), email and website addresses.

I N 1910 AN 18-YEAR-OLD HIGH SCHOOL DROPOUT BOARDED A TRAIN FROM Nebraska to Kansas City, Missouri, with two shoeboxes of postcards under his arm. He moved into the YMCA, where he operated his wholesale card business until the YMCA complained about the large mail volume. He called on drugstores, bookstores and gift stores to promote his products. A few years later he opened a store and expanded his inventory to include greeting cards.

Now more than 100 years later, the little business that Joyce C. Hall started with a shoebox is a $4 billion company known worldwide as Hallmark Cards Inc., which includes products in 30 languages in 100 countries and 40,000 retail outlets in the U.S. Although the traditional paper cards still abound, Hallmark greetings now come with iPhone and iPad applications, recordable storybooks and cards geared to Hispanics and African-Americans.

Corporate communications have changed as well. These days information about Hallmark is on Twitter, YouTube, Facebook, blogs and several company websites. Press releases are offered online in printable formats, audio, video, and via email and mobile news alerts.

Joyce C. Hall, founder of Hallmark, at age 18 in 1910.

Joyce C. Hall, founder of Hallmark, chaired the company for 56 years.

A Hallmark card from the 1920s.

"The company that defined the 20th-century greeting card is now redefining it, adding choices like e-cards and greeting card software, and exploring the possibilities for other means yet to come," according to the company's website.

CHANGES IN PUBLIC RELATIONS

Hallmark is an example of how corporate communications are changing. The public relations professional today needs to be skilled in multimedia, multitasking and multicultural awareness.

"Writing beyond traditional media relations is required for a range of digital content, such as websites, newsletters and content-marketing related to white papers, case studies, research and journalistic-quality articles," according to Howard Sholkin, director of communications and marketing at IDG (International Data Group). "The social Web — growing at tremendous speed — requires an understanding of different platforms (LinkedIn, Twitter and Facebook) and how they can be effectively applied to public relations and marketing programs," he wrote in a blog for the Public Relations Society of America.

A Hallmark card for the 21st century.

Defining Public Relations

Social networks are changing the way public relations practitioners reach their publics and deliver content. But the purpose of public relations transcends technology, according to Harold Burson, founder of the largest P.R. agency in the world. "My greatest frustration as a lifelong public relations professional is that so many of my fellow professionals cannot define public relations in its totality," he said in a speech at Boston University. "The overall role of public relations is to motivate a person or a group to take a specific action. No new invention or methodology can ever change the basic human characteristic of communicating ideas with the basic purpose of influencing agreement or support or otherwise."

Past, Present and Future

The first press release was created in 1906 after a Pennsylvania Railroad train wreck in Atlantic

MULTIMEDIA COACH

PUBLIC RELATIONS practitioners need to target their audiences in many ways — print, email, blogs, photos, audio, video, online and social media. Add information in Spanish or other languages for bilingual users and in brief formats for mobile media. The press is no longer the only target audience. Bloggers, customers and millions of social media users are consumers in the corporate communications universe.

Here are some suggestions for improving convergent communications in the coming years:

- Provide a corporate blog. Follow some P.R. blogs such as these suggested by the Public Relations Student Society of America: Culpwrit (*www.culpwrit.com*), by Ron Culp focusing on guiding careers in public relations; Edelman 6 a.m. (*www.edelman.com /conversations/6-a-m*) by Richard Edelman, CEO of Edelman PR; @briansolis. (*www .briansolis.com*) by Brian Solis, author of *Putting the Public Back in Public Relations* and other books.

- Provide multimedia. Use podcasts and video interviews to complement print and online stories.

- Include more data graphics and applications for mobile media.

- Understand how to use mobile tools and provide content in various platforms.

- Provide good content — no matter what platform you use.

City, New Jersey, where 50 people were killed. Ivy Lee, a publicist who represented the railroad, issued a public statement from his client, and he is credited with creating this type of public relations message. For the next 100 years, the press release didn't change much.

These days the press release will probably be online or in text or video format, posted on Twitter or Facebook or distributed to mobile media. The term "news release" is preferred by many communicators because the information is now distributed to a larger audience than the media, but the terms are interchangeable.

Press releases still play an important role in news reporting. "As the press scales back on original reporting and dissemination, reproducing other people's work becomes a bigger part of the news system," according to a report by the Pew Research Center. "We found official press releases often appear word for word in first accounts of events, though often not noted as such."

Many of the tools publicists have used in the past, such as press releases and media kits, will continue to have value, but their form and substance will change. "It's pretty clear where the press release will go next: It's going to get shorter, link to more sources; be focused on simplification and explanation; and it'll come in many more flavors," according to David McCulloch, director of public relations at Cisco Systems.

WRITING SKILLS FOR PRESS RELEASES

Many press releases are not read all the way through, but most editors or recipients of your release will at least skim the releases to find out if there is some newsworthy information. Community newspapers and local television stations rely heavily on press releases about events in their area.

If you want your news event to be covered, you need to consider that you are competing with many other events and stories that these media will cover. How do you get the attention of the assignment editors? Here are some tips for writing your releases:

- **Target your audience.** Make sure that your information is newsworthy for the publication. Check the name and spelling of the person who should receive the release. Don't use nicknames (unless you are very familiar with the source), and make sure that you have the correct gender. Don't send duplicate releases to several editors. You might also send a copy to a reporter assigned to the beat covered in your press release. Ask if the publication prefers a faxed release, an email release or other type of delivery via the Web.

- **Find a newsworthy angle.** If you are targeting a local newspaper or TV station, localize the angle. The qualities of timeliness, local interest, new information and unusual nature are the main factors in determining newsworthiness.

- **Identify the news element in the headline and lead.** Don't make your intended reader wade through several paragraphs to determine if the event or news you are touting should be covered.

- **Use inverted pyramid order.** Write a basic news lead that answers the most important questions — who, what, when, where and why.

- **Consider a visual element.** If you are targeting a television station, the visual impact is crucial. List photo opportunities for print and video possibilities for television and the Web.

- **Include key words that can be picked up by a search engine** (SEO — search engine optimization) if you are posting your press release on a company website or other online site such as Facebook.

- **Relate your information to your audience.** How will readers or viewers be affected in this target area? Why is your information or event important to them?

- **Keep your information factual.** Avoid adjectives, superlatives and promotional language.

- **Provide diverse sources.** Consider how to include multicultural segments of the community in your projects, visuals and materials.

- **Allow lead time.** Send your releases in advance of the publication's deadlines. A magazine might have a lead time of several months. Some TV stations might prefer only a few days of lead time. Check with the publication or organization for preferred advance notice. Include the release date, preferably "For Immediate Release," unless there is some important reason for an "Embargoed Until . . ." date.

- **Use active voice.** Who did what, not what was done to whom.

ETHICS

ETHICAL DILEMMA: How truthful should you be when you are faced with a conflict between protecting your client and dealing with the media?

The case: You are the public relations director for a company that manufactures portable baby cribs. The chief executive officer of your company informs you that two babies died when their cribs collapsed. However, he is reluctant to issue a recall because more than 100,000 cribs of this particular model were sold, and it would cost the company a fortune.

He says the product development team warned him a few years ago that the sides of the crib were not secure, but that to replace the design would have been too costly. He wants you to reassure the media that the cribs are safe and that there is no proof the deaths of these children were a direct result of any faulty crib parts. If the news media ask, he wants you to deny that the company ever had any indication the cribs might be defective.

Will you lie or withhold information to protect your employer? What steps will you propose to the CEO?

Ethical values: Truth, credibility, fairness, loyalty to your client.

Ethical guidelines: The Public Relations Society of America offers these guidelines in its code of ethics:

■ Be honest and accurate in all communications.

■ Reveal sponsors for represented causes and interests.

■ Act in the best interest of clients or employers.

■ Disclose financial interests in a client's organization.

■ Safeguard the confidences and privacy rights of clients and employees.

■ Avoid conflicts between personal and professional interests.

You can find the entire code of ethics at *www.prsa.org/AboutPRSA/Ethics/CodeEnglish.*

■ **Use present tense when possible.** In most cases you will want to promote an event or some information in a timely manner, not after the fact.

■ **Check grammar and spelling.**

■ **Make sure you include contact information for you and your company:** Your name, phone numbers, email and the company address and phone contacts.

EMAIL PRESS RELEASES

Online press releases must be shorter than print ones, so the information can be seen on the first screen.

■ Limit the release to one or two screens, about 600 words at most. However, if you are targeting your release for mobile media, keep it even shorter. Use single-spaced copy; a space between paragraphs is optional.

- Target your audience. Ask sources whether they prefer to receive releases by email. Don't send unsolicited email. Personalize the release if possible.
- Write a brief summary of the topic in the email subject line.
- Headings: Insert company name and contact information at the top, FOR IMMEDIATE RELEASE and date of release. Insert a space before the headline.
- Write a clear summary headline. Insert another space.
- Write a summary lead with basic information: who, what, where, when. Make sure that it is visible in the first screen.
- Use lists to itemize information when relevant.
- Avoid adjectives and superlatives. Keep the writing simple and newsworthy.
- Proofread. Email is notoriously filled with typos, spelling and style errors. Sloppy work is a poor reflection on you and your client.
- Don't send attachments. Your users may not be able to open your documents.
- Insert links at the bottom to relevant information. For example, if your release is about a survey the company has done, include a link to the complete survey.

SOCIAL MEDIA

SHORT, SUBSTANTIVE, SCANNABLE. Those are three essential concepts for social media messages. Make sure you have some timely, newsworthy information to share. Although some of the basic information such as contact information is the same for all press releases, messages in social media should have other qualities to encourage readers.

What are some effective ways to write corporate content for social media? Jakob Nielsen, a world-renowned authority on online usability, offers these tips based on studies he conducted of corporate use on Facebook, Twitter, MySpace and LinkedIn.

- **Post current and timely information:** If you post too rarely, you will lose users; if you post too frequently, you will crowd out other messages — a major annoyance. Post timely updates.
- **Provide useful content:** Messages with substance and timeliness scored highest.
- **Write for the medium:** The shorter the message, the more important the writing. Don't just repurpose other information.
- **Focus on one topic or subject per message.**
- **Place key words at the beginning of the message.**
- **Write in a conversational, informal tone.**
- **Link to other content within the social network rather than to external sites.** Make links short and readable.
- **Proofread your messages.**
- **Engage in two-way conversation.** Respond to questions from followers and fans within 24 hours.

- Put the contact information (office and cell phone numbers, fax, email and any related website) at the bottom of the release.

STRUCTURE OF PRESS RELEASES

Press releases differ very little from basic news stories. Although some press releases may have feature leads, most use a summary lead that gets to the main point quickly. If you use a soft lead, put the nut graph high in the release, preferably by the second paragraph.

These days most press releases and media kits are distributed via email or online. But you may need to mail or fax a paper copy to some organizations, so you still need to know how to write a print version. Printed versions are also necessary at functions such as press conferences, speeches, product demonstrations, ceremonies, trade shows and other places where you might need to hand out information.

Here are some basics for print releases:

Style Use one side of the paper. Double-space the body copy (or use 1.5-line spacing). Keep the release short, preferably one page and no more than two. Use Associated Press style for releases to newspapers and most magazines.

Number Pages If the release continues to more than one page, write "more" at the bottom of the first page, and number each page.

Timeliness Send out press releases in advance of the intended publication date. Although most press releases say "FOR IMMEDIATE RELEASE," you should send them out several days or a few weeks before an event is going to occur.

Major Elements in This Order

- **Company name** or logo at the top and company's address (street, city, state and ZIP code) or website if the company is only on the Web.
- **FOR IMMEDIATE RELEASE:** preferably in caps and boldface.
- **Date of release:** This could be placed under the previous item or attached to the dateline.
- **Contact information:** Place contact information justified on the left side of the page. Write "CONTACT," followed by the name, title, phone numbers (telephone, cell and fax) and email address of the person to contact. This information can be placed on the left or right side; it can be single spaced.
- **Headline:** Skip two lines after your contact information. Boldface is optional but suggested. Although some firms prefer writing the headline all in capital letters, websites such as PRWeb recommend that headlines be written with uppercase and lowercase letters. Limit the headline to one line, especially for Web releases.

- **Dateline:** This is the city of origin for your press release, followed by the state abbreviation if not a major city. You may put the date here, preceded by a hyphen.
- **Lead:** A direct lead is preferable, including who, what, when and where, but a feature lead immediately followed by the key information is acceptable.
- **Body:** Briefly summarize the key points. Include a quote or comment from a company official if possible. Keep paragraphs short. Use lists if you have key points.
- **Ending:** End with a brief sentence or paragraph about the company — if relevant. Repeat a contact or other relevant source for further information. Include a website if available. Skip a space and type a symbol for the ending: three # # # or — 30 —. Your format should look like this:

ORGANIZATION NAME ON LETTERHEAD

Heading information can be single-spaced.

FOR IMMEDIATE RELEASE   **CONTACT:** *This information can be in single space.*

Date of release   Name, title of contact person

                                                                         Telephone number

                                                                         Cell phone number

                                                                         Fax number

                                                                         Email address

Leave some space before the headline.

HEADLINE

Double-space body copy.

DATELINE — [Location for the origin of the release (in capital letters) plus a dash, followed by the first line of the lead]

Lead: Preferably start with a hard-news lead, especially on releases for news events or announcements.

Body: Write tightly. Limit copy to one page if possible, no more than two. If you have two pages, write "more" at the end of the first page, and number the pages.

Ending: As part of the ending, you could tell where more information is available, such as graphics and websites. A standard ending for a corporate press release includes a few lines about the company, including the company website.

— 30 — or # # #

Here is an example of a press release that was sent to newspapers, including *USA Today*, which published the story on the front page.

PRESS RELEASE — PRINT VERSION

Crayola, LLC.

1100 Church Lane

P.O. Box 431

Easton, Pennsylvania 18044-0431
[Company telephone number]

FOR IMMEDIATE RELEASE

Contact: Mark J. O'Brien
Media Communications
[office telephone number; cell phone number]
[email address]
[date]

CRAYOLA INTRODUCES NEW CRAYONS THAT ARE LITERALLY 'OFF THE WALL'

EASTON, Pa. — Parents can put away the scrub brushes and stain remover, thanks to Crayola LLC. The maker of Crayola products has introduced a totally off-the-wall product — washable crayons.

Unlike the billions of crayons produced before them, Crayola washable crayons are made from a patented formula that washes from most surfaces, including walls and fabric.

"Washable crayons address our No. 1 consumer complaint — getting crayon marks off different surfaces," says Mark O'Brien, Crayola spokesperson.

"Each year we receive thousands of calls and letters regarding crayon stains, mainly from parents of preschool children. With the introduction of washable crayons, parents can breathe a little easier when it comes to crayon mishaps."

The difference between traditional and washable crayons is in their formulas. Washable crayons contain special water-soluble polymers found in many health and beauty aids. This allows them to be removed from most surfaces by simply using soap and water. Tests have shown washable crayon marks can even be removed from walls and fabric one to two months after being stained. However, crayon marks are easiest to remove if washed soon after they happen.

Crayola washable crayons are nontoxic and available in two sizes. The So Big size, for younger children, comes six to a box and has a suggested retail price of $2.99. Boxes of eight, large-size washable crayons will sell for approximately $2.59.

# # #

Web Press Release

Web releases are generally shorter. A Web or email press release could include contact information at the top of the screen but should repeat it or include it initially at the bottom of the release so viewers don't have to scroll back to find it.

Here is a press release on the Hallmark website that also offered photos; note that it is written in single space with embedded links:

HALLMARK LAUNCHES NEW IPHONE AND IPAD APPS IN TIME FOR THE HOLIDAYS

One app helps find stores and store specials; the other celebrates the holidays with games and a special story.

KANSAS CITY, Missouri — Two new iPhone and iPad applications from Hallmark are set to help make holiday shopping easier and time with family merrier.

HALLMARK APP

The free **Hallmark app** launches with a Hallmark Gold Crown® store locator that will include driving directions as well as information about products and special offers available in stores. Users also can use the app to make a call to a store located by the application.

JINGLE ALL THE WAY APP

To celebrate the holidays, Hallmark also introduces the free **Jingle All the Way app** to bring a new dimension to family story time. This app complements Hallmark's new *Jingle All the Way* Interactive Storybook and Story Buddy, a book about a husky pup that finds a home for the holidays and a plush dog with voice-recognition software that responds with barks, whimpers and other sounds when certain lines from the story are read.

The application includes a narrated version of the story and the option to record your own voice reading the story. The plush dog interacts with these readings as well. The app also includes kid-friendly musical games and puzzles.

To install the new Hallmark applications, users will need the most recent version of iTunes and an iPhone, iPad or iPod Touch with OS3.1.3 or higher.This new app from Hallmark joins the existing hoops&yoyo™ **Smiles:)** and **fun@work** apps that provide a daily dose of funny from characters hoops&yoyo.

ABOUT HALLMARK CARDS, INC.

Hallmark makes the world a more caring place by helping people express what's in their hearts and spend time together — a privilege few other companies in the world enjoy. Hallmark greeting cards and other products are found in more than 40,000 retail outlets in the U.S., including the network of flagship Hallmark Gold Crown® stores. The brand also reaches people online at Hallmark.com and on television through Hallmark Hall of Fame original movies and cable's top-rated Hallmark Channel. Worldwide, Hallmark offers products in more than 30 languages

Courtesy of Hallmark Cards Inc.

Hallmark "Jingle All the Way" interactive storybook.

available in 100 countries. This privately held company is based in Kansas City, Missouri, and is led by the third generation of the founding Hall family. *corporate.hallmark.com* for more details.

List Format

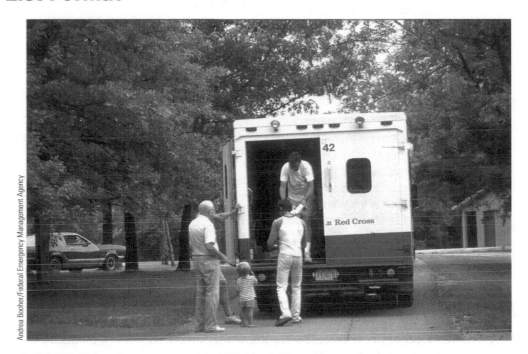

Andrea Booher/Federal Emergency Management Agency

The Red Cross used a list format for this press release to quickly summarize the event it is promoting.

Another form that would work for email, Web distribution or print is a simple list of the basics: who, what, when, where, why and how. Here is an example from the American Red Cross of Alaska:

PRESS RELEASE — DATE

Red Cross Smoke Alarm Drive

Contact information

Photo opportunity:
Anchorage Fire Department Engine Number 5 will meet Red Cross staff and volunteers for a photo opportunity at the Benson Park at 10:30 a.m. on Jan. 15. The American Red Cross emer-

gency response vehicle will also be at the event with coffee and hot chocolate for the community and volunteers.

WHO: American Red Cross of Alaska and the Anchorage Fire Department

WHAT: Anchorage citizens will show their concern for the safety of their neighbors by helping the American Red Cross of Alaska distribute free smoke detectors and batteries. The group will visit at least 1,000 homes and will be attended by firefighters from the Anchorage Fire Department.

WHEN: Saturday, Jan. 15 (year), 10 a.m.–1 p.m.

WHERE: Smoke detectors and batteries will be given away in the neighborhood bordered by Benson to the north, 36th Avenue to the West and C Street to the east.

WHY: Working smoke detectors are a crucial tool in the early detection of domestic fires, which can dramatically assist with the prevention of the loss of life and reduction of injuries. According to statistics, up to 50 percent of the smoke alarms in the U.S.

don't work because there is not an operable battery in the smoke detector. We have chosen this time of year to distribute smoke detectors because most house fires occur during the months of December, January and February.

HOW: This event is made possible by a generous grant from the Allstate Foundation.

Note: For more information, please call Heather Adams at 907-000-0000. The American Red Cross is a humanitarian organization, led by volunteers, that provides relief to victims of disaster and helps people prevent, prepare for and respond to emergencies.

Contact information repeated here.

VIDEO PRESS RELEASES

The video versions of press releases are known as VNRs, which are basically news stories produced for television. They include footage with a series of video images plus sound bites of quotes from sources in the story. In many cases the VNRs are so well done that TV stations can air them as polished news stories without even editing them. And therein lies the ethical problem.

Many small stations that have limited resources have used these VNRs produced by the U.S. government without attributing the source, thus making the video sound as though the station produced the story. Because these releases are promotional in nature and not balanced news stories, if the station does not indicate the source of the release, the audience can be misled. That isn't the fault of the public relations practitioner; it's the responsibility of the station to attribute the source.

The use of VNRs without attribution became so widespread that the Radio Television Digital News Association issued guidelines for use of them. "Television and radio stations should strive to protect the editorial integrity of the video and audio they air. This integrity, at times, might come into question when stations air video and audio provided to newsrooms by companies, organizations or governmental agencies with political or financial interests in publicizing the material," according to the RTDNA guidelines. The organization's code of ethics says that electronic journalists should "clearly disclose the origin of information and label all material provided by outsiders."

Mitzia Williams, a counselor at the University of Maryland University College, helps a prospective student fill out forms for tuition assistance.

The advantages of these video releases are that they are cost-effective for the TV station, which doesn't have to expend resources to shoot the video, and they provide the station with images and sound bites that could be inserted into locally produced news stories.

The format for video press releases includes the following elements:

- A disclaimer giving the news organization permission to use the material without charge.
- A list of the contents, often including the timing of each element.
- B-roll, which is video footage and natural sound that news stations can insert into stories.
- Interviews and sound bites from sources.
- Contact information.

BACK TO SCHOOL

More Education Means Greater Earnings

Date:
Slug: College Costs
Synopsis: How and why students are handling the ever-increasing cost of college.

Video Source: The U.S. Census Bureau
Super Information: (times to be inserted after client approval)
:XX (the time for the sound bite)
Mahlet "Mimi" Goitom
College student
University of Maryland
:XX

Dr. Sandy Baum
Senior policy analyst
College Board
:XX
Louis Kincannon
Director
Location: Washington, District of Columbia.

SUGGESTED LOCAL ANCHOR LEAD-IN: DESPITE THE RISING COST OF COLLEGE, AMERICANS ARE MORE EDUCATED THAN EVER, AND THE CENSUS BUREAU HAS JUST RELEASED INFORMATION THAT SUGGESTS INVESTING IN A COLLEGE DEGREE PAYS FOR ITSELF. HERE IS THE STORY.

(Open with shots of Mimi working in financial aid office)

VO: MAHLET GOITOM, (mah-hoh-leat goy-tum), OR MIMI, A THIRD-YEAR PUBLIC HEALTH MAJOR, IS ONE OF MANY STUDENTS RELYING ON BOTH FINANCIAL AID AND WORK TO PAY THE EVER-INCREASING COST OF COLLEGE.

(Cut to Mimi on camera)

SOT: "The main way that I'm dealing with the increased finances is by taking out loans, and I've also become an RA to help my parents with the burden of paying for college."

(College campus shots transition to a graphic)

VO: THE MOST RECENT CENSUS DATA SHOWS COLLEGE GRADUATION RATES AT AN ALL-TIME HIGH. AT LAST COUNT, 27 PERCENT OF ADULTS 25 AND OVER HAD A BACHELOR'S DEGREE. AND ACCORDING TO EDUCATION EXPERTS, THAT NUMBER MAY CONTINUE RISING BECAUSE TODAY'S STUDENTS

HAVE ACCESS TO A LOT MORE FINANCIAL AID.

(Cut to Sandy Baum, on camera)

SOT: "Over 100 billion dollars of student aid was distributed to college students last year. The reality is that grant aid is growing rapidly, loans are growing even more rapidly, and there is help out there for students to pay these rising college costs."

(College campus shots transition to Census Bureau graphic)

VO: MIMI, LIKE MANY OTHER COLLEGE STUDENTS, PUTS IN THE LONG HOURS BECAUSE SHE BELIEVES IT WILL PAY OFF IN THE FUTURE. AND THE EXPERTS SAY SHE'S RIGHT.

SOT: (Kincannon) "There's no doubt there is a strong relationship between education and earnings. The more education you have, the likelier it is you'll have a higher income. For example, high school graduates earn about $30,000 yearly, whereas college graduates earn nearly 75 percent more."

(Shots of Mimi)

VO: AND THAT WILL HELP STUDENTS LIKE MIMI CARRY THE BURDEN OF DEBT FROM STUDENT LOANS.

(Cut to Mimi, on camera, cut to shots of Mimi walking) SOT: "An undergraduate degree is essential for any career path, and I think it's definitely worth it to take out a loan."

THIS IS HANNAH HAINES.

(Local anchor tag)

SUGGESTED LOCAL ANCHOR TAG: FOR MORE CENSUS DATA ON EDUCATION, GO TO *WWW.CENSUS.GOV.*

PUBLIC SERVICE ANNOUNCEMENTS

Public service announcements, commonly called PSAs, are messages that TV or radio stations will air without charge, provided that the messages have noncommercial and nonpolitical content. In print media they are considered public service advertisements. Because they are used without charge, they are usually very brief. In broadcast media, PSAs generally run from 15 seconds to one minute. You should check with the stations for their requirements of formats and submission dates. In general they contain information that could be considered useful or beneficial to the audience.

- At the top of your script, write a slug, the length of time for the PSA (usually in seconds) and the agency that produced it.
- Start with a hook, a strong statement that will grab the listener's or viewer's attention.
- Read your copy aloud because the message will be heard by the audience.
- Keep it brief, and include only the most crucial information.
- Include the dates and times of any event you are promoting.
- Use broadcast style of all capital letters and double-spacing for a video script.
- End with some statement that either requests an action by the listener or offers more information.
- For television broadcast of video PSAs, send your video with the PSA text.

Your format should look like this:

From: Name of organization and address

Contact: Name of contact person with phone numbers (telephone, fax and cell) and email address

Length: Time it takes to read the PSA

Message: Type the PSA message in paragraph form.

Disclaimer: At the bottom of the page, briefly describe the organization, and specify that it is nonprofit.

Here is a 15-second PSA from the Federal Trade Commission:

THE FEDERAL TRADE COMMISSION SAYS ANYONE WITH A PHONE COULD BE A VICTIM OF A SCHEMING TELEMARKETER. DON'T GIVE AWAY YOUR CREDIT CARD OR BANK ACCOUNT NUMBERS ON THE PHONE. IF YOU HAVE ANY DOUBT ABOUT AN OFFER YOU HEAR ON THE PHONE, CHECK IT OUT AND GET IT IN WRITING. A MESSAGE FROM THE FEDERAL TRADE COMMISSION AND THIS STATION.

# # #

Courtesy of the Federal Trade Commission

Let's Say Goodbye to Fraudulent Telemarketing

Video PSA

MULTICULTURAL AWARENESS

Bob Nichols/U.S. Department of Agriculture/Creative Commons

Ed Avalos, Undersecretary of Marketing and Regulatory Programs for the U.S. Department of Agriculture, celebrates Hispanic Heritage Month at USDA.

If you want to find out how to reach 23 million Hispanics, Manny Ruiz will help you. He'll send you a daily blog, at your request, to keep you informed with articles and resources about publicizing and marketing to the Hispanic audience. Manny and his wife, Angela Sastaita-Ruiz, co-publish the Hispanic PR Blog, a leading marketing site for Hispanic public relations and social media (*www.hispanicprblog.com*). They are also the authors of the U.S. Hispanic Social Media Guide.

"If you scour the Latino Web as often as I do, you'll notice that one of the biggest trends right now is that not only are Latinos definitely engaging more through social media but that they are producing unique content as bloggers as well," Ruiz said in the guide.

Latinos and African Americans lead all other racial groups in the use of mobile media and cell phone ownership as well, according to a study by the Pew Internet and American Life Project.

Other studies confirm that minority groups are critical audiences for public relations and marketing professionals. As mentioned previously, Hallmark has the Sinceramente line of cards and products geared to Hispanics and the Mahogany line geared to African-Americans. Most of the major U.S. government agencies offer bilingual information in English and Spanish.

PRSA also features a website devoted to articles and blogs, and a diversity toolkit to help chapters develop multicultural resources *(www.prsa.org/Diversity)*.

MEDIA KITS

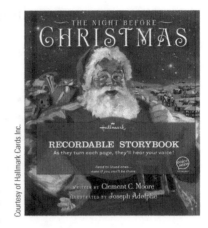

A Hallmark recordable storybook

Public relations practitioners often use media kits to promote corporate products. Printed versions of these kits are usually included in decorative folders that contain a variety of press releases, fact sheets about the company and its products and sometimes samples of the company's products.

These days more media kits are being produced for the Web. They still contain fact sheets and news releases, but online they also offer multimedia information in audio and video, PDF files containing images of the products, plus fact sheets, backgrounders and links to other information. They may also include interactive features. If you are planning a media kit for the Web, consider how many Web pages you will need for the information, and create links to each page. Most major corporate sites have a Press Room link to Web pages, with information about the company, press releases, products and contacts.

A good media kit should contain these items:

- **Attractive Cover:** The kit is usually contained in a folder with the company name and logo if it will be produced as a print product.

- **Brief Letter or Note:** A very brief explanation of the purpose of the kit should be provided for the editor. It could be on the inside of the cover.

- **Press release:** The first item after the editor's note should be a press release.

- **Fact Sheet:** Present information about the organization in simple list form. You might use headings such as *Who, What, Where, When, Why* and *How*. Fact sheets might also briefly itemize vital statistics about the organization or the issue, such as statistics on obesity if you are promoting a weight-loss product.

- **Backgrounder:** A backgrounder is information that can provide in-depth information that supplements the news, such as statistical research or historical developments that led up to the event you are promoting. Backgrounders might also include a feature story, such as a profile of a company executive. Don't include information in the backgrounder that should be in the press release. This is additional material, not a substitute for news.

- **Story Ideas:** The story idea sheet is optional, but if you include it, try to offer suggestions for localizing the information. This sheet should be written in list form or short paragraphs. You might also include suggestions for photos, video opportunities or graphics. The cover letter for your media kit should briefly state what is included. On the Web, you can create a navigation bar or box with links.

For example, the Hallmark online media kit for its recordable storybooks includes a fact sheet, a news release and links to multimedia. "Recordable storybooks feature exclusive voice-capture technology that enables a person to record each page of a book and have it played back over and over as the recipient turns the pages. The recording will not be lost, even when the batteries need to be replaced," according to the fact sheet. These links are included in the online media kit:

- Read and share recordable storybook stories on Facebook.
- Watch "Connecting Families, Creating Memories" on YouTube.
- View a recordable storybook video demonstration on Hallmark.com.
- Related images of storybooks in downloadable formats of low to high resolution.

JOB SKILLS — ADVICE FROM THE PROS

Networking is one of the most important skills for public relations practitioners. It helps to attend conferences so you can meet people face to face, but now you can network with hundreds of accomplished professionals without leaving your computer or smart phone. Resources for students and professionals abound on Twitter, Facebook and public relations organizations. Here are some helpful resources for public relations and marketing advice:

Social networking is critical for job seekers.

- PRSA (Public Relations Society of America, *www.prsa.org*): This is one of the most comprehensive sites offering blogs; several online magazines; and, perhaps most important for P.R. students, a job center with career resources and mentors to help you with résumé writing, interviewing skills and job networking. You'll find complete information on how to build your portfolio.
- New pros have great advice for students in their blog, *prnewpros .prsa.org.* Crystal Olig, a former chair of this blog group, offers these tips for networking: Attend events, dress smart, bring business cards, prepare questions and follow up with emails.
- PRSSA, the Public Relations Student Society of America, offers career guidance and internship opportunities. It also provides a skills inventory that lists effective written communication at the top of the list. Other essential skills include persuasive speaking, problem solving and multitasking. The website also gives complete advice on cover letters, résumés and networking at *www.prssa.org.*
- Twitter (*twitter.com*) is a fast way to skim hundreds of sources and links to blogs. Just type in "P.R.," "P.R. jobs" or "P.R. skills," and you'll find scores of entries. Check out "pr2020" for useful tips and trends.
- Create your own list of helpful blogs and sites from Facebook, Twitter and P.R. organizations and agencies. Find a place where you might like to work, and follow that company or agency.

Here is some inspiration from Elizabeth Albrycht, author of the CorporatePR blog and an expert in new technologies for public relations: "Be prepared for the unexpected. The one constant in PR is change. Stories change, people change, clients change, jobs change, technologies change, fads change, trends change. ... P.R. is generally NOT glamorous. There is nothing fun about stuffing press kits at 4 a.m. in a crappy conference center hotel room when you have an 8 a.m. press conference. The P.R. person rarely gets thanked when things go well and is the first to be blamed when things go badly. However, one of the great things about P.R. is you can immediately see the results of your work. You can make a difference."

EXERCISES

1 **Press release (hard-news style):** Gather information from an organization for an event on your campus or in your city. Write a press release announcing the event.

2 **Social media:** Create an account on Twitter. Find at least five public relations sites, corporate sites or professionals to follow. Follow the discussions for at least a week. Write an analysis of each site, critiquing the good and bad information. What was helpful, annoying, a waste of time or useful? Critique the writing as well. With only 140 characters allowed, were the postings clear? What enticed you to click further?

3 **Media kit:** Study a company in your community. Devise a media kit to promote some product or aspect of the company. This activity may require some coordination so many students do not bother the same firm. If a team of students or the whole class is studying a large company, divide the responsibilities so that students are studying different aspects of the company.

4 **Press release (feature style):** As the contact, use your name, phone number and email address. The company is Excaliber Entertainment Inc., 1955 Larkspur, San Antonio, Texas 78213. This information is adapted from a press release for a former online contest site owned by Excaliber. You may use a direct or creative lead. Assume that the website still exists for your press release, which should be limited to one page.

Who: *www.vaultcracker.com*, a contest website.

What: Sponsoring the contest "Junkiest Dorm Room in America."

When: Use now through the next two months.

Where: *www.vaultcracker.com*.

Why: To promote the new website.

How: The contest will award $300 to a college student whose pictures of his or her dorm room are judged the junkiest. Second prize is $100. The contest is open to all students who are enrolled full time at a college or university in the United States.

Comments: From Richard McNairy, founder and president of *www.vaultcracker.com*: "We know how busy college students are and we wanted to turn a negative into a positive. I'm sure students with messy rooms get criticism from others. Now two students with junky rooms will be able to brag about the fact that they earned cash because of their junky rooms."

More information: Visit *www.vaultcracker.com*.

5 **Email press release:** Write a one-page email press release (about 150 words) based on the following information; use your name, phone number and email for contact information:

The U.S. Department of Commerce's census bureau released a report today about the value of various college degrees. The report is called "What's It Worth? Field of Training and Economic Status." The data are from a panel of the Survey of Income and Program

Participation. College graduates who work full time and have a bachelor's degree in engineering earn the highest average monthly pay ($4,680), whereas those with education degrees earn the lowest ($2,802), according to the report. "Majoring in a technical field does pay off even if you don't finish a four-year degree," said Kurt Bauman, co-author with Camille Ryan of the report. "The average person with a vocational certificate earns around $200 more per month than the average high school graduate; but if the certificate is in an engineering-related field, the boost in earnings is close to $800." At the top of the earnings scale were those with professional degrees, such as doctors and lawyers ($7,224 per month), followed by full-time workers with master's degrees ($4,635), bachelor's degrees ($3,767), high school graduates ($2,279) and those without a diploma ($1,699).

Business was the most popular field of training beyond high school; 7.5 million people had bachelor's degrees in business and earned a monthly average of $3,962. An additional 1.9 million had master's degrees in business administration or other advanced degrees in business. The average monthly earnings of people with master's degrees in business was $5,579. Of people with managerial jobs, 46 percent had a bachelor's degree or higher degrees. Of people in professional occupations, 71 percent held a bachelor's degree or higher degrees. By comparison, no more than 8 percent of those in craft, service, farm and production occupations had completed this much education. Associate degrees generally require a two-year course of study, but people took an average of more than four years to complete them. Bachelor's and higher degrees took an average of five or more years to complete.

6 **Public service announcement:** Write a 15-second public service announcement (about 65 words) based on this information:

This message is from the Federal Emergency Management Agency. It's about tornadoes. They can be deadly. Tornadoes strike nearly every year, with the most powerful winds on Earth. Remember these three tornado danger signs: (1) Before a tornado hits, the wind may die down and the air may become very still. (2) Tornadoes can be nearly invisible, marked only by swirling debris at the base of the funnel. An approaching cloud of dust or debris can mark the location of a deadly tornado. Seek shelter immediately. (3) Tornadoes generally occur near the trailing edge of a thunderstorm. When a thunderstorm moves through your area, be alert for tornadoes. For more information on tornado preparedness, visit the FEMA website at *www.fema.gov*, or contact the Red Cross. Plan ahead to survive the next tornado, and listen to this station for more emergency preparedness information from FEMA.

7 **Promote a product:** Working in small groups, create a new product and a company name and address. Use your name and contact information. Each person in the group should then write a press release promoting this product.

8 **Usability study:** Conduct your own informal usability study by visiting the websites of three to five corporations that interest you. On each site, search for basic P.R. information described in this chapter and note your findings. Do the sites contain the basic contact information that you would need, such as phone numbers, addresses and key corporate officers? Do the sites contain a good description of the company's purpose? What other information do you think these websites should contain?

FEATURED ONLINE ACTIVITIES: Log on to the MindTap for Rich's Writing and Reporting News to access a variety of robust additional material, including this chapter's learning objectives, activities, comprehension quizzes, and more!

COACHING TIPS

Check your story for **accuracy.**

Seek documents to **substantiate sources' claims.**

Seek sources with **alternate points of view.**

Role-play: If you were the source or the source's attorney, what would you find **libelous or objectionable** in the story?

Check for the **latest charges or disposition** in police and court cases.

Don't copy information from a website without **attribution or permission.**

Don't use Twitter, Facebook or other social media photos, text or video **without permission.**

Don't use online information or social media you can't **verify, especially if it includes accusations** about a person.

CHAPTER 14
Media Law

© Anonymes/Shutterstock.com

Congress shall make no law respecting an establishment of religion, or prohibiting the free exercise thereof; or abridging the freedom of speech, or of the press; or the right of the people peaceably to assemble, and to petition the Government for a redress of grievances.

—THE FIRST AMENDMENT TO THE U.S. CONSTITUTION

267

T

EST YOUR KNOWLEDGE OF THESE LEGAL ISSUES:

1. You are the online editor of your campus newspaper. A person using a pseudonym has posted a message on your website that could be libelous. If you don't remove the posting, the paper will be liable for the information in the message if a lawsuit is filed. True or false?

2. You have visited a website that has a graphic you want to use in your campus newspaper or your radio station's website. The site does not contain any copyright notice, so you can use the graphic without permission. True or false?

3. Any columns labeled "opinion" or editorials published in your newspaper cannot be considered libelous regardless of the information they contain. True or false?

4. You are posting a video on YouTube. If you use just a portion of a popular song in your video, you will not be violating copyright laws. True or false?

Many legal issues arising from the increasing use of social networking sites, blogs and other online media do not have clear-cut answers. However, the questions posed here have legal precedents. Here are the answers to the first three questions, which are adapted from information on the Student Press Law Center (*www.splc.org*), and the answer to the last question, which is explained on the YouTube website (*www.youtube.com*):

Question 1: False The paper is not liable for messages posted by a third party. The federal Communications Decency Act grants immunity to website operators and Internet providers for messages posted by a third party. But if you create part of the message by editing it, you could be considered a "content provider," and you might be liable in a lawsuit. In addition, because the Web is a global medium, you could be liable in other countries. It is probably a good idea to check the postings and delete ones that you think are offensive or potentially libelous.

1101 Wilson Blvd.
Suite 1100
Arlington, VA 22209, USA.
Telephone: 703.807.1904

Do you have questions about your legal rights and responsibilities as a student journalist or media adviser? Or are you just interested in more information about press law? The SPLC Resource Center can help you find answers.

Courtesy of the Student Press Law Center

Question 2: False All material on the Internet is copyrighted as soon as it is created. It does not need to have a copyright notice to be protected by U.S. copyright laws. However, some images may be available without permission if they are from most U.S. government sites or from websites that say permission is granted for specific use. In many cases the site may grant permission to use images on personal pages, but not for commercial use.

Question 3: False You may express opinions without impunity, but if you publish an allegation that is false and damaging to a person's reputation, you can be sued for libel no matter where it is published in a newspaper, on a website or in a broadcast medium. You can criticize someone as a bad performer without being libelous, but if you falsely accuse the performer of being a drug addict, that would be libelous.

Question 4: False You are violating copyright by using all or a portion of a song or video that you did not create yourself. The YouTube site specifically states: "If you're not sure if something will violate someone's copyright, the safest thing to do is to create something completely original, with images and audio you've created. . . . If you've recorded something from a DVD, videotaped your TV screen, or downloaded a video online, don't post it unless you have permission."

LIBEL

"Libel is essentially a false and defamatory attack in written form on a person's reputation or character. Broadcast defamation is libel because there is usually a written script. Oral or spoken defamation is slander," according to Donald Gillmor and his co-authors in *Mass Communication Law: Cases and Comment*. The "script" is not limited to a news story, the authors explain; it can take the form of headlines, photos, cartoons, film, tape, records, signs, bumper stickers and advertisements.

Several libel suits have also resulted from messages that people posted to online discussion groups. If the defamatory statements are published — whether online or in print — they can still be considered libelous.

Truth is a defense in libel suits. Anyone can sue or threaten to sue for libel, claiming injury to his reputation. The real concern is whether the person has grounds enough to win. The key factors to consider are whether you published untrue information that hurt the reputation of an identifiable person and whether you were either negligent or reckless in failing to check the information:

- Are you publishing something that may not be truthful?
- Are you carelessly publishing something that is inaccurate?
- Are you publishing something accusatory that you haven't checked out?
- Are you publishing something that clearly identifies a person and harms that person's reputation?

If your answer is yes to any of those questions, you could be in trouble for libel.

New York Times Co. v. Sullivan

Those standards were the ones the U.S. Supreme Court applied in 1964 in a landmark libel case, *New York Times Co. v. Sullivan*, and the standards have been applied since then to public officials.

The New York Times case stemmed from an advertisement the newspaper accepted in 1960 from a group of people in the civil rights movement. The group was trying to raise money for the Committee to Defend Martin Luther King. The ad claimed that King had been arrested seven times and that his home had been bombed. It also claimed that black students who had staged a nonviolent civil rights demonstration at Alabama State University had been the target of police brutality. The advertisement accused the police department in Montgomery, Alabama, of being armed with shotguns and using tear gas to subdue students.

Even though the police commissioner, L.B. Sullivan, had not been named in the advertisement, he sued for libel. He contended that the mention of "police" in the ad referred to him as the Montgomery police commissioner and that the ad contained factual errors that damaged his reputation. He claimed that the police did not ring the college campus or padlock the college dining hall, as the ad had claimed. Furthermore, Dr. King had been arrested four times, not seven, and three of the four arrests had occurred before Sullivan was commissioner.

Sullivan won in the lower courts and the Alabama Supreme Court. But the U.S. Supreme Court reversed the decision in its landmark ruling about "actual malice." Malice, in this context, does not mean ill will or intent to harm someone; it means that you published something knowing it was false or carelessly published information without checking whether it was true or false. The justices wrote:

> The constitutional guarantees require, we think, a federal rule that prohibits a public official from recovering damages for defamatory falsehood relating to his official conduct unless he proves that the statement was made with "actual malice" — that is knowledge that it was false or with reckless disregard of whether it was false or not.

The court placed the burden of proving libel on the plaintiff, the person who is suing. The justices made this a constitutional issue, applying the First Amendment right of a free press to publish matters of public concern. In the ruling, Justice William Brennan wrote the following:

> Thus we consider this case against the background of a profound national commitment to the principle that debate on public issues should be uninhibited, robust, and wide-open, and that it may well include vehement, caustic, and sometimes unpleasantly sharp attacks on government and public officials.

The *Times v. Sullivan* ruling applied only to people who are public officials. The application was later broadened to include "public figures."

Public Officials

For purposes of libel law, who is a public official? Elected officials and candidates for office are definitely considered public officials. Appointed

Justice William Brennan

Library of Congress Prints and Photographs Division

officials may or may not be. Here are the criteria: Do they have authority to set policy in the government, and are they under enough public scrutiny to have easy access to the media?

The Supreme Court defined public officials this way in *Rosenblatt v. Baer*, a case about the status of appointed officials:

> It is clear, therefore, that the "public official" designation applies at the very least to those among the hierarchy of government employees who have, or appear to the public to have, substantial responsibility for or control over the conduct of government affairs.

Is a police officer a public official? Courts in Pennsylvania are split on that decision, but most courts have ruled that law enforcement officers are public officials because they have the power to make arrests, a form of control in government. However, teachers, professors and other employees in a public education system are not usually defined as public officials because they are carrying out policies set by other officials of the school district or university. But if they achieve fame or notoriety, they may become public figures.

Public Figures

Who is a public figure, and why is the distinction between public officials and public figures important? People may be considered public figures if their achievements or notoriety places them in the public eye or if they seek attention by voluntarily thrusting themselves into a public controversy. But if they are brought into the public spotlight involuntarily, they may not be public figures. A court will usually determine whether the person qualifies as a public figure.

Like public officials, public figures also bear the burden of proving that the information in contention was libelous. The person or organization being sued does not have to disprove libel. The courts identify three types of public figures: pervasive, vortex and involuntary.

A "pervasive" public figure is a person who has gained prominence in society or great power and influence. Well-known entertainers and athletes and people who voluntarily seek public attention are in this category.

A "vortex," or "limited," public figure is a person who has voluntarily thrust himself into a public controversy to influence the outcome. The Supreme Court has stated that people in this category are not public figures for all aspects of their lives, but only for the aspects that relate to their role in a particular public controversy. A key point is the "voluntary" concept. An individual does not automatically become a public figure if he is thrust into a newsworthy situation; the involvement in the controversy must be the person's choice. Access to the media is another factor in determining whether someone is a public figure. The person must have enough regular and continuing access to the media to counter criticism and expose falsehoods.

Sen. William Proxmire, U.S. Congress

Consider the case of *Hutchinson v. Proxmire*. In 1975, when the late Sen. William Proxmire issued his annual "Golden Fleece" awards, which satirized some government-funded research projects as wasteful, he issued a press release targeting a researcher who was using monkeys to study stress. The scientist, Ronald Hutchinson, sued Proxmire for damaging his reputation and subjecting him to public ridicule by falsely claiming Hutchinson's research was wasteful. Key to the case was determining whether Hutchinson was a public figure.

Proxmire claimed the scientist was a public figure because he had received federal grants and had access to the media when they contacted him about receiving the Golden Fleece award. A federal district court agreed with Proxmire and dismissed the suit. But Hutchinson appealed.

The U.S. Supreme Court ruled that Hutchinson was not a public figure because he was not willingly involved in a public controversy until Proxmire caused it. The court said Hutchinson did not automatically become a public figure by being thrust into a newsworthy situation. Also, the court determined that Hutchinson did not have regular and continuing access to the media. He was sought out by reporters only to respond to Proxmire's criticism. Hutchinson ultimately received $10,000 from Proxmire.

The third type of public figure, "involuntary," is someone who does nothing voluntary to garner attention or to get involved in a public issue but finds himself in the middle of a public controversy anyway. Courts have found that this category rarely fits an individual in a libel suit.

Private Figures

The difference between being a public or private figure is crucial because the standards for proving libel can differ. Many states have made it easier for private persons to prove libel than for public figures. The Supreme Court has left it up to the states to determine their own standards of liability for private figures:

> We hold that, so long as they do not impose liability without fault, the States may define for themselves the appropriate standard of liability for a publisher or a broadcaster of defamatory falsehood injurious to a private individual.

The court made this ruling in a 1974 case, *Gertz v. Welch*. Elmer Gertz was a Chicago lawyer who claimed he had been libeled when a John Birch Society magazine, *American Opinion*, published an article labeling him a Communist. He sued the publisher, Robert Welch. Even though Gertz was a prominent lawyer, the Supreme Court ruled that he was a private person under the circumstances of this case. The court also declared that because private people don't have the same access to the media to defend themselves as public officials, they shouldn't be held to the same strict standards in proving libel.

In *Gertz v. Welch*, the court decided that a private individual needs to show only that the material was published with carelessness or negligence instead of proving actual malice, which means publishing with knowledge or reckless disregard of falsity. But all libel plaintiffs, public and private, have to prove the material is false and damaging to their reputation.

Even though the Supreme Court left it up to states to determine their own libel standards in cases involving private figures, the *Gertz* case paved the way for allowing private people to abide by less rigid standards than public officials and figures. Many states have followed the "simple negligence" standard in the *Gertz* case. Others require private individuals to abide by the same "actual malice" standard as public individuals.

"Negligence" in this context means you failed to exercise reasonable care in doing your job as a journalist. That type of care might include talking to all sides of a controversial issue, using relevant documents, taking accurate notes and checking your information for accuracy before publishing it.

Architect of the Capitol photograph/U.S. Capitol

THE FIRST FEDERAL CONGRESS · 1789

WITHOUT FREEDOM OF THOUGHT
THERE CAN BE NO SUCH THING AS WISDOM
& NO SUCH THING AS PUBLICK LIBERTY
WITHOUT FREEDOM OF SPEECH
BENJAMIN FRANKLIN 1722

Oil painting showing the First Federal Congress of 1789

THE IMPORTANCE OF ACCURACY

Accuracy is paramount for a good journalist. Every mistake you make jeopardizes the organization's credibility with readers and viewers. Because of that credibility factor, newspapers throughout the country print corrections every day, many for the incorrect spelling of names. That's another reason why you should always double-check the names in your stories.

Accuracy in the media is also affected by the growing use of social media networks for reporting. Sources are not always reliable or identified, especially in tweets, and the rush to publish in this highly competitive news world can lead to inaccurate information. With press credibility at an all-time low, it is crucial to verify your sources when you use Twitter, Facebook and other social networking sites for reporting.

Anonymous Sources

In addition to verifying sources, it is also important to identify them. However, when doing investigative reporting or getting confidential sources, particularly in government, sources often refuse to divulge information unless they receive a promise of anonymity. Most news organizations prefer to avoid that promise, but reporters still depend on these anonymous sources.

Federal Shield Law

Most states have laws that protect reporters from revealing their sources if a case comes to court where testimony from the source is needed. But there is no federal law offering such protection, even though attempts to pass one have been proposed for many years. In several instances reporters who have refused to reveal their sources in federal cases have been sentenced to jail.

In 2013 a federal shield law, The Free Flow of Information Act, was proposed in Congress. The latest version of the bill contained a provision of "judicial discretion," which gives a judge the power to extend the shield law's provisions to any person "if the judge determines that such protections would be in the interest of justice and necessary to protect lawful and legitimate news-gathering activities under the specific circumstances of the case."

Earlier versions of this bill disputed the definitions of a journalist, but the most recent version says the law could apply to a "covered journalist," meaning a person who "disseminates news or information" not yet invented. This broader interpretation of a journalist would apply to citizen journalists, freelancers and possibly bloggers and social media reporters, depending on the judicial discretion application.

The bill proposed in the Senate imposes these conditions: Journalists would only be granted protection from revealing sources in federal cases if alternative sources have been exhausted; if testimony is critical to the investigation; if the source's identity is necessary to prevent terrorism or harm to national security and if the disclosure outweighs the public interest in the news dissemination.

The bill still must pass in Congress and be signed into law by the president before it can become law.

State laws that protect journalists from revealing sources vary. The Reporters Committee for Freedom of the Press offers a website listing those laws at *www.rcfp .org/reporters-privilege*.

Showing Copy to Sources

Should you show your story to sources or read it to them before you publish it? Many of your sources will ask you to do that. And many editors will say you shouldn't. They claim the risks are too great that sources will recant what they have told you or ask you to delete any information that puts them in a bad light.

If you don't show the entire story to your source, it is considered acceptable — even wise — to ask a source about any technical information you may not fully understand. You can read what you have written and ask the source to check its accuracy.

Corrections

The most common cause of lawsuits is carelessness. Most news media don't publish material they know or suspect is false.

Although newspapers and broadcast media get sued by people targeted in major investigative projects, the majority of libel suits stem from much less important stories. Incorrect captions, defamatory headlines, an inaccuracy in a police story or a feature can result in a libel suit.

Printed corrections or oral retractions on radio or television don't prevent libel suits. They may assuage an angered source enough to forestall a lawsuit, or they may be evidence of the news organization's good faith, but corrections do not undo the harm of inaccurate published material. It's up to a jury to decide whether you were negligent, careless or reckless in your disregard for the truth.

Even when you use the word "alleged," meaning that the accusation is a charge without proof, you are on dangerous ground. This word, although widely used by reporters in police cases, does not save you from libel. It is better to attribute the information to official sources or records.

If you don't name the person against whom the accusation is made, you still can be sued for libel. A person who can claim he was identified — either by enough information to describe the person physically or by position — can then sue.

Nor does attribution save you. Say that a candidate for mayor tells you his opponent is a crook. You print the statement and attribute it to the candidate. The opponent could sue you and your organization. Just because you named the source of the statement, you cannot avoid responsibility for it. And if it isn't true and you haven't documented it as true, you could be considered guilty of reckless disregard for the truth.

If you are going to print or broadcast any accusations that could be defamatory, you should always check with the person being accused and ask for a response.

Cross-checking may not save you from libel, but it at least gives you a chance to prove you were not reckless.

There are times when you can publish accusatory or damaging information, especially when you are writing about crime. You have certain privileges as a member of the press, and so do some of the officials who deal with you.

Privilege

Privilege — in a legal sense — comes in two forms: absolute and qualified.

Absolute Privilege This means that public officials, including law enforcement officials, can make statements in the course of their official duties without fear of being sued for libel. This form of privilege extends to court proceedings, legislative proceedings, public and official meetings, and contents of public records. For example, if Senator Proxmire had announced his Golden Fleece awards on the floor of the Senate instead of in a news release, he would have had absolute privilege and could not have been sued by Hutchinson, the researcher who claimed he was libeled.

Qualified Privilege As a member of the media, you have "qualified privilege." You may print defamatory statements made by people who are absolutely privileged as long as you are being fair and accurate, and the information is from a public proceeding or public record. But if your report contains errors, you could lose that qualified protection.

If, during a public meeting, a city council member calls another member a crook, you may print the accusation. If the same city official makes the same comment to you during a telephone interview or after the meeting, you can't print it without risking libel. The key is that the defamatory statement must be made in an official capacity during an official proceeding. Or you may use, with attribution, something stated in court records. But you must make it clear that the accusations were made by other people in records or meetings and are not proven fact.

Suppose that a police officer tells you something about a suspect. You may print this information if the officer is acting in an official capacity and if the information is documented in a public record, such as a police report or court files. However, you still should be careful about how you word accusations in crime stories. The police officer may say the man stabbed his wife, but you may not say the same thing without attribution. If the information is not stated in a public record, such as a police report or court record, it can be libelous. Generally, statements made outside of the court by police are not privileged, but some states may extend privilege to these comments.

Never call anyone a murderer unless the person has been convicted of murder in court. Suppose that a man has been murdered and you go to the neighborhood for reaction. A neighbor says the man's wife killed him. The neighbor isn't an official acting in an official capacity, and the wife hasn't been convicted. The neighbor's comments could be libelous, and you could be sued for printing them.

Don't call a suspect a "robber" or use any other accusatory term before the person is convicted. Use terms such as "the suspect," "the man accused of murder," or "the woman charged with the robbery."

Person of Interest In recent years police have been using another term, "person of interest," to describe someone who is being investigated in a crime but has not been arrested or charged with anything. Although the term appears to be a synonym for "suspect," it does not have any legal definition and can implicate people who are just being questioned.

The term has become known as "the Richard Jewell rule," because it was used in reference to Richard Jewell, the man who was initially accused of being responsible for the 1996 Olympic Park bombing incident, but was never charged. He was cleared of any wrongdoing, but when he died in 2007, news stories still associated him with the wrongful accusations in the bombing incident. The lesson from that is to be careful how you characterize people in criminal investigations and to think before you publish names of people who have not been officially charged with crimes.

Neutral Reportage

Another type of privilege, called "neutral reportage," has been recognized in about 10 states. It gives the news media First Amendment protection in writing accusations about a public official or public figure in a public controversy as long as the reporter states them accurately and neutrally. If one official or person considered responsible and newsworthy accuses another public figure of wrongdoing, you may print the information as long as you get reactions of the accused or other participants.

Under neutral reportage you aren't responsible for determining whether the accusations are true. However, many states don't extend this type of privilege to the media, so it's always safer to beware of printing unsubstantiated accusations.

The best defense for a reporter is the "truth" defense, proving that what you wrote is true. What you can do and what you should do may differ. You may have the right to print statements from court records or meetings, but if you think they could be untrue or unfair, should you print them? Those are the kinds of ethical decisions journalists must make. Most editors advise this: When in doubt, leave it out.

Fair Comment and Criticism

Suppose you are writing a review of a play, concert or book, and your review is very negative. Can you be sued? Yes. You can always be sued. But you are protected under the right of fair comment.

Writers of editorials, analysis stories, reviews and other criticism may express opinions, but they may not state inaccurate facts. A factual error can be grounds for libel; an opinion is protected.

To qualify as fair comment, a comment must generally be on a matter of public interest; it must be based on facts known or believed to be true; and it may not be malicious or made with reckless disregard for the truth. In this case also, truth is considered a good defense.

ETHICS

ETHICAL DILEMMA: You are attending a school board meeting as a reporter. During the public comment portion of the meeting, a woman accuses a male guidance counselor in the high school of having had sex with students. This is a small town, with only one high school and two guidance counselors, both male. The school board says it will conduct an investigation. You are on deadline and must get the story in right after the meeting. You can't reach either guidance counselor for his reaction. The comment was made at a public meeting, and it is part of the public record. Even if you have the legal right to publish this information, what are your ethical concerns? Will you include this information in your story?

INVASION OF PRIVACY

Issues of privacy involve ethical decisions, not matters of accuracy. However, with the proliferation of invasion of privacy lawsuits, a journalist should understand the legal issues. Privacy is not a right guaranteed by the U.S. Constitution. In privacy cases, damage is usually considered the mental anguish that results from wrongfully revealing to the public some part of the plaintiff's life. Truth may not be enough of a defense in privacy cases.

The courts have acknowledged four grounds for invasion of privacy lawsuits: intrusion, public disclosure of private and embarrassing facts, false light, and misappropriation of a person's name or image without permission.

Intrusion Into a Person's Solitude

Eavesdropping, harassing someone and trespassing on private property can be considered intrusion. So can going onto private property and using a telephoto lens, listening behind doors and using any device to enhance what the unaided eye can see or the unaided ear can hear. In other words, a journalist who uses subterfuge to obtain and publish confidential material could be risking a suit for invasion of privacy. The intrusion can be either physical or mental.

In *Dietemann v. Time Inc.*, two *Life* magazine reporters were sued for going undercover as husband and wife to do a story on a plumber, A.S. Dietemann. The plumber was believed to be practicing medicine with herbs. The so-called healer told the female reporter she had cancer and prescribed an herbal cure. The female reporter taped Dietemann's comments, and her partner took pictures with a concealed camera. Even though the plumber later pleaded no contest to a charge of practicing medicine without a license, he sued the magazine company for invasion of privacy. A California court awarded him $1,000. An appeals court upheld the award and said that the undercover methods, used without Dietemann's consent, were an invasion of his privacy. "The First Amendment is not a license to trespass, to steal, or to intrude by electronic means into the precincts of another's home or office," the court opinion said.

Unlike libel suits, publication isn't required for someone to claim invasion of privacy in this type of case. Truth isn't a defense either.

Public Disclosure of Private Facts

Publishing facts such as information about a person's sex life or medical history that the public considers offensive could be considered invasion of privacy, even if they are true. But if the facts are taken from the public record, such as court documents, they will probably be considered fair to publish.

In 1975 the Supreme Court ruled in *Cox Broadcasting Co. v. Cohn* that a television station in Atlanta was within its First Amendment rights to publish the name of a rape victim even though state law prohibited doing so. The victim's family had sued for invasion of privacy, claiming a private fact had been disclosed. The family had won, but Cox appealed the decision to the U.S. Supreme Court. The court said the news media had the right to report matters on the public record.

Information not on the public record is more susceptible to lawsuits. The courts have ruled that the media may be invading privacy if the private facts in question would be offensive and objectionable to a reasonable person and would not be of legitimate public concern. Community standards of what is "offensive" may vary from one place to another. That's why these are difficult cases for courts to decide.

Publicity That Puts a Person in a False Light

If a published story or picture gives the wrong impression and is embarrassing to the person, the possibility exists that the court will consider a "false light" verdict. For example, in one case a television station doing a story about teenage pregnancy took pictures of a young woman walking down the street. The television station did not say she was pregnant, nor did the station identify her. However, she claimed the picture put her in a false light — indicating that she was a pregnant teenager — and she won her lawsuit against the station.

False light is related to defamation, but the story or picture does not have to defame a person to be considered false light. It does have to portray the person inaccurately. Truth is a defense in these cases. Generally, the plaintiff has to prove that the media showed actual malice by knowingly publishing false information.

The case often cited here is *Time Inc. v. Hill*, because it was the first false-light case to reach the Supreme Court. James Hill, his wife and five children were held hostage in their suburban Philadelphia home by three escaped convicts in 1952. After the incident, the Hills moved to Connecticut. A few years later, *Life* magazine was planning to publish a review of a play partially based on the incident. The magazine took the cast of the play to the Hills' old home and photographed the actors in some scenes from the play.

James Hill sued, saying the pictures in *Life* gave readers the impression that the scenes portrayed the family's real experiences. Hill initially won his suit. But it eventually went to the Supreme Court, which ruled that Hill would have to prove actual malice on the part of *Life* magazine. The court sent the case back for retrial to a lower court, but Hill dropped the suit.

Use of a Person's Name or Photo Without Permission

This doctrine applies when the picture is used for commercial purposes, such as advertising or promotion. For example, use of an athlete's photograph to promote a product without his consent could be grounds for a lawsuit. The easiest way to avoid this kind of lawsuit is to have the person sign a consent form.

Television personality Vanna White sued Samsung Electronics when an advertisement the firm used featured a robot that resembled White as she appeared on the game show "Wheel of Fortune." White claimed her image was appropriated without her permission, and a court agreed.

ONLINE LEGAL ISSUES

The Internet is spawning many new legal issues and laws regarding free speech vs. pornography, libel, copyright and privacy.

Retired Associate U.S. Supreme Court Justice John Paul Stevens

Communications Decency Act

The first major test of free speech on the Internet to reach the U.S. Supreme Court was the Communications Decency Act (CDA) of 1996, a federal law that restricted distribution of indecent material on the Internet to people under age 18. The American Civil Liberties Union challenged the law, which was ruled unconstitutional by a federal three-judge panel in Philadelphia, but the government appealed the ruling in *Reno v. ACLU*.

In 1997 the U.S. Supreme Court struck down portions of the act that censored online material. In the ruling, Associate Justice John Paul Stevens wrote that the CDA's "use of undefined terms 'indecent and patently offensive' raises special First Amendment concerns because of its obvious chilling effect on free speech."

One area that was not struck down was a little section that has become a big issue for Internet providers, bloggers and other people who post messages on any Internet or social networking sites. Section 230 of the act says, "No provider or user of an interactive computer service shall be treated as the publisher or speaker of any information provided by another information content provider."

As mentioned at the start of this chapter, that means that if someone posts a libelous message to your website, you are not responsible for the content of it unless you created part of it. Courts have held that this part of the act protects you even if you edit or delete the offensive material. If you are only providing the website or service, you're safe, but if you contribute to the content, you could be held responsible.

Zeran v. America Online

Online providers can thank Kenneth Zeran for that protection. He was just at home in Seattle, running his publishing business from his house in April 1995, when his phone began ringing every two minutes with callers issuing death threats. The calls began just six days after the bombing of the federal building in Oklahoma City where 168 people died.

An anonymous person had posted Zeran's telephone number on an America Online message board, telling readers to call him because he was selling T-shirts, key chains and other memorabilia about the bombing, with such offensive slogans as "Visit Oklahoma . . . It's a BLAST!!!" Oddly enough, Zeran wasn't even a member of AOL, and the person who posted the message had a trial membership and was never identified because AOL didn't keep records of nonsubscribers.

To make matters worse, an announcer for a classic rock radio station in Oklahoma City read the message on air and encouraged listeners to call Zeran and tell him how they felt about what he was doing. Zeran sued the radio station on grounds of defamation, false light, invasion of privacy and intentional infliction of emotional distress, but the court ruled in favor of the radio station on all counts. The court ruled that the only charge applicable to broadcast was slander, and there was insufficient evidence to establish injury to Zeran's reputation or that his emotional stress was "severe" enough to prevent him from conducting his daily affairs.

More significant was his suit against AOL on charges that the service was responsible for the defamatory messages and was unreasonably slow in removing them. This was the first libel case against an online service provider to reach the U.S. Supreme Court. Zeran's case was initially dismissed in 1997 by a U.S. District Court, which ruled that Section 230 of the Communications Decency Act of 1996 protected online service providers from liability for subscribers' material. In 1998 the U.S. Supreme Court upheld that decision. So AOL was not at fault, and Zeran got nothing for his troubles.

SOCIAL MEDIA

THE LIABILITY OF BLOG-GERS: Although the law is specific regarding protection for Internet service providers from material posted by their users, it is not as clear regarding bloggers. "Bloggers can be both a provider and a user of interactive computer services," according to "Bloggers' FAQ," an article on the Electronic Frontier Foundation website (*www.eff.org/issues/bloggers/legal*). "Bloggers are users when they create and edit blogs through a service provider, and they are providers to the extent that they allow third parties to add comments or other material to their blogs. Your readers' comments, entries written by guest bloggers, tips sent by email and information provided to you through an RSS feed would all likely be considered information provided by another content provider," according to the EFF article. But the courts have not ruled on whether you would be responsible for defamatory material if you selected the information from other blogs to post on your site.

Liability on Social Networking Sites: Julie Doe (known as Jane Doe in the lawsuit) was a 13-year-old teenager from Texas when she created a profile on MySpace. The next year a 19-year-old man, also from Texas, saw her profile and contacted her. They began communicating and later spoke on the phone. In 2006 the two met in person, and the man sexually assaulted her, according to a lawsuit she and her mother filed against MySpace Inc. and its partner News Corporation. The charges were negligence, gross negligence, fraud and negligent misrepresentation for failing to protect underage users from sexual predators. The court ruled that MySpace was not responsible for the content on its site and dismissed the charges against the social networking service.

Although MySpace has changed its form from social profiles and is now geared mostly to music and entertainment, the case was the first to address whether that portion of the Communications Decency Act that protects Internet providers from liability for information posted by a third party can be applied to a social networking site.

Liability on Twitter: When is a negative tweet an opinion or a potential libel suit? Amanda Bonnen posted a tweet about her landlord stating: "Who said sleeping in a moldy apartment was bad for you? Horizon really thinks it's okay." But the landlord, Horizon, didn't think the tweet was OK and filed a $50,000 lawsuit against her for defamation. A judge dismissed the case on the grounds that the tweet was "too vague." Bonnen's lawsuit was only one of several involving Twitter messages. Rock star Courtney Love was sued for libel by a fashion designer who claimed Love posted false and defamatory messages about her on Twitter and on a Facebook page. Love paid $430,000 to settle the suit. These cases show that social media messages are an emerging area for legal cases.

The issue regarding retweeting is less clear. The Twitter site says, "We encourage and permit broad re-use of Content." However you are still responsible for the copyright of your material. "You retain your rights to any content you submit, post or display on or through the Services. By submitting, posting or displaying content on or through the Services, you grant us a worldwide, non-exclusive, royalty-free license (with the right to sublicense) to use, copy, reproduce, process, adapt, modify, publish, transmit, display and distribute such content in any and all media or distribution methods (now known or later developed)."

Privacy of Text Messages: If you use your employer's equipment to post text messages to a social media site while you are at work, does your employer have the right to check your messages? A case involving that issue was the first of its kind to reach the U.S. Supreme Court. A California police officer used his city-issued pager to send private text messages, some of which were sexually explicit. When his employer reviewed the messages, Officer Jeff Quon claimed his privacy rights were violated as guaranteed by the Fourth Amendment, which protects citizens against unreasonable search and seizure.

The Supreme Court was unanimous in ruling that because Quon used city equipment, he didn't have a right to privacy especially because the city had a written no-privacy policy regarding the pager. However, the Court did not apply this ruling broadly. To be safe, you should check your employer's policy. To be even safer (and ethical), you should just work when you are at work.

Electronic Frontier Foundation

BLOGGERS' LEGAL GUIDE

Bloggers legal guide on the Electronic Frontier Foundation site (*www.eff.org*)

Children's Online Privacy Protection Act (COPPA)

The Communications Decency Act originally contained provisions to protect children from obscene and indecent Internet material, but those parts were struck down by the Supreme Court as violations of the First Amendment's right to free speech. However, these other efforts succeeded:

- COPPA, which took effect in 2000 and was revised in 2013, makes it a federal crime — with penalties of $16,000 per violation — to collect information from children under 13 and use it for commercial purposes that could be considered harmful to minors. The revised rule widens the definition of children's personal information to include identifiers such as cookies that track children's activity online, geolocation, videos, photos and audio recordings. It requires operators of websites or online services directed to children under 13 to give notice to parents and get their consent before collecting, using or disclosing any personal information they collect from children.

- The Children's Internet Protection Act (CIPA), passed in 2000, also attempts to protect children by requiring public schools and libraries that receive federal funds to install software that would block online material considered "harmful to minors," basically pornography and obscenity. The law was challenged as unconstitutional by the American Library Association, but in 2003 the Supreme Court upheld it. In addition, more than 21 states have enacted laws to require Internet filtering software in public schools or libraries to limit children's access to sexually explicit online information.

These types of legal issues are certain to continue as the government attempts to regulate the Internet.

COPYRIGHT

If you take pictures or documents from a website that does not contain a copyright notice, are you violating copyright laws? Absolutely. The 1976 U.S. Copyright Act protects everything that you or others write the minute the information is offered in "a fixed form," which includes online or print information. The law was amended later to make a copyright notice optional on all works published on or after 1989. Prior to that date a notice was required to receive copyright protection. It's always safe to include the copyright symbol and notice on your website or material, even if it isn't mandatory.

Fair Use

How much information can you copy without infringing on a copyright? Of all the copyright laws, fair use is the murkiest. "The distinction between what is fair use and what is infringement in a particular case will not always be clear or easily defined. There is no specific number of words, lines, or notes that may safely be taken without

MULTIMEDIA COACH

THE DAYS OF producing content only for print or only for broadcast are over. Whether the content you produce is geared to mobile phones, tablets or websites, the material will probably include print, video and social media references.

Can you include some video from YouTube or a social networking site in your material? Can you include a photo you found on the Internet or on Facebook? Is it OK to use the video or photo if you credit the source? If you read an article you like on the Internet, can you email it to a friend? The simple answer to all these questions is no. However, there are exceptions.

If you use information from social networking sites or online sites for writing academic papers, blogs or any other purpose, here are a few tips on how you can prevent online legal problems:

- Don't copy material from the Internet (including images) or use it in your blog, your Facebook site or other social networking sites without permission. Many images are offered free for personal use, but check the site notices to be sure.

- Don't write any defamatory messages to an online blog or other site.

- Avoid writing defamatory or derogatory comments in personal email messages. Email is often passed to other users without the permission or knowledge of the source.

- Consider the accuracy of material you find on the Internet. Check the site owner and organization to make sure that you are using a responsible site. You should also verify the accuracy of any information from the Internet.

- Check the posting dates of online material to determine whether the information is still accurate. Much online information may be outdated.

---

permission. Acknowledging the source of the copyrighted material does not substitute for obtaining permission," according to the U.S. Copyright Office.

The fair use doctrine of U.S. Copyright laws says the ruling depends on whether the material you are copying is for commercial or nonprofit educational purposes, the amount of material taken and whether the material copied will affect the value of the copyrighted work. For example, if you copied an entire chapter of this book without permission, the publisher would probably not consider that "fair use" because it would affect the sale of the book. If you take an audio or video of a commercially sold item and post it on your website, that would also fail to qualify as fair use.

Photos, screenshots and other material from websites are also copyrighted, so if you put them on your website, you should either get permission or check to make sure that the creator of that material has posted a notice that you may use the material without separate copyright permission.

Creative Commons One exception is Creative Commons, a nonprofit organization that offers copyright licenses allowing people to share their materials. The licenses specify whether the information may be reproduced for noncommercial or commercial use and what type of attribution is needed.

To determine whether you are free to use information especially from online sources, check the webpage for a copyright notice or other disclaimers and terms of service.

Public Domain If the site says the information is in the public domain, that means the work is publicly available without copyright restrictions. Most U.S. government websites and publications are in the public domain. Other works that were published in the U.S. before 1923 also qualify because their copyright expired; and those published before 1964, if the copyrights were not renewed.

Although many unresolved issues remain about intellectual property rights for online materials, additional laws to protect software and online materials were enacted in the late 1990s.

- The No Electronic Theft Act, signed into law in 1997, provides penalties of up to five years in jail and fines of up to $250,000 for copying software or online materials, even if you don't make a profit.

- The Digital Millennium Copyright Act of 1998 provides a broad range of penalties, including criminal offenses from $500,000 to $1 million and up to 10 years imprisonment, for copying online materials for commercial advantage or private financial gain.

More cases continue to come before the courts regarding peer-to-peer file sharing of music. Rulings are pending on other cases involving companies that furnish the software for file sharing, and these issues are likely to continue. Whether it is material for a blog, a profile in a social networking site or other online matter, most sites that host such content specify terms about posting pornography, defamatory messages or other unacceptable material that could be libelous. The nature of communication is changing rapidly, and so are the legal decisions, but the concepts of accuracy and fairness are timeless.

EXERCISES

1 Actual malice: Write a paragraph explaining "actual malice" and "reckless disregard for the truth" as defined by the U.S. Supreme Court in *Times v. Sullivan*.

2 Libel potential scenario: You are the editor of your local newspaper. A U.S. senator has decided to seek re-election. Five women who worked for him several years ago say he sexually harassed and abused them while they were in his office. The women refuse to be named. Their allegations range from stories that he plied them with drugs and alcohol and then sexually abused them to accusations of rape. All the women are reputable, including a political lobbyist and a former secretary to the senator, but none has gone to the police. As a result, you have no record of formal complaints about their allegations. However, three years ago a formal complaint by a former employee charged him with sexual molestation, but the charges were dropped. Will you print these women's allegations and use his name? If you do, will the senator have grounds for a libel lawsuit?

3 Privacy issue 1: A candidate for city council in your community had a nervous breakdown 10 years ago. The candidate's opponent has slipped you a hospital document confirming this fact. Should you print the story? Why or why not? If you do, does the candidate have any grounds to sue you for invasion of privacy?

4 Privacy issue 2: You are a photographer who went on assignment to the county fair. You snapped a picture of a woman whose skirt blew up to her shoulders, exposing her underwear, as she emerged from the fun house. Your editor decided that this picture captured the fun mood of the fair and used it. The woman is now furious and is suing the paper for invasion of privacy — disclosure of a private fact. Discuss whether she has grounds for a lawsuit and whether you think you should have taken the picture.

 MindTap

FEATURED ONLINE ACTIVITIES: Log on to the MindTap for Rich's Writing and Reporting News to access a variety of robust additional material, including this chapter's learning objectives, activities, comprehension quizzes, and more!

COACHING TIPS

Examine all your **alternatives.**

Consider all the parties who will be affected. Do you need **other points of view?**

Weigh the **benefits and harms** of your decision.

Justify why you are making this decision.

Be **careful about what you post on social networks.** Your opinions and your personal information could conflict with your job.

CHAPTER 15
Media Ethics

© Faveninch/Shutterstock.com

If someone is going to be hurt by what gets printed or broadcast about them, then journalists need to provide a reason — a good reason — for going with it. "That's my job," doesn't cut it. Nor do appeals to First Amendment freedoms.

—**DENI ELLIOTT,** *Poynter–Jamison Chair in Media Ethics and Press Policy, University of South Florida*

C

ASE 1: YOU ARE A REPORTER FOR YOUR CAMPUS NEWSPAPER or TV station. A gunman entered one of the classrooms and began shooting, injuring three students before he fled. You check Facebook, where you find comments and photos from other students who were at the scene. You are on deadline and don't have much time to check the information on the site. Should you use the Facebook photos and comments if you attribute them to the names listed under the material?

The Associated Press Stylebook states: "You should never simply lift quotes, photos or video from social networking sites and attribute them to the name on the profile or feed you found them under." If you don't have time to check the accuracy of the information, don't use it.

Case 2: You are covering a campus rally on abortion issues. You have interviewed people from both sides of the issue — pro-life and pro-choice. You have also written a blog expressing your strong belief in the pro-life movement. Is it ethical for journalists to express their opinions in a blog or on social media sites if they are also covering the issue for news?

Many news organizations are developing guidelines to prohibit journalists from blogging or posting comments on social networks that might compromise their objectivity or fairness when covering news. The Radio Television Digital News Association offers these guidelines: "Be especially careful when you are writing, tweeting or blogging about a topic that you or your newsroom covers. Editorializing about a topic or person can reveal your personal feelings. Biased comments could be used in a court of law to demonstrate a predisposition, or even malicious intent, in a libel action against the news organization, even for an unrelated story."

Case 3: You are the editor of your campus news site, and you receive a tip that a local landlord is discriminating against students of color in renting apartments near your school. You assign a black reporter and a white reporter to go undercover to investigate the situation. The black reporter applies for an apartment, and the landlord says there are no vacancies. A few hours later the white reporter applies for an apartment, and the landlord shows him three vacant apartments that are available. Is it ethical to report this information without revealing that you are reporters?

A pro-choice rally

Night Owl/Creative Common

Pro-life supporters participate in the annual "March for Life" in Knoxville, Tenn.

Although most news organizations say deception should be used as a last resort, they still use it to a certain extent in investigative stories. However, before you publish any material you acquired in a deceptive manner, you should reveal your identity and seek comments from the sources you investigated.

Here are some other common ethical questions:

- Is it ethical for you to accept free food while you are covering a news event such as a political dinner or a sports activity?

- If you have granted confidentiality to a source, should you reveal the person's identity if the source proves to be unreliable?

- Is it ethical for a journalist to express personal opinions in a blog or Facebook page about a topic the reporter covers for the news in an organization?

Those are just a few of the typical questions the Ethics AdviceLine for Journalists receives (*ethicsadvicelineforjournalists.org*). The AdviceLine is a free service for professional journalists sponsored by the Chicago Headline Club Chapter of the Society of Professional Journalists and Loyola University Chicago Center for Ethics and Social Justice. The service will put journalists in contact with experts who will discuss the ethical dilemma on the phone at 866-DILEMMA. The Society of Professional Journalists also offers a hotline to provide advice about ethical issues at 317-927-8000 x208, or check online at *www.spj.org/ethicshotline.asp*.

Some of those ethical dilemmas have existed for many years without clear resolution, but social networks are creating new ethical problems for journalists. Ethical dilemmas have been included in every chapter, but in this chapter we'll examine some major cases and some approaches that can be used to make ethical decisions.

SOCIAL MEDIA

THE OVERALL ETHICAL guideline for social media is this one from the Radio Television Digital News Association: "As a journalist, you should uphold the same professional and ethical standards of fairness, accuracy, truthfulness, transparency and independence when using social media as you do on air and on all digital news platforms."

Although that is a good suggestion, some of the ethical dilemmas created by social media pose unique situations. Because readers and viewers get their news from several sources, truth can be elusive, and the lines between fact and opinion are often blurred.

One of the most common concerns in the media involves separating personal and professional material. Here are some guidelines about this issue from news organizations:

- From NPR: "Recognize that everything you write or receive on a social media site is public. Anyone with access to the Web can get access to your activity on social media sites. And regardless of how careful you are in trying to keep them separate, in your online activity, your professional life and your personal life overlap. . . . You must not advocate for political or other polarizing issues online. This extends to joining online groups or using social media in any form (including your Facebook page or a personal blog) to express personal views on a political or other controversial issue that you could not write for the air or post on NPR.org."

- From *The Roanoke Times* and the Poynter Institute, which collaborated in developing social networking policies: "Information gathered online should be independently confirmed offline. Interview sources in person or over the phone whenever possible. Verify claims and statements. Be transparent with the audience as well as sources. Let them know how you contacted people, in what context you gathered information and how you verified it (or didn't)."

- From RTDNA (Radio Television Digital News Association) social media and blogging guidelines: "When using content from blogs or social media, ask critical questions such as:

  - What is the source of the video or photograph? Who wrote the comment and what was the motivation for posting it?

  - Does the source have a legal right to the material posted? Did that person take the photograph or capture the video?

  - Has the photograph or video been manipulated?"

For other guidelines, check the Associated Press Stylebook section on social media guidelines.

CONFLICTS OF INTEREST

Students line up for a sorority rush at Purdue University. If you are a member of a sorority or fraternity during its rush, is it a conflict of interest if you cover the event?

Some of the most common dilemmas for journalists are conflicts of interest. If you are just beginning in journalism, you may not be aware of all the ways you might have conflicts. For example:

- Suppose you are a member of the GLBT (gay, lesbian, bisexual, transsexual) group in your college or university. Should you be assigned to cover the group's activities? Even if you are not an official member, but you are gay, should you still avoid covering the group's activities?

- If you belong to any other club or organization on campus, do you have to avoid covering its activities?

- If your boyfriend or girlfriend is running for an office or has a major role in a university group, do you have to avoid reporting or writing about him or her or his or her group?

- If you are actively supporting a local or national political party or candidate, can you cover any political stories of that party or the opposing one?

- If you want to date a source or if you get involved with your editor romantically, what should you do? Is it OK to date the source *after* you finish an assignment involving that person? Do you have to resign from the organization if you want to continue a relationship with the editor?

The simple answer to most of these questions is that you should avoid reporting or writing any story in which you have a personal relationship or competing loyalties.

Follow this advice from the Society of Professional Journalists: "Avoid conflicts of interest, real or perceived" and "remain free of associations and activities that may compromise integrity or damage credibility." The primary concern about conflicts of interest is that readers or viewers won't be able to trust that your reporting and writing are truthful and unbiased. That is also why these recommendations apply to social media.

Romantic liaisons are more difficult. You can't legislate love. In many cases news organizations will not have a problem if you date a source *after* the assignment, unless that person is an ongoing source in your beat. In that case, you should change your beat.

More problematic — and more common — are relationships that occur in the organizations between reporter and editor. If the organization is large enough, you can switch to another editor or change your beat. If not, you may just have to avoid any appearance of favoritism. And even worse, if the relationship fails, avoid any display of emotion in the office.

Almost all news organizations — collegiate and professional — prohibit journalists from obvious conflicts of interest such as writing about personal relationships or covering clubs, activities and political organizations in which they are involved.

Some college and professional news organizations require staff members to sign a disclosure form listing all the organizations, financial interests and political and personal relationships they have that could conflict with their news gathering responsibilities. Even if you don't sign a disclosure form, you should reveal any conflicts to your editor — or your professor — before you accept an assignment.

Conflicts of interest can extend beyond relationships. These are some of the other factors that pose conflicts of interest and are prohibited at many news organizations:

- **Gifts:** You should not accept gifts from sources before or after you cover a story. The Associated Press Stylebook suggests that caps, mugs and items of nominal value less than $25 might be the exception. The Society of Professional Journalists is more specific: "Refuse gifts, favors, fees, free travel and special treatment, and shun secondary employment, political involvement, public office and service in community organizations if they compromise journalistic integrity."

- **Free tickets:** Most organizations allow reporters to accept free tickets to a concert or performance if they are reviewing or writing about the event; otherwise you should pay for them.

- **Hospitality:** If you are interviewing someone at a restaurant, it's preferable to pay your own way.

- **Trips or free transportation:** If you are covering a campus or local athletic event that requires you to travel with the team or to the event, it may be difficult to pay your own way if the university or organization does not have a travel budget. Whenever it is possible, it is preferable to reimburse or pay the travel costs.

In all other cases, use your common sense. If the situation is going to make it appear as though you did not report the news fairly and accurately, take steps to avoid a real or perceived conflict of interest.

DECEPTION

A case of deception that generated considerable media discussion in the 1990s was the Food Lion/ABC-TV case. ABC television network reporters lied on job applications to get hired by the Food Lion supermarket chain, and they used hidden cameras and microphones to record employees processing food and discussing meat department practices. The reporters for "Primetime Live" then produced a story accusing Food Lion of selling rotten meat, fish and cheese. Food Lion didn't challenge the facts but instead sued for trespass and won a $5 million judgment. But the trial judge said that was too much and cut the award to $315,000. ABC appealed, and a federal court later reduced the award to just $2 — a dollar for trespassing and another dollar for breaching employees' legal duty of loyalty to an employer.

Could the reporters have gained the story any other way? ABC doesn't think so, but many other journalists have questioned the use of deception in this and other situations.

Although print and broadcast media have used hidden cameras for many years, they proliferated in television news magazine shows during the 1990s. One reason was the improved technology of cameras, which could be small enough to be hidden in tie clips. But media critics charged that a more common reason for using hidden cameras was sensationalism.

Deception remains controversial in ethical terms. Before using any form of deception, ask yourself if there is any other way to get the story. Louis Hodges, professor emeritus of ethics at Washington and Lee University, suggests that you apply three tests: importance, accuracy and safety. Ask yourself these questions:

- Is the information of such overriding public importance that it can help people avoid harm?
- Is there any way you could obtain the information through conventional reporting methods, such as standard interviews or public records?
- Are you placing innocent people at risk? For example, you should not pose as a nurse, law enforcement officer or employee in a job for which you might not be trained.

Deceptive reporting techniques are fraught with risks, such as lawsuits for invasion of privacy. On the other hand, deception may be the only way to reveal matters of great public concern. Even with such reasoning, using deception may still be unethical.

PLAGIARISM

The subjects of plagiarism and fabrication have been discussed in several other chapters in this book. Why so much attention to practices you surely wouldn't engage in? Even though technology has made it easier to plagiarize because accessibility to thousands of news sources is so easy, stealing words from someone else without attribution is not a new phenomenon. Nor is fabrication, which is making up quotes, adding false description and basically passing fictional material off as news.

Despite considerable publicity about Jayson Blair, a *New York Times* reporter who plagiarized and fabricated stories he wrote for the newspaper, journalism students and veteran journalists are apparently not getting the message that plagiarism and fabrication are serious infractions that can lead to firing and ruined careers. Blair had fabricated quotes and plagiarized several of his national stories for the *Times*, even claiming to interview sources he never contacted. The discovery of his deception led to his dismissal and a front-page story in the newspaper revealing his misdeeds. The case also resulted in the resignation of two top editors at the *Times*. This highly publicized case brought shame to the paper and awareness of plagiarism as a major problem in the media, but it didn't prevent it from continuing — even at *The New York Times*.

Size doesn't seem to matter when it comes to plagiarism. From college newspapers and small newspapers to large newspapers, scores of journalists have been fired for plagiarism. Every year more cases of plagiarism and fabrication in the media are uncovered, and they don't even include plagiarism of research papers in college. Nor do they include plagiarism in blogs, websites and social media.

Definition of plagiarize: "To take (ideas, writing, etc.) from another and pass them off as one's own" — from Webster's New World College Dictionary. If you copy material from someone and don't cite the source, you are plagiarizing. If you take someone else's article but change some of the words, is that plagiarism? Yes, according to this definition from plagiarism.org: "Changing only the words of an original source is NOT sufficient to prevent plagiarism. You must cite a source whenever you borrow ideas as well as words."

However, using someone else's idea for a news story is usually not considered plagiarism. U.S. copyright laws don't protect ideas. In the news business, it is considered good practice to localize a national story idea or to use an idea from another newspaper and do original reporting. The key is "original reporting." If you use all the same sources and the same anecdotes from another publication or broadcast, it may not constitute plagiarism, but it raises ethical questions.

The best practice is to cite your sources and if you use their exact words, make sure you use quotation marks around them.

PRIVACY ISSUES

Some of the most wrenching ethical dilemmas the media face involve people's privacy. You may have the legal right to publish certain information, but do you have the ethical right?

To understand the ethical concerns, it may help to define "ethics." Ethics is the study of choices about what we should or should not do, whereas morality is concerned with behavior. So ethics can be considered the process of making decisions about the way a person behaves. Some of these privacy issues involve public officials, celebrities, rape accusers and photo subjects in the news.

Public Officials

Would you print information about the sex life of a politician? When is the private life of a public figure relevant? When does it serve the public interest to publish such details?

In the summer of 1987, reporters and editors at *The Miami Herald* decided that the private life of a politician was relevant. Former Sen. Gary Hart was seeking the Democratic nomination for the presidency. Rumors of Hart's infidelity to his wife had circulated for months, and during the campaign the rumors called into question his character and credibility. When asked about the rumors, Hart challenged reporters to "follow me around . . . They'd be very bored." Acting on a tip that Hart had a relationship with a Florida model, *Herald* reporters staked out his townhouse. They revealed that Hart spent the night with the woman, Donna Rice. Hart never admitted that the relationship with Rice was sexual. Nevertheless, he withdrew his candidacy the day before *The Washington Post* was set to reveal evidence about his involvement in another affair.

At the time of this incident, although previous presidents and presidential candidates had engaged in extramarital affairs, their private lives had not been dissected in public. The sexual affairs of President Kennedy were not revealed until long after his assassination. But the Gary Hart case changed the nature of political reporting.

The nature of sexual revelations in political reporting changed even further during Bill Clinton's second term as president, when former White House intern

Former Sen. Gary Hart, D-Colo., (on the right) was the subject of news about his sexual relationships.

Monica Lewinsky testified to a grand jury that she had engaged in a sexual relationship with the president during her internship. Clinton denied the allegations when he testified in a court case brought against him by an Arkansas woman, Paula Jones, who claimed sexual harassment against Clinton when he was Arkansas governor. Then the day after his testimony, in a dramatic reversal of his previous denials, he admitted on national television that he had engaged in an "inappropriate relationship" with Monica Lewinsky.

The media followed Lewinsky day and night. Competition for any tidbit of information was keen. The media published unsubstantiated rumors, including sexual details, and relied heavily on anonymous sources and other media for news. That changed when Kenneth Starr, a special prosecutor investigating Clinton for obstruction of justice and perjury, released a grand jury report that contained graphic sexual details of the Clinton–Lewinsky relationship. The majority of newspapers in the United States either printed the entire report in a special section or posted it on their websites. Many newspapers offered a disclaimer that the content might be considered offensive. This report laid the groundwork for impeachment hearings on the charges that the president had committed perjury under oath when he originally denied having an affair with Lewinsky.

In November 1998, almost four years after the case began, Clinton agreed to pay Jones $850,000 to drop the case. But it didn't prevent him from being impeached.

Despite the serious turn the case took, media critics and the public still questioned whether the media had acted responsibly in relying heavily on anonymous sources and publishing rumors in the early stages of the saga. And the debate raged about whether a politician's private life should be dissected in public. The ethical dilemmas these stories posed will continue to be debated for years.

Reporters also face other ethical dilemmas about privacy when covering politicians. For example, is it in the public interest to reveal the criminal background of a candidate if he withdraws from the race before you can print the story?

Editors at the campus newspaper of the University of Kansas faced this dilemma after they found out that a candidate for student government had been convicted of indecent solicitation of a child six years earlier. When the candidate learned that the newspaper was planning to print the information, he held a press conference to resign his candidacy. He claimed it was because he had just learned he was HIV positive. At the same time, he resigned as director of the organization representing gays and lesbians on campus. He never referred to his criminal record, nor would he answer reporters' questions.

Two tickets to the impeachment trial of President Bill Clinton on Jan. 14, 1999

Courtesy of the Gerald R. Ford Presidential Library and Museum

Was his criminal record relevant to the public now that he was no longer a candidate for office or leader of the gay rights group? What harm would the publication of his record cause him? The student's friends pressured the editor not to run the story, saying it would cause their friend immense personal suffering when he was already suffering from the HIV-positive news. In addition, they said, he had already paid his debt to society by serving time in prison.

Stephen Martino, editor of *The University Daily Kansan* at the time, said the decision was the most difficult one he ever had to make as an editor. He said he decided to run the information because it was relevant; it was why the candidate resigned. Martino said the candidate had learned about his HIV-positive status three weeks earlier and had made no attempt to resign then. "To my way of thinking, omitting the truth is the same thing as lying. Had the *Kansan* not reported the full story as it knew it, it would have been accused of a cover-up, and its credibility would have been destroyed," Martino wrote in an editorial page column the day the story ran on the front page.

Angry students protested the next day by dumping copies of the *Kansan* on the lawn in front of the newspaper offices in the journalism school.

Naming Suspects

Consider another case that has given the media an ethical black eye. A pipe bomb had exploded in a park on the site of the Olympic games in Atlanta on July 27, 1996. One

University of Kansas students dump the campus newspaper to protest a story.

person was killed, and 111 others were injured. Initially, a security guard at the site, Richard Jewell, was declared a hero for alerting police to the bombing. Three days later, Jewell became a suspect when law enforcement officials leaked his name to the press.

Most newspapers withhold the name of a suspect until formal charges are filed. But this was a case of great national interest. Would you have published his name? The *Atlanta Journal-Constitution* did, stating that Jewell was a "target" of the investigation. That was just the beginning.

For the next 88 days, Jewell was profiled and followed by the media, and his past, present and future were the subject of news stories. Only one factor was missing: He was never charged in the crime. On Oct. 26, 1996, the FBI apologized and publicly admitted that Jewell was no longer a suspect. Eric Rudolph, accused of this bombing and several others at women's clinics where abortions were performed, was subsequently charged with the crime, convicted and sentenced to life in prison.

But Jewell claimed that his life had been ruined. In an emotional press conference after he was vindicated, he said: "For 88 days, I lived a nightmare. . . . Now I must face the other part of my nightmare," he said. "While the government can tell you that I am an innocent man, the government's letter cannot give me back my good name or my reputation."

Federal Bureau of Investigation

Eric Rudolph made the FBI's Ten Most Wanted Fugitives list and was later convicted of the Olympic Park bombing.

Jewell died in 2007, but news stories and obituaries still bore headlines identifying him as the Olympic Park bombing figure or suspect. The case has become a classic example in media ethics literature as a warning about the harm media can cause in naming or pursuing suspects before they are formally charged with a crime.

Rape Cases

Whether to name rape accusers is another continuing ethical debate in the media. Because of the stigma associated with rape, most news organizations withhold the names of people who claim they have been raped. The accuser cannot legitimately be called a "victim" until the case is decided.

That issue became apparent in a scandal involving three Duke University lacrosse players accused of rape. The case involved all the elements of a TV drama — racial conflict (a poor, black single mother with a troubled background who was earning money as a stripper versus three white students from wealthy families), a prosecutor who refused to release evidence that would have cleared the suspects, a prestigious university protecting its reputation, and a community torn by racial tension surrounding the case.

The case began when one of two strippers hired to dance at a party for the lacrosse team accused three of the players of raping her. The three players she identified were charged with rape, kidnapping and sexual offense. But DNA tests of the three players and all the other lacrosse team members did not match the rape-kit swabs taken from the woman at the hospital where she was examined after the party.

However, Durham County District Attorney Michael B. Nifong withheld this DNA evidence from the players' defense attorney and issued statements to the press calling the athletes "hooligans." Although the accuser changed her version of the story several times, the prosecutor persisted in trying the case. After a yearlong investigation, the players were exonerated and the district attorney was disbarred for unethical behavior.

"This woman has destroyed everything I worked for in my life," one of the players said on CBS's "60 Minutes" after the players were exonerated. "She's destroyed two other families, and she's brought shame on a great university. And worst of all, she's split apart a community and a nation on facts that just didn't happen and a lie that should have never been told."

The accused players were named in the press, but the accuser was not named until the case was resolved. After all the charges were dropped, one of the players said he would probably always be known as that Duke lacrosse player in the rape case. For that reason, the players' names will not be used in this textbook.

Although unrelated to that case, in 2013 the accuser, Crystal Mangum, was convicted and sentenced to 14 years in prison for the murder of her boyfriend. The headlines listed her as the "Duke lacrosse accuser."

Most news organizations still protect the accuser and name the suspects in rape cases, and the Duke case is unlikely to change those policies.

Geneva Overholser, professor at the University of Southern California Annenberg School of Journalism, is a staunch advocate for naming both the accuser and the accused. Years ago when she was editor of *The Des Moines* (Iowa) *Register,* she wrote a column saying the stigma of rape would be reduced if it were treated like any other crime and the names of rape victims were used.

Overholser still feels strongly that failing to name both parties in a rape case only prolongs the stigma of the crime for women. In a column for the Poynter Institute, she wrote: "The responsible course for responsible media today is this: Treat the woman who charges rape as we would any other adult victim of crime. Name her, and deal with her respectfully. And leave the trial to the courtroom."

Photo Subjects

Many privacy issues involve photographs. Should a photographer take a picture of a grieving mother whose son has drowned, even if she doesn't want the picture taken? At what point is a photograph an invasion of privacy?

Another concern for photo editors is taste: what readers or viewers need to see versus what they want to see. For example, should newspapers, websites or TV publish pictures that depict gore and tragedy even if they would upset readers and viewers? This issue is even more relevant these days when so many photos are posted on the photo-sharing site, Flickr, and on social media sites.

The media faced those ethical decisions when they received graphic video and photographs of Iraqi prisoners who were abused by U.S. soldiers at the Abu Ghraib prison outside Baghdad during the war in Iraq. The story, initially aired by CBS on "60 Minutes" and subsequently detailed in a *New Yorker* magazine article by Seymour M. Hersh, revealed torture inflicted on the prisoners by U.S. soldiers. Although *The New Yorker* did not print the photos, CBS showed some video, and *The Washington Post* published some photos in the newspaper and more photos and video on the *Post's* website. The photos, released to newspapers around the world, showed naked prisoners being taunted and humiliated by soldiers. One of the most dramatic photos showed two U.S. soldiers smiling in front of a human pyramid of naked prisoners. Another showed a soldier holding a leash around a naked man's neck.

The *Post* posted this note on its website with the photos: "Some of these photos may be disturbing because of their graphic or violent nature." The *Post* and other news organizations cropped or blurred photos that showed the prisoners' genitals. Both *The New York Times* and *The New York Daily News* ran a front-page photo of a naked prisoner being menaced by dogs used by the soldiers. Television news anchors also gave a warning to viewers about the graphic nature of the images they were about to see.

The public was incensed, and editors throughout the country wrestled with what they should print or air. In many cases, news organizations offered more photos on their Web pages but limited images in print. But Leonard Downie, then editor of *The Washington Post*, echoed the sentiments of many other news editors when he was quoted in the article as saying, "We decided that the importance of the news was the most important consideration."

Such ethical dilemmas arise daily at newspapers, television stations and websites, although rarely involving photos as graphically disturbing as these. But how do editors make those decisions, and how can you decide what is ethical?

MULTIMEDIA COACH

A YOUNG WOMAN was on the verge of jumping from a bridge in Seattle that is well known for suicides. A journalist approached the scene. First he called 911 and reported the situation to police. Then he posted a message on Twitter about the plight of the girl. Within minutes scores of other people began demanding updates on Twitter. Traffic by the bridge backed up, and one woman who complained that she had been stalled in traffic for an hour yelled, "Jump already," as did a few other drivers. The journalist tweeted minute-by-minute coverage of her actions and posted a photo of her as she stood by the bridge railing. Was it ethical for him to report her actions as they were happening?

Police negotiators came and talked the girl out of jumping. But the reporter said he knew the situation was ethically challenging and that he tried to avoid an online spectacle. However, he also felt that he couldn't ignore the situation, and he got caught up in the demands for updates on Twitter.

Although the news media rarely report suicides, times have changed because of convergence of print, TV and online media, especially mobile media. News is more immediate than ever. Journalists don't need a newsroom or a computer to report breaking news; they simply need a mobile phone. If the journalists don't respond immediately, citizens will report news on social media. Speed is not synonymous with accuracy.

News will continue to be delivered across many platforms and by many "citizen journalists." In some cases, that means journalists will publish first and think later. And the purveyors of news are not limited to journalists.

As a result, it is even more important to apply the code of ethics of the Society of Professional Journalists to multimedia news. Some of those basic principles state:

- Seek truth and report it. Journalists should test the accuracy of information from all sources.

- Identify sources whenever possible.

- Minimize harm. Show compassion for those who may be adversely affected by news coverage.

- Be accountable. Journalists should clarify and explain news coverage and invite dialogue with the public over journalistic coverage.

Whether it is a photo or a story, ethicist Louis Hodges suggests this guideline for privacy issues: Publish private information about public officials or public figures if it affects their public duties. But for victims of crime, publish private information only if they give their permission, because these are people with special needs and vulnerability.

ETHICAL REASONING

Journalists use several methods to justify their decisions. In most ethical dilemmas, editors and reporters discuss the issue and the consequences of publication before making the decision. They consider how newsworthy the story is and whether the public really needs this information. The process of ethical reasoning generally involves these three steps:

1. Define the dilemma. Consider all the problems the story or photograph will pose.

2. Examine all your alternatives. You can publish, not publish, wait for a while until you get more information before publishing, display the story or photo prominently or in a lesser position, or choose other options.

3. Justify your decision. Weigh the harms and the benefits of publication, or weigh such factors as relevance and importance of the story to the public.

The Poynter Institute Model

Robert M. Steele headed the ethics program at the Poynter Institute for 14 years before joining the faculty of DePauw University as a distinguished professor of ethics. While at Poynter, he developed these questions to help journalists make decisions in ethical dilemmas:

- Why am I concerned about this story, photo or graphic?
- What is the news? What good would publication do?
- Is the information complete and accurate, to the best of my knowledge?
- Am I missing an important point of view?
- What does my reader need to know?
- How would I feel if the story or photo were about a member of my family or me?
- What are the likely consequences of publication? What good or harm could result?
- What are my alternatives?
- Will I be able to clearly and honestly explain my decision to anyone who challenges it?

ETHICS

ETHICAL DILEMMA: Your campus newspaper has received an advertisement that promotes the revisionist point of view that the Nazi Holocaust of World War II never occurred. The ad, accompanied by a $125 check, was sent by the Committee for Open Debate on the Holocaust, an organization run by Bradley R. Smith from his home in Visalia, California. He sent the advertisement to colleges all over the U.S. In a cover letter he urges campus editors to run the ad to promote dialogue and to support the First Amendment.

When the University of Miami campus newspaper, *The Miami Hurricane*, ran the ad, nearly 400 students demonstrated outside the newspaper. A wealthy alumnus threatened to withdraw a $2 million gift but later recanted when the school promised to offer courses on the Holocaust. Other school newspapers have refused to print the ad. You know that this ad will offend many people on your campus and in your community, but you want to uphold the First Amendment. Will you run this ad or reject it and return the check? Justify your decision.

CODES OF ETHICS

Many news organizations have devised codes of ethics that govern the behavior of employees. These include policies about accepting gifts or freelance assignments as well as guidelines about conflicts of interest.

Staff members who violate these policies at newspapers can be fired, and many have been. In some cases, reporters have been fired for entering into business relationships with a source or for using for personal gain information they get from sources. Journalism societies, such as the Radio Television Digital News Association and the Public Relations Society of America, also have basic codes of ethics to guide members.

Principles common to all the codes include adhering to accuracy, telling the truth, minimizing harm and avoiding conflicts of interest.

For links to codes of ethics, check the website for this chapter.

EXERCISES

1 Apply ethical reasoning, using the Poynter Institute guidelines, to the following cases (or to other cases described in this chapter):

- An anonymous source tells you that a U.S. senator for your state has voted against many gay rights issues even though he is gay. You have heard other rumors that the senator is homosexual, but the senator has denied that the rumors are true. What will you do about this story?

- You have heard rumors that your local nursing home is abusing its clients. However, no complaints have been filed with state regulatory agencies or with the police. You have contacted some of the clients' family members, who say they are concerned but have no proof. Will you go undercover as a volunteer aide at the nursing home (no special training required) to investigate?

2 Discuss the ethical dilemma, described in this chapter under "Public Officials," about revealing the criminal record of the student government candidate who resigned before the story could be published. What would you do if you were the editor of your campus publication or broadcast station? Do you agree or disagree with the decision made by the editor of *The University Daily Kansan*?

3 You are writing a story about problems of online pornography and the groups that oppose it. The story will be published on your campus website. Will you link to the pornography sites that the groups find objectionable?

 MindTap

FEATURED ONLINE ACTIVITIES: Log on to the MindTap for Rich's Writing and Reporting News to access a variety of robust additional material, including this chapter's learning objectives, activities, comprehension quizzes, and more!

CHAPTER 16
Multicultural Sensitivity

Language is the source of misunderstandings.
—**ANTOINE DE SAINT-EXUPÉRY,** *The Little Prince*

COACHING TIPS

Seek sources from **different racial and ethnic backgrounds** for all kinds of stories, not just stories about minorities.

Ask your sources **how they prefer to be addressed.**

Ask yourself if you would write the **same type of description for a man as for a woman,** for a white source as for a person of color, for a disabled person or member of any other ethnic or special group.

WHAT DO YOU THINK OF WHEN YOU HEAR THE WORD "ALIEN"?

Does it conjure up an image of a creature from outer space? Now add the word "illegal," and you get a term that the National Association of Hispanic Journalists (NAHJ) considers derogatory.

"The association has always denounced the use of the degrading terms 'alien' and 'illegal alien' to describe undocumented immigrants because it casts them as adverse, strange beings, inhuman outsiders who come to the U.S. with questionable motivations," according to the NAHJ in a news release. Even more objectionable to the association are headlines using the word "illegals" as a noun.

"Using the word in this way is grammatically incorrect and crosses the line by criminalizing the person, not the action they are purported to have committed. The NAHJ calls on the media to never use 'illegals' in headlines."

Instead of terms such as "illegal aliens" or "illegal immigrants" used by many news media, the NAHJ prefers the terms "undocumented worker" or "undocumented immigrant."

The Associated Press Stylebook agreed in 2013 when it banned the term "illegal immigrant," and went even further by changing its acceptable definitions to the following: "Except in direct quotes essential to a story, do not use the terms 'illegal alien' 'an illegal,' 'illegals' or the term 'undocumented.' Acceptable variations include 'living in or entering a country illegally or without legal permission.'"

As the population of the U.S. continues to change, journalists and public relations practitioners need to be aware of such concerns about terminology and other issues in a multicultural society.

By 2050 more than half the population in the country will be a mixture of Hispanics, Asians and blacks, with Hispanics making up nearly 29 percent of the residents, according to the U.S. Census Bureau. The Asian-American population will have the next largest increase, going from 5.1 percent to 9.2 percent of the population.

Both old and young populations will also have dramatic increases. The number of people over age 65 will more than double, to 20 percent of the population by 2050, but more than half of all children in the U.S. will be minorities by 2023, the Census Bureau reports.

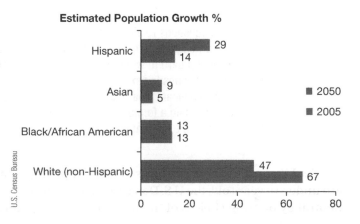

Estimated Population Growth %

U.S. Census Bureau

The U.S. Census Bureau says that by 2023 half of all American children will be minorities.

THE LANGUAGE OF MULTICULTURALISM

Race is not the only issue creating confusion and consternation over language. Terms for gender, sexual orientation, religious affiliation and nationality can all create negative interpretations among different groups.

Gender-Neutral Language

You may be a freshman in college, but not in any state-funded school in Washington. If you are in your first year of college in that state, you are a "first-year student." You can't be a fireman or a policeman there either — only a "firefighter" or a "police officer" if those words are in any state documents.

In 2013 Washington passed a new law banning "gender-specific" words in state laws. Nor is Washington alone. Several other states, including California, Hawaii, Maryland, New York and Rhode Island, have gender-neutral requirements for state documents, and other states are considering them.

The trend to avoid using terms for gender or sexual orientation that might offend people isn't limited to states. If you are applying for a federal student loan from the U.S. Department of Education, you don't need to specify "mother" and "father" anymore. "Parent One" and "Parent Two" can substitute on the forms where the department is trying to establish the student's legal parents regardless of their marital status or gender. This change in language will "provide an inclusive form that reflects the diversity of American families," said Arne Duncan, secretary of education.

The new regulations are in keeping with a Supreme Court decision that declared portions of the Defense of Marriage Act unconstitutional that barred the federal government from recognizing same-sex marriages that were legalized by states. The Education Department issued this explanation:

> For all FAFSA questions related to marital status, applicants who are married or the married parents of dependent applicants must respond as married without regard to whether the marriage is between individuals of the same sex or opposite sex. This applies if the applicant and applicant's spouse, or the applicant's parents, were legally married in any state or jurisdiction (including a foreign country), without regard to where the couple resides or where the student will be attending college.

And if you were born overseas and are applying for a passport for the first time or are under 16 years old, the U.S. Department of State also wants to make sure it is gender neutral by offering choices of "mother," "father" or "parent" on its application form.

In these cases, the government has made the decision for you to avoid terminology that might be considered offensive by the gay, lesbian, bisexual or transgendered community. But gender-neutral language involves only a fraction of the terms that can cause communication problems. And even when you think you are being sensitive, language preferences change.

For example, "African-American" is the term preferred by many blacks, but it is not accepted at all newspapers and television news organizations. "Chicano" is preferred by Mexican-Americans in some parts of the country, yet it is offensive to many older members of the group. "People of color" is a term preferred by many organizations with a majority of nonwhite members.

How can a journalist know the proper term to use? Any terms that might be acceptable today could be out of vogue tomorrow. The easiest solution is to ask how the source prefers to be addressed. But journalists have many other guides, starting with The Associated Press Stylebook. In addition groups representing various cultural and racial communities also have style guidebooks.

The National Lesbian and Gay Journalists Association has published a stylebook that offers helpful information for terms that are often used, but not clearly interpreted. For example, when it is relevant, should you write about someone's "sexual orientation" or "sexual preference"? The association's stylebook says avoid "sexual preference," which is a politically charged term implying that sexuality is the result of a conscious choice. Instead the stylebook recommends "sexual orientation." You can download the stylebook free at *www.nlgja.org/files/NLGJAStylebook0712.pdf.*

Definitions of Race

Meta G. Carstarphen, author of several books and articles about race and gender, discovered that journalists have a difficult time defining race. In a study she conducted, 40 percent of the journalists defined race as skin color or physical characteristics and 28 percent defined it as ethnicity. The remainder gave various definitions involving social and political differences.

Other terms related to race, diversity and multicultural topics are equally confusing.

"Diversity is the street where I live, and I would argue the neighborhood that all of us inhabit," Carstarphen wrote in a blog. "One definition I found online equates diversity with 'variety' and 'multiformity.' Diversity in some ways is too placid a term, connoting just the right mix of different elements, operating in a perfect balance with all of its parts. But I think the experience of diversity involves a sometimes raucous, sometimes contentious and sometimes blissful set of interactions."

Courtesy of Meta Carstarphen

Meta G. Carstarphen, graduate director, Gaylord College of Journalism and Mass Communication, University of Oklahoma

Racial Identifiers

The way the media identify minority groups is often considered contentious.

The Asian American Journalists Association (AAJA) conducts a "Media Watch" group to keep tabs on racial identifiers it considers offensive. The organization writes letters to editors or publishers when it finds stereotypical or negative portrayal of Asian-Americans, such as this note to *The Wall Street Journal* in reference to an article entitled "Furniture — Coping with the Asian Invasion."

> "Asian invasion" implies something ominous and dangerous; it also reinforces the bigoted belief — it continues to fester in some quarters of our society — that people of Asian descent are foreigners who are to be kept out at all cost.

The newspaper editor responded, saying no bigotry was intended but also thanking the association for calling the item to his attention.

In another case, the group objected to comments a radio station sports commentator made about Asian golfers at the U.S. Women's Golf Championship at Interlachen, Minnesota. "The fact of the matter is that we have these kids named Kim, Park and Lee out there. . . . It's hard to tell one of these kids from the other for us who don't follow LPGA golf real closely."

The association wrote to the radio station saying it found the comments offensive because "they reinforce the stereotype that all Asians resemble each other."

> The remarks take on a racial overtone with the implication being "well, they all look alike anyway, don't they?" Asia is a large continent with a diverse cross section of cultures, languages and physical characteristics. One could not imagine a sports columnist implying that all golfers from Europe are identical in appearance.

In a another letter to an editor at KTNV-TV in Las Vegas, Nevada, the president of AAJA complained about a phrase:

> We want to caution you on the use of the phrase, "yellow faces," in describing Asian-Americans. It is a misnomer and an outdated one at that. Asian-Americans are not yellow-skinned, after all.

The organization provides a stylebook for terms and issues referring to Asian-American and Pacific Islanders (*www.aaja.org/aajahandbook*).

It is not the only organization that offers a style guide for terms to improve sensitivity to a racial group. The National Association of Black Journalists (NABJ)

Courtesy of U.S. Marine Corps

Students attend a journalism workshop operated by the National Association of Black Journalists, which also offers a style guide.

also offers a stylebook as a resource to supplement the Associated Press Stylebook (*www.nabj.org/?styleguide*).

When referring to African-Americans, the association says "African," "African-American" and "black" are acceptable. But it adds:

> Not all black people are African-Americans (if they were born outside of the United States). Let a subject's preference determine which term to use. In a story in which race is relevant and there is no stated preference for an individual or individuals, use black because it is an accurate description of race. . . . Do not use race in a police description unless the report is highly detailed and gives more than just the person's skin color. In news copy, aim to use black as an adjective, not a noun. Also, when describing a group, use black people instead of just blacks. In headlines, blacks, however, is acceptable.

The term "people of color" is also acceptable as a synonym for minorities, according to the style guide.

ETHICS

ETHICAL DILEMMA: This photo was taken of the celebration at the end of a three-day conference of the Black Student Government at the University of Kansas and published in the student newspaper. African-American students at the university complained. Why? Do you think there is anything insensitive about this photo?

After students complained, the editor of *The University Daily Kansan* wrote this column:

....

Newspapers have a responsibility to present the news in a way that portrays the reality of an event or issue. At the Kansan we take this responsibility seriously. But in regard to the photos used to illustrate the 16th annual Big Eight Conference on Black Student Government, our coverage was irresponsible. . . .

By including photos that represented only four hours of a three-day event, we misrepresented the conference. But even worse, we perpetuated a stereotype.

The photos were of African-Americans dancing and singing. On the sports page that same day, five African-American athletes were pictured. Those were the only photos of African-Americans in that issue.

Dancing, singing and slam dunking: These are too often the only images of African-Americans that newspapers provide to their readers. I or someone else in the newsroom should have realized before the photos were printed that we were perpetuating this stereotype of African-Americans.

My goal for this column is to help our readers understand what we did and why we were wrong for doing it. We have learned from our mistake. We hope others will learn from it, too.

....

Photo by Daron J. Bennett/University Daily Kansan

This photo caused a controversy at the University of Kansas.

For "diversity," the guidebook gives this broad definition:

> Catchall term to describe a condition or environment that is multira-
> cial and multicultural; being representative or reflective of the multi-
> ethnic society. Diversity is not synonymous with affirmative action, is
> not limited to race and is not government-mandated. A company can
> have a diverse staff mixing races, ages, sexes, sexual orientation, etc.

MINORITIES IN THE NEWS

Multicultural sensitivity involves not only the sources you use but also the kinds of
stories you choose. Innumerable studies have been conducted to show how women
and minorities are portrayed in biased or stereotypical fashion. Minorities are often
featured in stories about crime but excluded as sources in general stories about life-
styles, the economy and other stories where experts are cited. Conversely, women and
minorities are often portrayed as unusual if they have operated a successful business
or accomplished some of the same newsworthy feats as white males.

Mervin Aubespin, former president of the National Association of Black Journalists,
said one way the media can become more sensitive to the needs of minorities is

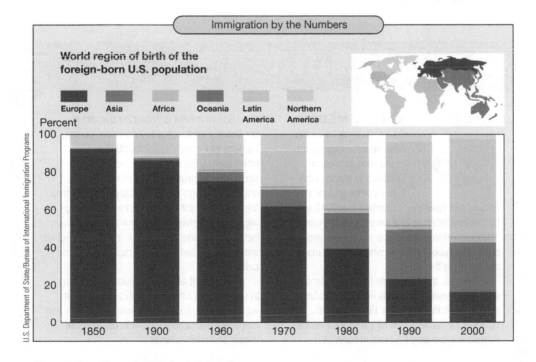

Changes in regions of origin for immigration

to hire more minorities. As the U.S. population becomes more diverse, the need for minority representation in the media workforce and in media coverage is only going to increase. But newspapers and broadcast media do not reflect the nation's diversity.

The big picture of minority employment in television news and newspapers has changed very little in the last 20 years, according to Robert Papper, a Hofstra University professor who conducts an annual survey of broadcast news employment.

The minority population in the U.S. is 36.6 percent, but it is only 21.4 percent in the TV workforce, according to Papper's 2013 survey for the Radio Television Digital News Association. Percentages are even lower at newspapers, where minority journalists make up only 12.4 percent of newsroom employees, according to a survey by the American Society of News Editors.

Aubespin said hiring minorities is only the first step; editors have to encourage minority reporters to express their diversity. One of the problems is that white editors "really want black faces that write like whites," he said. "There is no formula, no one way to write about a minority group. The best guideline is to treat each person as an individual. We are as different as you are."

Stories about terrorism have created another problem for journalists. The media are often blamed for stereotyping Muslims and Arab-Americans in connection with these stories. The Society of Professional Journalists offers these guidelines for countering racial, ethnic and religious profiling:

- Do not represent Arab-Americans and Muslims as monolithic groups. Avoid conveying the impression that all Arab-Americans and Muslims wear traditional clothing.

SOCIAL MEDIA

SOCIAL MEDIA SITES such as Twitter have become major communication venues for Latinos and blacks, who lead all other groups in texting and tweeting, according to a 2012 study by the Pew Internet and American Life Project. "Minority Internet users are more than twice as likely to use Twitter as white Internet users," according to the study.

Overall, the Pew study found 67 percent of Internet users use social networking sites, according to the study. For Hispanics that figure is 72 percent. It is 68 percent for African Americans, but only 65 percent for whites.

Social media is "coloring the world we live in," according to Ana Roca-Castro, founder of Latinos in Social Media (*latism.org*), the largest organization of social media professionals of Hispanic origin. "Through blogging, they have planted themselves right at the epicenter of merging worlds: between tradition and modernity, between off-line and on-line, between English and Spanish, between American and Latino cultures."

Women of all cultures outnumber men in using social networking sites (71 percent women versus 62 percent men) and blacks and Hispanics outnumber whites in using social media on mobile phones.

- When describing Islam, keep in mind there are large populations of Muslims around the world, including in Africa, Asia, Canada, Europe, India and the United States. Distinguish between various Muslim states; do not lump them together as in constructions such as "the fury of the Muslim world."

- Avoid using word combinations such as "Islamic terrorist" or "Muslim extremist" that are misleading because they link whole religions to criminal activity. Be specific: Alternate choices, depending on context, include "al-Qaida terrorists" or, to describe the broad range of groups involved in Islamic politics, "political Islamists." Do not use religious characterizations as shorthand when geographic, political, socioeconomic or other distinctions might be more accurate.

- Ask men and women from within targeted communities to review your coverage and make suggestions.

GENDER DIFFERENCES

The principles for coverage of gender are the same as they are for coverage of ethnic minorities. Make an effort to include female sources as experts in general stories, not just stories geared to women. Seek diversity of opinion, but write about people as being all equal. When you write about a woman, don't include descriptive details about her appearance unless you would also include descriptive details about a man's appearance.

How can you avoid sexism and gender stereotypes? In addition to the gender-neutral language described earlier, here are some other tips from in *The Gannetteer*, a magazine for employees of Gannett newspapers:

- "Avoid stereotypes in illustrations and graphics.

- Avoid calling groups of people men, unless they are all male. A congressional group should be called lawmakers or members of Congress, not Congressmen.

- Avoid referring to women by their first names in stories. This is almost always patronizing, and not usually done to men.

- Avoid describing women with adjectives that dwell on sexual attributes. Ask yourself whether you would describe the walk of an IBM executive as 'suggestive' if you were profiling a man, or would the walk just seem 'confident'? Ditto for 'feisty.' When is the last time you saw a man described as 'feisty'?

- Be careful with 'first' stories: the first woman to pick up the garbage for a living, fly into space or run for the school board. (*However, if it is a first, it may be worth mentioning, but it does not have to be the focus of the story.*)

- Avoid phrases that carry an element of surprise such as 'smart and dedicated woman.' Is it unusual that someone who is smart and dedicated is a woman too?

- Beware of approaching any story with the subconscious idea that it is more of a man's story or a woman's. Almost always we quote women in stories about child care. Why not men? A lack of child care is just as big a problem to them — or should be."

MULTIMEDIA COACH

THE INTERNET IS a multicultural Mecca for sources. More than a dozen journalism organizations devoted to racial and ethnic groups offer websites with sources and research. Here are some ways you can use the Web to improve your coverage of diversity:

■ Subscribe to blogs and social networking sites about diversity.

■ Do a search for blogs about diversity and racial issues.

■ Read ethnic newspapers online.

■ Check minority journalism organizations for sources.

■ Check online diversity organizations for internships, job opportunities, scholarships and guidelines to help journalists become sensitive to diversity.

■ Check network and cable news stations, and analyze the coverage of people of color as well as the reporters and anchors.

GUIDELINES FOR WRITING ABOUT SPECIAL GROUPS

Every group has some special needs and concerns about language. A man who uses a wheelchair probably doesn't consider himself handicapped (a derogatory term). However, he may have a disability that requires him to use a wheelchair. A person who has AIDS is not a victim, but rather an AIDS patient or a person living with AIDS. And not all people over age 65 are ready for the stereotypical rocking chair.

You cannot be expected to memorize dictionaries for each special interest group. However, if your beat is a specialty that frequently deals with aging, disabled people, AIDS or some other minority interest, you could call an umbrella organization and ask for guidelines. Most organizations have these printed.

Your first source, however, should be the people you interview. Ask them how they prefer to be addressed. Next, consult the Associated Press Stylebook, which includes guidelines under such listings as "handicapped," "disabled" and "AIDS." You'll minimize trouble by avoiding the use of adjectives to describe people.

People with Disabilities

Do not characterize someone as disabled unless that condition is crucial to the story. Avoid the word "handicapped," unless the person uses it to describe himself. If the disability is a factor, don't say "disabled people." Instead, use "people with disabilities." Avoid such terms as "crippled" and "deformed."

These Paralympic athletes are participating in a wheelchair race. Avoid describing people as "handicapped" or "wheelchair bound," and try to be specific about a disability if necessary.

Many euphemisms — such as "physically challenged," "partially sighted" and "physically inconvenienced" — have come into vogue. However, disability groups object to such euphemisms because they are considered condescending. The AP Stylebook also says to avoid euphemisms such as "mentally challenged" and descriptions that connote pity, such as "afflicted with" or "suffers from" a particular disease. Just say the person has multiple sclerosis or other applicable disease.

Heather Kirkwood, a former journalism student at the University of Kansas, is legally blind but can see with the use of various aids. She doesn't like being called "visually challenged" or "partially sighted." She prefers the term "blind." But she says organizations representing blind people disagree with her and insist that the distinction between partially and fully blind should be made.

"As far as political correctness, my own feelings are that it isn't the word, it is what the word means," Kirkwood says. "Saying 'visually impaired' instead of 'blind' doesn't really change the way the blind are viewed in society. What matters is what comes to mind when you say the word 'blind.' Progress is changing what it means to be blind, not changing the word for it."

Kirkwood acknowledges that many stories about people with disabilities have that same "gee whiz" factor as stories about successful women.

"As far as the 'amazing factor,' that must really confuse people," she says. "Many blind people truly believe they are amazing. That is because we are taught to think that from a very early age. . . . The biggest problem we face is not blindness, but rather the public's perception of blindness."

Here are some more tips:

- When interviewing people with disabilities, do not speak louder unless the person has a hearing impairment. A common complaint of people who have disabilities unrelated to their hearing is that everyone treats them as though they were hearing impaired. Treat people with disabilities exactly as you would any other source.

- Avoid overcompensating by writing about people with disabilities as though they were superhuman. The hidden implication is that all people with disabilities are without talent and that your source is unusual.

- Avoid writing about people with disabilities as though they don't have any faults.

- Avoid using adjectives as nouns to describe a group of people with disabilities, such as "the deaf" or "the retarded." Say "people who are deaf "or "people with mental retardation." For people who are blind, "visually impaired" is a preferred term.

- For mental illness, avoid such terms as "crazy" and "demented." "Psychotic" and "schizophrenic" should be used in context — and only if they are the proper medical terms. Preferred terms are "people with emotional disorders" or "people with psychiatric illness," "mental problems" or "mental disabilities."

- Avoid "gee whiz" stories that stress how amazing it is that this person could accomplish anything special, given his disability.

Stories About Aging

If there were ever a group especially prone to "gee whiz" stories, it would have to be people over age 65. Most newspaper feature stories treat people in this age group as absolutely amazing just because they walk, run, dance or accomplish anything. People over 65 are usually described as "spry," sometimes "feisty," but always "remarkable."

The population in the U.S. is aging, and people over age 65 are among the fastest-growing group in the country, according to the U.S. Census. But for many years the journalists who wrote about them were considerably younger, and much of the coverage revealed a lack of understanding and sensitivity even though the intent may have been well meaning.

Consider this feature:

This place hops.

The food's tame, the dance steps slower than they used to be, the stiffest drink comes from the water fountain.

Still the Gray Crowd jams the Armory Park Senior Citizens Center.

Typically, 1,200 men and women gather daily for gossip, games, and yes — even to cast some plain old-fashioned goo-goo eyes.

— *The* (Tucson) *Arizona Daily Star*

U.S. Army Sgt. 1st Class Michael Carden/Department of Defense

Senior veterans participate in the Golden Age Games.

Or the story will feature a twist — surprise, surprise, they're old!

The teams, each with two rows of participants, face one another. As the blue balloon floats through the air, the two seemingly docile teams transform into aggressive competitors.

You'd think they were teenagers. They were . . . perhaps 50 or more years ago.

— *Tulsa* (Oklahoma) *World*

Make age a factor, not the focus of a person's accomplishments. Readers can decide for themselves if the person's accomplishments are surprising because of the person's age. Especially avoid the astonishment factor: "Isn't it amazing this person can accomplish such and such at this age?"

Here are some general guidelines for dealing with people of this age:

- When writing about people over age 65, avoid such adjectives as "gray-haired" or other terms unless you would use the same type of description if the story were about a younger person with blond or brown hair.

- Avoid stereotypes. Don't introduce rocking chairs or similar stereotypical images if the people in the story aren't using them.

- Avoid the "graying population," "senior citizens" and other group designations unless you are writing a trend story. And then use such a term only if it is relevant, necessary and appropriate — for example, if a group uses the term in its own name, as in Gray Power.

- Avoid saying such things as "She doesn't consider herself old," unless she says it. Even though you are meaning to extend a compliment, by writing such denials you are introducing a stereotype.

AIDS Stories

In the last 20 years, medical developments have improved the life span of people living with AIDS, but the disease still carries a stigma. It is a subject that still requires the reporter to use great sensitivity.

Jacqui Banaszynski, a distinguished professor at the University of Missouri School of Journalism, says one of the reasons AIDS stories differ from other stories is the social stigma. "The disease is one story, the social context of the disease becomes another story. If you ignore the opportunity to deal with the societal revulsion, you miss the whole crux."

Banaszynski knows firsthand how difficult it can be to interview people with AIDS. She did it long before the disease was understood and before medicines existed to prolong the life of patients with AIDS. Death was the only certainty when she wrote a series that won the 1988 Pulitzer Prize for feature writing.

The rules change for this kind of story, Banaszynski says. "You have to be empathetic. On the other hand, you have to be honest and true to the reader who may be hostile to the subject. You walk a fine line between not blaming and not whitewashing."

Banaszynski, then a reporter for the *St. Paul* (Minnesota) *Pioneer Press*, spent 15 months reporting how a Minnesota farmer, Dick Hanson, and his partner Bert Henningson lived and died with AIDS.

Readers don't want to read about AIDS or deal with it, she says. So she decided that the best approach was to portray these two men as two ordinary Minnesotans who had a commonality with readers. "If Joe and Suzy Reader could not relate to two gay pig farmers, they could relate to two men who plant impatiens, feed kittens and tend a vegetable garden, because that's what all Minnesotans do." In her introduction, she stresses that this is a story about people living — as well as dying — with AIDS:

Death is no stranger to the heartland. It is as natural as the seasons, as inevitable as farm machinery breaking down and farmers' bodies giving out after too many years of too much work.

But when death comes in the guise of AIDS, it is a disturbingly unfamiliar visitor, one better known in the gay districts and drug houses of the big cities, one that shows no respect for the usual order of life in the country.

The visitor has come to rural Glenwood, Minnesota.

Dick Hanson, a well-known liberal political activist who homesteads his family's century-old farm south of Glenwood, was diagnosed last summer with acquired immune deficiency syndrome. His partner of five years, Bert Henningson, carries the AIDS virus.

In the year that Hanson has been living — and dying — with AIDS, he has hosted some cruel companions: blinding headaches and failing vision, relentless nausea and deep fatigue, falling blood counts and worrisome coughs and sleepless, sweat-soaked nights.

He has watched as his strong body, toughened by 37 years on the farm, shrinks and stoops like that of an old man. He has weathered the family shame and community fear, the prejudice and whispered condemnations. He has read the reality in his partner's eyes, heard the death sentence from doctors and seen the hopelessness confirmed by the statistics.

But the statistics tell only half the story — the half about dying.

Statistics fail to tell much about the people they represent. About the people like Hanson — a farmer who has nourished life in the fields, a peace activist who has marched for a safer planet, an idealist and a gay activist who has campaigned for social justice and now an AIDS patient who refuses to abandon his own future, however long it lasts.

The statistics say nothing of the joys of a carefully tended vegetable garden and new kittens under the shed, of tender teasing and magic hugs. Of flowers that bloom brighter and birds that sing sweeter and simple pleasures grown profound against the backdrop of a terminal illness. Of the powerful bond between two people who pledged for better or worse and meant it.

"Who is to judge the value of life, whether it's one day or one week or one year," Hanson said. "I find the quality of life more important than the length of life."

Much has been written about the death that comes from AIDS, but little has been said about the living. Hanson and Henningson want to change that. They have opened their homes and their hearts to tell the whole story — beginning to end.

— Jacqui Banaszynski, *St. Paul* (Minnesota) *Pioneer Press*

Ground Rules for Sensitive Questions

When you write about AIDS, you have to ask about dying, and you have to ask about sex. How do you approach either of these sensitive questions?

"The only thing to do is to set it in context," Banaszynski says. "When I get to it, I ask as directly as I can: How many men did you sleep with? I don't warn them that this is a hard question. I set that up in the ground rules. I say, 'We're going to talk about a lot of personal things, and a lot may be embarrassing. You don't have to answer, but I'll try to get you to answer.' If you ask honestly and directly with no judgment in your voice so there is no shame involved, they will answer. If you are embarrassed, they will pick it up. I ask the question as matter-of-factly as I would about the weather."

Banaszynski says people are really very eager to tell their stories. "I think you can ask anybody any question if you are nonjudgmental and a good listener. Nobody listens anymore."

When she wrote the stories, she also did something that is not general practice in journalism. "I called each person involved in the story and read them their quotes, and I told them the context. For example, in one case I said, 'I set you in the context of a fight with your family.' Then I told them, if you can convince me that I have erred or been insensitive, I'll consider changing it." Only one person complained. She didn't take out any of his comments, but she added a sentence that appeased him.

She also took the newspaper to Hanson and Henningson the night before it hit the morning newspaper stands, so they could see it first. "They couldn't change anything, but that's just courtesy. If they allow me to invade their privacy, I owe them that courtesy."

Banaszynski says the ground rules are different when you are writing about people who are not accustomed to dealing with the media. "These people don't know the rules. I have more responsibility to tell them what I'm going to be writing, the general thrust and what I'm trying to do."

Banaszynski predicts that it will get increasingly difficult to interest the public in AIDS stories. "The one thing you always have to remember about AIDS is that it has an overlay of homosexuality," she says. "It is a stigmatized disease that the public doesn't want to read about. You have to get past a big barrier of rejection.

"You have to focus on the common denominator. This could be your brother or neighbor or your doctor. AIDS serves as an extreme example of all the challenges in reporting more than other stories. You have got to find ways to have it connect to everyone's life."

EXERCISES

1 **Multicultural story ideas:** Interview members of various ethnic and racial groups in your community or on your campus about their concerns and the kinds of stories they think newspapers are not writing about them. Devise 10 story ideas based on your interviews.

2 **Sexism, ageism and racism:** Develop your own media watch group or become a member of one. Look for examples of language, description or other elements of stories that you think are sexist, racist or ageist. Find at least five examples in print, broadcast or online media that you think would be offensive to a minority group.

3 **Gender coverage:** Using highlighters of two different colors, read the news sections of your newspaper for a few days. Use one color to mark the female sources quoted and the other color for the male sources. Analyze the types of stories that feature women more than men, and vice versa. Also try to determine whether multicultural sources are used in the news stories.

4 **Multicultural profile:** Interview a person on campus who is a member of a minority group — whether because of the person's race, ethnic background or sexual orientation. The focus should be this person's feelings about how the media treat

members of his or her minority. Get some background about the person.

Then ask questions related to the focus. Some questions to include might be these:

- How do you prefer to be addressed? How do you think the media portray people in your minority group? Are the portrayals positive or negative? (Ask for specific examples.) Have you ever experienced insensitivity or prejudice because of your race, ethnic background, disability or special interests? (Please specify.)

- Have you ever been interviewed by the media? Was your experience good or bad? (Please specify.) What advice would you give to reporters about coverage of minorities such as yourself? (Again, ask for specifics.) Write your findings in the form of a mini-profile.

Here are some additional questions that Meta Carstarphen asks her students to pose in similar interviews:

- Tell me about where you were born and grew up. Do you think the racial attitudes at your home are different from the ones you experience here?

- How do you describe yourself physically? When do you think about race? What makes that happen?

- Would your life be different if you were another gender or a different race? Why or why not? If so, what ways would those differences be evident?

5 Perceptions of language: As you read the following terms, write the first *descriptive* words that come to your mind; then discuss whether your perceptions are stereotypes:

Texas	African-American	lesbian
ghetto	gay	truck driver
Hispanic	Asians	firefighter
Jewish	Native Americans	basketball player
Irish	Catholics	inner city
alien	immigrant	minority

6 Advertising: Watch advertisements on television for one or two days, and analyze whether they are more inclusive of racial groups than other media. Discuss which racial groups are most represented in television advertisements. Compare those ads with print ads in your newspaper or in magazines you read. Are the ads in one medium more racially diverse than in another? Discuss how men and women are portrayed in ads, especially on television. Do the ads reflect or promote stereotypes?

 MindTap

FEATURED ONLINE ACTIVITIES: Log on to the MindTap for Rich's Writing and Reporting News to access a variety of robust additional material, including this chapter's learning objectives, activities, comprehension quizzes, and more!

CHAPTER 17
Profiles and Obituaries

Everybody's got one good story to tell. If you talk to them long enough, you'll find it. Nobody has lived a totally uneventful life.

—**ALAN RICHMAN,** *Writer, GQ (Gentlemen's Quarterly)*

COACHING TIPS

For profiles:

Show the source **in action.**

Do background research to **find unusual questions** the subject will enjoy discussing.

Check social media (Facebook, You Tube, Twitter, blogs etc.) for background.

Find a **unifying theme** for your profile.

For obituaries:

Ask yourself **what made this person memorable?**

Check the **accuracy of spelling** and information in profiles and obituaries.

ALAN RICHMAN ENTERS THE DARK MANHATTAN HOTEL BAR TO await the arrival of Robert De Niro. The famous actor has agreed to meet with Richman for 15 minutes to decide whether he will grant the writer an interview for *GQ (Gentlemen's Quarterly)* magazine.

Richman is accustomed to writing celebrity profiles, but this time he is nervous. De Niro hates to be interviewed.

It's 6:45 p.m. The meeting is set for 7 p.m. Richman paces in the lobby. At 7:17 p.m. De Niro arrives. He startles Richman by asking him what his first five questions would be.

Richman is trying to come up with five questions the actor will like. He isn't prepared. The words don't come.

The actor says two questions will do.

I haven't said a coherent word yet and I've blown 60 percent of this interview. Later, I'm told that I should have asked him about Brando. He loved Brando in "The Freshman," wants to do character roles like that, ones in which he doesn't have to carry the film.

I don't think of that. I choke and ask the obvious. I ask him why he's agreed to consider an interview if he hates them so much.

— ALAN RICHMAN, *GQ*

De Niro says in jest that he's agreed because of the clothes he'll get by being photographed for *GQ*. Richman doesn't tell him he won't get to keep the clothes. The writer is ready to pose his second question.

He never gets the chance. De Niro says he has to go, and he leaves without agreeing to the interview.

Richman is stuck. He still has to write the profile for *GQ*. So he calls De Niro's friends and associates.

"After the interview failed, I went back and called all those people to figure how to make the story work," Richman says. "I asked them, what question could you ask that he (De Niro) would answer. Everybody told me something about De Niro you couldn't ask."

One actor who worked with De Niro said, "I don't think I'd ask him about his family or his love life. He's pretty private."

Another friend warned Richman not to talk about world politics, sports, fine wines or clothing because "he doesn't know a lot about those things."

Those and other comments about De Niro were probably more insightful than the actor would have been about himself. And that was the theme of the profile: how to interview a celebrity who doesn't like to be interviewed.

Richman had broken one of his major rules for conducting celebrity profiles. "You've got to nail them with a question they like," Richman says. "They are so bored. I always ask myself, 'What question can I ask this guy that he'll enjoy answering.' It takes thinking."

He didn't do enough thinking before he met De Niro to set up the interview. But he's had better luck with other celebrities and athletes in the 40 years that he has been a sportswriter in Philadelphia, a columnist and writing coach for *The Boston Globe*, a reporter for *The New York Times* and a profile writer for *People* magazine.

These days, Richman has become a celebrity in his own right as the most award-winning food writer in history. As a food and wine critic for *GQ*, he has reviewed restaurants all over the world. He also teaches writing skills as dean of food journalism and new media at The International Culinary Center in New York.

Richman's varied career reveals how many possibilities exist for a journalist. He tells his students that although they may be writing about food, good writing skills are more important than the subject.

Celebrities are considered worthy of profiles because they have accomplished something more special than the average citizen. However, many profiles focus on people in the community who have done something noteworthy but do not have celebrity status.

"Everybody's got one good story to tell," Richman says. "If you talk to them long enough, you'll find it. Nobody has lived a totally uneventful life."

To find that story, Richman uses what he calls the "Columbo school of interviewing," named after the deceptively naïve TV detective. "I sort of hang around looking harmless. I try to be as unthreatening as possible. Then I use a weave-and-jab style of questioning. You can't be afraid to be a little bit rude," he says. "If the point of the interview is that they were a bigamist, I'll say: 'We all want to have two wives; tell me how you got away with it.' If it's a profile of a man growing award-winning roses, I'll say: 'I can't believe someone would spend 15 years to grow a decent rose.'"

You may have a different interviewing style, but before you even get to the interviewing stage, you should research your subject's background. If possible, try to get a résumé or an academic vita if you are interviewing a professor. Check social media and online sites, but don't rely on the information.

"I don't trust press releases or clips," Richman says. "I always ask the background stuff." Sometimes background questions can be boring. So Richman just puts his subjects on notice. He tells them:

"It's that time now; I've got to ask these questions." Basically they think I have some secret that I'm going to ask them like "Tell me about when you were 11 years old and you slept with a goat." Then I tell them, "I've got to go over your life." They're relieved. I don't mess around and pretend it's going to be fun. It's more like, do me a favor. You never know what you are going to get.

Many reporters seek background from the profile subject's friends and family *before* they conduct the main interview. In De Niro's case, Richman had no choice. He had to contact the actor's friends *after* the interview failed, but he prefers that method anyway — with this caveat:

> One of my rules is never call up friends or acquaintances of stars and ask what they think of the person, because they will always lie. If you were doing a profile of Hitler, most journalists would call Goebbels and Himmler and they would say, "What a guy!" Instead, ask them for facts or anecdotes.

TURNING POINTS

Walter Dawson, a former editor for *The Commercial Appeal* in Tennessee, said that regardless of the profile subject, "the heart and soul of a profile is making sure the reader understands the twists and turns and intricacies of human life." Dawson said writers should consider the following universal elements:

- **Patterns:** Some lives build to a climax, as for a law school student who becomes a judge.

- **Decisive moments or turning points:** Most lives take turns along the way. Take the law school student; perhaps she wanted to be a great defense lawyer but became a prosecutor instead. Or maybe your subject was an accountant who became head of a river-rafting company.

- **Future:** Every profile subject has a future, and you need to ask your subject what could lie ahead. Let the person speculate, especially about career goals. Ask the impertinent question: If this career doesn't work out, what could you do? The answers about the future could also provide an ending for the profile.

THE GOAL METHOD

To discover those turning points and other qualities of your profile subject, consider using the GOAL method (goals, obstacles, achievements, logistics). Questions about obstacles the person faced can provide some of the most interesting parts of your profile. Don't stick to any order, but consider some of these questions as they arise naturally in the conversation:

Walton LaVonda/U.S. Fish and Wildlife Service

Check online and social media sources to find background and questions your source might want to discuss.

PROFILE PLANNING TIPS

Choose your subject:

- Why is this person newsworthy?

- What will be your focus of the profile?

- What has this person done that would be of interest to readers?

- Does this person contribute to your college or university behind the scenes?

- Has this person received an award, written a book, started a new course or program?

- Is this person new in the job?

- Is this person retiring after a long stay at your college or university?

- If the profile subject is a student, is he or she head of an organization or an athlete,

or has the person achieved an unusual accomplishment?

- Do you have a backup plan for another interview subject in case your first choice cancels the interview?

Background research:

- Check the Internet and social media sites.

- Ask for a résumé or vita.

- Get a photo.

- Ask coworkers, students or other people about the person (before the interview) to get tips on questions to ask. (You also could interview these people after the interview). Check everything you can about the person's background before the interview.

Determine the focus of your profile while you conduct the interview.

- **Goals:** What were your original goals? What are your current and future goals?
- **Obstacles:** What obstacles did you face in accomplishing your goals, and what new problems loom?
- **Achievements:** What pleasures or problems have these achievements brought?
- **Logistics:** What background (logistics of who, what, when, where) led to your current situation? How has your past influenced you?

BASIC ELEMENTS OF PROFILES

Focus What is the main idea of the profile? What makes this person newsworthy? Why are you writing about this person now? Those questions should be answered in the nut graph.

Theme What is the difference between a nut graph and a theme? The nut graph is the reason for the story, but the theme is an angle or recurring idea that weaves throughout the story. Some general themes for profiles might be overcoming adversity; succeeding against odds; or coping with failure, illness or serious problems.

Background Profiles should not be written in chronological order. The subject's background should be inserted where it fits best, often in the middle of the story. But in some cases, when the background is the most interesting or crucial element, it may be the lead or in the beginning of the story, as in this example about a New Orleans detective who overcame adversity to become a successful detective.

Background

NEW ORLEANS — The white frame house on Barrone Street is small and gated, just as it was when Jacklean Davis was a shy, serious-eyed little girl in a world of grown-up horrors.

Here, 12 blocks from the muddy brown Mississippi River, Davis was raised by a prostitute, raped by a sailor, sexually molested by an uncle and pregnant at age 16. By then, folks in the neighborhood were whispering that Davis was headed for the same hard life as the aunt who had reared her: selling herself to strangers. In a sense they were right — but in an entirely different way.

Now 34, Jackie Davis cruises the city in a police car — not just any cop but the most successful detective in New Orleans, this humid capital of good times and jazz that also happens to be one of the deadliest cities in the South, with 346 murders last year.

Nut graph

— MATTHEW PURDY, *The Philadelphia Inquirer*

Here are some other elements to include in profiles:

Age and Physical Description: Help the reader visualize your profile subject. But use description only when it is relevant to the topic you are discussing. Make the details work for you. In this example from a profile of Willie Darden, a convicted killer who was interviewed while he was awaiting execution in a Florida prison, the writer weaves in the age and physical description by relating them to the pressure of waiting for death:

Darden maintains a normalcy, a serenity that is surreal. His forehead is not cleaved by worry lines. His hair has not gone gray. He lifts his shackled hands and displays unbitten fingernails. "Calmness is a nice thing to have in times of stress," he says.

He gives his age as 62, but prison records say he is 52. He looks 42. It's as if the man has not only cheated the executioner, but time itself.

Or maybe time just stops when there is no future.

"Prison does tend to sustain one's youth," Darden says with an ironic grin. "You're not doing anything that you would normally do on the outside — such as working hard every day. You've got no family problems. The wear and tear, so to speak, is on the inside."

— RICHARD LEIBY, *South Florida Sun-Sentinel* (Fort Lauderdale, Florida)

Other Points of View: Seek anecdotes and comments from friends, family, colleagues and other people affected by the person at work, such as students for a profile about a professor or employees for a profile about a manager.

Visuals Use graphics as a way to visualize your story in both the planning and writing stages. Outlining your profile by planning a facts (highlights) box can help you determine what topics to include in your story.

If the background is boring, break it out of your story. You can put key dates and such information as birthplace, education, career moves or similar items in a box. But if that information is an interesting and crucial part of your story, leave it in the body of the profile. You also can use a box to add information that doesn't fit well into your story but might be of interest, such as hobbies, favorite books, a favorite saying or a major goal. The major goal should also be mentioned in your story, but it works well in a facts box.

Several newspapers, magazines and websites use graphic devices to substitute for written profiles; others use highlights boxes to enhance profiles. For example, *The Kansas City* (Missouri) *Star* Sunday magazine profiles celebrities with blurbs following these headings:

- Vital statistics (occupation, birthday, birthplace, current home, marital status and so on)
- My fantasy is . . .
- If I could change one thing about myself, it would be . . .
- The best times of my life . . .
- Behind my back my friends say . . .
- These words best describe me . . .

Those are also good questions to ask for your profile even if you don't use the items in a visual tool. However, if you mention topics in a graphic, you don't have to repeat them in the story.

MICRO PROFILE

Can you describe yourself or your profile subject in six words? Consider the poignancy of these six words: "For sale, baby shoes, never worn." Those words were written by Ernest Hemingway when he was challenged to write a six-word story to win a bet, although it has never been proven conclusively that he was the author. But Pete Berg, a freelance TV producer and Web designer was inspired by the story to create a website seeking contributors of six word stories (*www.sixwordstories.net*). Many of the entries are also poignant, clever and convey a complete story in such a succinct form. Check it out for inspiration.

Using that concept, try to condense your profile into six words that would leave a lasting impression.

Or use the concept of Twitter to write a Twitter profile in 140 characters. What is the dominant impression you want to create? Those ideas might help you form your focus by considering the most important elements to include in your profile before you write the story.

SNAPSHOT PROFILES

Brief profiles showing a slice of life or vignettes of people are excellent formats for the Web or for a package of stories as sidebars to a main in-depth story, especially now that many stories are being tailored to small screens. An idea that works well is a package of stories about diversity on campus, with profiles of international students or those from varied ethnic and racial backgrounds. A major story about an upcoming election in your town might also lend itself to these snapshot profiles of the candidates.

Julie Sullivan, a Pulitzer Prize–winning journalist, mastered the art of writing snapshot profiles several years ago when she won an award for short news writing from the American Society of Newspaper Editors.

Sullivan takes voluminous notes but discards about half of them. "I write everything down. I don't trust my memory," she says. She also stresses observation. "Pay attention to details, from the right spelling of names to finding out the date of people's birthdays."

How does she know which details to include in her stories? "I write what I remember without looking at my notes. What details stand out?"

She is also selective about the limited quotes she includes. "I really think readers glaze over quotes," she says. "I do few quotes because I think most people are pretty plain-spoken and simple. You don't need to use it just because it's in quotes."

Her tips for writing briefly: "Trust your instincts about what is important, what struck you during the interview. The rest is chaff."

The profile that follows was part of a series about the problems of low-income residents in a deteriorating Spokane apartment building, the Merlin. As you read this profile, consider what information came from observations and what came from questions. And then decide how you could say it all in as few words.

DONALD 'JOE' PEAK

Joe Peak's smile has no teeth.

His dentures were stolen at the Norman Hotel, the last place he lived in downtown Spokane before moving to the Merlin two years ago.

Gumming food and fighting diabetes have shrunk the 54-year-old man's frame by 80 pounds. He is thin and weak and his mouth is sore.

But that doesn't stop him from frying hamburgers and onions for a friend at midnight or keeping an extra bed made up permanently in his two-room place.

"I try to make a little nest here for myself," he says.

Chock-full of furniture and cups from the 32-ounce Cokes he relishes for 53 cents apiece, Peaks' second floor apartment is almost cozy.

A good rug covers holes in the kitchen floor, clean-looking blankets cover a clean-looking bed. Dishes are stacked neatly in the kitchen sink.

But cockroaches still scurry across his kitchen table.

"I live with them," he says with a shrug. "I can't afford the insecticides, pesticides, germicides. I don't have the money."

With a $500 per month welfare check and a $175 rent payment, Peak follows a proper diet when he can afford it. He shops at nearby convenience stores where he knows prices are higher but the distance is right. He has adapted to the noisy nightlife in the hallways and sleeps when he is too exhausted to hear it.

Part Seminole Indian, Chinese and black, the Florida native moved to Spokane 20 years ago to be near relatives in Olympia. He quit school at 13 to help earn the family income and worked a string of blue-collar jobs. Along the way, someone started calling him Joe.

His voice is lyrical, his vocabulary huge, but Peak's experience with whites is long and bitter.

When conditions at the Merlin began worsening three months ago, junkies and gray mice the size of baby rats moved in next door. He hated to see it, but he isn't worried about being homeless.

He's worried about his diabetes. He's frightened by blood in his stool and sores on his gums. He wonders whether the white-staffed hospitals on the hill above him will treat a poor black man with no teeth.

— JULIE SULLIVAN, *The* (Spokane, Washington)
Spokesman-Review

ORGANIZING THE PROFILE

There is no one way to organize a profile, other than having a lead, a body and an ending. Just make sure that you have a focus. Descriptive show-in-action leads, anecdotes, contrast leads and scene-setting leads work particularly well in profiles. As with any lead, make sure you back up the lead with information that supports it later in the story.

The body of the story can be organized in many ways:

Supporting Themes Block each concept, use all relevant material, and go on to the next concept.

Time Frames Start with the present, go to the past, go back to the present, and end with the future. Or use some variation of the time frames, possibly starting with the past and then proceeding to the present.

MULTIMEDIA COACH

CHECK THE INTERNET and social media for background on your profile subject, but don't rely on the information. Make sure that you check the accuracy of the information you get. The following tips apply to profiles for print, broadcast and the Web:

- Start with a simple search for the person's name in Google (*www.google.com*) or other search engine.
- Check out any articles or books written by or about the profile source. If the person has written books, read one, or at least read summaries on the Amazon website (*www.amazon.com*).
- Check for personal and academic websites and online résumés the person might have — especially if you are interviewing professors.
- Check athletic records in sports sites for profiles of athletes.
- Check fan sites for celebrities or athletes. These sites may contain links to articles or other information. Use them only as a guide; don't trust information from personal sites.
- For profiles about candidates, check voting records of incumbents and campaign contributions at sites such as FollowTheMoney (*www.followthemoney.org*) for candidates

to state offices and the Federal Election Commission (*www.fec.gov*) for candidates to federal offices.

- Check social networking sites such as Facebook, LinkedIn, YouTube, Twitter and others for personal pages and comments about your subject.

Broadcast Profiles

- Think visually in the planning stage before you do the reporting. Background research is essential so you can ask interesting questions that will elicit good responses from your source.
- Show and tell. Write to the video, and show your subject in action.
- Read your script aloud.
- Don't introduce your sound bites by parroting what the source will say.

Web Profiles

- Plan audio, video and graphic elements that may accompany your profile.
- Consider breaking out facts or other highlights into boxes.
- Plan links that might provide background or other elements of the profile.
- Consider writing the profile in sections; offer readers the choice of reading the parts linked on separate Web pages or on one page.
- Consider a question/answer format that is easy to read on the Web.

Chronology Look for a place in the story where chronological order might be useful, but don't write the entire profile in chronological order. A chronology might be helpful for the background. It might also work if you are writing the profile in narrative style. In some cases, however, the story might lend itself to chronological order if a situation unfolds in that sequence. Just make sure that your nut graph tells readers why you are writing about this person now.

Point/Counterpoint If the subject lends itself to pro-and-con treatment, you might consider this method. It can be helpful in profiles of politicians. You can include reaction quotes from other people after each controversial point is made.

Sections Splitting the story into separate parts may work if the profile is very complex. For example, if you are doing an in-depth profile of a politician or crime victim or crime suspect, you might organize it in sections, either by time frames of the person's life, issues or different points of view.

Q and A The question/answer format is becoming popular as a format for profiles. It works well in print and on the Web.

Several types of endings work well with profiles. A quote kicker can be used to summarize a source's feelings about the subject or to recap the subject's accomplishments. Or, with a circular ending, you can return to the lead for an idea and end on a similar note. An ending with a future theme tells what lies ahead for the person.

Those are some of the techniques Roman Stubbs, a former University of Montana student, used to win first place in profile writing by the Hearst Journalism Awards program. His profile of former Montana University football player Jimmy Wilson used a sections technique to describe how Wilson shot his friend, was charged with murder, went to prison and endured two trials before he was acquitted. The first section starts with the past time frame:

> He sat at his grandmother's dining room table late on that sweltering June night, dreaming. Eating his ribs and collard greens in silence, pondering his future with each bite.
>
> For Jimmy Wilson, there were only seven hours left before deliverance. Duffel bags packed, alarm clock ready. At five o'clock in the morning, he was going to rise out of bed and drive 17 hours from his Southern California home to Missoula, Montana, and love every minute of it. When he arrived on the University of Montana campus for summer workouts they would see a polished cornerback, a reinvented man.
>
> This was his year. To show what an All-American candidate was all about. To send the message that his legendary hits for this program were about to get a lot more vicious. And to make all those people who mocked his NFL dream think twice before they judged that dream again. Nothing was going to get in his way.
>
> A half hour later, Jimmy Wilson had an AK-47 pointed to his chest.

The next section describes how the shooting occurred, and the following sections describe how Wilson waited in jail for his trial and the outcome. To find out what happened to Wilson, you can read the entire profile, "Gladiator School," on the Hearst Journalism Awards site (*www.hearstfdn.org/hearst_journalism/competitions.php?type=Writing&year=2010&id=13*).

OBITUARIES

Obituaries are also profiles, but the subjects are dead. However, you don't write about the person's death; you write about his life. Marilyn Johnson, a magazine writer and editor, is so fascinated by obituaries that she wrote an entire book about the genre called *The Dead Beat*.

"The obituary pages, it turns out, are some of the best-read pages in the newspaper," she wrote. "Obituaries are history as it is happening. . . . Tell me the secret of a good life."

Jim Nicholson, a former obituary writer for the *Philadelphia Daily News*, became so famous for his obituaries that he was nicknamed "Dr. Death" by his coworkers.

Jim Nicholson, former obituary writer for the *Philadelphia Daily News*.

Courtesy of Jim Nicholson

He called his obituaries "character portraits," filled with details of how the person lived, "warts and all," he says.

Obituaries tend to be flattering portraits. But Nicholson says they should be true portraits. He believes someone's bad habits and criminal background, if they exist, should be part of an obituary. Many editors would disagree. And families are not likely to be happy with unflattering material. Generally, news editors weigh whether a criminal background was a crucial part of the person's life and if the crime was highly publicized. If a person was arrested at one time for shoplifting or for another misdemeanor, most editors would recommend omitting such information. When you are faced with such decisions, it is wise to confer with an editor.

"Cleaning up someone's act after he or she has died does not serve the cause of the deceased or loved ones," Nicholson says. "A sanitized portrait is indistinguishable from any other. It is the irregularities that give us identity. The ultimate acclaim may be when a reader thinks, 'I wish I had known this man or woman.'"

Like the obituary for Lawrence Pompie "Mr. Buddy" Ellis, a retired maintenance man who was a leader in his church:

> He came to be known affectionately among friends as "Dial-A-Prayer" for his unceasing availability to those who wanted him to pray with them. If he couldn't meet personally with someone, he would pray with them on the telephone, said his wife, Fannie, who shared 38 years with him. . . . At 5-foot-7 and 205 pounds, Ellis loved to eat. "He loved everything about a pig," said his wife, "and if he didn't watch out, he'd catch his grunt."
>
> — JIM NICHOLSON, *Philadelphia Daily News*

SOCIAL MEDIA

THE SUBJECTS are dead, so you might not think about checking their blogs. But the deceased person might have created a blog that provides insights to his thoughts. To find interesting tidbits about the people who died, you can check "twituary," an obituary list on Twitter.

Obituary writers have their own blog, the "Obituary Forum" (*obituaryforum.blogspot.com*), where you can learn how they feel about their craft.

If the person had a Facebook page, it may contain posts from friends that will reveal much about his life. Other social media sites like YouTube might also provide information about your subject. Family members may also have personal websites worth checking. Don't copy material from these sites without permission, but use them to gather information that will reveal the kind of character portraits Jim Nicholson suggested.

The Importance of Facts

A misspelled name or a factual error is a major problem in any story; in an obituary it is disastrous. So you should check every fact, every name, every reference. And you should check with the funeral director and the family to make sure that the person you are writing about is dead.

Someone from the *Detroit Free Press* didn't do that. And the death of Dr. Rogers Fair turned out to be greatly exaggerated, as Mark Twain would say. Fair, a Detroit physician, woke up one morning to read in the newspaper that he had died of cancer. The newspaper had received the obituary information by telephone from a woman who claimed she was Fair's aunt. And the reporter didn't call back to check with family members or a funeral home.

Fair, 40, claimed the "aunt" was a 21-year-old woman who was infatuated with him. She had wooed him with flowers and love notes, but when he rejected her and began dating another woman, he began receiving harassing telephone calls, bomb threats and vandalism to his home.

"She is obviously an obsessed person," Fair told the *Free Press*. "She has stated that if she can't have me, nobody else can."

The follow-up story was an embarrassment to the paper:

The obituary for Dr. Rogers Fair in Tuesday's *Free Press* took a lot of people — especially Fair — by surprise.

"My beeper was just jumping off the hook," the 40-year-old physician said Tuesday. "My secretary called me. She was in tears. . . . "

The erroneous report of Fair's demise was the second phony obituary published by the *Free Press* in recent years. The first prompted a revision of reporting practices, requiring all obituary information phoned in by friends and relatives to be confirmed either by a funeral home or law enforcement officials.

But Fair's obituary wasn't properly double-checked, and a woman identifying herself as Fair's aunt was able to hoodwink the *Free Press* with details of his death.

— *Detroit Free Press*

Most newspapers have free or paid death notices — announcements from the family about the deceased. In addition, funeral directors and families call the newspaper to request an obituary. Almost all newspapers will publish an obituary about anyone prominent in the community.

Generally, reporters scan the paid death notices to look for interesting people, long-term residents or those active in community service. Then you make the phone calls — or double-check the validity of the ones you have received by calling a funeral home, checking the phone book, and calling the family back or calling other relatives and friends. And, as in any other story, you check newspaper clips or databases and the Internet.

Calling people about death isn't easy. But it isn't as difficult as you might expect, especially for obituaries. Most families are grateful because this is the last story — and more often the only story — printed about their loved ones. Usually, someone in the family is prepared to deal with the media.

The easiest way to start gathering information is with the funeral director, if one has been selected. The funeral director should have the basic information and should be able to tell you which family members to call and their phone numbers.

Obituary Guidelines

Obituary writing follows some basic forms, even when you are writing a special profile. All obituaries, no matter how long or short, must contain the same crucial information:

Background Research Before you use anything from a website for background research, make sure that you check it for accuracy. Was the site dated? Does it have an author? Is the site credible? Do not use anything you can't verify. If you do include something from a website, cite your source.

Name: Use full name, middle initial and nickname if it was commonly used. Enclose the nickname in quotation marks.

Identification: How do you describe a person's life in one brief phrase? That's not so easy to do, but most obituaries start with a lead that identifies the person and summarizes the main accomplishment of his life. Usually, people are identified by occupation or community service. Always try to find something special to use following the name, such as "John Doe, a retired salesman" or "Jane Doe, a homemaker who was active in her church."

Age: In some cases, a family will request that you withhold the age. You should confer with an editor about honoring this request.

Date and Place of Death: Use the day of the week if the death occurred that week, the date if it was more than a week prior to the obituary. State the name of a hospital, if applicable, or other location where the death occurred.

Cause of Death: This fact is not required at all newspapers, especially if the cause of death was suicide or AIDS-related, or when the family requests that the cause be withheld. However, some news organizations require the cause of death, regardless of stigma or family wishes. So check your organization's policy before you gather the information. You may have to inform family members of the policy.

If a suicide occurs on a college campus, the news spreads quickly. Should it be mentioned in a campus newspaper story or obituary? That's an ethical dilemma that campus news editors and directors have debated. If it is public and well known around the school, one approach is to do a general story about suicide, which is a significant issue on college campuses. In most cases, however, suicide is not mentioned in the obituary out of respect for the family.

Address: Tell where the person lived when he died and previous areas of residence for any major length of time. Broadcast obituaries rarely use the specific address.

Background: Specify major accomplishments, organizations, educational background, military background and any other highlights. When people are very active in their church, mosque or synagogue, this fact should be mentioned in the obituary.

Survivors: Use the names of immediate family members (husband or wife, with her maiden name; children; brothers and sisters). Grandchildren are usually mentioned only by number: "He is survived by five grandchildren." New complications are arising these days because of changes in family relationships. Many news publications now list unmarried partners as survivors. In the future these relationships may also be a standard part of obituaries.

Services: Specify the time, date and location.

Burial: Name the place, and provide memorial information when available. When the death occurred a week or more ago, it is customary to start with information about the service or a memorial if that has not yet been conducted.

This example about the death of a local citizen follows all the basic guidelines; it also includes information about contributions:

Lucy Davis Burnett, a Dallas native and longtime civic leader, died of cancer Saturday at her home. She was 79.

A graduate of Woodrow Wilson High School in Dallas and Mary Baldwin College in Staunton, Virginia, Mrs. Burnett was active in numerous cultural and civic affairs.

She was past president of the Southern Methodist University Lecture Series, vice president of the Dallas Junior League and president of the Junior League Garden Club.

She was a founding member of the Dallas Slipper Club and also held memberships in the Dallas Women's Club, the Dallas Arts Museum League, the women's division of United Way of Dallas and Highland Park United Methodist.

She is survived by her husband, F.W. Burnett of Dallas; a daughter, Lucy Chambers of Vancouver, British Columbia; a son, F.W. Burnett Jr. of Dallas; and six grandchildren.

Services for Mrs. Burnett will be at 2 p.m. Tuesday at Highland Park United Methodist Church.

Memorials may be made to Children's Medical Center of Dallas, the Dallas Chapter of the American Cancer Society or a charity of the donor's choice.

— *The Dallas Morning News*

Here are some style tips:

Names of Services: Mass is celebrated, not said. The word is capitalized. Find out the exact wording you should use for the particular mass, such as Mass of Christian Burial. Likewise, ask for the proper wording of a service for other denominations.

Courtesy Titles: Although many newspapers and TV news organizations have eliminated courtesy titles (Mrs., Mr., Ms., Miss) for news stories, several keep them for obituaries. Again, you must check your newspaper's or broadcast station's policy.

Mass Communication Specialist 3rd Class Robert Stirrup/U.S. Navy

U.S. Naval officer reads a Dr. Seuss book to kindergarten students.

Titles for Religious Leaders: Check the proper title for a rabbi, minister or priest. When writing about a priest, do not use "Father" or "Pastor" for the title. Use "the Rev." (the reverend) followed by the priest's name: "the Rev. Vince Krische." For a rabbi, use "Rabbi" before the name on first reference: "Rabbi Jacob Katz." On second reference for clergy, including priests, use only the last name. But for second reference to high-ranking clergy, use "Cardinal," "Archbishop" and so on. Check The Associated Press Stylebook for specific religious titles.

Here is a feature obituary for Dr. Seuss that follows the guidelines. The story begins with the writer's death, some basic information about his accomplishments and then a chronology of his life. It ends with information about survivors. No information was available about services at the time, but if it had been, it would have been included at the end.

Theodor Seuss Geisel, alias Dr. Seuss, whose rhymed writing and fanciful drawings were loved worldwide and helped teach generations to read, died Tuesday night at his home in La Jolla.

Geisel's stepdaughter, Lea Dimond, told reporters the world-famous author died with his family around him. No other information was released regarding the cause of death, but Dimond said Geisel, 87, had been ill for several months.

In the 1950s and '60s, Geisel's books gave millions of children relief from the drab textbook adventures of Dick and Jane. His 48 children's books were translated into 18 languages and sold more than 100 million copies.

Geisel also drew most of the fanciful illustrations in his books, creating a menagerie of Whos, grinches, ziffs and zuffs, talking goldfish and loyal, sweet elephants. He was awarded a special Pulitzer Prize in 1984 for his contribution to children's literature.

Geisel's tales were filled with his own moral concerns, particularly for the environment and world peace. "The Lorax" warns against polluting the environment, while "The Butter Battle Book" tells of an arms race between creatures who disagree about whether it is better to eat bread with the butter side down or up.

When asked recently whether he had any final message, Geisel told a reporter from the *San Diego Union:* "Whenever things go a bit sour in a job I'm doing, I always tell myself, 'You can do better than this.' The best slogan I can think of to leave with the USA would be 'We can do this and we've got to do better than this.'"

Geisel was born in Springfield, Massachusetts. His father was a brewer and superintendent of parks, which included the zoo, where Geisel said he started drawing animals.

He graduated from Dartmouth College in 1925, having drawn cartoons for the school humor magazine. He went to England to study literature at Oxford University, but dropped out, in part, after receiving encouragement in his artistic ambitions from another American student, Helen Palmer. She became his first wife a few years later.

Geisel spent a year in Paris, where he got to know Ernest Hemingway, James Joyce and other writers. He returned to the United States in 1927, hoping to become a novelist.

He wrote humor for the magazines *Judge* and *Life*, adopting his now-famous pen name, Dr. Seuss, as a spoof of scientific developments.

Among his most famous books are "The Cat in the Hat," "Green Eggs and Ham" and "Horton Hears a Who!" which was made into a popular TV special, as was "How the Grinch Stole Christmas!"

He moved to La Jolla soon after the end of World War II. During the latter part of the war he served in the Army, helping director Frank Capra make training and documentary films. Two Geisel documentaries, "Hitler Lives?" and "Design for Death," co-written with his wife, won Academy Awards for their producers in 1946 and 1947.

After the war, Geisel's work continued to be translated to movies, with his cartoon short "Gerald McBoing Boing" winning an Oscar in 1951. He turned his attention to television in the 1950s, designing and producing cartoons, including the Peabody Award–winning "How the Grinch Stole Christmas!" and "Horton Hears a Who!". . .

Geisel did not have any children of his own. His first wife died in 1967. He later married Audrey Dimond, who has two daughters from a previous marriage. He also is survived by his niece, Peggy Owens, and her son, Theodore Owens, of Los Angeles.

— LAURA BLEIBERG, *The Orange County* (California) *Register*

EXERCISES

1 **Twitter or six-word profile:** Write a Twitter or six-word profile of yourself. For inspiration check Six Words at *www.sixwordmemoirs.com* or Six Word Stories at *www.sixwordstories.net*.

2 **Celebrity profile:** Plan a celebrity profile of someone you would like to interview. If you enjoy sports, plan a profile of an athlete on your campus. Use Alan Richman's tips, and plan an interesting question you would use to begin the interview, as well as a preliminary theme you might pursue.

3 **Profile coaching:** Coach a classmate on writing a profile. Ask your classmate some of the basic coaching questions: What's it about? What is the focus? Do you have a theme? Were there any

patterns, any turning points? What anecdotes do you remember as most interesting? What is the point — why should the reader care? What order are you considering? As the writer discusses the profile, you as the coach can ask questions that occur to you.

4 **Slice-of-life snapshot profiles:** Using the theme of "A Day in the Life" of your campus or your community, write vignettes about people and places. Each person in the class can take a different part of the campus or community.

5 **Personal profile:** Write a blog or memo about a turning point in your life or a significant experience that might make you worthy of a profile. Pairing

up with a classmate, exchange your memos and interview each other for a profile. Then write your profiles and share the results with your partner.

6 **Obituary:** Gather information from news clips, magazines, online sources and social media about a celebrity or otherwise prominent person in your community who is still alive. Write an obituary, including comments the person has made and comments about the person.

FEATURED ONLINE ACTIVITIES: Log on to the MindTap for Rich's Writing and Reporting News to access a variety of robust additional material, including this chapter's learning objectives, activities, comprehension quizzes, and more.

Be sure to check out the "Extended Profile/ Obituary" NewsScene scenario for an interactive writing exercise that will help to reinforce many of the themes presented in this chapter.

COACHING TIPS

Do your homework. **Check clips and online sources** for background about the speaker or issue.

Include audience reactions and responses to questions at speeches, meetings and news conferences.

Try to get as many good **quotes and sound bites** as possible.

Write a **highlights box** to accompany your story, especially for the Web.

Get the **full text of speeches** and documents from meetings to post on websites.

Record audio or video to post on the Web.

CHAPTER 18

Speeches, News Conferences and Meetings

© R. Gino Santa Maria/Shutterstock.com

The comments officials make during a meeting are for public posturing. Some of the best quotes you get are after the meeting when you ask them to explain why they did or said something.

—**MARK FAGAN**, *Reporter*

T'S A QUIET SUBURBAN NEW ENGLAND TOWN WITH TALL CHURCH SPIRES
and historic buildings, including the birthplace of Noah Webster, author of the first American dictionary. The center of town resembles a Norman Rockwell postcard, with tree-lined streets and brick sidewalks bordering specialty stores, coffee shops and boutiques.

A typical town meeting might be sparsely attended by a handful of residents interested in zoning changes or budget requests such as the one to purchase new parking meters to replace coin-operated ones.

So when a town hall meeting about the new health care law drew hundreds of people sporting signs protesting or supporting the law, this quiet town of West Hartford, Connecticut, reverberated with impassioned voices. The demonstrations before and after the meeting were more newsworthy — and more interesting — than the speeches inside the town hall.

When you cover speeches, meetings and news conferences, your observations are as much a part of the story as the scripted comments from speakers.

That's the advice of Mark Fagan, who covered meetings of the city council in Lawrence, Kansas, for many years.

"The comments officials make during a meeting are for public posturing," Fagan says. "Some of the best quotes you get are after the meeting when you ask them to explain why they did or said something."

West Hartford residents protest health care reform at a town hall meeting.

Used with permission from Sage Ross

A resident in favor of health care reform demonstrates at a West Hartford town meeting.

That advice also applies to someone from the public who speaks at a meeting. "A person may speak for 30 seconds and afterward she'll tell you, 'My kid needs a safe place to walk because he was attacked two years ago,'" Fagan says. "Don't just sit in the meeting if the person leaves; follow him or her out and get those additional comments."

What you write before the meeting is even more important, Fagan says. He writes at least one story to tell readers what officials will discuss at their next meeting. He also provides timely tweets about meetings and events on his beat before, during and after the events. If people don't know what officials plan to do, they won't get a chance to participate in government.

Although many newspapers and TV news programs are curtailing local government meeting coverage because the news is sometimes dull, Fagan thinks that's a mistake. Meetings are where officials make decisions that affect the public.

"I'll write stories sometimes and no one (from the public) will show up at a meeting, and I wonder if what I do makes a difference. Then a city commissioner will say, 'I got about 20 phone calls after your article.' So I know people are reading them."

Even if people don't read his stories or attend the meetings, Fagan thinks it's important for reporters to be there as watchdogs for the public. "I put the commissioners' comments in the paper, and everyone knows where they stand," Fagan says. "That's a great power of the press."

ETHICS

ETHICAL DILEMMA: You have the political beat on your campus newspaper. You are covering a speech of one of the candidates for student government. You write a fair and balanced article about the speech for your campus newspaper. However, on your personal blog, you express your opinion that you think the candidate is a jerk who should never be elected. The candidate complains to your editor that you should be taken off the beat and should not be allowed to cover this election. Do you have a right to express your opinions about the election on your blog, which is not connected to your campus newspaper?

Ethical guidelines: The Radio Television Digital News Association has created social media and blogging guidelines. The organization says this about image and reputation: "Remember that what's posted online is open to the public (even if you consider it to be private). Personal and professional lives merge online. Newsroom employees should recognize that even though their comments may seem to be in their 'private space,' their words become direct extensions of their news organizations. . . . Avoid posting photos or any other content on any website, blog, social network or video/photo sharing website that might embarrass you or undermine your journalistic credibility. When you work for a journalism organization, you represent that organization on and off the clock."

Do you agree?

Whenever you are covering a meeting, it's important to look beyond what officials say publicly. Fagan says reporters should ask questions before and after the public event to find out how the story affects readers and viewers.

"An item on a meeting agenda may say they are going to award bids for highway improvements on North Second Street," he says. "I look at that and say, 'What does that mean?' Are they going to widen the street? This is the only artery that connects downtown and an old neighborhood. Are they going to close the road to traffic for eight months? This is how officials plan to spend taxpayers' money. You need to find out how it affects readers."

STORIES ABOUT MEETINGS

The decisions that affect readers' daily lives — such as where they take their trash, get their water and send their children to school — are made by local government officials at meetings. Countless surveys conducted by news organizations reveal that local news is near or at the top of the list of the kinds of stories readers and viewers want. Yet meeting stories are often written without explaining their real impact on the reader.

All states have open-meeting laws requiring officials who have the authority to spend public funds to conduct their business in public. These boards may conduct executive sessions behind closed doors for certain discussions, such as personnel matters or collective bargaining, but all decisions must be made in a public meeting. Although open-meeting laws vary from state to state, most of them require public agencies to give advance notice — usually 48 hours — of their meetings and to conduct public hearings.

Understanding the System

When a board makes a decision at a meeting, you need to understand what kind of authority that board has. Suppose you are covering a zoning board meeting. The board is discussing a zoning application from a developer for a major shopping center. If the board approves a zoning change, is that the final decision? Probably not. Most zoning boards are advisory and must submit their recommendations to a city or county board of officials for final approval. That is essential information to include in your story.

If you are covering meetings of your university administration, find out who can make the decisions and which boards are advisory. Who can raise the tuition — school officials or a board of regents? Is the action taken at a meeting a recommendation or a ruling? You need to explain the system as well as the next step in an action.

Writing the Advance

Many times, knowing what is going to happen at a meeting is more important to readers than knowing what did happen. A story that tells readers what is being proposed can alert residents to make their concerns known before a measure is adopted by local officials. A pre-meeting story is called an "advance."

An advance is especially crucial if local officials are planning to conduct a public hearing about an issue. If the public doesn't know about it, how can the public be heard? You can tweet about an advance, but you need to link it to a full story for important issues.

City and school boards usually publish an agenda in advance of their meetings. This agenda lists the items to be discussed, although new items can and usually are presented.

When you receive an agenda, look through it for items that might be of special interest to readers. Call board members and ask for comments, or ask them to discuss the items they expect to be most interesting or controversial. If the issue has been in the news previously, check clips or blogs and call other interested parties. If you are writing an advance for a public hearing, make sure that you give the time and location of the hearing.

The following excerpt from an advance includes the time and location of the meeting:

> The stage is set for changing the city's human relations ordinance to include protections for homosexuals.
>
> Lawrence city commissioners will accept public comment on a proposal to add the words "sexual orientation" to the city's anti-discrimination ordinance at next week's meeting, which begins at 6:35 p.m. Tuesday at City Hall, Sixth and Massachusetts streets.

Covering the Meeting

Arrive early. Find out the names of board members (usually they have name tags), and find out who is in charge.

Ask board members, especially the head of the board, whether you may talk to them after the meeting. If you know people in the audience who are leaders of a group favoring or opposing a controversial issue, greet them and tell them you would like to get comments after the meeting.

Check items on the agenda, and get any background that you need.

Check the consent agenda, a list of items on the agenda that the board will approve without discussion. They may include bids for approval or other points the board may have discussed in work sessions.

Don't remain glued to a seat at a press table. When members of the audience give public comments, get their names and more comments. Many times they will leave immediately after their testimony. Follow them out of the meeting. You can catch up with the action inside later. Or sit in the audience. Sometimes the comments of people attending the meeting are more interesting than the ones the board members make.

Stay until the end, unless your deadline prohibits staying. The most important issue could emerge at the end of a meeting, when the board asks for new business or public comments. Or something dramatic could happen. The mayor could resign. Violence could erupt. You never can tell, especially if you're not there.

Writing the Story

First, how not to write it: Do not say the city council met and discussed something. Tell what they discussed or enacted. This is the kind of lead to avoid:

> The 41st Annual Environmental Engineering Conference met yesterday at the Kansas Union to discuss solutions to environmental problems.
>
> Representatives of the Kansas Department of Health and Environment, the Environmental Protection Agency and other organizations spoke to about 180 people who attended the conference.

So what did they say? This lead reveals nothing.

Some meetings are long. They can be boring. Avoid telling the reader how much you suffered listening to board members drone on and accomplish nothing in a long meeting. The reader doesn't care how much you suffer. The reader wants the news. If the length of the debate is crucial to the story, you should include it. But if the meetings are usually long, and the time element is not a major factor related to the focus, don't mention it.

Here are some points to include in your story:

Type of Meeting and Location Give this information, but if the city council or school board meets all the time in the same building, don't mention the location.

The Vote on Any Major Issue For instance, say "in a 4–1 vote . . . " If the issue is particularly controversial, say who voted against it — or for it, if an affirmative vote was more controversial. If the measure was approved unanimously, say so. However, don't give the vote for every minor item.

The Next Step If a major issue or ordinance cannot be adopted until a public hearing is conducted, tell readers when a hearing is scheduled or what the next step is before the action is final.

Impact on Readers Explain how the decision will affect them.

Quotes Use only quotes that are dramatic, interesting or crucial to the story.

Background of the Issues What do readers need to know to understand what has happened?

To write the story, select one key issue for the focus. If the board approved several other measures, add them at the end: "In other business." If several important actions occurred, consider breaking another key issue into a separate story, if possible. If not, try a lead mentioning both items, or put the other key point in the second paragraph and give supporting background later. For example, "City commissioners yesterday approved plans for the city's first shopping mall but rejected plans for a new public golf course." Then proceed with the discussion about the shopping mall.

Although many meeting stories are written with summary leads, especially if the news is significant, they do not have to follow that form. If you think a softer lead is appropriate for the type of news that occurred, you can use it. Try an impact lead that emphasizes how readers and viewers are affected by the action or lack of action that occurred at a meeting.

Here are a few matters of style for meeting coverage:

- "Board" is a collective noun and therefore takes a singular verb: The board discussed the issue at "its" meeting, not "their" meeting. If this approach seems awkward in your story, say that the board *members* said *their* next meeting would be Tuesday.

- Capitalize "city council," "city commission" and "school board" when they are part of a proper name — such as the Rockville City Commission — and when the reference is to a specific commission in your town — the City Commission. If you are not referring to a specific city commission but just saying most municipalities have city commissions, use lowercase letters.

- Capitalize the titles of board members or other officials when they come before the name, as in "Mayor John Corrupt." If the title follows the name — "John Corrupt, the mayor" — use lowercase letters.

- For votes, use "3–1," not "3 to 1."

Stories about meetings can take a hard, soft or advance-impact approach. Whichever one you use, make the story relevant to readers. Here's how:

Summary lead: what happened

LAGUNA BEACH, Calif. — Despite neighbors' objections, a North Laguna Beach couple were given permission Tuesday to adorn their home with a 17-foot-high outdoor sculpture of 30 water heaters and two house trailers.

Vote

The City Council, after viewing a scale model of the artwork, voted 3–1 to endorse the sculpture. It will climb around a pine tree in the back courtyard of Arnold and Marie Forde's home.

Dissenting vote

Mayor Neil Fitzpatrick dissented, saying the sculpture infringed on neighbors' views. Councilwoman Martha Collison was absent.

Reaction

"It's a victory for the freedom of expression," said Los Angeles artist Nancy Rubins, who will craft the sculpture. "It would have been a sad day if a community that sees itself as supporting the arts struck down an artwork in a private yard."

Impact: so what

The sculpture had been the focus of an intense neighborhood battle.

Residents who live near the Fordes have called the sculpture junk and complained that the artwork would block their view and spoil the neighborhood character.

More reaction

David DeLo, who lives across Cliff Drive from the Fordes, said he was considering challenging the council's action in court.

Next step

"If the council wants to place a piece of junk in a residential neighborhood, that's their prerogative, but this council has been overturned before," he said.

Backup: conditions of council action

To appease neighbors, the council approved the sculpture on the condition that the Fordes place it as low as possible in the yard and landscape the area with another tree and a hedge. The additional plants should hide the sculpture from neighbors, officials said.

Future kicker

The $5,000 sculpture will take a week to build. Rubins said she did not know when it will be finished.

—HARRISON FLETCHER,
The Orange County (California)
Register

SOCIAL MEDIA

SOCIAL MEDIA TOOLS are ideal for reporting and delivering information about speeches, news conferences and meetings.

- Use Twitter to post updated information during a news conference or meeting. Encourage readers to tweet about the issues.

- Post video of a speech or interesting news conference on YouTube.

- Encourage readers and viewers to blog about the issues in a news conference or meeting, especially if the subjects are controversial.

- Follow community, business or government agencies on Facebook, Twitter and other popular social media sites.

- If you are a public relations practitioner, post tweets and news releases on social media sites.

- Add share tools to your story to encourage reader and viewer communication.

STORIES ABOUT SPEECHES

Before you cover a speech, you should prepare for it by finding out as much as you can about the speaker and the issue. Be sure to check the clips, blogs and online databases.

With a prominent speaker, you can often get the text of the speech in advance. But be careful not to rely on it. The speaker may depart from the prepared text. However, you can still use the prepared text. Just say, "The speaker said in prepared remarks" or "in a written text." Reporters sometimes have to rely on the written version, especially if their deadlines come before the speech or news conference is over.

During the speech, try to get full quotes of the important points (especially if they vary from the written text), and jot down reactions of the speaker and the audience. Note when and if the speaker shows emotion and how the audience responds. Write follow-up questions to ask the speaker after the speech or news conference.

Try to get an aisle seat. If someone asks a good question after the speech or meeting and then leaves, you should follow that person out of the room quickly, so you can check the name and get more information.

Your story should always include some basic information:

- Size of the audience.
- Location of the speech.
- Reason for the speech.
- Highlights of the speech, including good quotes.
- Reaction of the audience, especially at dramatic points during the speech.

Although you need to include this basic information, don't clutter the top of your story with it — unless it is crucial to the event. Write the story just as you would any other good story.

You can lead with a hard-news approach that emphasizes a main point the speaker made or a soft-news approach that describes the person or uses an anecdote from the speech. Just don't lead with a no-news approach: Someone made a speech. Tell the reader what the speaker said.

For example, here is the kind of lead to avoid; this one appeared on a story in a campus newspaper:

> Students from Gay and Lesbian Services spoke yesterday to a psychology class about their lives and experiences.

What did they say? It's better to focus on some interesting point they made.

Speakers usually don't make their strongest points first and follow in chronological order, so your story shouldn't be written in that order. Put the most emotional or newsworthy information first. Then back it up with quotes and supporting points.

Sometimes the most interesting information isn't what happens during the speech. It can be what happens after the speech or outside the place while the person is speaking, especially if there is a protest or other major reaction to the speech.

Russavia/Creative Commons

Dachau Concentration Camp, one of the Nazi prison camps where a Holocaust survivor described his childhood

You can also use storytelling techniques for speeches. In the next example, a journalism student used narrative and descriptive writing to convey the drama of a speech by a survivor of the Holocaust. Notice where the writer put the basic information: when, where and how many people attended the speech.

Zev Kedem huddled in silence with his grandparents in a pigeon coop above his family's apartment while soldiers searched for them. His grandparents were prepared to swallow vials of poison as the soldiers tried the metal door they hid behind.

The door held. And the soldiers went on.

The year was 1942, and so begins Zev Kedem's story of survival that began over 70 years ago as Adolf Hitler orchestrated the Holocaust.

A "Schindler's List" survivor, Kedem spoke for over an hour as he told the story of his childhood in a Nazi concentration camp to 750 people in the Union Ballroom last night.

— GAIL JOHNSON

Here is a basic speech story that starts with a summary lead followed by a backup quote in the third paragraph. Note that the basics of location, audience size and reaction are lower in the story.

REPORTER NOTES LOWER STANDARDS IN JOURNALISM

Half of the reporting duo that unearthed the Watergate scandal, which led to the downfall of President Nixon, railed Saturday against what he characterized as another downfall: the media's fascination with the "loopy and lurid."

Former *Washington Post* reporter Carl Bernstein took aim at trash television, inaccurate reporting and media monopolies, primarily that of mogul Rupert Murdoch. The media are fascinated with celebrity, gossip and manufactured controversy, and pander to viewers and readers, adding to the "triumph of trash culture," he said.

"The greatest threat to the truth today may well be in our own profession," said Bernstein, who spoke for more than an hour at Budig Hall. His speech was sponsored by Kansas University's Student Union Activities.

Although every society has an "idiot subculture bubbling beneath the surface," Bernstein said a constant diet of certain television talk shows could cause it to boil over.

The problem needs to be addressed at the root level, with reporters refusing to limit their horizons and keep digging for the "best obtainable version of the truth," he said. "Really great reporting almost always comes from the initiative of the reporter, not the editor," said Bernstein.

— CHRIS KOGER, *Lawrence* (Kansas)
Journal-World

MULTIMEDIA COACH

WHEN YOU COVER speeches, meetings and news conferences, plan to provide additional coverage on the Web, including audio and video if possible.

■ Write or broadcast a story advancing coverage of meetings, and post highlights or a complete meeting agenda on the Web.

■ Tape the event to post sound bites or the entire speech or news conference on the Web.

■ Get a complete copy in digital form of budgets, proposals, speeches or other documents to post on the Web.

■ Be prepared to post a breaking news story of the event online, and plan a more complete follow-up story for the next print or broadcast edition of the news.

■ Focus on the significance of a news conference or meeting; find people who are affected by the news before, during or after a meeting or news conference.

■ Plan a highlights box of the key points in a speech, news conference or meeting for print, broadcast or Web publication.

STORIES ABOUT NEWS CONFERENCES

News conferences are like speeches, except that the questions reporters ask after a news conference are often more important than the prepared comments the speaker makes. The answers to those questions are an important part of the story — and sometimes are the story. Consider news reports after the U.S. president conducts a news conference. His prepared remarks often are less interesting than his answers to the press corps.

Do your homework. Before or after the news conference, research the issue. If the conference is about a local crime, check files or background to provide perspective. How many other crimes of this nature have occurred? If the conference is about a city issue, how does the information affect your readers and viewers? Don't just recite the news; interpret it so that your audience can understand how the issues affect them.

Stories about news conferences must include the following information:

■ Person or people who conducted the news conference.

■ Reason for the news conference and background.

■ Highlights of the news, including responses to questions.

■ Location, if relevant.

■ Reaction from sources with similar and opposing points of view.

Stories about news conferences are like most other news stories. Although reporters' questions may prompt the most interesting information, the answers are usually incorporated into the story without references such as "In response to a question" or "When asked about . . . "

Leif Skoogfors/Federal Emergency Management Agency

When covering a press conference, include responses to reporters' questions.

Centers for Disease Control and Prevention

Graphics enhance presentations at press conferences, especially if stories will be posted on the Web.

Many news conferences these days are conducted by audio or video or teleconferences, especially from federal government agencies. However, the principles of coverage are similar to conferences attended in person.

Here is a story based on a press conference by the Centers for Disease Control and Prevention about a report on binge drinking among women and girls.

Summary lead–main point; reason for press conference

Binge drinking is a significant but underestimated problem among women and adolescent girls, according to a new report from the U.S. Centers for Disease Control and Prevention.

The report found that nearly 14 million U.S. women binge drink about three times a month, and consume an average of six drinks per binge. Binge drinking is defined as consuming four or more drinks on an occasion for women and girls.

Location — where, when

"Drinking too much, including binge drinking, causes about 23,000 deaths among women and girls in the United States each year," Dr. Thomas Frieden, director of the CDC, said at a press conference in Atlanta Tuesday.

Supporting quotes

"It puts women at increased risk for many health problems such as breast cancer, sexually transmitted diseases, heart disease, and unintended pregnancy," he said. "Pregnant women who binge drink expose a developing baby to high levels of alcohol, which can lead to fetal alcohol spectrum disorders and sudden infant death syndrome," he said.

Highlights

The report was based on data the CDC researchers collected from 278,000 women through the Behavioral Risk Factor Surveillance System. The key findings included:

- About one in eight women and one in five high school girls report binge drinking.
- Binge drinking was most common among white and Hispanic women and among women with household incomes of $75,000 or more.
- Half of all high school girls who drink alcohol report binge drinking.

Reaction

Dr. Robert Brewer, head of the CDC's alcohol program, said that binge drinking is not a new problem among women and girls, but there are special concerns because they metabolize alcohol differently than males and reach higher blood levels faster.

"It is alarming to see that binge drinking is so common among women and girls, and that women and girls are drinking so much when they do," Brewer said. "The good news is that the same scientifically proven strategies for communities and clinical settings that we know can prevent binge drinking in the overall population can also work to prevent binge drinking among women and girls."

EXERCISES

1 **Speech story:** If possible, cover a speech on campus or in the community.

2 **Online speeches:** Go to YouTube and search for speeches. You can find graduation speeches by

Bill Gates (*www.youtube.com/watch?v=AP5VlhbJwFs*) or famous speeches, including Martin Luther King's "I Have a Dream" speech, which is also available on other online sites.

 MindTap

FEATURED ONLINE ACTIVITIES: Log on to the MindTap for Rich's Writing and Reporting News to access a variety of robust additional material, including this chapter's learning objectives, activities, comprehension quizzes, and more. Be sure to check out the "City Council" and/or "Big Fire" NewsScene scenarios for an interactive writing exercise that will help to reinforce many of the themes presented in this chapter.

CHAPTER 19

Government and Statistical Stories

I'm convinced there's not a beat that you can't use database reporting for. The biggest shortage in journalism is people with computer-assisted reporting skills.

—JENNIFER LAFLEUR, *Data Journalism Editor, Center for Investigative Reporting*

COACHING TIPS

Use **impact leads** to explain how readers and viewers are affected.

The more complex the information, **the simpler your sentences** should be.

Avoid **jargon**.

Write for your readers and viewers, not your sources.

Use analogies to help readers understand numbers.

Think about graphics before you write your story. **Use charts** for numbers.

Post digital versions of budgets and government proposals on the Web.

© Haywiremedia/Shutterstock.com

JENNIFER LAFLEUR WASN'T LOOKING FOR A DATE, BUT SHE WANTED to find the best places to meet single people. Using a census database, she found the information she needed — and something she didn't want. "I threw out the data for prisons," she said. "They had a high level of single men, but not men I'd want to date." Combining the statistics with some old-fashioned reporting, she discovered that the best place to meet single men was in grocery stores.

"After I did the story, an 85-year-old woman called me and said, 'I loved your story, honey, but could you do it by age?'" LaFleur said.

LaFleur is senior editor for data journalism at the Center for Investigative Reporting. She also trains journalists throughout the country how to use databases and the Internet. She reels off stories she has reported from databases — for example, what color cars get the most tickets, how many dead people voted in an election, what names are most popular for the dogs in a community. And more serious stories about bus drivers with drunken-driving records and how the government funds schools that don't exist.

Hillcrest Rural Schools in north-central Kansas is set to get nearly $7,000 in federal stimulus money to help its disadvantaged students. Only one glitch: The district doesn't exist anymore. It closed in 2006 when it was merged into another nearby district.

Jennifer LaFleur trains students in computer-assisted reporting at the University of Kansas.

Courtesy of Jennifer LaFleur

Hillcrest is one of nearly 14,000 school districts or local education agencies nationwide that the U.S. Department of Education reported would get stimulus funds under its Title I program.

But some of those districts are phantoms because they were dissolved or merged.

In Kansas, 11 school districts that no longer exist are on the U.S. Department of Education's distribution list for stimulus funds. They set to receive nearly $600,000.

(www.propublica.org/article/phantom-school-districts-tagged-for-stimulus-dollars-925)
—JENNIFER LAFLEUR, *ProPublica*

"I'm convinced there's not a beat that you can't use database reporting for," she said. "The biggest shortage in journalism is people with computer-assisted reporting skills."

The term "computer-assisted reporting" often refers to the use of databases, but it also refers to use of the Internet to find sources, documents and information about millions of topics. You can download many government databases directly into your computer and analyze them in a spreadsheet program such as Excel or in a relational database program that allows you to find and compare data.

A staggering amount of federal government data is available on the Web. But some of the state or local information you want might not be accessible online, especially in small communities. You have to ask officials for it, and they may be reluctant to give it to you.

LaFleur says reporters should try to find the person in a government agency who knows about computers and data. "It's usually a guy named Leon who works

MULTIMEDIA COACH

WHEN YOU COVER government agencies, think in multimedia terms. Don't just plan to write a story or script for a print or broadcast publication: Plan to provide complete versions of proposals and budgets on the Web. Get a digital version of a local government budget, school district test scores, government proposals and important statistics to accompany stories on the Web.

Here are some other tips for using the Web for government statistics and information:

- Check the date the information was posted; many reports may not be current. Contact the agency by phone or email to find out if more current information is available.

- Check your city, school district and state sites for background information on government stories.

- Check whether advocacy agencies and other groups in your community have websites. Use these sites for sources in reaction and human-interest stories.

- Add graphics to explain statistics or digital maps to identify locations in your stories.

in the basement," she says. "I go to whatever agency I'm covering to find out how they do what they do. I also try to be overly cheery. I never first go in and demand a computer file."

After you get and analyze your data, don't flood your story with statistics. LaFleur bristles when people say computer-assisted stories are about numbers. They may contain only a paragraph or two of numbers, which could make the difference in the focus, but the stories still require good reporting and writing techniques.

REPORTING TIPS

Here are some tips for covering local government:

Human Interest: Make government relevant to readers by finding people who are affected by the actions of government agencies. Using social media tools, you can find sources to contact. But don't forget the old-fashioned reporting technique of going into the community and talking to people face to face.

Bulletin Boards: Check them for job offerings and other announcements that could result in stories.

Memos and Letters to and from City Officials: Check with the city clerk or administrative assistants for access to files about any issue involving public funds. Most of these — except for personnel and labor matters — are public records.

Planning Commission: Check agendas for meetings, and develop sources in planning offices. Seek information not only about future plans but also about the past. Some great stories can result from plans gone awry.

Consultants: Check who gets consulting contracts and fees, and investigate previous studies on the same subject.

Zoning Meetings: They can be full of human interest. People care about what is going up or down in their neighborhood.

Legal Notices: Check them for bids and other notices. Government agencies must advertise for any major purchases. Check with disgruntled bidders for major contracts. Many good stories lurk behind these seemingly boring subjects.

Audits: Read them carefully. They can reveal misuse of public funds.

Union Leaders: Cultivate heads of unions in school districts and cities as sources. They know what is going on behind the scenes.

Non-officials: Get into the schools and write about what teachers and students are doing, or talk to people working in government offices. Spend some time learning about what they do, how they do it and whether they do it. Many good stories can result from finding out how lower-level employees work in government.

A Naval officer volunteers at an elementary school in an Adopt-a-School program.

The System: Learn how it works. Are officials in your town following the laws? If you don't know how government is supposed to operate, you won't be able to find out if it is working properly.

Records: Check expense accounts, purchasing vouchers and other records pertaining to issues or officials you are covering.

Offices: Check all the offices in your government building, and find out what kind of work the people in them do. For example, do you know the function of every office in your campus administration building? You could find features or great news stories just by checking what the people in these offices do.

The Internet: Many communities, local police departments and school districts have Web pages offering a wealth of information and documents. You can find sources, news releases and databases on their sites. In addition, websites for state and federal government agencies abound.

VISUALS

Before you write your story, think not about what you can put in it; think about what you can pull out of it, especially when you are writing stories with statistics. Use highlights boxes, facts boxes and charts to break out key concepts of a proposal or budget. Then you don't need to clutter the story with the same information.

Consider empowerment boxes, information that tells readers what the story means to them and what they can do. These boxes should contain information about where they can call for help, more information or other facts that would be useful. Once you have decided what can be displayed visually, you can present the remaining information verbally.

Here's an empowerment box from the *Reno* (Nevada) *Gazette-Journal* that accompanied a story about overdue parking tickets. The city adopted late fees that would add $30 to tickets not paid within a month.

TO PAY

- Pay at the city clerk's cashier office, using cash, check or Visa or MasterCard.

TO PROTEST

- Make an appointment. The hearing officer is setting aside time in Room 204 at City Hall. Call 334-2293.

ETHICS

ETHICAL DILEMMA: You are the news producer for your campus television station. Spring break is approaching, and every year at this time sexually transmitted diseases become rampant. The Centers for Disease Control and Prevention offers a video explaining the types of diseases and how to treat them. The video quality is excellent, and it features unidentified students and a doctor explaining risks and treatment. You don't have the staff or time to produce your own video on the subject, and the one you have seems perfect. After all, it's a news release, so you are entitled to use it without any copyright violation. Will you use the video news release? Will you identify the source as the CDC?

Guidelines: The Radio Television Digital News Association says this in its code of ethics: "Clearly disclose the origin of information and label all material provided by outsiders." However, a *New York Times* investigative story revealed that many television stations are using video news releases from the government without identifying them as government sponsored. The problem has become such a concern that the Boston University Department of Journalism adopted a resolution condemning the practice. It states in part: "We find particularly objectionable the use of 'phony reporters' hired by one agency or another who deliver complete reports, including sign-offs, without ever mentioning their affiliation and, in some cases, misrepresenting it. We also condemn those stations that knowingly run news segments, written, shot and recorded by the government with no identification as to the source of the material. We regard these practices as unethical journalism that run the high risk of confusing or even deceiving the public."

Centers for Disease Control and Prevention media tools.

■ Hearing times are from 5–8 p.m. on Nov. 4 and Nov. 6; 1–4 p.m. on Nov. 8; 5–8 p.m. on Nov. 13 and Nov. 14.

WRITING TIPS

After you have found good information for your stories, how can you make them readable?

One way is to avoid "jargon," stilted or technical words and phrases that officials use, but readers don't. Writing coaches call this artificial language "journalese," long words or phrases instead of short ones that would be clearer. Examples: "medication" for "medicine"; "restructuring" for "changing"; "funds" for "money." When you need a loan from a friend, do you ask to borrow "funds"?

Clichés are another common form of journalese in government stories. Journalists love to use words related to heat and cold: "heated debate," "hotly contested," "blasted," "chilling effect," "cooling-off period." In this example, the reporter strained the lead by picking a holiday that had nothing to do with the story, just so she could use these "heated" terms:

> The Fourth of July is four months away, but insults and accusations exploded like fireworks at the tumultuous Board of Supervisors meeting yesterday.
> The firecracker was Republican Supervisor John Hanson, who blasted his colleagues by calling them "crooks."

Here are some other tips:

Use Short, Simple Sentences The more complex the information, the simpler and shorter the sentences should be:

| *Complex* | The City Commission last night approved a resolution to authorize the city staff to apply for funding through the systems enhancement program of the state Department of Transportation for a $3.6 million project for the expansion of U.S. Highway 77 from two to four lanes for 2.2 miles between Interstate 70 and Kansas Highway 18. | The City Commission last night agreed to apply for $3.6 million from the state Department of Transportation to expand a portion of U.S. Highway 77 from two to four lanes.

The project would widen the highway for 2.2 miles between Interstate 70 and Kansas Highway 18. | *Simpler* |

Keep the Subject and Verb Close Together Long clauses and phrases before the verb make it hard for the reader to remember what the subject is — who said or did what. Use subject–verb–object order.

Complex	Rather than having government inspectors sweep through businesses, finding violations and imposing fines, in Maine, officials at the federal Occupational Safety and Health Administration, in an effort to improve work conditions and save the government money, are urging employers to identify health and safety problems and then to work with the agency to correct them.	A federal agency is urging employers in Maine to find and correct health and safety problems in their businesses instead of having government inspectors seek violations and impose fines. The move is an attempt by the federal Occupational Safety and Health Administration to improve work conditions in businesses and save the government money. *Simpler*

Use Vigorous Verbs Whenever possible, replace "to be" verbs and other bland verbs with words that help to paint a picture of the activity you are reporting.

> A 42-year-old St. Joseph man escaped a blazing house without serious injuries when he grabbed a coffee table, hurled it through a picture window, and then, like a movie stunt man, leaped through the jagged glass to escape the heat and flames.
>
> —**TERRY RAFFENSPERGER,** *St. Joseph* **(Missouri)**
> *News-Press*

Avoid Starting Sentences with 'There' The word "there" forces you to use a weak "to be" verb, such as "is," "are," "was" or "were."

Weak	There was sadness expressed among local people gathered Thursday night to watch their team lose by two points in the NCAA finals.	Local people expressed sadness as they gathered Thursday night to watch their team lose by two points in the NCAA final. *Strong*

Interpret Information Tell readers how they are affected.

> The value of real estate in the county jumped roughly $83 million in one year — an increase of about 27 percent.
>
> What does all that mean to the average homeowner? Most likely a lower tax rate — called a mill levy — and perhaps a lower tax bill for some, Douglas County Administrator Craig Weinaug said.

Translate Jargon Explain terms in concepts or comparisons that the reader can understand.

> A spot inventory of Jeanne Johns' freezer shows the usual stuff. Ice cream. Frozen peas. TV dinners.
>
> Acid rain.
>
> Acid rain? You bet.
>
> Johns, who lives in Haslett, is one of four Michigan volunteers in the Citizen Acid Rain Monitoring Network. The network has more than 300 stations nationwide to monitor acid rain. ...
>
> She measures the acidity on a pH scale ranging from 0 to 14, with 0 being the most acidic. The scale increases tenfold, meaning a 4.0 reading is 10 times more acidic than 5.0.
>
> Normal precipitation is usually about 5.6. A pH of 5.0 is equal to the acid content in cola. Frogs die if placed in water with a pH of 4.0. Battery acid is 1.5.
>
> —KEVIN O'HANLON, *Lansing* (Michigan)
> *State-Journal*

Vary the Pace Avoid writing huge blocks of complicated concepts and complex sentences. Follow long sentences and long paragraphs with a short sentence.

Focus on a Person to Explain Impact The way an issue affects one person makes it clear to many. That's the concept of *The Wall Street Journal* formula, and it can be used effectively in government stories. Lead with an anecdote about a person; then go from the specific to the general. It's the "one of many" technique.

> Linda Green paid $42,000 in 1982 for a house on a half-acre lot in Fontana, banking on the equity that would build over the years.
>
> But if Fontana's new general plan is approved, Green is fearful her property may be worth no more than the day she bought it.
>
> The proposed plan would change the zoning on her half-acre so no additional homes could be built on it, making the site less attractive to buyers.

> Green is not alone in her fears. She was among several landowners complaining Monday that the revised general plan — a blueprint for Fontana's growth — will put their properties in less profitable zoning areas.
>
> "I bought my land as an investment. If they zone it down, I will lose my money, and I worked hard to put my money into it," Green told the planning commission during the first public hearing on the new 20-year plan.
>
> More than 130 people attended the hearing.
>
> —TONY SAAVEDRA, *The* (San Bernardino, California) *Sun*

Use an Impact Lead or Explain Impact in the Story Tell how the reader will be affected by a bureaucratic action or proposal.

> A $10,000 car would cost $25 more in taxes, a $40 power saw an extra dime and a $4 six-pack of imported beer a penny extra in Rockford if Alderman Ernst Shafer, R-3rd, gets his way.
>
> Shafer wants Rockford to join the push in Springfield for a 0.25 percent increase in the sales tax. Locally the sales tax would rise from 6.25 to 6.5 percent under the proposal.
>
> —BRIAN LEAF, *Rockford* (Illinois) *Register Star*

Avoid Boring Quotes You don't have to quote an official to prove you talked to him. If you can express the official's point better in your own words, do so.

Use the Pull-Quote Test Are your quotes strong enough to be broken out as pull quotes? That's one way of testing whether they are worth using in a story.

Use Conversational Style Write the story as though you were having a conversation with a friend. Here is how one reporter used the conversational style in the lead of a government story:

> How'd you like an airport for a neighbor? Or maybe a landfill or an incinerator?
>
> Probably about as much as government officials like trying to find a site for these things.
>
> But what if you could negotiate noise insulation for your airport-area home? Or an agreement requiring the incinerator to douse its fires if it didn't burn hot enough to eliminate most pollutants?
>
> Those alternatives were offered Wednesday to a roomful of Twin Cities area public officials frustrated by their protracted and often doomed efforts to make people accept controversial facilities they don't want.

Ropable/Creative Commons

A landfill serves as a creative lead for a government story about undesirable locations for development.

> In an area where officials are looking for places for new landfills, a new airport, light-rail transit routes and other public works projects, the Metropolitan Council sponsored yesterday's conference in an effort to see if there's a better way.
>
> There is, they were told by a specialist in how to make the risks of such facilities more acceptable to their neighbors.

—STEVE BRANDT, (Minneapolis) *Star Tribune*

Use Lists Use them in the middle or at the end of the story, especially to explain key points of an issue. Lists are particularly helpful in stories with numbers or explanations of proposals. They are also helpful for stories distributed on mobile media because readers can scan the information quickly.

Avoid the City-Dump Syndrome Be selective. Use only quotes and facts that you need. Don't dump your notebook into the story.

Use the Blocking Technique If you have more than three speakers, block the comments from each one, and then do not use the sources again unless you reintroduce them. The reader can't remember all the officials by second reference only.

Read Aloud If you read all or parts of your story aloud, you will catch the cumbersome phrases.

SOCIAL MEDIA

GOVERNMENT AFFECTS people's lives, but too many stories just parrot news releases or report coverage of meetings. If you don't help readers and viewers understand how the information affects them, chances are that they won't read or watch the information you are trying to convey. Social media tools provide journalists with more ways than ever before to connect with their communities and devise stories that will reflect people's concerns.

Reporters used to go to barber shops or beauty parlors, local beer halls and other gathering places to find out what people in the community were discussing. That's still a good idea, but now the gathering places are online. With social media such as blogs, Twitter, Facebook and others, you can reach far more people and engage them in issues that concern them. You can also use social media sites to follow blogs or Twitter sites of politicians, governmental agencies and citizens who are interested in community issues.

Many of the federal government agencies post information on social media sites, including the U.S. Census Bureau, which is a treasure trove of statistical information.

U.S. Census Bureau

Follow Us

Keep up to date on the 2010 Census by downloading the Apportionment Countdown Clock and following us on Twitter, Facebook, YouTube and Flickr.

STATISTICAL STORIES

Jennifer LaFleur writes about numbers all the time, but they rarely appear in the leads to her stories. She knows how to relate to readers and make sense of statistics. Here are some of the techniques you can use in stories with statistics:

Use Analogies Whenever you are referring to large numbers, comparisons with something familiar to readers are especially helpful. This is an analogy from a story about pollution in Alabama's rivers:

> Each minute, about 30 million gallons of Alabama river water, or the equivalent of what it would take to fill 60 Olympic-sized swimming pools, flush into Mobile Bay, washing over oyster beds in the northern part of the bay closed to harvesting.
>
> —DAN MORSE, *The* (Montgomery) *Alabama Advertiser*

Round Off Numbers In most cases it is better to round off numbers — for instance, to $3.5 million instead of $3,499,590. Make it easy for the reader to grasp large numbers. This is especially important in broadcast stories.

Avoid Bunching Numbers in One Paragraph Spread numbers out over a few paragraphs rather than glutting one sentence or paragraph with them. Another good technique is to present numbers in lists.

Interpret Numbers Show the impact on readers in terms they can understand.

University enrollments might offer clues for dating prospects.

A 10-year analysis of enrollment patterns at Kansas University and five other state universities revealed two dating tips for college students:

- Men hoping to improve dating prospects might consider attending Emporia State University, where 60 percent of students are women.
- Women interested in more dating opportunities should look to Kansas State University, the only state university in the area with more men than women.

—TIM CARPENTER, *Lawrence* (Kansas) *Journal-World*

Use Storytelling Techniques

Even statistical stories can lend themselves to storytelling.

Statistically speaking, last month was Nate Payne's best chance in 16 years to get a job.

Payne is a resident of Pennsylvania, where the unemployment rate in March jumped to a 16-year low.

But statistics didn't do a thing for Payne, 29. He was laid off last month from his job as a heavy-equipment operator for a paving contractor and hasn't worked since.

He spent yesterday morning waiting for an interview with a job service counselor in the Pennsylvania Employment Service office at Broad and Master Streets.

He had plenty of company. At least 50 other men and women had come to the office by 10 a.m. to confirm that they had not found jobs and were still eligible for unemployment payments or to see whether any jobs were available that met their requirements.

Payne's assessment: "It's really grim this time."

—ANDREA KNOT, *The Philadelphia Inquirer*

Use Graphics Try to get the numbers out of your story and into a separate graphic. You need to mention some of the numbers, but always consider whether a chart, graph or diagram could convey the information better.

BUDGET STORIES

Budget stories are hard to write and even harder to read if you flood them with a lot of numbers. And in broadcast stories, numbers are worse to hear. You can't avoid using numbers in all stories, but don't put several numbers in the same sentence or paragraph. Whenever you are writing about numbers, you must analyze what they mean. Most reports list numbers in comparison to a previous year or time frame. Always put numbers in perspective in two ways:

- **Explain change:** Do the numbers show an increase or decrease from a previous period?

- **State the significance:** What do the numbers mean, and why are they important? Explain what is interesting or important about these statistics in a way that will make readers care. You can even use a transition such as "Here's what this means to you."

This graphic is a visual way to convey information from a survey by the U.S. Census Bureau for money that can be earned after graduation in different fields.

Consider these basic questions:

- **Who** is most affected by the budget? Who are the winners and losers?

- **What** are the major changes in a budget? How does it compare with previous years? Don't just say the budget or tuition has increased by 10 percent; give the figures and state the current tuition.

- **When** do the new proposals go into effect? Not all budgets have immediate ramifications.

- **Where** are the increases and decreases in the budget?

- **Why** are the cuts or additions to the budget being proposed?

Budget planning starts several months before the budget is approved. Learn how to interpret the proposed budget by asking a financial officer of the city, school or agency to explain it to you before the budget is released. If he can't brief you on this year's proposal, use last year's budget to learn the system. In most cases, officials will be willing to cooperate because they want you to present the facts accurately.

Basically, budgets have two sections:

- **Revenues:** The income, usually derived from taxes — primarily property taxes in municipalities. But there also are sales taxes, income taxes and fees. Look for clues about how the revenue will be raised. Will property taxes increase?

Used with permission of Sage Ross

Explain how budgets and taxes will affect people.

If you are covering a university budget, will tuition be increased? Find out how the revenue source will affect your readers.

- **Expenditures:** Where most of the money will be spent. Will some departments be increasing expenses more than others, such as police or fire departments? If so, why? Will salaries be increased or more people be hired? How do the expenditures for this year compare with those of the past few years?

Generally, budgets include figures from the previous year or past few years. Look for major increases and decreases in revenues and expenditures.

Before a government agency can adopt a budget, it must conduct public hearings, where the public can comment about the budget. If the budget proposal is at the hearing stage, be sure to include the dates of the hearings in your story. Taxpayers often want to attend hearings to protest cutbacks, tax increases or to request money for programs they support.

Budget and Tax Terms

If you want to explain budgets, you must know what these terms mean:

Assessments and Property Taxes Common in municipal budgets, where taxes are based on real estate. Homeowners pay taxes based on an assessment, or estimated value, of their property. A city property appraiser determines this amount based on a number of factors: size of the property, number of bedrooms, construction and so on. For example, suppose you decide to buy a condominium or a house selling for $160,000. That is its "market value," the price it sells for on the market. Some communities base their tax on the full market value, but most use only a percentage of the total value. The property is given an "assessed value," a value for tax purposes. If your community bases its tax on half the market value, your house would be assessed for $80,000. Your annual property taxes equal some percentage of the assessed value.

Employees of the U.S. Government Printing Office prepare the federal budget.

Capital Budget Money used to pay for major improvements, such as the construction of highways or new buildings. Capital is often raised by selling bonds, and people who buy the bonds receive interest. The government then uses the money and repays the bonds, plus interest, over a period of years in what is called "debt service." The process is much like buying a house: The bank lends you money; you live in the house and repay the loan plus interest on a long-term basis, often over 30 years.

Deficit When government spends more money than it receives. Most municipalities and states require a balanced budget: The expenses must be the same as the income. The difference between the expenditures and the income is the deficit, or debt.

Fiscal Year The year in which budgeted funds will be spent. In government, the budget term often starts on July 1 and goes to June 30, instead of the calendar year. So if you use a fiscal year, give the dates: "in this fiscal year, which starts July 1." Or if you are writing about when the money will run out: "in this fiscal year, which ends June 30."

Mean An average; the sum of all the figures divided by the number of items in the survey. If the salaries of 100 journalists total $3 million, they have a mean salary of $30,000. The salaries of the 100 journalists in the survey would be added and then divided by 100 to get the mean.

Median An average; the value in the middle of a range. If 15 journalists in a survey earn from $20,000 to $65,000, you would list all the salaries in numerical order and find the one in the center of the list. The eighth number in the list would be the median.

Mill Unit equal to $1 for every $1,000 that a house is assessed. Local school and city taxes are based on mills. Explain the impact of these taxes clearly. If the school tax rate is 25 mills, your story should say, "The tax rate is 25 mills, which equals $25 for every $1,000 of assessed property valuation." Or you could insert a definition: "A mill equals $1 for every $1,000 of assessed value on a property." Then give an example: "Under this tax rate, a homeowner whose property is valued at $80,000 (multiplied by 0.025) would pay $2,000 in school taxes." Try to avoid using the term "mills"; just

Members of the press cover the unveiling of the U.S. budget at the Government Printing Office.

say the tax rate will be $25 for every $1,000 of assessed property value. Follow with a specific example so residents can figure out how much their tax will be.

Operating Budget Money used to provide services (police, fire, garbage removal and so on) and to pay for the operation of government. Most of the money for this budget comes from taxes.

Other Taxes Wage tax, income tax and sales tax. Cities and states often charge these additional taxes. Check when you write your budget stories to determine whether they will be increased or decreased. If they will stay the same, say so.

Per Capita The rate per person. For example, if a community has 50 murders and a population of 175,000 people, the per capita murder rate would be determined by dividing 50 by 175,000, to yield 0.000286. However, such a small number is hard to comprehend, so it might be multiplied by 100,000 to give a number per 100,000. In this case the rate would be 28.6 murders for every 100,000 people.

Reappraisal State or local decision to re-evaluate properties in the community, usually to increase their values. This action almost always generates good stories because it affects people dramatically.

A groundswell of protest over the mass reappraisal of Atlanta and Fulton County property is threatening to become a wholesale tax revolt.

> Thousands of homeowners have turned out at meetings throughout the city and county to express displeasure with their new assessments, in some cases more than double last year's.
>
> At the South Fulton County Annex, more than one thousand people gathered Monday to talk about fighting the assessments.
>
> "My assessment went up 190 percent and I'll gladly sell my home to the county for what they think it's worth," said Mitch Skandalakis, a leader of the Task Force for Good Government, as the crowd roared.
>
> —MARK SHERMAN, *Atlanta Constitution*

Writing Techniques

Impact is crucial in budget stories. So are graphics. A chart or list of key numbers can make a story more presentable. Also get reactions from city officials, residents at public hearings or the people most affected by budget cuts. If you are writing about university budgets, get reactions from administrators, students, professors and the officials whose departments will be affected most.

Here are some key points to include in a budget story, not necessarily in this order:

- Total amount of the budget (rounded off when possible — $44.6 million instead of $44,552,379). Most budgets are supposed to be balanced, so the figure applies to both revenues and expenditures.
- Amount of increase or decrease.
- Tax or tuition levy, or how funds will be raised (impact on reader, comparison to current tax).
- Major expenditures (major increases and decreases in department funds).
- Consequences (impact on the government or agency — cuts in personnel, services, and so on).
- Historical comparisons (how budget compares with previous year and past few years).
- Reactions from officials and people affected by increases or decreases.
- Definitions and explanations of technical terms.

Here is a way of explaining impact in a lead that is not cluttered with statistics:

> Pinellas School Superintendent Howard Hinesley has proposed a list of budget cuts for the next school year that will mean fewer textbooks, fewer teachers and fewer administrators if School Board members approve them next Wednesday.
>
> —PATTY CURTIN JONES, *St. Petersburg* (Florida) *Times*

Library of Congress Prints and Photographs Division

A Philadelphia row house neighborhood.

Don't forget that budgets affect people. Here is an example of an anecdotal-narrative approach to an advance on the city budget:

It was 8:05 on a Monday in August, Rosemary Farnon remembers, when her husband, Tony, called the police to report that their row house in the Juniata Park section had been ransacked.

Amid a shambles of overturned furniture, scattered papers and food taken from the fridge, the Farnons nervously and angrily waited nearly five hours before an officer appeared. He explained apologetically that the local police district had no cops to spare.

Theirs is one story, from one neighborhood, but it typifies what is happening across Philadelphia:

Taxes are up and services are down — and residents are unhappy about it.

So Rosemary Farnon and hundreds of thousands of taxpayers will be listening closely Thursday when the mayor proposes the budget for the coming fiscal year, which begins July 1.

—DAN MYERS AND IDRIS M. DIAZ,
The Philadelphia Inquirer

EXERCISES

1 Census for dating prospects: David Cuillier, director of the School of Journalism at the University of Arizona, created this exercise to teach students how to find the best and worst places for dating prospects by U.S. Census data. It is similar to the research Jennifer LaFleur did for her story, but now you can tailor the material for your own interests. Here's a variation of his exercise:

- Go to the U.S. Census Bureau website at *www .census.gov*, and find the states with the highest and lowest male-to-female ratios: *www .census.gov/prod/cen2010/briefs/c2010br-03.pdf*.

- Scroll down until you reach Table 3, and check which states have the highest ratios of males to females; then check Figure 5 for the states with the median age you prefer. Next, scroll to Table 4, "Ten Places with the Highest and Lowest Sex Ratio: 2010."

- Go back to the main Census page (www .census.gov).

- Click Quick Facts. Use the interactive map or pull-down bar to select a state. Check the statistics for that state, and narrow your search to a county or city to find population statistics that suit your purpose.

- Alternative route: On the main census page, pull down Data on the top menu, to Easy Stats. Choose a state from the pull-down menu, click on a topic of interest, such as Jobs, and check the results.

- For more detailed statistics such as same-sex couples, statistics for educational attainment as well as others, check the main menu under People and choose the statistics you want to search.

2 Taxes: Figure your taxes using the following method:

- You own a condominium that is worth $100,000 on the market. The city appraises residential property for tax purposes at 11.5 percent of its market value. What is the assessed value of your property?

- Using your assessed value as calculated in problem a, figure your tax rate as follows:

  a Write your assessed value:

  b Divide the assessed value by 1,000, because a mill is a $1 tax on every $1,000 of assessed property value. Write that figure:

  c The tax levy in your community is 125 mills. Multiply the amount in problem b–2 times the tax levy to figure your tax bill. Write the result:

- Last year your taxes were $1,250. Using the answer from problem b–3 for this year's taxes, figure your tax percentage increase.

- The city had a tax rate of 125 mills last year and is raising it to 137.5 mills this year. What is the percentage increase?

3 Your dream home: Envision the home you would like to own. How much will it cost? If you want a swimming pool, sauna and other amenities, make sure that you figure them into the price, along with the land value in your community or wherever you want to live. When you figure the selling price, that's the market value.

Now figure your taxes. Your community assesses property at 30 percent of its market value for tax purposes. The tax rate for city and schools combined will be 75 mills. How much will you pay in taxes?

 MindTap

CHAPTER 20
Crime and Punishment

© Liv Friis-larsen/Shutterstock.com

The police beat is all about people, what makes them tick, what makes them become heroes or homicidal maniacs. It has it all: greed, sex, violence, comedy and tragedy.

—**EDNA BUCHANAN**, *Former Police Reporter,*
The Miami Herald

COACHING TIPS

Role-play: What would you want to know if you were affected by this crime?

Gather enough details to **recreate the crime scene** as though you were witnessing it.

Avoid the jargon of police or other legal authorities. If you don't understand a term, chances are the reader may not know it either.

Always include the **background of the case,** no matter how many days a crime story or trial continues.

Double-check your story for accuracy, and make sure that you don't convict someone of a crime before a judge or jury does.

Check the Internet and sex offender registries for **background** of suspects.

T

HE POLICE BEAT, WHICH OFTEN INCLUDES THE FIRE DEPARTMENT, is considered an entry-level job. Most reporters move on to other beats after a few years of covering crime stories. Edna Buchanan did not. She covered the police beat at *The Miami Herald* for more than 20 years before resigning to write books. But while she was at the *Herald*, she turned police reporting into an art form and won a Pulitzer Prize.

A soft-spoken woman, she writes with a strong punch. One Pulitzer Prize juror said, "She writes drop-dead sentences for drop-dead victims. She is never dull." Consider:

> There was music and sunlight as the paddle wheeler Dixie Bell churned north on Indian Creek Thursday. The water shimmered and the wind was brisk. And then the passengers noticed that the people in the next boat were dead.

Buchanan is most famous for the lead she wrote on a story about a man who shoved his way to the front of a line at a fried chicken restaurant. The counter clerk told the man to go to the end of the line and wait his turn. He did. But when he reached the head of the line again, the restaurant had run out of fried chicken. He battered the clerk fiercely, and he was shot fatally by a guard in the restaurant. Her lead: "Gary Robinson died hungry."

"In truth, Edna Buchanan doesn't write about cops. She writes about people," *Herald* editors wrote in the Pulitzer entry. Buchanan is the first to admit that. "You learn more about people on the police beat than any other beat," she said at a convention of investigative reporters.

She said she had reported more than 5,000 violent deaths. How did she keep from getting upset by them and burned out on the job?

> The thing that keeps you going is that you realize you can make things better. You may be affected like everyone else by a terrible tragedy, but you're in a position to do something about it. That's the real joy of this job. We can be catalysts for change. We can bring about justice. Sometimes we are all the victim has got. Police stories do make a difference.
>
> You've got to be accurate and fair and very, very careful, particularly in crime reporting. A news story mentioning somebody's name can ruin their lives or come back to haunt them 25 years later. It is there in black and white on file. It's like a police record; you never outlive it. You can do terrible damage. So you knock on one more door, ask one more question, make one last phone call. It could be the one that counts.

When Buchanan made those phone calls and someone hung up on her, she just redialed the number and said, "We were cut off." The second time, she might have gotten a relative or someone else who was willing to talk, or the first person might have changed his mind. But she didn't try a third time; that would be harassment, she said.

CRIME STORIES

Buchanan gathered her information from interviews and records. And then she wove them into stories with leads that hooked the reader. She said that crime reporters need to talk to witnesses and get color, background, ages and details — what people were wearing, doing and saying when they became crime victims or suspects.

Police have the right to protect the crime scene and limit access to the press. If the crime scene is on public property, reporters and photographers can get as close as police will allow. If the crime scene is on private property, access is at the discretion of the police or the owners of the property.

Police may limit access to the press at a crime scene.

Records

If you have the police beat, you should check the daily police log, also called the "blotter," to see the list of all crimes recorded by police for that day. The log will list the names of the victims and the nature of the crimes. This is public record and should be available to the press and anyone else. However, the reports filed by the officer at the scene and records to cases under investigation may not be available.

Although the incident reports contain the names of the officers who filed them, many police departments with a public information officer do not allow reporters to talk to the arresting officers. If access is permitted, try to talk to the arresting officers, especially in a major crime.

For details about arrests, check the jail log, which should contain the suspect's name and address, birth date, sex, race, occupation, place of arrest and charges.

Previous Criminal Records Check to see if a suspect has a previous criminal record. If someone has been convicted of a crime, that court record should be available in the court jurisdiction where the person was convicted — unless the record is sealed by order of a judge. If the person was charged with a crime and found not guilty or charges were dropped, that record is also public. You need to look up the court file (and get the case file number) under that person's name and probably the year of the court case.

The court file should contain all pertinent information, including names of the lawyers involved, description of the crime and all motions filed in the case. Most important, it will tell what happened — the disposition of the case — including specific terms of the sentence or probation or dismissal. Many court records are posted online in searchable databases.

In some cases, a person convicted of a minor crime can have his record erased — "expunged" — after a number of years, with permission of the court. In other cases, a judge may permit certain records to be sealed, meaning that they will be withheld from the public and available only to law enforcement officers.

University Records In 1986, Jeanne Ann Clery, a 19-year-old student, was raped and murdered in her third-floor dormitory at Lehigh University. Her parents later learned that 38 violent crimes had been committed on the Lehigh campus in the previous three years, but the university was not required to divulge those statistics. Connie and Howard Clery wanted to make sure that their daughter's death was not in vain.

As a result of their efforts, a landmark federal law was enacted, requiring all colleges and universities that have federal student financial aid programs to publish an annual report listing three years of crime statistics. The law, originally called the Campus Security Act, was amended in 1998 and renamed the Clery Act in memory of Jeanne Clery.

However, universities may withhold names on crime reports because of another federal law. The Buckley Amendment to the Family Educational Rights and Privacy Act prohibits government agencies from releasing any personal data about students and employees in institutions that receive federal funding. But in 1992, a new federal law exempted campus records from the restrictions of the Buckley Amendment. Universities are still not compelled to release information on crime records, but they will no longer risk losing federal funds if they do release the names.

Another change added to the act after the shootings at Virginia Tech in 2007 requires institutions to have a plan notifying the campus as soon as an emergency is confirmed. Check out the Clery Act and related information at the Clery Center for Security on Campus (*clerycenter.org/summary-jeanne-clery-act*).

Records of Juvenile Offenders All states have laws restricting the release of records that identify "juvenile offenders," people under age 18. The names are withheld by all branches of the juvenile justice system, including the social services system, but a judge can authorize their release. If a juvenile is being tried as an adult — a decision that is made by a judge — or if the juvenile's name is mentioned in open court, the name can be used. This sometimes happens when the crime is particularly heinous or the juvenile has an extensive criminal record.

Most newspapers and broadcast stations have policies to withhold the names of juveniles, but that is more of an ethical decision than a legal one. The media may use the name if they receive it by legitimate means.

Use of Names Many newspapers and TV news stations also withhold the names of suspects in crime stories until they have been formally charged with the crime. Being arrested means only that someone has been stopped for questioning in a crime.

Many news organizations withhold the name of the person arrested until formal charges have been filed.

U.S. Immigration and Customs Enforcement

The person becomes an official suspect after charges are filed in a court, usually at a hearing called an "arraignment." (The process will be explained in the section about courts.)

Person of Interest: In recent years, police have begun releasing the name of a suspect as a "person of interest" before actual charges are filed. This term is used most often when police have good reason to believe the suspect will soon be charged with the crime, but it is controversial because it casts suspicion on someone who may not be involved in the crime.

Some news organizations also withhold the names of crime victims to protect their privacy. A growing controversy at newspapers and television stations is whether to withhold the names of complainants in rape cases. Again, the policy varies, but most of the media do not publish the names.

When names are used in crime stories, always get the full name, including the middle initial, and double-check the spelling. Do not rely on police reports; many names on reports are spelled incorrectly. Check the names in telephone directories whenever possible. If a discrepancy exists between the name in the phone book and the one the officer gave you, call the officer again or go with the information from the police.

Using full names with initials helps reduce confusion and inaccuracies; there could be a dozen John Smiths in the community. John T. Smith is more specific, especially when followed by age and address.

Wording of Accusations
Remember that all people are innocent until they are proved guilty in court or until they plead guilty. When a suspect is arrested, the person is not officially charged with anything. A person can be arrested after an officer gets a warrant or on suspicion of a crime. But the police cannot charge anyone with a crime; a member of the district attorney's office must file the charge officially with the court (more about that later). As a result, you must be careful with wording, so you don't convict a person erroneously. Most media wait until the person has been charged with the crime, except in sensational cases when the arrest is important news.

If you are writing about an arrest before the official charge, do not say, "Sallie R. Smith was arrested for robbing the bank" (that implies guilt). Do say, "Sallie R. Smith was arrested in connection with the bank robbery." If you are writing about the suspect after charges have been filed, say, "Sallie R. Smith was charged with bank robbery" or "Sallie R. Smith was arrested on a charge of bank robbery."

Also be careful before you call anyone a crime victim. If a person was killed or visibly injured during a crime, it is probably clear that the person is a crime victim. In other cases, the suspect has to be proved guilty before you can say the other person is a victim. You can say "the *alleged* victim," or, if applicable, you can call the other person the accuser — for example, "The accuser in the rape trial . . ."

Use the official charges when possible. If they are very awkward, and they often are, don't use them in the lead. For example, one man who was accused of robbing a jewelry store was also accused of carrying a gun. But police didn't charge him with possession of a gun. They charged him with possession of an instrument of crime. And there are varying degrees in the charges, such as first-degree murder, which should be cited. But don't cite the other qualifications, such as Class E felony (a category for the crime) unless you are going to explain what they mean and why the reader must know. If categories are used at all, it is for explanation of the penalties: "The crime is a Class E felony, which carries a penalty of . . . " It is still preferable to explain the penalty without the category, which is meaningless to readers.

Alleged: The word "alleged" is dangerous, so avoid it whenever possible. It means to declare or assert without proof. If you allege carelessly, you can be sued. Do not say, "Smith allegedly robbed the bank." You, the writer, are then the source of the allegation — and a good candidate for a libel suit. You can say, however, "Police accused Sallie R. Smith of robbing the bank" or "Police said Smith robbed the bank". An accusation is OK if it comes from police (and they are citing charges on record), not if it comes from you. Other permissible uses include "The bank was allegedly robbed" or "the alleged robbery," although such uses are not preferable.

Here's an example of the proper use of "alleged": When basketball star Kobe Bryant was accused of rape, it would be accurate to say the "alleged rape" when referring to the incident because it was never established that the accuser was actually raped; Bryant claimed that the sex was consensual. The case was dismissed when the woman who accused Bryant of sexual assault decided not to testify. The woman also had to be considered an "alleged victim" because the charges were never proved.

Also be careful when using the word "accused." Follow the Associated Press Stylebook guidelines: A person is accused *of,* not *with,* a crime. In addition, you should not say "accused bank robber Sallie R. Smith" (this convicts her). Instead, say, "Sallie R. Smith, accused of the bank robbery . . . "

Attribution

In crime stories, make sure that you attribute all accusatory information and much of the information you received secondhand (not by direct observation). Factual information does not need attribution. For example, the location of a crime is usually factual. If someone has been charged with a crime, you can state that as a fact.

To reduce the use of attribution after every sentence, you can use an overview attribution for part of your story, especially when you are recounting what happened: "Police described the incident this way."

Newspaper or Television Archives

The first thing you should do before you write your story is check newspaper clips in your library, TV file tape or online archives. They may make a big difference in your story. Don't rely only on information you may get on the Internet.

A reporter for *The Hartford* (Connecticut) *Courant* covered the case of a man arrested on a charge of rape. Small story for a big paper. But the reporter checked clips and discovered that the man had been previously arrested on rape charges and was free on bail when he was charged with another rape — a much bigger story.

Check newspaper clips, TV file tape or online archives in your library for background information.

Three months later, a different reporter was making police checks. A man had been accused of rape. The reporter checked the clips. It was the same man charged with a third rape, which occurred when he was free on bail, still awaiting trial in the first rape case — a very big story. And this story led to a major front-page follow-up story on the system in Connecticut that allows rape suspects to be released on bail, no matter how many times they have been arrested and charged with that type of crime. ("Bail" is the amount of money, set by a judge, that the suspect has to deposit with the court to be released from jail pending a hearing or trial. If the suspect flees, the bail money goes to the court.)

One caution: Clips and tape on file in your news organization's database may not be up to date. They may contain stories of someone's arrest, but not the disposition of the case. Always check to see whether charges were dropped or the person is still awaiting trial or was convicted.

Guidelines for Reporting Crime Stories

In any story you will seek good quotes and answers to the five W's. Here are the basic questions to ask and the basic information to include in crime stories:

Victims: Get full names, ages, addresses and occupations, if available (use if relevant).

SOCIAL MEDIA

SOCIAL MEDIA has changed the nature of crime reporting. It does not replace the need for checking with police and other sources, but it is an invaluable additional tool for police and reporters.

Many police agencies use social media to seek citizen tips for solving crimes. The FBI uses Twitter, Facebook and YouTube as well. Like many other departments, the Boston Police Department keeps citizens informed on its Twitter page. In fact, when law enforcement agencies concluded their manhunt for the suspect in the Boston Marathon bombings in 2013, the Boston Police Department didn't call a press conference to announce the news. Instead, the department used its Twitter page to post these two tweets: "Suspect in custody. Officers sweeping the area. Stand by for further info." And a second tweet: "CAPTURED!!! The hunt is over. The search is done. The terror is over. And justice has won. Suspect in custody."

Social media is even more valuable for reporters. Journalists can follow police agencies' social media sites for reports, tips and documents that were not accessible online in the past. But another indispensible use of social media is the ability to acquire sources. With social media, you can invite readers to submit leads, tips and personal stories about a crime or subject.

If you are covering a breaking news crime, Twitter, Facebook and Flickr and other social media sites can provide on-the-scene reactions from sources. However, in this age of instant news, you need to exercise caution about publishing information you get from social media without checking it for accuracy and validity. You also need to avoid using information you receive from anonymous sources on social media sites.

Suspects: Get full names, ages and addresses, if available; if not, get a description. Guidelines about whether to include race or ethnic background are changing. Check your organization's style. A general rule is to avoid mentioning race or ethnicity unless it is crucial to the story or to a description of a suspect.

Cause of Fatalities or Injuries: Also describe the injuries, where injured people have been taken and their current condition; check with hospitals. In stories involving property, specify the causes and extent of damage.

Location of Incident: Don't forget to gather specific information for a graphic or map.

Time of Incident: Be as specific as possible.

What Happened: Make sure that you understand the sequence of events; always ask about any unusual circumstances.

Arrests and Charges Filed: If people have been arrested, find out where they are being held, when they will be arraigned (a hearing for formal charges) or when the next court procedure will be. If they have already been arraigned, find out the amount of bail.

Eyewitness Accounts: Comments from neighbors may also be relevant. Be careful about using accusations against named individuals. When in doubt, leave them out.

In addition to gathering the basic information, you may want to try some of these other reporting techniques:

Role-Play Imagine that it is your car in the accident, your home that was burglarized or burned in a fire, your friend or relative injured in a crime. What information would you want to know if you were personally affected by the story?

Play Detective What information would you want to gather to solve the crime?

Gather Graphics What information would you need to diagram the car accident, draw the crime scene or a locator map, write a highlights box or a chronology of events or design a chart or graphic depicting how and where the crime occurred? Ask questions to gain the information you will have to convey to the artist who will draw the graphics for your story or for locating the crime scene on a Google map or other online mapping program.

Marti Gatlin/U.S. Marine Corps

A police dispatcher is often the person who answers reporters' phone calls and reports the daily crime log for the media.

Use the Telephone Often you will gather information for crime stories over the telephone. Usually you will get the information from a dispatcher or public information officer who was not at the scene and is just reading a report to you. Make sure that you ask police officials to repeat any information you did not hear clearly. Also ask the police officer releasing the information to give you his full name and rank. Police often identify themselves only by title and last name, such as Sgt. Jones. Ask the officer to spell the names of all people involved; you can spell them back to double-check the accuracy.

Stories About Specific Types of Crimes

For the first version of a major crime story, a hard-news approach is preferred. With the instant changes that mobile and online media provide, be prepared to update the leads continually. For follow-up stories and sidebars, consider some of the storytelling techniques.

Motor Vehicle Accidents Vehicle accident stories usually are hard-news stories unless there is an unusual angle. In addition to following the basic guidelines, make sure that you have this information:

- Speed, destination and directions of vehicles and exact locations at the time of the accident.
- Cause of accident, arrests, citations and damages.
- Victims' use of required equipment, such as seat belts and bicycle or motorcycle helmets.
- Weather-related information, if relevant.
- Alcohol- or drug-related information, if relevant.
- Rescue attempts or acts of heroism.

It is customary to lead the story with fatalities and injuries. This example is structured in inverted pyramid form:

Summary lead: delayed identification, fatality and cause

A Santa Ana boy was killed when a van rear-ended the car he was riding in while it was stopped at a turn signal, police said. The van's driver was booked for vehicular manslaughter.

Identification

Robert Taylor, 10, died at UCI Medical Center in Orange.

When, where, other injured people

The 3:17 p.m. accident at First and Bristol streets in Santa Ana also critically injured the boy's mother, Griselda Taylor, 29,

and his sister, Lynelle, 8. An 8-year-old boy in the car sustained minor injuries, police said. His name and relation to the Taylors were not released.

Taylor was waiting on the eastbound side of First, in the left-turn lane, at a red light when a van driven by Don Currie Edwards, 49, struck the back of her car, police said. The impact pushed her

What happened and who was involved

Condition of injured people; hospital sources

car into the intersection, and it was then struck by a west-bound car driven by Phillipe Hernandez, 18.

Taylor sustained a broken neck. She was in guarded condition at Western Medical Center in Santa Ana, hospital officials said. Lynelle sustained critical head injuries, police said.

Edwards was treated for minor injuries and arrested, police said. Hernandez was not injured.

—The Orange County (California) *Register*

Burglaries and Robberies A burglary involves entry into a building with intent to commit any type of crime; robbery involves stealing with violence or a threat against people. If you are away and a person enters your home and steals your compact disc player, that's a burglary. If you are asleep upstairs and the person is downstairs stealing the player, that's still a burglary. But if the person threatens you with force, that's a robbery. A burglary always involves a place and *can* involve violence against a person; a robbery *must* involve violence or threats against a person.

For both burglaries and robberies, ask the basics: who, what, when, where, why and how. Then add the following:

- What was taken and the value of the goods.
- Types of weapons used (in robberies).
- How entry was made.
- Similar circumstances (frequency of crime or any odd conditions).

In burglary and robbery stories, mention in the lead any injuries or deaths. Keep the tone serious when the story involves death or serious injuries. In other cases, use your judgment, and lead with any unusual angles. If there are none, stress what was taken or how the burglars entered the building, if that is the most interesting factor.

Whether you write a hard or soft lead depends on how serious the crime was, whether it is the first story on the crime and whether you have enough interesting information to warrant a soft approach.

Here's a hard-news version of a burglary story:

FAIRBANKS, Alaska — A Fairbanks man was charged with burglary after he broke into a home, took off his clothes and fell asleep in the homeowner's bed, police said.

Jordan Anderson, 28, will be arraigned today in district court where he will also face a criminal mischief charge.

Alaska State Troopers said Anderson told them he had been smoking synthetic marijuana, a legal substance that is a blend of spices and herbs sold in head shops. They said Anderson claimed he went to bed in the house on Goldhill Road because "God had told him to."

In this burglary story, the tone is lighter and a soft lead is used because of the subject matter:

Someone took Burger King's "Have It Your Way" slogan too literally this week and stole a three-foot-wide Whopper hamburger display costume from a van parked in northeast Salem.

Shannon Sappingfield, a marketing representative for local Burger Kings, said the missing burger was made of sponge.

The Whopper was in a van parked at Boss Enterprise, 408-A Lancaster Drive NE. The company owns nine local Burger Kings.

When Sappingfield came to work about 6 a.m. Tuesday, she saw that the van's window had been broken. The cardboard box containing the Whopper costume was missing; two other boxes containing a milk shake costume and a french fry costume were untouched.

"I'm not convinced they realized what they had until they were away from the site and opened the box," she said.

She estimated that the costume was worth about $500. But to get another one, the company would also have to buy another milk shake and french fry costume, which cost $500 each.

— (Salem, Oregon) *Statesman-Journal*

Homicides "Homicide" is the legal term for killing. "Murder" is the term for premeditated homicide. "Manslaughter" is homicide without premeditation. A person can be arrested on charges of murder, but he is not a murderer until convicted of the crime. Do not call someone a murderer until then. Also, don't say someone was murdered unless authorities have established that the victim was murdered — in a premeditated act of killing — or until a court determines that. Say the person was slain or killed. Some additional information to gather:

- Weapon (specific description, such as .38-caliber revolver).
- Clues and motives (from police).
- Specific wounds.
- Official cause of death (from coroner or police).
- Circumstances of suspect's arrest (result of tip or investigation, perhaps at the scene).
- Lots of details, from relatives, neighbors, friends, officials, eyewitnesses and your own observations at the crime scene.

For many first-day stories about death, you may choose to use a hard-news approach. You should get the news about the death in the lead. But if there is a more compelling angle, you could put it in the second or third paragraph. Again, you must use judgment in deciding whether the story lends itself to a hard-news or a storytelling approach.

This is a hard-news approach to a homicide story:

A 32-year-old man was charged Tuesday with killing his former girlfriend when she wouldn't leave the back porch of his home.

Lester Paul Stephens of 3357 N. 2nd St. was charged with first-degree intentional homicide while armed in connection with the death of Ruby L. Hardison, 42. Hardison was shot in the head Saturday.

According to the criminal complaint, Stephens told police that he and Hardison recently had ended their relationship. But Hardison came to Stephens' home Saturday and began knocking and banging on the door and front window.

Stephens told police he got upset about the noise, and went to the back door to tell her to leave him alone. Then he went back inside and got a .32-caliber semiautomatic pistol and walked back to the porch, the complaint says.

Stephens told Hardison to get off the porch and go home, then fired one shot in the air to scare her away.

The complaint says that he then put the pistol to the right side of her head, and after they continued to argue, the gun discharged.

Stephens, who faces life plus five years in prison if convicted, was being held on $50,000 cash bail. A preliminary hearing was scheduled for April 30.

—The Milwaukee Journal

ETHICS

ETHICAL DILEMMA: An 18-year-old student at your university has accused three men on the college football team of raping her at a party on campus. The men have been arrested and arraigned on rape charges. You are the editor of your campus newspaper's website. Your website and other print and broadcast media on campus have a policy against naming accusers in rape cases, but they do not prohibit naming the accused parties after they have been arraigned. However, the local newspaper has published the names of the suspects, and their names are being posted on several social media sites.

The Twitter site for your campus is buzzing with tweets about the incident. Several of the tweets are ranting about why the media publish the suspects' names, but not the name of the accuser. The tweets are also defending the football players and questioning whether the woman is telling the truth. The case is even getting national attention.

At this point you have not named any of the parties involved, but the pressure is mounting, particularly because the suspects' names are all over the Internet, and they are on the police records.

Do you think it is fair to publish only the suspects' names, but not the accuser's name? Will you withstand the pressure from the public and your followers on social media? What will you decide?

Epilogue: This scenario is adapted from a case at Hofstra University, where five men were accused of raping a female student in a dormitory bathroom. The men's names were published in local and national media. After police obtained a cell phone video of the incident, the woman recanted her story and admitted that she'd had sex with the men, but it was consensual.

Edward N. Johnson/U.S. Army Garrison Humphreys/Public Affairs Office

In stories about fires, include the number of fire companies that responded, any injuries or fatalities and how long it took to get the fire under control.

Fires

Although fire stories may not be crime stories, unless arson or other criminal behavior was involved, police reporters are often responsible for fire stories. Here are the important elements:

- Time fire started, time fire companies responded, time fire was brought under control.
- Number of fire companies responding, number of trucks at scene.
- Evacuations, if any, and where people were taken.
- Injuries and fatalities (make sure that you ask whether any firefighters were injured).
- Cause (ask whether arson is suspected — intentional setting of fire), how and where fire started.
- Who discovered the fire, extent of damage, insurance coverage.
- Description of building.
- Estimated cost of damages.
- Presence and condition of smoke detectors or sprinkler system (especially in a public building or apartment building, if city requires them).
- Fire inspection record, fire code violations (usually for a follow-up story, especially in public buildings).

When fatalities or injuries occur in a fire, they should be mentioned in your lead, preferably a hard-news lead. If no one is injured or if heroic rescue attempts are involved, a soft lead may be appropriate. Follow-up stories and sidebars provide many opportunities for storytelling techniques.

These examples follow most of the guidelines for reporting fires:

Child alerts family to duplex fire

Print version

A child in an East Anchorage duplex alerted his family that the house was on fire Tuesday morning, leading to a safe evacuation and only minor injury to one person.

The family of four — one adult and children ages 6, 8 and 12 — were at their rented duplex unit on Northwind Avenue, near Muldoon Road, when the child roused everyone as smoke detectors started sounding, said Tom Kempton, Anchorage Fire Department spokesman.

The first firefighters arrived on the scene about three minutes later, at 7:43 a.m., Kempton said. Crews found smoke streaming from an upstairs window and the family waiting outside. The adult had a minor burn to the hand but didn't have to go to a hospital, Kempton said.

Firefighters had to wake residents in the attached duplex unit and get them out, Kempton said. But that half of the building wasn't damaged.

The fire apparently started in an upstairs bedroom. Crews kept the blaze to that area, though the rest of the unit had smoke damage, Kempton said. Firefighters declared the scene under control just before 8 a.m. Damage is estimated to be $40,000 to $50,000, and the cause of the fire is under investigation.

The occupants reportedly do not have renter's insurance. The Alaska chapter of the American Red Cross is providing the family with food, clothes, shoes and lodging.

—KATIE PESZNECKER,
Anchorage Daily News

Family left homeless after fire

Broadcast version posted on the TV station's website.

Anchorage, Alaska — Two Anchorage families are safe, but one is homeless after a duplex fire this morning in the Muldoon area.

The Anchorage Fire Department says the blaze broke out about 8 a.m., in a child's bedroom at 8151 Northwind Ave. The child alerted the rest of the family while fire crews went to the adjoining unit to make sure neighbors escaped safely. Firefighters were able to safely evacuate all people and pets from the home.

The cause of the fire is not yet known.

The American Red Cross of Alaska is assisting the family who was displaced. They did not have renters insurance.

—MARIA DOWNEY, *KTUU*

U.S. Department of State/Bureau of International Information

COURT STORIES

Court cases are full of drama. They are the stuff of television series and movies. Yet print and online stories about them are often dull. Even if you use a hard-news approach to report a conviction or testimony, you can still use storytelling techniques of dialogue, description and narrative writing for portions of the story so the reader can experience the human drama that filled the courtroom.

To cover courts, you need a basic understanding of the process and the terminology that is used. Court procedures vary from state to state and even in counties within states. You need to find out how the system works in the area where you are working.

Whenever you hear a term you don't understand, seek a definition. Go by this guideline: If you don't understand something, chances are the reader won't either. It's up to you to make the story clear.

Here are some basic guidelines for writing court stories:

- Get reactions, facial expressions and gestures of the defendant and the accusers, attorneys, relatives and other people affected by the case, especially in trial stories and verdict stories.
- Use descriptive detail and color — lively quotes, dramatic testimony and dialogue.
- Translate all jargon, and avoid legal terminology.
- State exact charges in the story.
- Give the background of the crime, no matter how many stories have been published about this case.
- Include the name of the court where the trial or hearing is being held.
- Get comments from defendants, prosecutors, defense attorneys, plaintiffs (the people who brought suit or filed charges), relatives and jurors in all verdict stories.
- In verdict stories, include how long the jury deliberated. Also include how many jurors were on the case; not all cases have 12-member juries, the most common number. In all cases, however, the length of deliberations is part of the story.
- Write the next step — the next court appearance or, in verdict stories, plans for an appeal if the defendant is found guilty.

Criminal and Civil Cases

Court procedures fall into two categories: criminal and civil cases. Criminal cases are violations of any laws regulating crime. If you are arrested on suspicion of drunken driving, you could be charged in a criminal case.

Civil cases involve lawsuits between two parties. If your landlord says you have not paid the rent or you have damaged your apartment, he can bring a civil lawsuit

MULTIMEDIA COACH

CHECK THE WEB for background of criminal suspects. Start with a basic search engine, and check sex offender registries — even if the person is not charged with a sex crime.

- Check the Web for perspective on issue stories. For example, if you are writing about a local school shooting, check online for a listing of recent school shootings or similar statistics in other crimes.
- Search blogs and social networking sites for messages suspects may have sent.

against you. Divorces, malpractice, libel, contract disputes and other actions not involving criminal law are civil cases.

FEDERAL COURTS AND STATE COURTS

The court system functions on two levels: a federal level and a state level. Federal courts have jurisdiction over cases involving matters related to the U.S. Constitution (such as civil rights), federal tax and antitrust matters and any other federal laws. Federal courts also hear cases between people from different states. Here is the hierarchy of the federal court system:

- **U.S. District Court:** This is the lowest level of the federal judicial system, where most cases involving federal issues are first heard.
- **U.S. Court of Appeals:** There are 12 of these courts for geographical areas, plus the U.S. Court of Appeals for the District of Columbia Circuit. It is the intermediary court, where cases from the federal district courts are appealed.
- **U.S. Supreme Court:** This is the highest court in the nation. Cases may be appealed to this court, but the justices do not have to rule on all the cases.

Most states also have three levels of courts: a trial court, an appeals court and a state supreme court for appeals of the last resort on the state level. Cases from the state's highest court may be appealed to the U.S. Supreme Court if there is a federal angle, such as a constitutional matter — a First Amendment issue, for example — or a civil rights violation.

The names of the state courts can be confusing. In one state a superior court may be a trial-level court, whereas in others it may be an appellate court.

There also are municipal courts, where violations of local laws, such as traffic laws or city ordinances, are heard.

In addition, within the state system there are juvenile courts (for cases involving people younger than age 18) and probate courts, where disputes involving wills and estates are heard.

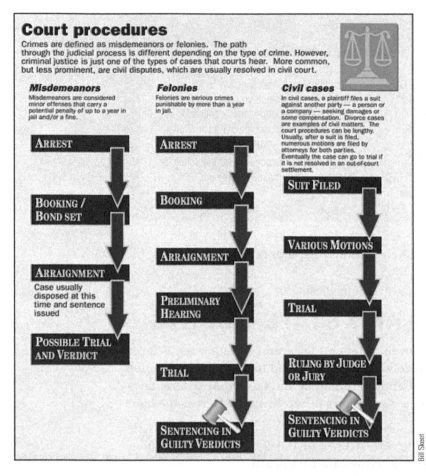

Court procedures

Crimes are defined as misdemeanors or felonies. The path through the judicial process is different depending on the type of crime. However, criminal justice is just one of the types of cases that courts hear. More common, but less prominent, are civil disputes, which are usually resolved in civil court.

Misdemeanors

Misdemeanors are considered minor offenses that carry a potential penalty of up to a year in jail and/or a fine.

Felonies

Felonies are serious crimes punishable by more than a year in jail.

Civil cases

In civil cases, a plaintiff files a suit against another party — a person or a company — seeking damages or some compensation. Divorce cases are examples of civil matters. The court procedures can be lengthy. Usually, after a suit is filed, numerous motions are filed by attorneys for both parties. Eventually the case can go to trial if it is not resolved in an out-of-court settlement.

Misdemeanors:
ARREST → BOOKING / BOND SET → ARRAIGNMENT (Case usually disposed at this time and sentence issued) → POSSIBLE TRIAL AND VERDICT

Felonies:
ARREST → BOOKING → ARRAIGNMENT → PRELIMINARY HEARING → TRIAL → SENTENCING IN GUILTY VERDICTS

Civil cases:
SUIT FILED → VARIOUS MOTIONS → TRIAL → RULING BY JUDGE OR JURY → SENTENCING IN GUILTY VERDICTS

Bill Skeet

Process of criminal and civil cases.

When you write your court story, find out the proper name of the court — whether it is called a district court, a circuit court or a common pleas court — and write that in the story.

Criminal Court Process

Crimes are classified as misdemeanors or felonies. *Misdemeanors* are considered minor offenses that carry a potential penalty of up to a year in jail and/or a fine. *Felonies* are more serious crimes punishable by more than a year in prison. Criminal procedures differ from state to state, but there are some general processes in the court system that you should understand. The diagram outlines court procedures for both criminal and civil cases.

Terms Used in Court Reporting

You should become familiar with these terms so you can better understand and explain court proceedings:

- **Acquittal:** Finding by a court or jury that a person accused of a crime is not guilty.
- **Adjudicate:** To make a final determination or judgment by the court.
- **Affidavit:** Sworn statement of facts.
- **Appeal:** Plea to ask a higher court to review a judgment, verdict or order of a lower court.
- **Appellant:** Person who files an appeal.
- **Arraignment:** Court hearing in which a defendant in a criminal case is formally charged with the crime and given a chance to enter a plea of guilty, not guilty or no contest (nolo contendere). At this time, bail is usually set.

- **Bail:** Amount of money set by the court that the defendant must guarantee to pay if he does not show up for a court trial. If the defendant can't raise the money through a bail bond company or personal sources, he stays in jail.

- **Bond:** Written promise to pay bail money on the conditions stated. The bond for bail is usually 10 percent of the total amount of bail set. The term is often used interchangeably with bail. Very often, a person will borrow money from a bond company. Then if the person flees, the bond company loses the money.

- **Brief:** Legal document filed with the court by a lawyer, stating the facts of the case and arguments citing how laws apply to this case.

- **Change of Venue:** Procedure to seek a change of location of the trial, usually when defense attorneys contend that the defendant can't get a fair trial in the current location because of too much pretrial publicity.

- **Charge:** Official allegation of criminal wrongdoing.

- **Civil Suit:** Lawsuit to determine rights, duties, claims for damages, ownership or other settlements in noncriminal matters.

- **Complaint:** Formal affidavit in which one person accuses another of violating the law.

- **Condemnation:** Civil action to acquire ownership of property for public use. When a municipality wants to build a road or sidewalk, the government will condemn the property to gain right of way.

- **Contempt:** Action that disregards the order or authority of the court. A lawyer who screams obscenities at the judge will probably be found in contempt of court.

- **Defendant:** In a civil case, the person being sued. In a criminal case, the person charged with breaking the law.

- **Deposition:** Written statement of testimony from a witness under oath.

- **Discovery:** Pretrial examination of a person (including depositions), documents or other items to find evidence that may be used in the trial.

- **Dismissal:** Order to drop the case.

- **Docket:** List of cases pending before the court. A trial docket is a list of cases pending trial.

- **Extradition:** Procedure to move a person accused of a crime from the state where he is residing to the state where the crime occurred and where the trial will be conducted.

- **Felony:** Major crime punishable by a sentence of a year or more. Crimes such as robbery, homicide and kidnapping are felonies; lesser crimes such as shoplifting are misdemeanors. Legally, a felony is defined as a crime punishable by death or imprisonment in a state prison.

- **Grand Jury:** Group of citizens selected by the court to investigate whether there is enough evidence or probable cause that a crime occurred and that the person should be charged, or indicted.

- **Hung Jury**: Jury that cannot reach a unanimous verdict, a requirement in most criminal trials.

- **Indictment:** Recommendation by the grand jury that there is enough probable cause to charge a person or group of people with the crime under investigation. The grand jury hands up an indictment to the judge (because the judge sits on a platform higher than the jury); the judge hands down rulings. It's preferable to use the word issued.

- **Injunction:** Order by the court instructing a person, group or company to stop the action that was occurring, such as picketing. For example, an injunction can order a group to stop marching outside an abortion clinic.

- **Innocent:** The term "not guilty" is preferable in court cases. The Associated Press Stylebook previously recommended using the term "innocent" in case the "not" in "not guilty" was dropped from typesetting, but that is no longer the case. AP now recommends using "not guilty."

- **Misdemeanor:** Crime less serious than a felony; crime punishable by less than one year in jail and/or fines.

- **Mistrial:** Trial that is set aside or declared invalid because of some mistake in proceedings or, in a criminal trial, because the jury cannot reach a unanimous verdict.

- **Motion:** Request for the court to make a ruling or finding.

- **Nolo contendere:** Latin for "I will not contest it" (no contest). This plea has the same effect as a guilty plea, but it is not an admission of guilt. It means the person will not fight the charge. If you agree to pay a fine for a traffic ticket but do not agree that you were speeding, you are pleading no contest. This type of plea is used as a form of bargaining to get the defendant a reduced charge in exchange for his agreement not to protest and to eliminate the need for a trial. Use the English term "no contest" in a story, and explain briefly that it is not an admission of guilt.

- **Plaintiff:** Person who sues in a civil case. The defendant is the one being sued.

- **Plea:** Defendant's response to a charge, stating that he is guilty, not guilty or not willing to contest the charge.

- **Plea bargain:** Agreement between the prosecutor and the defendant (or defense attorney) to accept a lesser charge and a lesser sentence in return for a guilty or no-contest plea. Plea bargaining is used extensively as a way to eliminate court trials. Once the defendant pleads guilty or no contest, there is no need for a trial. However, a plea bargain must be approved by the court.

- **Probable Cause:** Determination that there is enough evidence to prosecute a criminal case. Police officials also need probable cause — enough reason to believe a crime is being committed — when they seek a search warrant or any other warrant for a person's arrest.

- **Probation:** Condition in which the person is released from serving a jail sentence if he meets certain terms, such as serving in the community, entering drug treatment or accepting whatever restrictions the judge decides.

- **Recognizance:** Literally, "recognition." A person may be released from jail based on his own recognizance — meaning the recognition of a previously good reputation. This ruling is essentially the judge's way of saying that, because of the person's reputation, he is not considered a high risk for skipping the next court hearing or trial.

- **Subpoena:** Court order commanding a person to appear in court or to release documents to the court.

- **Summary judgment:** Procedure in a civil suit asking the court to give final judgment on the grounds that there are no further questions and no need for a trial.

- **Summons:** Document notifying a defendant that a lawsuit or complaint has been filed against him.

- **Suspended sentence:** Court order stating that the punishment of the defendant will be suspended if certain conditions are met. A person who receives probation gets a suspended sentence.

- **Temporary injunction:** Court order to stop an action, such as a protest, for a specific amount of time until a court hearing and ruling whether the action should be enjoined, or stopped permanently.

- **Tort:** Civil case involving damages, pain, suffering or other allegations of wrongdoing.

- **True Bill:** Indictment issued by a grand jury.

- **Verdict:** Decision by a jury about guilt or innocence.

- **Warrant:** Court order directing law enforcement officials to arrest a person. A search warrant gives officials authority to search a premises.

Court Story Examples

A court case is a continuing saga. From the time a person is arrested until the case is resolved, whether in a trial or a settlement, you will write many stories about it. But never assume that the reader is familiar with the case, no matter how sensational it may be. Always include the background.

Whether you take a soft or hard approach, make sure that your nut graph explains who is being accused of what, and place it high in the story.

U.S. Administrative Office of the U.S. Courts on behalf of the Federal Judiciary

U.S. Judge Howard Matz with a student counterpart in a mock trial in federal court in Los Angeles.

If information is part of a court record, you may use it as fact — but it still may not be true. It's up to a judge or jury to decide whether the claims in court documents and trials are true. So you need to attribute your information, although not necessarily in the lead.

Unlike other stories, many court stories do not appear balanced. On any given day, one side in the case may present its arguments, so you won't always have a story that seems fair to both parties. The testimony will be biased; you should not be.

Some reminders:

- Explain charges and background.
- Describe defendants and witnesses.
- Specify the court where the proceeding takes place.
- Tell how long the jury deliberated in verdict stories.
- Tell a good story.

When the verdict is issued in a major trial that has garnered interest locally or nationally, a hard-news story is appropriate. A soft lead also may work, but make sure that you put the verdict very high in the story. The following example uses a hard news lead and includes all the major points needed for a court story at the end of a trial.

INTERNET ROMANCE KILLER GETS 30 YEARS

Summary lead
A judge gave confessed Internet romance killer Theodore Manning 30 years in prison Thursday after a jury found him guilty of voluntary manslaughter, not murder, in the death of Nikki McPhatter, a Charlotte airline employee.

Length of deliberations and charges
The Richland County jury of seven men and five women deliberated for almost 10 hours over two days before finding Manning guilty of the lesser charge. Murder would have meant life in prison without parole.

Jury reasoning and background
But the jury sided with the defense, accepting the argument that the 2009 killing was a spur-of-the-moment action during a lovers' quarrel and not premeditated. They focused on the couple's wrestling over the gun that killed McPhatter, instead of what Manning did next: looting McPhatter's ATM accounts, stuffing her body in the trunk of her car, driving the car to rural Fairfield County and setting it on fire to try to cover up his crimes. Still, in the end, Judge Thomas Cooper could have given Manning from two to 30 years behind bars. He chose 30.

"I have no sympathy for you whatsoever," a grim-faced Cooper told Manning in front of more than a half-dozen of McPhatter's weeping friends and family members who asked for the maximum sentence.

The verdict was a defeat for 5th Circuit Solicitor Barney Giese, whose office earlier had turned down a request for a plea agreement while trying to persuade the jury to return a verdict of murder.

And the verdict came despite Giese's argument that McPhatter had been shot "execution-style," in the back of the head. Under South Carolina law, Manning, 30, will be eligible for parole after serving 85 percent of his sentence, or 25½ years.

Manning had confessed to the killing, taking the witness stand to defend himself. But he told the jury that although he shot and killed McPhatter, it happened during a quarrel and that he never meant to do it.

Moreover, Manning testified, another girlfriend pressured him into disposing of McPhatter's body in the way he did.

There were no witnesses, and by Manning's own admission, he lied repeatedly to law officers trying to gather information about what happened to McPhatter.

Length of trial

The verdict climaxed a hard-fought, nine-day trial over in one of the most sensational, widely publicized murder cases in Richland County in recent years. It illustrated the perils of Internet dating where two people can use cyber dating services to link up with romantic partners who are completely outside a person's normal circle of friends and family.

Manning and McPhatter met on Tagged.com and had no mutual friends. When she disappeared in May 2009, police had few immediate leads. McPhatter's frantic friends only knew that she had been seeing a man named "Teddy" in Columbia.

Deputies were able to crack the case by using high-tech and shoe leather investigative techniques that led to another Manning girlfriend, Kendra Goodman, who told police where McPhatter's body was and who had killed her.

Background

Confronted, Manning confessed but said it was an accident, that McPhatter was angry because she wanted more from their relationship. Manning told police he didn't want a more extensive relationship with McPhatter — that he had been seeing six girlfriends simultaneously, keeping each one in the dark about the others.

Reactions

More than a half-dozen family and friends of McPhatter rose to speak before Cooper's sentencing. Each cried or choked back tears.

Latoya McPhatter, McPhatter's oldest sister, her words punctuated by sobs, said: "My sister was a very sweet, jolly person. She was my biggest fan. She used to tell me when she was a little girl that she wanted to be like her big sister. I will always miss her. My heart is so heavy now."

She added, "I don't have any hatred in my heart for nobody,

Trial highlights

but just please — give her some justice." She collapsed sobbing into her seat. . . .

Giese and his deputy, Luck Campbell, sought to convince the jury that Manning's treatment of the body was so horrific, and his attempted cover-up so extensive, that he should be convicted of murder.

Ironically, Cooper is known for often giving criminals less than the maximum penalty so they can have hope to rehabilitate themselves.

But, in this case, Cooper said, he agreed with Giese.

Manning's "desecration of the body" made him think the same as Giese, Cooper said, giving Manning the maximum time behind bars.

—JOHN MONK, *The State*, (Columbia, South Carolina)

Most court stories are serious, but some have a humorous angle. Here is a lighthearted story in a conversational style that tries to involve the reader. It is an example of how a plea bargain works — or in this case, how it didn't work out very well. This story is written in storytelling form with the clincher at the end; unfortunately, the headline gives the twist away.

MAN GAMBLES ON PLEA, LOSES

You're the defendant. You make the call:

You're Marvin E. Johnson, 40, convicted three times of drug possession.

You're facing a minimum 15 years in prison without parole if convicted of being a felon in possession of a handgun.

On Wednesday, the jury at your federal trial in Kansas City deliberates three hours without reaching a verdict. On Thursday, the jury deliberates three more hours and announces it is hopelessly deadlocked. A hung jury and a new trial loom on the horizon.

The prosecutor, Assistant U.S. Attorney Rob Larsen, offers a deal. If you plead guilty, he'll reduce the government's sentencing request to a range of 15 to 22 months.

While you ponder that deal, the jury buzzes. It has a verdict.

Do you:

A) Sign the plea agreement and serve at least 15 months in prison? Or

B) Roll the dice with the jury's verdict? If it's guilty, you get at least 15 years; if it's not guilty, you walk away.

On Thursday afternoon, Marvin E. Johnson signed the plea agreement.

Five minutes later, the jury found him not guilty.

"I'm sure glad I struck that plea agreement," Larsen said.

"I can't win for losing," said Johnson's defense lawyer, John P. O'Connor.

—TOM JACKMAN, *The Kansas City* (Missouri) *Star*

EXERCISES

1 Crime story: Although the police report shown on the next page is labeled "Standard Offense Report," it is not standard everywhere. Each state has its own form; however, this one is similar to many. Most of the report is self-explanatory, with some exceptions. The case number is important for reporters; if you want to follow the case through the court system, you need this number, which stays the same for all actions in the case. Time is computed as military time, from one to 24 hours. Where the stolen property is listed, codes are used to signify the type of property. A complete code sheet is usually on the back of the police report. Write a story based on the following report.

You called the police to ask more about the theft of the bird because that was unusual. The police told you that the bird was valuable and that was probably the reason it was stolen. They told you there is no rash of bird burglars, although there had been some thefts of birds several months ago. But this bird theft does not appear to be related to those because other items were taken, the police said. Police are still investigating. Use yesterday as your time frame for the date of offense and today as the date reported.

2 Fire story: You are making a routine call to the fire department to find out if any fires occurred overnight. Fire Battalion Chief Stephen McInerny gives you this information:

A fire occurred in a ground-floor apartment in the 2700 block of Northeast 30th Place in your town at 1:12 a.m. today. Four fire engines and 16 firefighters responded at 1:15 a.m. Cause of fire: A stove was turned on, and some cookbooks and towels on the stove ignited. When firefighters arrived, they found a 2½-year-old cocker spaniel at the front door. Estimated damage: $9,000 smoke damage to apartment. Other units not affected. Apartment is uninhabitable. Dog's name is Tito.

McInerny said the dog apparently started the fire by jumping on the stove, using one of the

knobs for foothold. The setting on the burner was on medium high. The dog was apparently looking for food. The dog crawled to the front door. "The dog was clinically dead; it had no pulse and no respiration." McInerny said firefighter Bill Mock took the dog outside and gave it cardiopulmonary resuscitation and oxygen, and the dog came back to life. The dog was taken to the animal hospital and treated for smoke inhalation. McInerny said it is not unusual for dogs to be caught in house fires, but it is unusual for them to be revived from the dead. "That's twice in a little more than a year we've revived dogs that have been clinically dead as a result of a fire. We're getting pretty good at it."

You interview Mark Alan Leszczynski, who rented the apartment and owns the dog. He said he and a houseguest went to a bar before midnight and left the dog alone. "The dog is a little mischievous. I've caught him doing this before. He has a never-ending appetite. I had just reprimanded him for going into my houseguest's suitcase and stealing some candy."

3 Court terms: You may use your imagination for this exercise. The point of it is to see if you can use court terminology in the proper context and spell the words correctly. Use the following terms: "change of venue," "affidavit," "felony," "misdemeanor," "subpoena," "mistrial," "bond," "arraignment," "suspended sentence," "plea bargain."

Use those terms to write a story about this situation: A college student, 19, named Gold E. Locks, has been charged with a felony: breaking and entering into the home of Pa Pa Bear and his wife, Ma Ma Bear, who live at (you decide the address) with their child, Bay B. Bear.

4 Civil court case: Write a brief story about the following case, a petition for a name change, which was filed in the civil section of a county court (use your county court).

STANDARD OFFENSE REPORT
FRONT PAGE OPEN PUBLIC RECORD

On View √ Dispatched	Name of Agency	Agency No.	Case No.
√ Citizen	Your town police dept.	0230100	03-123456

Incident

Date offense started	Time	Date offense ended	Time	Date of report
Use yesterday's date	0700	Use today's date	------	Today's date

Location of Offense	Time reported	Time arrived	Time cleared
2339 Felony Lane	22:36	22:40	22:55

Offense

Description	Premise	Method of Entry	Type of Theft	Type of Force
Burglary		Force √ No Force	From building	Unknown

Victim

Name of Victim				Address					Telephone no.
Last First Middle				Street City State ZIP					555-1234
Smith Jon J.				2339 Felony Lane Your town Yours Yours					

Type of victim	Race	Sex	Age	Ethnicity	Height	Weight	Hair	Eyes	License	Social Security No
Individual	W	M	22	----	6-0	195	Blond	Blu	-----	131-300-0123

Reporting Person

Last First Middle				Address					Telephone no.
Doe James Brian				Street City State ZIP					555-4321
				2337 Felony Lane Your town Yours Yours					

Type of victim	Race	Sex	Age	Ethnicity	Height	Weight	Hair	Eyes	License	Social Security No
Individual	W	M	25	----	5-10	170	Br	Br	-----	171-009-0554

Property Description - Type of Loss
1=None 2=Burned 3=Counterfeit 4=Destroyed/damaged /vandalized 5=Recovered 6= Seized 7= Stolen 8 = Unknown

Type Loss	Property Code	Description	Est. Quantity	Value	Date Recovered
7	0618	Zenith VCR	1	300	-------------
7	0618	Sharp CD player	1	350	-------------
7	1002	Cockatoo (bird)	1	1,500	-------------

Reporting Officer	Badge No.	Date	Copies to
John Law	733	Today	Property Total 2,150

Description of incident

At 22:56 the office was contacted by Mr. James Doe, next-door neighbor of the victim. He was watching Mr. Smith's house while Smith was away. Doe checked the door to Smith's residence at 07:00 before he went to work. When he returned home at 22:30, he again checked Smith's residence and noticed that someone had pried the deadbolt lock on the front door. I was dispatched to the residence. I searched premises but did not find any suspects. When Mr. Smith returned home, he advised that items missing were VCR, CD player and cockatoo, who answers to the name of Homer. Owner described bird as white and 10 years old. He said the bird could say his name and had limited vocabulary of "damn," "rotten" and a few curse words.

IN THE CIRCUIT COURT OF (YOUR COUNTY, YOUR STATE)

Joseph Weirdo, Petitioner   Case No. 99 C638

PETITION

Comes now the petitioner, Joseph Weirdo, and prays his cause of action and states as follows:

1 That he resides at 700 Louisiana St., Your City, Your State.

2 That the petitioner requests a change of name from Joseph Weirdo to Joseph Weir.

3 That the current name of the petitioner has caused him great embarrassment and suffering.

4 That petitioner is a citizen in good standing and the request for the name change is not to avoid any legal actions against said petitioner.

5 That petitioner is not seeking for redress as a means of avoiding any debts owed to any parties.

6 Wherefore, petitioner prays for favorable judgment from the court.

Joseph Weirdo

City, State, ZIP Code

On behalf of himself

You call Joseph Weirdo, and he tells you he was tired of being kidded about his name. "I didn't want to go through life being a Weirdo," he says.

You check with Circuit Court Judge Jack Musselman, who approved the petition. He says he signs hundreds of these, but most of them are name-change petitions from divorced women, foster children who want to take the name of the family they have stayed with or people with "an extremely ethnic name." "I can't recall anyone looking to play games. A lot of times people are trying to avoid creditors. There's no way of checking that out."

The court clerk tells you that more than 300 people filed to have their names changed this year. It costs $200 to file the papers.

FEATURED ONLINE ACTIVITIES: Log on to the MindTap for Rich's Writing and Reporting News to access a variety of robust additional material, including this chapter's learning objectives, activities, comprehension quizzes, and more. Be sure to check out the "Trial" and/or "Music Download" NewsScene scenarios for an interactive writing exercise that will help to reinforce many of the themes presented in this chapter.

CHAPTER 21

Disasters, Weather and Tragedies

Death is always and under all circumstances a tragedy, for if it is not, then it means that life itself has become one.

—**THEODORE ROOSEVELT,** *26th President of the United States*

COACHING TIPS

Seek **human-interest stories** and anecdotes.

Check **social media** on Twitter, Facebook, blogs and other citizen journalism accounts.

Get information to **reconstruct a chronology of events.**

Use **descriptive and narrative** techniques.

Double-check all information; initial reports and statistics will change quickly.

Use **role-playing** reporting techniques: If you were a relative of someone in a tragedy, what would you want and need to know?

Plan **highlights boxes** and empowerment boxes to provide survival tips.

© jamdtravel/Shutterstock.com

DAVID HANDSCHUH WAS BURIED ALIVE. A PHOTOGRAPHER FOR the *New York Daily News*, Handschuh was driving to New York University to begin his first day as an adjunct professor of a photojournalism class. It was the morning of Sept. 11, 2001. He looked up and saw a mass of smoke. He turned on his police scanner and heard a voice screaming: "Send every piece of apparatus; the World Trade Center is on fire."

He called his newspaper and then called NYU to tell them to post a note that he would be "a little late this morning."

"All we knew is that it was an accident," Handschuh recalled. He said he turned his car around and crossed over the center divider of the highway to head toward the towers. As a photographer who had shot hundreds of fires, he knew many of the city's firefighters. He passed a fire truck with 11 firefighters who were waving to him. "All 11 firefighters in that truck died," Handschuh said. "They were on their way to their own funeral, and they didn't know it."

It was just one of many traumatic moments Handschuh would experience on that day and long after the terrorist attack of Sept. 11, 2001, in which 2,749 people died when two hijacked planes crashed into the World Trade Center towers in New York City. Terrorists had also hijacked two other commercial jetliners on that day and crashed one of them into the Pentagon; a fourth plane, headed toward Washington, District of Columbia, plummeted into a field outside of Pittsburgh, Pennsylvania.

Although many other tragedies have occurred since then, the terrorist attack on 9/11 will endure as one of the most significant events in U.S. history.

The first attack in New York was at 8:46 a.m., and Handschuh arrived at the scene at 8:48 a.m., one of the only times he remembers that day. "At that time only one plane had hit the towers," Handschuh said. "The streets of New York were eerily quiet, as though somebody had pressed a mute button." Eighteen minutes later the second plane slammed into the south tower.

Handschuh kept shooting photos. About an hour later the south tower started to collapse. "I was standing across the street," Handschuh said. "A voice in the back of my head said, 'Run.' It was like a wave at the beach. I was running one second and flying the next. The impact of the building tossed fire trucks. I wound up partially under a fire truck. I was buried alive. I never lost consciousness, I don't think. I couldn't move my legs. A fireman came and said, 'Don't worry, Brother, we'll get you out. You're hurt but you're alive.'"

For the next nine months he went through physical therapy. "I had to learn how to walk again," he said. His right leg had been completely crushed, and his left leg had also been "messed up." His nose and mouth had been clogged with ashes. His breathing and his lungs remain only at 50 percent capacity. But even now, several years after the 9/11 tragedy, that

David Handschuh.

The World Trade Center towers shortly after planes crashed into them.

experience scarred him in less visible but equally significant ways. He still pauses when he hears a plane overhead.

"I never want to photograph anyone dead or dying again," Handschuh says. So these days he is a food photographer.

In 2011, after 10 years of searching for Osama bin Laden, the leader of the al-Qaida terrorist organization responsible for the attack, a U.S. military team succeeded in finding and killing him at the compound where he was hiding in Pakistan. In announcing his death, President Barack Obama said, "For over two decades, bin Laden has been al-Qaida's leader and symbol and has continued to plot attacks against our country and our friends and allies. The death of bin Laden marks the most significant achievement to date in our nation's effort to defeat al-Qaida. Yet his death does not mark the end of our effort. There's no doubt that al-Qaida will continue to pursue attacks against us. We must — and we will — remain vigilant at home and abroad."

Cleanup at the World Trade Center disaster area in New York.

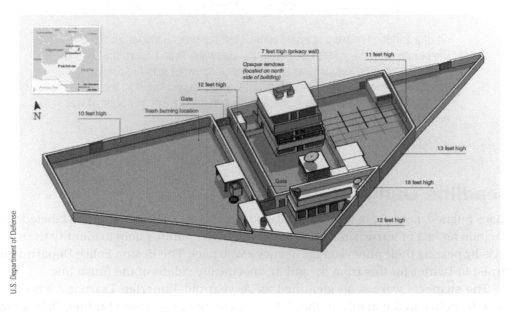

U.S. Department of Defense

Osama bin Laden hideout in Pakistan.

CHANGING CHALLENGES OF COVERING TRAGEDY

The changing nature of news presents greater challenges for reporters when they cover traumatic events. Instant news reporting with mobile and social media sources creates more need and less time for checking accuracy. Competition for breaking news adds chaos and more possibilities for mistakes. And journalists can also become victims of the tragedies by suffering from post-traumatic stress disorder because of the gruesome nature of these events. Compassion and coping methods have become part of the arsenal of skills journalists need for this type of reporting.

Boston Marathon Bombing

All of these factors collided in the Boston Marathon bombing on April 15, 2013, when two homemade bombs exploded near the finish line of the race, killing three people and injuring 264 others. The carnage from the scene was horrific. Shrapnel from nails, ball bearings and BBs sprayed from the bombs, causing 15 people to lose their legs and undergo amputations. Injuries to many of the other victims were described by doctors as "life changing."

Boston Globe reporter David Abel described the scene in a column for the Nieman Foundation for Journalism at Harvard University:

All of a sudden I heard a massive boom. I felt the ground shake, and saw the plume of white smoke rising from the sidewalk. Then I heard the second explosion. My first instinct was to try to figure out what was happening. It only took a few seconds to realize that it was an attack. I saw all the carnage afterward, and I will have these memories seared into my brain. It was some of the worst things I've ever seen.

Deadline Dangers

Chaos reigned, not only in the scene but also in the news coverage. The FBI labeled the situation an "act of terrorism" and initially sought the public's help to identify the suspects by posting their photos on the agency's Web page. The Boston Police Department turned to Twitter for tips from the public, specifically videos of the finish line.

The suspects were soon identified as 26-year-old Tamerlan Tsarnaev, who was killed by police in the manhunt that followed, and his 19-year-old brother, Dzhokhar, who was captured and faces 30 federal charges, including use of a weapon of mass destruction. Both were residents of Cambridge, Massachusetts, immigrants from the Chechen Republic.

The FBI said that although the brothers were not linked directly to any known terrorist groups, federal agents said they were motivated by extremist Islamic beliefs and learned to build their pressure-cooker bombs from an online magazine published by al-Qaida affiliates in Yemen. However, the FBI was criticized for failing to

The scene after the explosions at the Boston Marathon.

Aaron "tango" Tang/Creative Commons

follow through on a request from Russia's Federal Security Service to investigate the older brother, Tamerlan, who had been on a trip to southern Russia and was suspected of becoming linked to a terrorist group there.

But the FBI also criticized the media for publishing mistakes. Two days after the bombing, CNN and Fox News announced that an arrest had been made but later admitted that information was in error. "There have been a number of press reports based on information from unofficial sources that has been inaccurate," the agency said. The shootout with Tamerlan occurred the next day, and the arrest of Dzhokhar, who was captured alive with serious injuries, came the following day.

The death and injury toll also changed in the first few days, but that is a common factor in any tragedy. The rush to publish other facts based on social media or other unsubstantiated sources is a byproduct of the changing news-gathering methods.

Jason Fry, a freelance writer, said that the Boston massacre is an example of how events reported in real time are changing the nature of disaster coverage. In a column for the Poynter Institute, he wrote:

> The tools have changed, with Twitter an instant printing press for bite-sized bits of news, but the skills — a keen eye, empathetic ear, and a good list of contacts — have not. . . . News gathering and reporting — an intrinsically messy hodgepodge of verifying facts and debunking chatter — is now done in front of readers.
>
> Whether we like it or not, this isn't going to change — given readers' hunger for news on such days. . . . Readers want information from the beginning of the reporting process but still hold news organizations to the same standards that governed the final product. All of this adds up to a profound change — one we've only begun to grapple with.

Sandy Hook Elementary School Tragedy

Four months earlier, on Dec. 14, 2012, the nation and the world mourned the deaths of 20 children and six adults fatally shot by a gunman who burst into their elementary school and fired several hundred rounds from an assault rifle into two first-grade classrooms in the small town of Newtown, Connecticut. The gunman then shot himself. His mother was later found dead inside her home 2 miles away.

This tragedy, the worst mass shooting in an elementary school in the nation's history, posed even greater challenges for journalists in interviewing parents and townspeople, because the children who died — all 6 and 7 years old — were so young and the details were so devastating. The school principal, four teachers, the school psychologist and a teacher's aide were among the victims.

One-word headlines expressed the enormity of the tragedy: "Shattered" — *Connecticut Post;* "Unthinkable" — *The Day* of New London, Connecticut; "Horrific" — *The Kansas City Star;* "Why?" — *The Star* in Shelby, North Carolina; and "Unspeakable" — *San Francisco Chronicle.*

Initially the media made several mistakes based on misinformation that emerged in the chaos of the incident. Adam Lanza, the 20-year-old shooter, was mis-identified as his brother, Ryan Lanza. Compounding the error, several news outlets used photos from Ryan's Facebook account. Their mother, Nancy, was incorrectly described as a teacher at the school, but she had no position there. Police said Adam shot her several times in the head at their home before he headed to the elementary school.

More problematic was the armada of media that converged on this small town and pursued grieving parents and children for interviews.

Need for Compassion *Hartford Courant* reporter Bill Leukhardt understands the need for compassion, as a journalist and as a grieving relative. His stepdaughter was one of the teachers killed in the massacre.

"Kindness is what really resonates with people," he said at a symposium at the Columbia University Journalism School. "When people who knew victims don't want to be interviewed, leave them alone. Be respectful, be kind."

Another problem for the media in this tragedy was dealing with young children who were witnesses or were affected by the loss of their principal, teachers and friends. Julie Drizin, director of the Journalism Center on Children and Families, advises journalists to respect children's and parents' wishes not to talk and to interview children younger than 12 with a parent or adult present.

SOCIAL MEDIA

SOCIAL MEDIA played a strong role in the Boston Marathon bombing and the tragedy at Sandy Hook Elementary School. Journalists used Twitter extensively not only for breaking news information but also to acquire sources for interviews. However, Twitter has its limitations when you are trying to be sensitive with grieving sources.

Dan Petty, *Denver Post* social media/ engagement editor, said that in the past much of the reporting at tragedies came from meeting people at the scene. "Trying to show compassion in 140 characters can be a challenge for sure," he said in an interview with a Poynter Institute instructor. "You can come across as unpatient and abrupt on Twitter because you don't have the space to explain what you're trying to do. Twitter is a great first way to contact people, but from there, try to take it offline; you can explain yourself more."

Verification is another issue when you use social media. Christopher Cillizza, a political reporter for *The Washington Post*, offers this advice:

Better safe than sorry. The reality of a news environment driven by Twitter, cable television and constantly updating news on the Web is that the desire to be first has become all-encompassing. Everyone, of course, still wants to get it right, but in the race to be first, judgment about being right can get skewed.

"I think the most important thing for journalists to recognize is that a child who has been through a school shooting . . . has been traumatized," Drizin said. "They are in a state of shock, so you have to be careful not to re-traumatize them by forcing them to describe in great detail what happened."

Toll on Journalists Much emphasis has been placed on the need for journalists to be sensitive and to show compassion when dealing with victims of tragedy. But journalists are also affected and may suffer post-traumatic stress disorder as David Handschuh did after 9/11. He now spends some of his time coaching journalists on how to deal with stress at the Dart Center for Journalism & Trauma (*dartcenter.org*).

The center, based at the University of Washington, provides tips and tools to help journalists understand how to cover tragedies and how to cope with their own emotional stress that can result from this type of journalism. Until recently, little attention had been paid to the toll that disaster coverage can take on journalists who have to stifle their own emotions as they report and photograph the trauma of tragedy victims. But during these tragedies, journalists excel and suppress their own feelings to fulfill their mission to inform the public. Despite the personal toll, Handschuh stresses the crucial role of journalists by saying, "Our work became history."

ETHICS

ETHICAL DILEMMA: You are the news editor for a newspaper or television station in your community, and the photographer has shot images of dead bodies along with several other photos of an airplane disaster scene. The photos of the bodies strewn around the crash site are the most dramatic.

Until the disasters of 9/11 and subsequent images from the war in Iraq, most U.S. media did not run photos of dead bodies. However, that changed after the 9/11 terrorist attack.

Associated Press photographer Richard Drew captured a haunting image of a man falling headfirst from one of the twin towers of the World Trade Center. His photo became the subject of ethical discussions in newsrooms around the country as editors debated whether to use it. Many did.

Bill Marimow, editor of *The Philadelphia Inquirer*, was one of them. "The horror of the event determines the use of the photos," he wrote in an article for The American Press Institute. "There are so many other things that we can adjust to minimize the sensitivity aspect, but we must not minimize the horror of the event."

Do you agree? Would you print photos of dead bodies in the airplane disaster scene? If so, how will you justify it to the victims' families?

Ethical Guidelines: The National Press Photographers Association's code of ethics states, "Photographic and video images can reveal great truths, expose wrongdoing and neglect, inspire hope and understanding and connect people around the globe through the language of visual understanding. Photographs can also cause great harm if they are callously intrusive or are manipulated. Treat all subjects with respect and dignity. Give special consideration to vulnerable subjects and compassion to victims of crime or tragedy. Intrude on private moments of grief only when the public has an overriding and justifiable need to see."

Images from that tragedy will be seared in people's minds and in history. "We have to take those pictures," Handschuh says, "but we don't have to publish them. These were some very tough calls."

REPORTING TECHNIQUES

Before you venture out of the newsroom to report on a disaster, you should find out a few facts and take emergency precautions and supplies. Many major metropolitan newspapers have plans for covering disasters.

Cities also have disaster plans, and police and fire departments frequently conduct drills to test them. If you have a municipal beat, find out whether the government has such a plan, and get a copy of it. If a disaster occurs, a good follow-up story is to check whether the plan was effective.

These tips are not only crucial for reporters in print and broadcast media; they also apply to public relations practitioners who might work for nonprofit organizations such as the American Red Cross or other agencies.

In the event of a disaster, you should follow these basic procedures before leaving your office or home:

- Check a map or use your GPS application on your mobile phone to see what routes lead to the scene. Are there alternative routes in case major arteries are blocked?

- Find out whether temporary headquarters have been established for officials and media.

- Make sure that your cell phone is fully charged and that you have the right email addresses and phone numbers stored in your computer or cell phone. If you are calling in your story on deadline, remember that information changes frequently, and you will need to keep updating your editors.

- Take proper clothing, if necessary: boots, rain gear, a change of clothes (in cases of flood coverage) and emergency rations — food and beverages if you think you'll be stuck somewhere for an extended period, flashlight and so on. You could be reporting for a long time in an area without utilities. It's a good idea to have this emergency kit of supplies in your car at all times.

- Make sure that you have a full tank of gas for your vehicle.

- Take plenty of notebooks, pens and even pencils, which are better than pens or electronic gear in rainy weather. Don't rely on electronic equipment — cell phones, notebook computers, tablets or other e-media, — at the scene of a disaster.

When you are covering the breaking news of a plane crash or earthquake or you are in the middle of a major storm, the sources of information are disorganized and unreliable. The news changes momentarily. The death toll often changes radically within the first few hours and even weeks or months later in a major disaster. Chaos reigns. You get the best information you can from eyewitnesses and officials at the scene. And then you check back repeatedly.

How do you know what to ask? You always need to ask the basics: who, what, when, where, why and how. But another way of thinking about questions is role-playing, the "what if" technique of reporting. What if I were in this person's place? What if I were waiting to find out about a relative? What would I want to know?

For example, what if it is spring or winter break and you are expecting friends or relatives to visit you? Suddenly you hear over the radio that a plane has crashed at the international airport closest to you. What do you want to know? Make a list. Chances are that the information you want to know is the kind of information any reader would want to know: What airline, what plane, how many people died, who died, who survived, what caused the crash, how did it happen, where did it crash? Those questions will produce information for your lead and the top of your story. Then you gather details.

Think statistics. You need specifics: numbers of people killed or injured or evacuated for the story and for graphics that your newspaper or TV news program might display.

Think human interest. How did people cope? How did they survive? What are their losses? What are their tragedies? Three hundred people could die in a plane crash, but the human-interest stories of a few people make that crash vivid and poignant for the reader.

Think about narrative storytelling techniques for sidebars. How would you reconstruct the incident — what was the chronology? Try to gather information about the sequence of events if the story involves such disasters as explosions, plane crashes and other events that are not acts of nature. However, even with tornadoes, earthquakes, floods and hurricanes, it helps to get the sequence of events — specific times that events occurred, the minutes involved in destruction.

Think about helpful information for empowerment boxes. Where can people get more information, donate blood, volunteer their services and so on?

Sidebars

Sidebars are not synonymous with soft news. Many sidebars are human-interest stories, but they also can be hard-news stories or informational self-help stories. A sidebar is basically a story that gives the reader some new information or more information than the main story, called a "mainbar," can provide. The main story in a disaster story is comprehensive; each sidebar should be very narrowly focused on one topic. The mainbar can allude to information that is in the sidebar, such as a quote from an eyewitness, but the sidebar should not be repetitious. A mainbar without emotional quotes from people would be boring. However, an entire sidebar about the people who have been quoted extensively in the mainbar is too repetitious.

Here are some ideas for sidebars and some questions you can ask to determine whether you need them:

Helpfulness If I were the reader, what information would I find helpful? For example, if a disaster affects utilities, as in a flood, consider a sidebar on how to cope without electricity or fresh water. If it affects roads, consider a story about alternate routes, or when homes and businesses are destroyed, plan a story about how to get government aid.

Human Interest Is there a human-interest story that the reader might find compelling? Does someone have a story that is unusual?

Perspective Would the reader find it interesting to know the history of other disasters of this type?

The Location Is there a color piece that is compelling about the scene or a location affected by the disaster, such as a story about the hospital scene or the shelters where evacuated people were taken?

Other Angles Is there enough information worth telling about a specific angle of the story, such as the rescue efforts, the efforts of investigators or previous problems with that type of aircraft?

Analysis If your community has been working on a disaster plan, is there a need for an analysis piece about how rescue or government workers coordinated the disaster operations?

In most cases, especially in human-interest sidebars, you can use all the feature techniques of descriptive and narrative writing that you have studied. You should try to make the story vivid and compelling.

A sidebar still stands alone as a story, so you need to insert a reference to the main news — a brief line about the disaster or crash — especially if you have only one sidebar. If you have a huge package of several sidebars, you don't need to rehash the news statement in each one. You need to coordinate with the editor just how much of the main news needs to be in your story.

Graphics

Think in multimedia terms. Almost all disaster stories in print, broadcast and on the Web are accompanied by graphics — maps, illustrations, charts — to help the reader visualize where, when and how. The job of supplying information to the graphic designer or artist falls to the news reporter.

You need to gather details. Use a mapping application to pinpoint exact locations: cross streets and measurements in yards or feet of where the accident, explosion or plane crash occurred. Consider whether the incident lends itself to a graphic using the time of the accident. Get a chronology in minutes or hours.

Disaster Basics

Whether you are a covering a natural disaster, such as an earthquake, or another kind, such as a plane crash or explosion, you need to gather some basic facts. With the exception of the five W's, which come first, the rest of the items are not listed in order of importance.

Who How many people died or were injured, and how many survived? These numbers will change constantly, but "who" should be one of your first questions. In a plane crash, get the name of the airline, the flight number and type of aircraft, takeoff and destination sites and the number of passengers and crew members on board.

What and Why In many disasters, particularly airplane crashes, the cause is not immediately known. However, you should always ask and keep asking for follow-up stories. In natural disasters, get statistics about the height of rivers in floods, the intensity of earthquakes, the velocity of winds in hurricanes and similar information.

When and Where Find out exactly what time the disaster occurred and the location. Consider graphics and a reconstruction of the event.

Weather For a weather-related disaster, get the specifics. If it is a plane crash, always find out about the weather, which could have been a factor.

Where People Go In case of evacuation — as in floods, hurricanes and earthquakes — find out where people are finding shelter.

Hospitals Whenever people are injured, check hospitals.

Disaster Scene Gather every detail of sight, sound, emotion and other sensory feelings. You will need them for description in your stories.

Estimated Cost of Damages and Property Loss Initially, these accounts — from insurance agents, fire departments, police officials or state offices — are often inaccurate, but they add an essential element to the story.

Eyewitness Accounts Get accounts from eyewitnesses and survivors. People make the story real and emotional. You need them for quotes in the main story and for sidebars. Ask people to reconstruct where they were and what they were doing at the time of the disaster.

Government Agencies Involved In plane crashes, the Federal Aviation Administration and National Transportation Safety Board always get involved in investigations. In major disasters, find out whether the National Guard is helping and which federal, state and local agencies will provide relief.

Consumer Information Find out where to go to give blood, to get help with insurance or rebuilding, to get further information. Consumer information may be included in your story or in empowerment boxes.

Red Cross and Shelters Always check with the Red Cross and other relief agencies for their role and their needs.

Safety Precautions Check with police and fire departments and with electric, gas and water utility companies to find out about the precautions people should take. You could refer to dangerous conditions in the main story or in a separate story.

Roads Check highway departments to find out which roads are closed or dangerous and what alternate routes people can take.

Survivors List those who are known to be alive.

Victims The names of people who were killed are often not released for days, but try to obtain them from officials.

Crime Check with police to find out about looting or other post-disaster crimes or arrests in cases of human-created disasters.

Perspective Was this the worst, second-worst or ninth-worst disaster of its kind in a certain period of time? Check online sources or an almanac to find out how this disaster ranks against previous disasters of its kind. If it is the worst of its type, that information should appear high in the story.

MULTIMEDIA COACH

WHEN 33 PEOPLE died at Virginia Polytechnic Institute in 2007 during the worst campus shooting in U.S. history, social networking sites and blogs became a primary source for parents, students and other people desperately seeking information about their loved ones. The first video of the shooting was sent to CNN by a student who took the images on his cell phone. Other images of the campus after the shooting were posted on a photo-sharing site, Flickr.

The shooter, Seung-Hui Cho, a senior English major at Virginia Tech, began his rampage about 7 a.m. on April 16, and almost two hours later, he went to a classroom building and shot 32 students and professors before killing himself. The university was widely criticized for failing to alert students via text messages or other means after the first shooting. The tragedy prompted many universities to examine ways of notifying students, faculty and staff members in such crises. The event also emphasized the role that social networking sites play in conveying information during a tragedy.

Virginia Tech students posted messages on Facebook, blogs and other sites to find and provide information. And journalists turned to these sites as well to find sources for firsthand accounts of the tragedy.

This tragedy offers a lesson in how you need to think in multimedia terms when you cover a disaster.

- Plan to post information immediately to your organization's website.
- Check social networking sites and blogs for information, but don't trust the material as accurate. Check with the sources, if possible.
- Provide links on your company's website to consumer information such as the Red Cross and other agencies.
- Offer ways to have citizen journalists contribute to your reports.
- Provide perspective about similar tragedies by creating time lines or lists of other disasters.
- Use the Web to provide interactive graphics if possible.

Background Check the background of the airline involved in a plane crash or a business involved in a disaster. Readers will be interested in any history that may apply to this disaster.

Medical Examiner Check for information about progress in the identification of victims.

Interviews With Grief-Stricken People

You have a list of people who died. Your editor wants you to call the families of victims to get biographical data and reactions. What do you do? Quit your job? Cry? Get sick? Many reporters feel like doing all three. But there are sensitive ways to cover grief. And it's difficult, if not impossible, to avoid dealing with such situations if you are going to be a reporter. So here are some concerns students have expressed and some suggestions about how you can cover such stories.

What If the Person Hangs Up on Me? You could try calling back or try calling someone else. Another suggestion is to call a neighbor and ask whether he knows someone in the house who might talk to you. You don't have to ask for the person who is in the greatest pain. If you are on the scene and the person does not want to talk to you, you might give him a card (or a note with your name and phone number) and ask if you could talk at another time.

What Questions Do I Ask? Don't ask, "How do you feel about your son's death?" Obviously, the person feels terrible. You might instead ask specific questions about what the person was like — in other words, biographical questions. What was the person planning, or where was he going when the accident happened? Then you could ask for memories about the person.

What Is the First Thing I Should Say? Introduce yourself and state your purpose. You might also express your condolences.

What If I Start to Cry? You can be empathetic and even a little teary. Try not to weep. But be sincere. Do not fake your emotions.

What If the Person I'm Interviewing Starts to Cry? Stop interviewing, and ask whether you can get the person a glass of water or a tissue, or just be quiet for a while. You might also ask if the person would prefer you to come back another time, depending on the severity of the situation.

What If I Say Something Insensitive Without Knowing It? Apologize.

Why Do I Have to Interview People in Times of Grief? Because these types of stories make a news event more significant and real to readers. Because people relate to other people, not to vague generalities. And remember, for some people, talking about their pain is a form of catharsis. For others, grief is a very private matter. So some people will talk to you, and others won't. Respect their needs. You won't get every story, especially if reporters from other newspapers and television stations have already talked to them. But the ones you do talk to can be wonderful.

Here is an example of how reporters interviewed friends and relatives of people who died in a plane crash. Notice from the quotes that reporters did not ask, "How do you feel?" The quotes and backup information contain specific memories and details about the people who died.

GRIEF CUTS WIDE SWATH

Relatives draw close as horror sinks in

BY JON PEPPER AND RACHEL REYNOLDS

The names of the dead trickled out slowly.

Among them was a professional basketball player. A weight lifter. A high school cheerleader and a successful businessman. A nursery school teacher from St. Clair Shores.

There were boyfriends and girlfriends, granddaughters and grandsons, husbands and wives.

None of the dead were positively identified by this morning. The few names that trickled out came from friends and relatives.

Kurt Dobronski, 28, vice-president of a Scottsdale, Arizona, construction firm and a former star football player at Dearborn Edsel Ford High and Central Michigan University, had come home to Dearborn for the wedding of a friend and found his 10-day visit "the best vacation he ever had," said brother Karl Dobronski.

"Things were going great for him," Karl Dobronski said. "This is a shock." Things were also going well for Nick Vanos, a 7-foot-2 center for the Phoenix Suns basketball team. After playing only sparingly in his first two years in the National Basketball Association, Vanos was expected to start for the Suns this fall. He had come to Detroit to visit a girlfriend and boarded Flight 255 for his return to Arizona, team officials said.

"Nick Vanos was a young man who was just beginning to come into his own as a professional athlete and was about to take a giant step," said Suns general manager Jerry Coangelo. "It was very sad because he gave everything he had with his abilities. . . ."

Bill Horton of Phoenix lost his wife, Cindy, 37, who had been visiting her parents in Wisconsin. She had flown to Detroit to catch a flight to Phoenix. At midnight Sunday, he tried to calm his two stepchildren, aged 11 and 7. "They're hysterical," Horton said, sobbing. "How do you explain something like this to them?"

—The Detroit News

AIRPLANE CRASHES

You may never have to cover a major airplane crash, but small plane crashes occur in almost every community. The principles for writing and reporting the news are the same, regardless of the size of the crash.

Almost all the disaster-related information listed earlier also applies to an airplane crash. One of your first concerns should be the number of dead or injured people. Initially, you will get only estimates, and most likely they will be wrong. But some accounting of the death and injury toll should be in the lead.

Although an actual cause may not be known for months, ask anyway because you need some idea.

You should also seek the names, ages and hometowns of victims and survivors. In major plane crashes, the list of passengers and their status is usually not released for a day or more, until the relatives have been notified. The names and status of the pilots and crew members may be available sooner.

In addition to getting accounts from eyewitnesses, reactions from relatives or people at the airport and other human-interest stories, make sure that you get the following specifics: name of the airline and flight number of the plane; the type of plane and number of engines, especially for small planes; the origination and final destination sites.

Check for comments from the air controllers. The pilot's last words are usually not available until investigators get the plane's "black box" recording, but keep it in mind for follow-up stories.

Don't forget the perspective: how many plane crashes of this type have occurred in recent years or how this crash ranks in severity.

Here are excerpts from a plane crash story that illustrate most of the guidelines for disaster coverage in the first four paragraphs:

A Northwest Airlines jet with 155 people aboard crashed just after takeoff Sunday night at Detroit Metropolitan Airport, killing at least 154 aboard and two people on the ground.

A 4-year-old girl, found in the wreckage under the body of a woman assumed to be her mother, is thought to be the only surviving passenger.

Witnesses said the airborne plane, Northwest Flight 255, burst into flames before coming down at the intersection of Middle Belt and Wick roads. Several cars were hit on the ground, and at least two motorists were killed.

The Northwest jet was carrying 149 passengers and six crew members when it departed from Metro runway 3-center at 8:46 bound for Phoenix.

—Adapted from The Detroit News

Follow-Up Stories

All major disasters require follow-up stories for many days. The second-day story should attempt to explain the cause if that was not clear the first day. If the cause still isn't clear, you can lead with what officials are investigating. If there isn't any new information, you can describe cleanup attempts at the scene. The death toll should remain in the lead, especially if it has changed from earlier reports, or should be in the first few paragraphs. Other follow-up stories may focus on rescue efforts, human-interest elements, cost of rebuilding or any other related news.

In follow-up stories, you still need to mention what happened — when and where the plane crashed, when the earthquake occurred and so on. In successive stories, that information can go a little bit lower. But it should still be high in the story on the second day.

Here is the second-day lead on the mainbar about the plane crash in Detroit:

> Loose and broken parts caused the breakdown of four jet engines like those on Northwest Flight 255, which crashed Sunday at Detroit Metropolitan Airport.
>
> At least 154 people were killed after witnesses saw an explosion in or near the aircraft's left engine. However, the head of a National Transportation Safety Board team investigating the crash said other witnesses saw no such fire and "very preliminary" findings are that there was no failure or fire in the left engine.
>
> Documents describing the engine failures, known to the Federal Aviation Administration (FAA) and the National Transportation Safety Board (NTSB) since April, were obtained in Washington Monday.
>
> A U.S. Department of Transportation source claimed Monday that a serious fuel leak problem with the jet was reported by crew members less than two weeks ago. FAA officials refused to confirm such a report.
>
> In Romulus, workers began the soul-bruising task of collecting human remains from the crash site for identification by pathologists, friends and relatives.
>
> —RIC BOHY, FRED GIRARD, MIKE MARTINDALE
> AND JOEL SMITH, *The Detroit News*

NATURAL DISASTERS

All disaster stories should include the same basic information: death toll, survivors, eyewitness accounts, human-interest quotes from survivors and details of the scene and of recovery efforts. For natural disasters, add information about the natural forces at work, such as weather conditions.

Any time you are writing about a weather-related disaster, be sure to include a weather forecast. If you are covering floods, find out how high the river crested — if that was a factor — or the height of water in feet. If winds were a cause of the destruction, get the specific miles per hour of the wind velocity. In the case of an earthquake, find out the magnitude and the location of the epicenter. Explain in simple terms how the natural phenomenon occurred. A graphic may be better than words.

Tornadoes, earthquakes, hurricanes and floods all cause extensive damage and leave people homeless. Find out where people are finding shelter and what is being done to help them. Insurance is also a big factor in natural disasters. Include consumer information, such as areas that readers should avoid and the names of impassable streets, or how people can cope. Utilities are often affected, so make sure that you check about the safety of drinking water, food supplies and electricity.

Many of these consumer elements may be in sidebars. But when you write the first-day story, the format is similar to that of a plane crash or any other disaster. Give the basic facts and a death or injury toll in the lead.

FERNDALE, Calif. — A powerful earthquake rocked California's remote North Coast on Saturday, knocking brick facades off buildings, sparking fires that destroyed several businesses and two post offices and sending at least 35 people to hospitals with cuts, broken bones and chest pains.

—*Los Angeles Times*

Here are excerpts from a weather disaster story that include all the basic information and human elements. Note the vivid verbs, descriptive writing, pacing of long and short sentences and details of observation.

Ed Edahl/ Federal Emergency Management Agency

Floods inundate a mobile home park.

NAPA, SONOMA HIT BY FLOODS — AGAIN

Basic news lead

For the second time this winter, rain-swollen rivers flooded Napa and Sonoma county towns and vineyards Thursday, creating a colossal mess where weary residents were just getting their lives in order after fierce January storms.

Weather specifics

Howling out of the central Pacific, the storm slammed into the state late Wednesday with steady, torrential rain and winds blasting to 60 mph. And weather forecasters expect more of the same today.

But for a few brief respites, the relentless battering continued all day Thursday.

Power problems

Torrential rains overpowered small streams and larger rivers throughout the region, triggering floods and mudslides. High winds snapped electrical power to 540,000 customers from Big Sur to Eureka, closed highways and shut down shipping in San Francisco Bay. New snow blanketed the Sierra Nevada.

Numerous rivers and streams were at or near flood stage throughout Northern California. Among communities threatened by the rising water were Susanville, Tehama and Hamilton City along the Sacramento River.

Forecast

The National Weather Service warned residents to brace for another wave of rain spinning in from a strong low-pressure system in the northeastern Pacific before dawn today.

Forecaster Brandt Maxwell at the National Weather Service's Monterey office said some areas could get as much as two inches of rain today. "Of course, any amount is going to aggravate flooding."

The rain is forecast to taper off this afternoon, with showers tonight and Saturday.

A winter storm warning was issued for the Sierra Nevada with snow levels forecast to range from 5,000 to 6,000 feet today. As much as three feet of snow could fall above the 7,000-foot elevation, according to the National Weather Service.

History/ perspective

It's starting to look like January, when a disastrous series of storms caused widespread flooding and $300 million in damage, killed 11 people and displaced thousands throughout California.

For residents of Napa and Sonoma counties, still recovering from the floods of January, it was an all too-familiar story.

In St. Helena, a small town in the Napa Valley wine country, the Napa River flooded vineyards, homes, apartments and a mobile home park. Firefighters evacuated more than 1,000 people as the river rose to 19 feet — six feet above flood stage.

Several hundred others were rescued from the Vineyard Valley Mobile Home Park, which survived the January floods. On Thursday, two-thirds of the 300 mobile homes were under water.

Emergency workers in small boats evacuated people through waist-deep water that blocked access to apartment complexes. But even the rescuers had troubles. One rowboat, caught in the swift current, floated down the Napa River for five miles before another boat came to its rescue.

Human interest

Malia Barron Hendricks, about to give birth to her second child, and her husband, Charles, found the road to the hospital blocked by floodwaters. So they drove to a fire station where firefighters helped deliver a healthy baby girl. The woman and her newborn, Hope Bridget Hendricks, eventually were taken to St. Helena Hospital by an ambulance that had to negotiate flooded streets.

Shortly after the birth, the firefighters shared a bottle of expensive Napa Valley sparkling wine with the new mother and father.

By late afternoon, a sheet of water four feet deep covered much of the eastern Napa Valley, isolating flooded farmhouses in inundated vineyards.

Farther south in Napa, the river was expected to rise four feet above flood level, flooding Soscol Avenue, a main business artery. Helpless onlookers watched water creep into the street, growing deeper by the minute.

Mark Townsend, 41, owner of Soscol Antiques, hurriedly tried to waterproof his store, sealing the doors with tape and sandbags, putting his wares as high on shelves as he could, and hauling away the most valuable items in pickup trucks. He lost $10,000 worth of antiques in the flood two months ago.

"It's a little hard, but you have to remember we are going home tonight, and home will have booze and an espresso machine," Townsend said, "and there are a lot of people who don't get to go home tonight."

—FRANK SWEENEY, JANET RAE-DUPREE AND MICHAEL DORGAN, *San Jose* (California) *Mercury News*

WEATHER STORIES

Not all weather stories involve disaster coverage. Weather stories can be news or features about prolonged hot, cold, wet or dry spells or just a statistical roundup of rain or snow totals for the month or year. They also can be features about interesting aspects of the weather and the ways it affects people. When a major snowstorm or thunderstorm hits an area, a weather story is expected.

Weather stories also provide drama. In 2005, *Chicago Tribune* reporter Julia Keller won the Pulitzer Prize for reconstructing the terror created by a tornado that struck one block in downtown Utica, Illinois, where eight people who huddled in the basement of a bar were killed. Keller was initially reluctant to do the feature story after the event because it had been so thoroughly covered by the media as breaking news. But she persevered for seven months as she pored over weather documents and conducted hundreds of interviews to write a compelling narrative account of just 10 seconds when the "wicked wind" had ripped through the town nearly a year before. The Pulitzer judges called it a "gripping, meticulously constructed account."

Here is the lead on the first of three stories:

> Ten seconds. Count it: One. Two. Three. Four. Five. Six. Seven. Eight. Nine. Ten. Ten seconds was roughly how long it lasted. Nobody had a stopwatch, nothing can be proven definitively, but that's the consensus. The tornado that swooped through Utica at 6:09 p.m. April 20 took some 10 seconds to do what it did. Ten seconds is barely a flicker. It's a long, deep breath. It's no time at all. It's an eternity.
>
> If the sky could hold a grudge, it would look the way the sky looked over northern Illinois that day. Low, gray clouds stretched to the edges in a thin veneer of menace. Rain came and went, came and went, came and went. …
>
> The survivors would henceforth be haunted by the oldest, most vexing question of all: whether there is a destiny that shapes our fates or whether it is simply a matter of chance, of luck, of the way the wind blows.

Here are some other ideas for features about weather stories:

- Unusual patterns in weather for your area. Include why the weather patterns are occurring.
- Effects of weather on pets, businesses, people's moods, health. For example, many people suffer from seasonal affective disorder, a depressive state usually related to a lack of light in the winter.
- Insect infestation because of weather patterns.
- People whose occupations force them to work outside during very hot or cold spells.
- Effects of snow removal on city budgets: price of salt, sand, overtime for employees and so on.
- Excessive costs of air conditioning or heating on your school or city during hot or cold spells.
- Features about upcoming seasons.
- Consumer stories or sidebars about coping with extreme heat, cold, tornadoes, hurricanes, floods or earthquakes.

Regardless of whether you are writing a feature or a breaking news story, include these elements in all weather stories:

Forecast Always include the forecast for the next day or for an extended period, especially when you are writing about floods, droughts, weather-related fires, or hot or cold spells.

Unusual Angles If the weather is unusual for your area or for the time of year, include explanations from weather forecasters.

Human Interest Tell how people are coping. Focus on one or a few people who have interesting stories.

Warnings Explain how extremely hot or cold weather affects people, especially very young or old people. Tell how to cope with or prevent problems. Also include warnings about keeping animals safe. Include any road or traffic information, such as road or bridge closings and alternate routes.

Records Explain whether the weather has broken any records or come near to breaking records, especially if you are doing a roundup of statistics or a story about unusual weather. Even if no records have been broken, put the weather statistics in perspective by comparing them to other months or years or by using a graphic for the statistics.

Terms Check your Associated Press Stylebook for definitions of weather terms. If you use such a word as "blizzard" or "hurricane," define it by explaining how high the winds must be. In any flood story, explain the flood stages of a river and how far above or below flood stage the river is, or when it is expected to crest to its highest level.

EXERCISES

1 Grief reporting: How can you ask questions about grief? Try this classroom exercise: In groups of three or four, list all the fears and anxieties you have about interviewing people who are grieving. Then discuss some reporting techniques you can use to deal with each of these concerns. After compiling your concerns and solutions, discuss them with the class as a whole.

2 Disaster coverage: Brainstorm a package of stories about a disaster in your community. If you live in an area prone to weather disasters, such as earthquakes, tornadoes or floods, plan that type of coverage. Or you can brainstorm how you would cover a plane crash or an explosion in your community. List the stories you would do and places

you should go for reporting on the type of disaster you have identified.

3 Disaster plan: Develop a plan for how you would cover a weather disaster in your area. Make a list of agencies and sources you should contact. Write a list of key questions. Develop a sidebar of consumer information with links that you would post on your campus or community newspaper or news station's website.

4 Social media: Check Twitter, Facebook, YouTube and any other social media sites you think would be helpful to you in covering a disaster. Make a list of agencies that use social media sites you might follow. Note the type of information you can gather from these sites.

 MindTap®

FEATURED ONLINE ACTIVITIES: Log on to the MindTap for Rich's Writing and Reporting News to access a variety of robust additional material, including this chapter's learning objectives, activities, comprehension quizzes, and more.

Be sure to check out the "Tornado" and/or Big Fire" NewsScene scenarios for an interactive writing exercise that will help to reinforce many of the themes presented in this chapter.

CHAPTER 22
Media Jobs and Internships

© Adam Gregor/Shutterstock.com

I guarantee that a prospective employer who doesn't already know you (and maybe one who does) will check you out online before calling your references, or possibly even before reading your résumé. . . . Through a blog, social networks and/or your personal website, make it easy for me to see how good you are.

—**STEVE BUTTRY,** *Digital Transformation Editor for Digital First Media*

COACHING TIPS

Call the employer to ask who should receive your application. Find out the **person's title and gender** and how to spell his or her first and last name.

Research the companies to which you are applying by checking the Web or library resources.

Create an **online portfolio.**

Proofread your application carefully for spelling and typographical errors.

Be careful about information you post in blogs or social networking sites that potential employers can find.

Check **online job sites,** journalism organizations and public relations associations for internships and career opportunities.

ONCE UPON A TIME IF YOU WERE LOOKING FOR A JOB, YOU HAD to submit an application letter and résumé on paper. You still do for many media jobs. But these days employers don't limit their search for candidates to the printed applications they receive. They might also search Facebook, YouTube, Twitter and similar sites. So beware of what you post on social networking sites. Potential employers might check out your blogs and social networking postings to find out more about who you really are. A video on YouTube showing your antics during spring break might be fun to share with friends, but not with potential employers.

It's an asset to have multimedia skills. It is becoming increasingly essential to have an online portfolio. But don't forego the old-fashioned methods of applying for a job with a letter and printed résumé. That's especially important for media jobs, where writing well matters.

Good communication topped the list of most-desired skills sought by employers, according to recent surveys by the National Association of Colleges and Employers, a nonprofit association for college career services. Employers also cited the lack of communication skills as the major problem with new graduates.

"Many employers reported that students have trouble with grammar, can't write and lack presentation skills," according to a survey by the association. "Poor communication skills are often evident in the interview, where students are unable to articulate how what they have done relates or contributes to the position they are seeking."

As students in media classes, you probably have an advantage in gaining good communication skills. But you may not know how to market yourself well. Unless you know how to write a good cover letter and résumé, even the best grade point average may not get you the job. You may also need to market yourself with digital skills, especially in large corporations that circulate applications among their properties and companies that have a significant online operation.

Steve Buttry, a writing coach and journalism blogger, stressed the importance of having a good profile on social media networks and websites. "The first thing most people are going to do if they check you out is Google you," he wrote in his blog "The Buttry Diary." "If I want to learn about someone, I am going to pay more attention to what I can find about that person online by myself than to what he or she sends me or tells me. So you should investigate your online profile and see how you look to others. . . . The image you present online is not more important than the work you can do. But you may not get to show what you can do if you don't show someone first in your digital profile."

If you had 140 characters to describe yourself on Twitter, what would you say? That's one way of creating a good headline or lead for your digital profile. You can also use the concept for a printed cover letter and résumé. Now think about how you would describe yourself to a prospective employer in one sentence in print or online. How would you persuade an employer that you are special and worth hiring? How can you tailor your application to the organization where you want to work? And how do you find jobs or internships?

These are some of the questions and answers this chapter will cover to help you find and apply for media jobs.

FINDING JOBS AND INTERNSHIPS

Q: How do you find internships and jobs?

A: The journalism and mass communications program at your school is a good starting place. It may list job and internship opportunities on bulletin boards or your department website. Professors in your department usually have good contacts in your field of study, so check with them as well. If you are seeking an opportunity at a specific news or public relations organization, check the website for that company. If you don't want to be limited to media jobs, the Associated Collegiate Press(*www.aftercollege.com/organizations/associated-collegiate-press*)offers a more inclusive job site as well as general sites like *www.jobster.com* and *www.monster.com*. The next step is to check several of the websites offering jobs and internships in media careers, some of which are mentioned in the next few answers.

Don't limit your search to media jobs sites, even if you want to work in print, broadcast or public relations companies. Jobs abound for people with good writing and editing skills and media training — many in unlikely places. Consider some of these job ads:

- An ad from a national chain that sells pet products: "Online communications and community coordinator. Develops content on the company website, manages online discussions, pitches to bloggers. Must follow AP writing style and have ability to rapidly produce editorial and technical content."

- An ad from the Society of American Florists: "Writer/editor and reporter with a nose for news, a flair for creatively conveying it in writing and a talent for online and offline research skills. Writes news briefs for two weekly e-newsletters and posts content on the association's Facebook and Twitter profiles."

- An ad from a dental services company: "Social media strategist. Responsible for the company's engagement through social networks, primarily with consumers and also employees."

Welcome Students and Recent Graduates

U.S. Office of Personnel Management

The U.S. government site for students and graduates includes searches for internships and jobs.

As you can see, media-related jobs are available in many companies. In addition, the U.S. government offers an extensive list of media-related jobs ranging from $50,000 to more than $150,000. Just access *www.usajobs.gov* and search for "media" to find hundreds of job opportunities. In addition, the website offers a special section for students and tutorials on how to write good résumés and applications.

Q: How do you find internships and jobs in newspapers?

A: If you want a job or internship at a particular newspaper, first check the newspaper's website. Most newspapers list jobs and internship openings on their sites. Several umbrella websites list searchable jobs and internships by state. The American Society of News Editors (*asne.org*) is one of them with links under job resources. Another excellent searchable site for jobs and internships is JournalismJobs (*www .journalismjobs.com*). These sites and others listed on our website for this chapter will give you more specific information than a general search in Google or Yahoo, which will refer you to these sites anyway.

Q: How do you find internships and jobs in television or radio?

A: Some of the advice in the previous answer applies to broadcast jobs as well. First check the website of a specific station to see if job or internship opportunities are listed. The Radio Television Digital News Association (*www.rtdna.org*), the main organization representing the broadcast industry, is a good place to start. It offers a searchable job base as well as information about scholarships and career resources. Some websites specific to the broadcast industry also provide searchable job databases. For example, TVJobs (*www.tvjobs.com*) contains an extensive list of jobs in television and radio as well as an e-résumé database where you can post your résumé. Others include TV/Cable Jobs (*www.mediabistro.com /tvnewser-jobs*), TVandRadioJobs (*www.tvandradiojobs.com*) and more linked to social media sites.

Q: How do you find internships and jobs in public relations?

A: The public relations field is so broad that you can find opportunities in government, corporations, marketing and public relations firms. A good place to start your search is with the umbrella organizations representing public relations such as the Public Relations Society of America (*www.prsa.org*) and the International Association of Business Communicators (*www.iabc.com*). Both have searchable databases by location or position. If your school has a chapter of the Public Relations Student Society of America (*www.prssa.org*), you should consider joining because many student chapters offer networking and local job opportunities. Even if you don't have a local chapter, you can check the PRSSA site for internships and jobs. In some communities advertising and marketing firms combine with public relations positions, so you can check under advertising as well. For example, talentzoo (*www .talentzoo.com*) contains a searchable site for advertising, publishing, marketing and broadcasting.

Job fairs are good places to network for jobs and internships.

If you want a public relations job in government, which offers many opportunities in local and national agencies, check your state government site or the U.S. Web portal (*www.usa.gov*), which has links to state and federal sites. Think broadly. Many organizations need publicists including hospitals, companies and nonprofit agencies, so you should consider opportunities in the location you desire.

APPLYING FOR A JOB OR INTERNSHIP

Q: How can you find out the name of the person to whom you should send your job or internship application?

A: Start by checking the organization's website, a search engine or telephone book to find a phone number for the company. Even if the name of the person in charge of hiring is listed on a website or in a publication, call the organization and find out who should get your application anyway. Accuracy matters in media. Websites may not be up to date, and printed directories are frequently incorrect because people change jobs before publications are reprinted. Get a specific person's name and title, and ask how to spell the person's name and whether the person is male or female. Don't make the mistake of addressing a letter to a female executive as "Dear Mr." or worse, "Dear Sir." Also make sure you spell the person's name correctly.

Q: Should you contact the editor or hiring officer first by email?

A: Sure, but be careful. Check your grammar and spelling before you send any email. Dan Lovely, a former metro editor at a Florida newspaper, said he liked to correspond with applicants by email so he could see how they communicate. He said if their emails were filled with typos or poor grammar, he wouldn't hire the applicants.

Q: Should you send your application via email?

A: Send an email application only if the organization requests it in that form. You can send an email query to find out whether the organization has a job or internship, but send a written cover letter and résumé as well unless the company specifies that it prefers email résumés. If so, make sure you take a print copy of your résumé with you if you get to the interview stage.

Many organizations request that you apply by filling out a form on their website. If you are applying to a company that has a major online operation and publishes primarily in digital formats, you should apply with an online application, links to your website and social media sites.

Q: Should you use your school email address or a personal one?

A: Use the email address you check frequently, and don't use a school address if you are graduating. Use a professional email login. If you have been using an address with a login like "sexybabe," "cuteblondechick" or "studguy," change it unless you are applying for a sex-related job. Don't use smileys or other emoticons and Internet abbreviations that are often used in chats or emails.

Q: How many résumés should you send out?

A: Apply to as many organizations as you like, but don't send a form cover letter. Make sure you target your cover letter (in print or digital form) to the specific organization.

Q: Should you just send a résumé to a company on speculation, without contacting an editor or hiring officer?

A: If the organization has posted a job ad, you can apply without an invitation from someone in the company. You can also post your résumé on a job or résumé site, but if you are seeking a job from a company that isn't advertising a position, it is preferable to contact someone there who has requested your material before sending it.

Q: Should you include your websites and blog addresses in a résumé?

A: Yes. These days so much information is online that you need to illustrate that you are capable of corresponding online and that you have knowledge of social media. If you have a media-related blog that is relevant to the job or internship you are seeking, it is a good idea to include a reference to it. Otherwise, keep your personal websites and blogs to yourself and your friends.

Q: Should you post your résumé on social networking sites such as Facebook or YouTube?

A: It doesn't hurt to post your résumé on social networking sites, but you need to be careful about other material you have on these sites. Prospective employers might check out applicants who have applied to see what other information they might learn about them. If you do post a video résumé on YouTube or another site, make it professional, as though you were speaking to the prospective employer.

Q: How many clips, scripts, graphics or other examples of your work should you include in a job or internship application?

A: In general, newspaper editors suggest at least six articles, preferably showing variety in styles such as features and hard news. For a broadcast job, enclose a few tapes, and for a Web job, make a copy of the sites you have created and include working links. For a public relations job, enclose a few samples you have created of news releases, brochures or other materials, especially examples of your writing ability.

Q: If you are a member of a minority ethnic or racial group, should you mention this in your cover letter or résumé?

A: A racial or ethnic minority background may be an advantage in some media jobs, particularly if the organization is in a community with a large population of minorities, such as Hispanics, Asians or African-Americans. Most news organizations are eager to increase the number of minorities on their staffs. You can refer to your racial or ethnic background judiciously in a cover letter and résumé by mentioning organizations or activities in which you have engaged that reflect this diversity or by explaining how your racial or ethnic background may help you in the job that you are seeking.

SOCIAL MEDIA

SOCIAL MEDIA can help you find a job or lose one. You can search for jobs or post your résumé on social media sites or you can post embarrassing photos and videos that will hurt your job chances.

Some of the social media sites you need for job hunting and posting your professional profile are LinkedIn, Facebook and Twitter. You also need an online portfolio with links to your website or blogs.

Twitter: Use Twitter to follow media organizations and leaders in your field. Input a term for the jobs you seek in the Twitter search box or use a search engine for Twitter such as *www.twitjobsearch.com*. Although not a part of Twitter, this search engine and others use Twitter listings. When you post your Twitter bio, it can be 160 characters, not the usual limit of 140 characters. You can link it to a full résumé or portfolio.

Facebook: You can search pages and groups for jobs, and you can also use the Facebook Marketplace for job searching. Follow a company or organization on Facebook to learn more about it before you apply. Use a professional photo and include the same information in your Facebook profile as in your LinkedIn profile.

Be careful about what you post on Facebook in the first place. Although you can remove information from your profile, copies may have been shared with other people and distributed. Check your privacy settings.

LinkedIn: This is a professional profile site that is useful for finding contacts and especially for posting your profile for job searches and related information (*linkedin.com*). It is wise to post your photo, but you should choose one that looks professional. Avoid the party photos, full-body shots and dramatic poses.

Joe Grimm, who wrote a job-recruiting blog for the Poynter Institute, says you should avoid some buzzwords such as "innovative" in your profile. When he searched LinkedIn for "innovative," it turned up 527,000 results. He offers this advice:

- Use phrases such as "innovative editor" instead of single words.

- Better yet, look for untapped words. Do a LinkedIn search for adjectives to find out which ones are overused.

- Use LinkedIn as a network by asking and answering questions that will end up circulating your name.

- Check your posts on any of these networks for spelling and accuracy.

For help in finding careers, jobs and advice on how to write cover letters, check out this government site, *myfuture.com*.

Q: What skills or qualities would be especially important to cite in your résumé?

A: Multimedia and social media skills are valuable for most media organizations. In addition, if you are bilingual or multilingual, that could be an asset in many media jobs. However, if you make that claim, make sure you are fluent in the languages you mention; do not exaggerate. If you say you are bilingual in English and Spanish, you could be interviewed by an employer in Spanish to test your fluency.

WRITING COVER LETTERS

Your cover letter gives employers their first impression of you. You may get all A's in your news writing and public relations classes, but do you know how to market yourself? That is the purpose of a cover letter, which is often more difficult to write than a news story because it is hard to write about yourself without appearing egotistical. However, you can use some of the same techniques that you use in a news story. Just as you need a focus in a news story, you need to get to the point of your cover letter quickly. Explain within the first three paragraphs that you are applying for a job or internship at this organization.

Paul Salsini, former staff development director and writing coach for the *Milwaukee Journal Sentinel*, said he evaluated cover letters carefully when he was reviewing job applications. "I can't stress how important it is for the applicant to write a cover letter that is both clear and interesting and tells me this person is a good reporter and writer," he said. "If they're just saying they want a job, that doesn't excite me. I want a letter to entice me into their clips and résumé. The cover letter is the only original thing they send."

One of the worst mistakes applicants make is that they fail to change the text in their word processors when they are sending out multiple applications, Salsini said.

He also was appalled by the mistakes in these job applications. One applicant misspelled "Milwaukee" throughout her application. Another said, "I've always wanted to work at the *Minneapolis Star*."

"Good for her," Salsini said. "Why should I care?" He also stressed that applicants should attach some explanation to their clips about how they wrote the story. "If they would just write a couple of sentences to explain whether this was their story idea and why the story was important, it would help to put the clip in context. It helps an editor understand the story. That doesn't take a lot of work and it is so important."

The same principles apply to broadcast jobs. When you submit a tape, you should include an explanation of how and why you did the story.

Cover letters can start with a straightforward approach like a hard-news lead or a more creative feature-type lead. Most important, avoid writing a form letter that you send to several employers. Each letter should be tailored to the company where you are seeking a job. To do that, you need to do research. Check out the organization's website. If it is a newspaper site, read the paper online for a few weeks. For a broadcast job, check out the station's site for news stories and personnel. For public relations, familiarize yourself with the material that company produces or clients the firm represents.

Internships and experience on campus newspapers, radio and television stations are important. Editors want evidence of how you report and write or what you can do as a copy editor, broadcast producer or reporter. They want clips of stories you have written or edited.

Technology has further complicated the job application process in the past few years. Many employers now scan applications into databases, so you need to keep your format simple and brief, preferably limited to one page each for the cover letter and the résumé. In addition, employers expect you to include an email address or cell phone number, whichever way you would be most accessible.

Cover Letter Tips

Make your first impression on the editor a good one. Use proper business letter form, and keep it brief — no more than one page. Editors and other employers are busy people. Double-check and triple-check your spelling. Make sure that all the names and titles are correct. A misspelled name, typo or other mechanical error can disqualify you for consideration.

Be straightforward — not cute, not boring. Start with why you are applying to this organization or something about yourself that makes you worth noticing. But get to the point quickly about why you are applying. Specify whether you are seeking an internship or a full-time job.

Before you write your cover letter and résumé, do some research about the organization to which you are applying. If you are seeking a job at a newspaper or magazine, read the publication. You can check the Web or online databases, such as Lexis/Nexis, or get copies of the publication.

If you are applying to a corporation for a public relations or advertising position, check databases, such as Standard & Poor's Register of Corporations, and business publications to learn something about the organization. Don't just cite facts about the company; weave the information into the paragraph in your cover letter that explains why you want to work for the organization. Most good websites have an "About Us" page that will give you some good background about the company.

Content of Cover Letters

Limit the cover letter to one page. Always address it to a specific person, never "Dear Sir" or "Dear Madam." Write a good lead that tells something about you, but don't make it too flowery. Follow with a nut graph — your reason for writing. If you prefer a direct approach, lead with your reason for the letter.

In the middle of your letter, explain why you are eager to work for this particular organization. Even though you are including a résumé, mention its high points. Make special note of any unusual skills you may have, such as fluency in a second language or relevant experience. If someone at the organization has encouraged you to apply, mention this person's name.

Write a few more paragraphs briefly explaining your experience, if any, and your major assets — why anyone should want to hire you — and why you want to work for this company. Then wrap it up with a brief paragraph thanking the editor for his attention.

Consider the lead to your cover letter as carefully as you would consider the lead to a news story. It's the attention getter.

A cover letter that starts "I am graduating in May from journalism school, and I am seeking an internship (or job)" will most likely land in the trash. Thousands of other applicants are also graduating from journalism schools. That lead reveals nothing special about you.

Here are some effective types of leads:

Direct Approach "Please consider me for a reporting internship (or job — and specify the type of position and the name of the organization) this summer." Follow with a line or two about who you are and why you are interested in this company. This approach does not reflect any creativity, but it is preferable to a strained lead.

Experience Approach If you had a good internship or have previous journalism-related experience, consider starting with a paragraph about what your experience was and why you are interested in or qualified for this job. If you are a graduate student or nontraditional student, you might refer to your previous experience and your reasons for studying journalism.

For example, Michael Strong was a nontraditional student who was once a massage therapist. His job application began, "How many reporters do you know who have experience meeting people when they are nude? That isn't exactly traditional training for a reporter, but I'm not a traditional candidate for a reporting job."

Although clichés aren't a good idea, University of Kansas graduate Tiffany Hurt made one work to describe herself, and she inserted her race subtly. "Good things definitely do come in small packages. Even though I only look 10 because I am 4 feet, 7 and a half inches, I am actually twice that age with the responsibilities and leadership of an ambitious college student. . . . On campus I am a member of the editorial board for the newspaper. In addition, I am the chairperson and editor of the newsletter for the Black Student Union."

Reference Approach The adage "It's not what you know but who you know" is still somewhat true when you are applying for a job or internship. If someone in the organization referred you to the company or if you have spoken to the recruiter, you can begin your cover letter by referring to that person or conversation.

Preferably by the second paragraph, explain the purpose of your letter — similar to a nut graph in a news story. State what type of job or internship you are seeking and why you are applying to this organization.

In the body, mention some highlights of your résumé or special skills that make you qualified or valuable for the position you seek. Elaborate briefly on any experience you've had related to this position. Try to tailor your comments to this organization rather than writing a form letter with a generic tone.

At the end, mention any enclosures, such as clips or videos. You may thank the person for attention to your application or provide any contact information that you think is necessary.

Autobiographical Approach Start with something about your background that made you want to become a journalist, public relations professional (or whatever type of career position you are seeking). If you use this technique, keep it short. Don't give your life story.

Several job websites offer sample cover letters and résumés, but you should use them *only* for format. Do not copy form letters or anything you find online. Such letters will lack the personal touch you need. For general advice, you can check these sites:

- Job searching at About.com: *jobsearch.about.com/od/letters/*

- Career resources at monster.com: *career-advice.monster.com/resumes-cover-letters/cover-letter-samples/jobs.aspx.*

- PRSA job center: *www.prsa.org/Jobcenter/career_resources/resource_type/tools_tactics/resume_cover_letter_help.*

- Government website with advice on how to build résumés and facts about careers: Myfuture.com, *www.myfuture.com.*

If you need help with a résumé, check this government site at *www.myfuture.com*.

ETHICS

ETHICAL DILEMMA: You have an internship at a local newspaper or television station. A few weeks after you start working, your supervisor asks you out on a date. You like your supervisor and think you could get romantically involved. Should you go on a date? What are the ethical problems of dating your supervisor?

Case 2: The newspaper or television station where you have wanted to work for a long time has hired you. You have established some roots and really enjoy your job. You've been on the job for about a year. You are very attracted to your editor, and he or she feels the same attraction to you. Should you get romantically involved? If so, what are the ethical problems and alternatives?

Case 3: You face a similar situation as in Case 2, but this time you are attracted to a source on your beat. Can you or should you get romantically involved? Do you have to give up a romantic relationship for your job? What are the ethical issues, and what alternatives are open to you?

ONLINE APPLICATION EXAMPLES

Check online application forms or instructions from major companies to get examples of the type of information companies are seeking. For example, Burson-Marsteller, the largest public relations company in the world, offers an internship application procedure on its website (*www.burson-marsteller.com*). In addition to submitting a résumé and cover letter, the company asks for the following:

- **Press release:** You've just been hired by Burson-Marsteller. Write a press release announcing your hire. Be creative.
- **Essay:** Write a one- to three-page essay on one of the topics listed, such as this one: How might you use research and insights to make a public relations campaign more impactful?

An application for a writing and editorial internship at Hallmark also requires a cover letter and résumé as well as responses to some questions that demonstrate your creative skills. For example, one question asks you to create a new product (cards or gifts) and follow it from conception to retail display as follows: "Identify your market, briefly describe your new product, give it a name, copy ideas and design descriptions for packaging if needed and copy ideas and design direction for the retail display."

These are just a few illustrations of how companies in public relations and other media organizations expect you to demonstrate your skills. As indicated above, in print and broadcast journalism, your clips and videos show your abilities in those fields.

RÉSUMÉS

Limit your résumé to one page, with a possible second page for references. Arrange your topics from most recent to previous, such as current experience followed by previous jobs. White paper is preferred. Content is more important than appearance. If you have a home page and online résumé, add the Web address to your résumé.

If your experience in previous internships or jobs is more interesting than your education, put the experience category first. If you have no experience or awards, eliminate the category; don't write, "None."

Bring copies of your résumé to job fairs where you could be interviewed.

Simone Chapman/Courtesy of the U.S. Air Force

You can start your résumé with an objective, a sentence that explains your job goal, or a summary, a paragraph that highlights your skills and accomplishments. Summaries are gaining favor with employers these days because they offer more information in a quick format than a vague objective.

Objective Limit your objective to one sentence. Tailor the statement to the type of job you are seeking.

- **Vague:** "Seeking to use my skills in public relations."
- **More specific:** "To use my journalism training at a small, community newspaper to gain experience in several types of reporting and writing assignments."
- **Specific:** "To use my communication skills and my background in graphic arts in a public relations and marketing firm with opportunities for creative expression and growth."

Summary The summary should be limited to a paragraph that highlights your skills and/or experience:

- "Campus newspaper editor and journalism major with internships at two major metropolitan newspapers. I am seeking a reporting position at a small to midsize newspaper with opportunities for advancement. Versatile skills include reporting, writing, copy editing and page design."

Here are some other tips:

- List your experience, education and other items in order of the most recent first.
- Make sure that your résumé is free of typos and spelling errors.
- List two or three references, and include phone numbers and email addresses where your references can be reached. Do not say "References available on request" unless you are posting this information online and the reference information would infringe on the person's privacy. Do everything you can to help the employer. By withholding references, you force the employer to spend more time checking on you. Make sure you ask the people you list whether they agree to be references for you. Don't assume they will or just list their names.
- Skip the fancy paper. Scannable résumés should be as simple as possible, on plain white paper with black type of at least 12 points. Your headings can be in larger type, but don't mix fonts. Also eliminate borders and underlining.
- Include five or six clips (or videotape for broadcast journalists, although scripts help in this area as well). Choose clips with good leads. Editors rarely read past a bad lead. Try to include a variety: features and hard news, short and long. Short is better, unless you have a major project. If you have some good enterprise stories, those you developed through your own ideas, include them. The significance of the news event is not important to editors; they want to see how you wrote more than what you wrote.
- When you copy your clips, don't reduce them in size. Cut them so they fit on standard-sized paper, even if you have to use more than one page for a story.

- Templates such as those offered in Microsoft Word are acceptable provided that you adapt them by adding or eliminating categories that don't apply to you. Consider using "Education" as your first topic heading if you are just graduating, but if you have considerable experience, list that heading first. Interests are optional, but references are not. Make sure that you add a heading for references because one is not included in the templates. Then list your references' titles, phone numbers and email addresses if they agree to be listed; make sure you ask them before using their names.

- Follow-up with a phone call. A week or two after you have sent your letter and résumé, call the organization to ask whether they were received and if you may come for an interview. Find out when the editor you are calling is on deadline or in meetings, and try to avoid these times.

MULTIMEDIA COACH

ONLINE RÉSUMÉS: Reading a résumé online is more difficult than reading it in print, so keep your Web résumé even shorter than your print one. Try to limit it to three screens. Don't just transfer the print résumé to an online version.

Use a different format, perhaps paragraphs or lists. Don't use the column structure you might use in print; online reading is vertical, not horizontal. If you use a one-screen design, don't offer too many links to separate categories for education, experience and so on. Endless clicking can be tedious for a potential employer. Put the basic information on one page, and link to clips or your portfolio.

Here are some other tips for Web résumés:

- **Background:** Don't use a dark background with white or light type. The type may not show up if an employer wants to print your résumé. If you really prefer this type of design, offer a printable version as well, with white background and black type.

- **Privacy:** Protect your own privacy and that of your references. Consider eliminating your address and phone number in online documents, especially if you post your photograph on your site. The same is true for your references. Although providing contact information for references is preferable in print, for online sites you may have to write "References available on request."

- **Create your own online résumé:** Many websites include résumé forms. Unless you are applying to a company that prefers you to use its online résumé form, create your own résumé, so you can demonstrate your ability to express yourself — a major qualification for media jobs.

- **Identify yourself:** If you are creating your own Web résumé, make sure that you put your name and email address on every page of your site. Don't use "I" or "Nancy's résumé" as an identifier.

- **Offer a printer-friendly résumé:** If you have a fancy website, offer a simple printer version. Recruiters will need to print your résumé and keep it on file.

- **Use key words:** Include terms that search engines will pick up.

YOUR NAME

Email: name@ . . .

Cell phone number

Permanent Address	**Present Address**
[If home address differs from address during the semester]	
Street	Street
City, state, ZIP code	City, state, ZIP code
Phone number with area code	Phone number with area code

Objective or Summary   List your career objective or a brief summary paragraph of your achievements and goals

Education: Years   University of . . .   Location

[Give dates, from most recent to previous.]

Degree expected: B.A. in journalism, [Date]

Major: Journalism with emphasis in magazine

Other colleges attended [If any]   Location

High school attended [Optional]   Location

Experience: [List any full-time or part-time jobs, particularly any related to your field, in order starting from the most recent. Give the dates. You may add a line or two explaining your job duties.]

January–May [Year]

Reporter, *The Daily Campus* newspaper; covered university administration

July–August [Year]

Reporting internship with *City Newspaper;* covered general news for city desk and features

May–August [Year]

Server Starving Students, [City, state]

Special Skills and Awards: [Omit this category if you have no special skills.]
Skilled in graphics programs and computer-assisted reporting
Fluent in Spanish
Scripps Howard Scholarship for College Journalism

Activities: [List only important activities and memberships, especially those that show leadership or skills related to the job you are seeking. This category may be omitted.]

References: [List only two or three people who have given you permission to list them. References may be listed on a separate page if you run out of room. List people's titles, addresses and phone numbers. Do not write "Available on request."]

Sample of scannable résumé.

ONLINE PORTFOLIOS

Even if you submit a printed résumé and cover letter, it's a good idea to have an online portfolio linked to the digital profile you should be creating. You don't have to know Web design to create your online portfolio; WordPress and Blogger, free online publishing tools, can do the work for you. Check out online portfolios of some successful professionals in your field for inspiration. One site that offers ways to create online portfolios of journalists is 10,000 Words at *www.mediabistro.com/10000words /tag/online-portfolios*.

Here are some suggestions about what to include:

- **Home page:** Include your name and email address. Many people just label their home pages "MyPage," and they fail to provide a name and contact information. Include a link to your online résumé.
- **Index:** Navigation menu or content page if you have several pages in your portfolio.
- **Writing and/or video examples:** Links to clips or video, brochures or public relations materials you have produced. You can provide the text in PDF format if that is preferable.
- **Multimedia files:** Images, sound files, multimedia Web pages
- **Social media links:** Provide links to your LinkedIn site, Facebook, Twitter or other social media sites that contain your professional information.
- **Blogs:** Link to blogs you have written if they demonstrate your media skills.
- **Update:** Keep your online résumé and other items up to date. List items in order of the most recent one first.

INTERVIEWS

The interview is your chance to explain how much you want to work for the employer and why you would be a good choice. It is also your chance to find out more about the employer and to assess whether you would really like to work there.

Here are some tips:

Dress Conservatively Wear the type of clothing that employees at that organization would wear to work. Women might wear casual attire such as a skirt and blouse or more businesslike outfits such as a suit or dress, depending on the company. Men should wear a suit or sport jacket with a shirt and tie.

Be Prompt Be on time for your interview. You may arrive 15 minutes early, but don't get there too early. Never be late. That's equivalent to missing a deadline. And that's equivalent to saying you are not fit for the job.

Be Prepared Be informed about the publication, organization or station. Read copies of the publication, particularly the most recently published ones, or view video on the station's website if possible. Public relations applicants should try to gather research about the company and the types of promotions the firm does. Memorize the names of key editors in advance.

Understand the Costs Some organizations will pay for your transportation and hotel. If not, be prepared to pay for them yourself. Small newspapers and other organizations may not have the budget for your travel costs. You have to decide whether the cost is worthwhile to you. If the organization is out of state, it's fair to ask whether your transportation and lodging costs will be reimbursed.

Concentrate When you are introduced to people, try to remember their names, especially those of key editors — such as the city editor or, if you are applying for a sports job, the sports editor. Homework helps.

Be Enthusiastic Your enthusiasm is your best asset, especially if you don't have experience. Show that you're interested in the job. Smile and enjoy the interview just as if you were doing an interview for a story. If you don't really want to work for the firm, don't waste everyone's time.

Be Polite Thank the editor or key person for granting you an interview, and thank the person at the end of it as well.

Be Pleasant Even if you are frightened, smile and be responsive.

Be Yourself Do not try so hard to make a good impression that you are insincere. Be honest about what you can and cannot do and what you want to learn. Never try to give a false impression of yourself.

Ask Questions The questions you ask are as important as the ones you answer. They show your curiosity and your concern about the job — qualities of a good reporter, editor or publicist.

Editors have their favorite questions, so it is hard to prepare for the interview. However, almost all of them will ask why you want to work for their organization and why you want to be a journalist. Try to be creative but sincere. "I've always wanted to write" is such a boring answer.

Here are some other questions that are popular with newspaper editors (similar questions are often asked in other fields):

Why Do You Want to Work for This Organization? The answers are up to you: Because you grew up in the area, want to remain in the area, are familiar with the community and so on. It's best to specify something you like about the organization if you are familiar with it. Or you could say you are seeking a variety of experiences, particularly if it's a small newspaper or television station, where reporters tend to do all types of stories. If it's a large organization, you could say you're attracted by the prestige of the publication or station or the chance to learn from very experienced journalists. If you are so eager that you will work anywhere, it's OK to say so. Just be honest.

Why Did You Want to Become a Journalist or Public Relations Practitioner? Because it's more interesting than selling used cars, because you seek adventure, because you love the language — whatever. Here is your chance to give your real reason. It could be that someone influenced you or that you just like the type of work.

What Are Your Goals As a Journalist? A preferred answer might be because you like the work of this paper or station and you are familiar with the community (if that's true). If your goal is to be a foreign correspondent, at this point you might consider joining the Navy. Small papers don't have much use for foreign bureaus. Again, be sincere.

What Books, Magazines and Newspapers Do You Read? Editors love this question. It tells them something about you.

What Other Interests Do You Have? This is another favorite question.

What Can You Do for this Organization, or Why Should I Hire You? Don't say you can turn the organization around or make it wonderful. But do say something about the types of stories you would like to do, or say that you would be willing to do all types of stories. Don't be arrogant.

What Do You Think of This Newspaper, TV Station or Public Relations Firm? Be cautious with this one. Don't say it's terrible and you can save it. Point out something good first. Then you might point out some weakness or area that you think could be improved. Perhaps you think it could use more human approaches to stories or more hard news. If you've read it, you have a right to your opinion. Just be diplomatic.

What Was Your Favorite Story (or Public Relations Project) That You Wrote or Produced, and Why Did You Like It? This is another question that gives insight into you — as well as your professional interests.

How Would You Cover This Issue? The editor might give you an example of a topic that is of concern in that community. You'll have to think and do the best you can to come up with some interesting approaches.

What Questions Do You Have? This question is very important. Here's where you get your chance to ask about the company, the workload, perhaps what the editors want or expect from reporters and copy editors. You could ask about a probationary period. You could also ask about salary, benefits and other compensation; generally, however, that shouldn't be your first question.

At the end of the interview, don't forget to thank the interviewer for his time and interest.

Interview Follow-Up After you have had an interview, wait a few weeks and then call to let the editor know you are aggressive and interested in the job. But don't be a pest.

Even if you are not interested in the job, send a note thanking the editor for the interview. That's just basic courtesy. And if you are interested in the job, the thank-you note lets the editor know something else about you: You're thoughtful.

EXERCISES

1 Tell your story in six words: This exercise comes from Anne McNeilly, an assistant professor at the School of Journalism, Ryerson University. (A similar exercise is in the social media chapter based on the website *www.sixwordstories.net*.) However, Professor McNeilly uses the concept to ask students to write a six-word bio and include an image or photo that illustrates the concept. Although she used the exercise to create a multimedia show, you can use this concept to create your home page of an online portfolio or résumé. Here are some of the examples from her students: "I want money but chose journalism"; "Waiting for a sign. Still hopeful"; "Missing mornings of Oreos with milk"; "University degree: bad credit, $40,000 debt."

2 Interview people in your field: Depending on your field of interest, interview three newspaper editors, television news directors, magazine editors or public relations employers about the qualities they seek in job candidates and the kinds of applications they want.

3 Describe yourself: Write a few descriptive paragraphs about yourself in the third person ("she" or "he"). This exercise will give you a clue to what makes you special, and it may help you find a lead for your cover letter.

4 Write a cover letter and résumé: Write a cover letter and a résumé for a job or internship you would be interested in getting.

5 Write an online résumé.

 MindTap

FEATURED ONLINE ACTIVITIES: Log on to the MindTap for Rich's Writing and Reporting News to access a variety of robust additional material, including this chapter's learning objectives, activities, comprehension quizzes, and more!

APPENDIX
Grammar and Usage

Library of Congress/Prints and Photography Division

The difference between the right word and the nearly right word is the same as that between lightning and the lightning bug.

—**MARK TWAIN**, *American Author and Humorist*

COACHING TIPS

When in doubt, **check it out.**

Don't depend on computer spellers and grammar checkers.

Don't turn in copy without **checking it for grammar,** spelling and style.

Keep a **dictionary and stylebook** on your desk as you write. Use them.

Check your **Associated Press Stylebook** for usage.

MANY NEWS ORGANIZATIONS REQUIRE YOU TO TAKE A grammar and style test if you are applying for a job as a reporter or copy editor. Public relations practitioners also need good writing skills. If you don't have a good grasp of grammar and usage, you won't be considered a good writer. And you can't rely on an editor or your computer to catch all your errors.

Now that you understand how to write a news story, this appendix will help you avoid these common errors in grammar, spelling and usage:

TEST YOUR KNOWLEDGE:

Who or *whom* should you contact for jobs and internships?

Will grammar have an *effect* or *affect* on your career?

Do you expect to go *further* or *farther* in your career if you get a good journalism background?

Do you know how the media *is* or *are* changing the way news is covered?

Does this sentence look *alright* to you? If it does, you need to study this appendix well.

The correct usage is in this paragraph: *Whom* should you contact for an internship? Check directories in your field. A good grasp of grammar will have a beneficial *effect* on your career, but poor grammar will *affect* your chances of getting a good job. You will go *further* in your career if you understand how the media *are* changing the way news is covered. It is never *all right* for you to write *alright*.

Despite the abbreviations and new language of tweets, u need 2 master grammar 2 b a gd writer. Whether news is delivered to your smartphone, tablet device, computer or in print form, it still must be well written and adhere to the principles of good grammar and style, preferably Associated Press style for most news organizations.

Should you send an *e-mail* or an *email*? Do you have a *website* or a *Web site*? Do you have a *smart phone* or a *smartphone*?

The AP Stylebook recently changed *Web site* to *website*, but it still insists that *Web page* is two separate words and the *Web* when used alone, should be capitalized. These words are joined and in lowercase: *website, webcam, webmaster* and *webcast*. And AP considers *smartphone* to be one word and spells *email* without a hyphen. As media terms keep changing or being created, the style for writing about them will inevitably evolve as well. But most news organizations and public relations firms still follow the AP Stylebook for print and online writing. You can follow the AP Stylebook on social media sites, Facebook and Twitter.

COMMON ERRORS

Advise/advice: *Advise* is what you do; *advice* is what you receive.

I *advise* you to study this chapter. If your professor has *advised* you to buy an Associated Press Stylebook, she gave you good *advice.*

Affect, effect: *Affect* is an active verb, and *effect* is a noun. Think of *affect* with an *a* for action and *effect* with an *e* for the end result. *Effect* can be used as a verb with *to,* as in "to effect change," but that is not a common use.

> Failing your style tests will *affect* your grade. But the *effect* on your writing will be more serious.

Aggravate/annoy: *Aggravate* means to make a condition worse; *annoy* means to irritate. People don't get aggravated; conditions do.

> If you continue to smoke, you will *aggravate* your lung disease.

> If you don't turn off your cell phone in class, you will *annoy* me.

A lot, alot: Two words, please. Always. If you can't remember, use *many* instead of *a lot.*

Alright: *Alright* is listed in the dictionary as *all right* in informal dialogue, but it is not all right, according to the Associated Press Stylebook, which says *never* use that spelling. Use two words, *all right,* to mean OK.

> It is not *all right* to use *alright.*

Altogether/all together: *Altogether* means completely or thoroughly. *All together* means people or items are all gathered in one place.

> It is wise to avoid addictive drugs *altogether.* The used books were dumped *all together* in a storage closet.

Among, between: *Among* is used with more than two items; *between* is used with two items.

> The conflict was *between* two students. The pay increases were divided *among* 10 employees.

Ampersand: Do not use the ampersand (&) as a substitute for *and.* This symbol should be used only when it is part of a company's name, such as Dun & Bradstreet.

Anxious, eager: *Anxious* means you are worried; *eager* means you are excited or looking forward to something.

> In your cover letter, don't say you are *anxious* to work for a company.

> Even if you are worried about the job, you are probably *eager* to get it.

As, like, as if, as though: Use *as, as if* or *as though* to introduce a sentence or clause with a verb. *Like* means "similar to" and should be used only to compare nouns or pronouns. Whenever you are confused, just see whether *similar to* would fit in the sentence. If the sentence or clause contains some action, use *as.* Think *a* for *as* for action.

> *As I said* (not *like I said*), she plays basketball *like* a professional. It looks *as if* she will become a professional basketball player.

Bad, badly: *Bad* is an adjective that modifies a noun, as in "You wrote a *bad* paper." *Badly* is an adverb that modifies a verb, as in "You played *badly* in the game." These words are used *badly* most of the time when used with the linking verb *feel.* "You *feel bad*" means that your health, emotional or mental state is bad. "You *feel badly*" means that your sense of touch is poor. (See *Linking verbs* for more explanation.)

Don't *feel bad* if you have made this common mistake, but don't write *badly* anymore in this context.

Before, prior to: *Before* is appropriate and less formal for most uses. *Prior to* is appropriate when the connection between the two events makes it clear that one event must precede the other.

Every passenger must show identification *before* a ticket will be issued. Every passenger must show identification *prior to* boarding the plane. (*Before* would also be acceptable here.)

Between, among: See *among*.

Between you and I or between you and me: Never use *I* in this case. *Between* is a preposition that must be followed by a pronoun in the objective case: *me, her, him, them, us*. Every time you are tempted to use *I,* mentally substitute *he* or *we*. You're not as likely to say "between you and he" or "between they and we."

Biannual/semiannual/biennial: *Biannual* means twice a year. So does *semiannual*. *Biennial* means every two years. Note that these words are not hyphenated.

Bimonthly/semimonthly/biweekly/semiweekly: *Bimonthly* means every other month; *semimonthly* means twice a month. Same with *biweekly* — every other week —and *semiweekly* — twice a week.

Board with singular verb: A reference to a board of directors or a board of education or any other board followed by a phrase describing it takes a singular verb, such as *is, was* or *votes*. The board is considered a singular entity; it's still one board even if it has 30 members. Ignore the modifying phrase.

The *Board of Education is* meeting tonight. The *Board of Regents votes* on the issue tomorrow. (If that sounds awkward, you might say, "*Members of the Board of Education are meeting* tonight.")

Can, may: *Can* means you are capable of doing something; *may* means permission or the chance to do something.

You *may* get a promotion if you *can* create Web pages or a complete website.

Clause, phrase: A clause is a group of words containing a subject and a verb. An independent clause forms a complete sentence; a dependent one depends on the rest of the sentence to make sense. Use a comma after an introductory clause. A phrase is a group of words without a subject or a verb. If you want to write well (that's a dependent clause), don't interrupt your subject and verb with a long clause.

Poor: The student, who was fond of writing long, complicated sentences with clauses between his subject and verb, was an English major.

Better: The student, who was an English major, was fond of writing long, complicated sentences.

Phrase: After the game, the fans celebrated at a local pub.

Comma: Use a comma between two independent clauses joined by a conjunction — *and, but, for, or, no, so, yet* — unless the clauses are short. Use a comma after an introductory clause unless it is short. Always put commas inside the quotation marks in a direct quote. Check the Associated Press Stylebook for a more complete discussion.

MULTIMEDIA COACH

ONLINE SITES with poor grammar and spelling errors lack credibility. Online news stories use Associated Press style. TV "crawls," the print that scrolls across the bottom of a screen, must also adhere to good grammar and usage even though these headlines are brief.

■ Proofread your copy carefully before you post anything online.

■ Most people's email messages are notoriously sloppy. Check spelling and grammar before you send your email messages, particularly if you are sending an email for an interview, an online résumé or other career-related activities.

■ Although broadcast journalists also use Associated Press style, the medium features the spoken word. Therefore, you may want to use a phonetic spelling of a name that is difficult to pronounce. But anything that is shown on the screen, such as a name or a title, should be checked for accurate spelling and grammar.

"When a sentence includes a direct quote (that's an introductory clause), the comma always goes inside the quotation marks," the professor said. "So does the period."

Comma splice: Never join two sentences with a comma. That's called a comma splice. Learn to love the period. If the sentences are closely related, you might use a semicolon.

People who use commas to join sentences are making a dreadful mistake; comma splices indicate bad writing.

Compared to/compared with: Use *compared to* when you liken one thing to another. Use *compared with* when you examine the similarities and differences of two or more items.

She is very smart *compared to* her sister. *Compared with* all the other students in her class, she is the best writer.

Complement, compliment: *Complement,* with *e,* means "to complete," also with *e. Compliment,* with *i,* means to flatter or praise.

"If you can't get a *compliment* any other way, pay one to yourself," Mark Twain said.

If you want a scarf to *complement* your outfit, buy one.

Consensus: This word means an agreement of opinion, so do not say *"consensus of opinion."* That's redundant.

After six hours of debate, the board of commissioners reached a *consensus* about building a new parking garage.

Council/counsel: A *council* is an appointed or elected group of people who give advice or make decisions. *Counsel* is the advice or consultation you receive.

She serves on the sorority *council*. The professor *counseled* me on how to apply for an internship.

Credible/creditable: *Credible* is believable. *Creditable* is deserving of credit, honor or esteem.

He gave a *credible* explanation for his absences.

The student made a *creditable* effort on the essay even though he didn't win the contest. The use of *creditable* in this case is awkward.

Criteria, criterion: *Criteria*, referring to the factors that will be used to judge something, is plural. If only one factor is involved, it is a *criterion*.

The *criteria* to get an A in this class are good writing, spelling, grammar and punctuation. The *criterion* for expulsion from the journalism school is plagiarism.

Currently, presently, now: *Currently* means "now"; *presently* means "soon," although it can mean "now." If you are confused, just use *now*.

She is *currently* in her senior year. The board will announce the winners *presently*.

Dangling modifier: A phrase or a participle (an adjective made from a verb ending in *ing*) is said to dangle if it is not placed directly before the noun or pronoun it modifies.

Dangling participle: After *studying* for three hours, the *test* was canceled. (The test did not study for three hours. The student did.)

Correct: After *studying* for three hours, the *student* learned that the test was canceled.

Desert, dessert: A desert is a barren place; a dessert is something to eat.

You probably won't find a delicious *dessert* in a *desert*.

Directions/regions: Capitalize regions of the country — *Midwest, North, South, West, Northeast, Southwest, East Coast* and *West Coast*. Use lowercase for directions: Go *west* and turn *east*.

She is hoping to get a job on the *East Coast*, but right now she lives in the *Midwest*.

He said the party is about five blocks *east* of the university.

Either, neither: Each of these words requires a singular verb and a singular pronoun. Think of *either one* or *neither one*. But if *either* joins a singular word and a plural word, the verb agrees with the closer subject.

Either student *is* qualified for the position.

Neither the president nor the vice president *is* available for comment.

Neither of the students *plans* to present *her* project tomorrow.

Either the president or several members *are going* to attend *their* fraternity's philanthropic event.

Embarrassment, harassment: These words are often spelled incorrectly. *Embarrassment* has two *r*'s and two *s*'s; *harassment* has just one *r*. You are probably embarrassed more than you are harassed, so give it the extra *r* for being a regular occurrence.

Etc.: This is an abbreviation for the Latin word *et cetera*, meaning "and other things." You can substitute *and so on* or *and so forth*, but it is best to avoid this term. It leaves the reader wondering what else should follow. As the late John B. Bremner, a renowned authority on usage, wrote, "Above all, don't use *etc.* as a cover for ignorance when you have run out of ideas."

Everyone, everybody, every one, each: Each of these words takes a singular verb and a singular pronoun. If the previous sentence sounds strange to you, mentally eliminate the prepositional phrase (of these words). The phrases that intervene between *everyone, each* and *everybody* and the verb or pronoun are what cause the confusion. If you really get confused, substitute all or another plural word for *everyone, each* or *everybody*.

> *Every one* of the students is seeking a good job in his or her field. (Stress the *one* in this sentence. You wouldn't say, "Everyone are" or "Everybody are seeking.")

Farther, further: *Farther* is distance; *further* involves length of time, quantity or intensity.

> How much *farther* do we have to drive?

> I'll give this *further* thought.

Feel: This word indicates a state of being or a sense of touch. Don't use it to mean "think" or "believe."

> You will *feel* bad if you don't get an A on the quizzes at the end of the chapter.

> You *think* or *believe* you are doing well (not you *feel* you are doing well) in the course.

Fewer, less: Use *fewer* to refer to a specific number of items that you can count; use *less* to refer to a collection of items, a period of time or a quantity. *Less* is often used with a sum of money.

> *Fewer* than 10 graduates took jobs in which they made *less* than $15,000.

Fragment: An incomplete sentence, sometimes just a word or phrase. (That is a fragment.) Fragments can be effective as a writing technique for emphasis but should be used cautiously and rarely.

Full-time/full time: Use the hyphenated version when you are using the word to describe something such as a *full-time* job. But use two words without a hyphen when it is not followed by a noun: He works *full time*.

Goes without saying: If it does *go without saying,* then why say it? This is a stupid expression often used in corporate memos.

Half-mast, half-staff: On naval ships and at naval stations, flags are flown at *half-mast*. Other flags are flown at *half-staff*, usually to commemorate a person or tragic event.

Hyphenate compound modifiers: When two or more adjectives are used together to modify a noun that follows them, use a hyphen. Don't use a hyphen for *very* or adverbs ending in *ly*. Do not use a hyphen if a compound adjective follows an action verb.

> The *3-year-old* child had a chronic ear infection. But: The child is *3 years old*. She was an *honor-roll student* in high school (compound adjective modifying *student*). But: The student was on the *honor roll* in high school (no modifier).

> The *part-time job* pays well (compound adjective modifying *job*). But: I work *part time* in the office (compound adjective after an action verb).

The student had a *poorly furnished apartment* (no hyphen after *ly* adverb).

A *very strong wind* blew off the roof (no hyphen after *very*). Limit the use of *very* in your writing; it's a weak modifier.

I, me: *I* does the action; *me* receives it. The same rule applies to the pronouns *he, she* and *we*. Don't use these words after the prepositions *to* or *with*. *I, he, she* and *we* are in the nominative case, meaning they should be used as subjects. *Me, her, him, us* and *them* are in the objective case and should be used as objects in sentences.

Whenever the newspaper needs someone to work overtime, Julie and *I* always get picked.

The chancellor gave the report to several journalism students and *me* to review before he made a decision.

If I were: Do not *use if I was*. *If* is a word used in the subjunctive mood, meaning it expresses a condition; it should always be used with *were*.

If I were you, I'd learn to use *were* with *if* when I mean it in a conditional sense.

If I were *he,* I'd probably reword the sentence, because it is correct, but it sounds weird.

If she were in my reporting class, she wouldn't use *was* in a sentence starting with *if*.

Irregardless: There is no such word, *regardless* of what you may believe and *regardless* of the fact that it is listed in the dictionary as nonstandard usage. Don't use it.

It's, its: Wordsmith John B. Bremner calls the misuse of *it's* and *its* "possibly the most sickening example of literary ignorance." *It's* is a contraction for *it is; its* is a possessive word meaning "belonging to it."

SOCIAL MEDIA

IF YOU WANT to join, not join together, a social media network such as Facebook, you can find *a lot* (not *alot*) of grammar resources. Just log onto Facebook, search for "grammar," and you will find GrammarGirl, who has many interesting posts. Additional entries in Facebook and other social media sites where you can find answers to some grammatical questions include:

- *The Elements of Style* or its authors William Strunk Jr. and E.B. White. This book, written in 1918, is one of the classic reference books for writers.

- Associated Press Stylebook: The style authority for most journalism organizations. You'll find posts on Facebook and Twitter.

- YouTube: If you are a visual learner, go to YouTube and search for English grammar and style. A number of entries will show you videos on proper punctuation or grammar issues.

- ACES: American Society of Copy Editors. Follow this organization on Twitter. You'll find timely posts and links to the society's blogs, which discuss many journalism issues and editing guidelines.

It's going to cost more to attend college next year because the university raised *its* tuition.

Join, not join together: *Join* means to connect. Can you *join* something apart? *Together* is superfluous.

Judgment: No *e*. There is no judge in *judgment*.

Lay, lie, laid, lain: *Lay* means to place or put something somewhere; it always takes an object when used in this sense. If you can substitute the verb *place,* use *lay. Laid* is the past tense. *Lie* means to recline. Its past tense is *lay,* and therein lies the confusion. It might help you to mentally use *down* with *lie* or to substitute *recline. Lain* is the perfect tense of *lie*.

Please *lay* the book on the desk. She *laid* the book on the desk yesterday.

Lie down and take a nap for a few hours. She *lay* on the beach for three hours yesterday and was badly sunburned.

He *had lain* on the sofa for three hours.

Layoffs/lay off: *Layoffs* without a hyphen is one word when used as a noun. When you *lay off* people as a verb, you must do it in two words.

Newspapers had many *layoffs* this year. The station was forced to *lay off* several reporters.

Less than/under: When you are using a collection of items rather than a specific number of items, *less than* or *under* is acceptable. For a comparison of a specific number, use *fewer than* (see *fewer*).

She makes *less than* $20,000 per year.

She makes *under* $20,000 per year.

He weighs *less than* 200 pounds.

He weighs *under* 200 pounds.

Like, as: See *as, like*.

Linking verbs: The *to be* verbs are linking verbs: *am, is, are, was, were, have been.* Verbs expressing the senses are also considered linking verbs: *appear, feel, smell, sound, taste, look.* Linking verbs join the subject with a predicate nominative, meaning a noun or pronoun in the same case as the subject. The pronoun that follows a linking verb could be used as a subject. The adjective after a linking verb modifies the subject and is called a predicate adjective.

It *is* she. She *is* it. (You wouldn't say "Her *is* it.") The food *tastes good* and the music *sounds good,* but I still *feel bad. (Good,* a predicate adjective, modifies *food* and *music,* not the verb. You wouldn't say "The food *tastes well* and the music *sounds well,* but I still *feel badly.")*

Lose, loose: If you *lose* your assignment, you're in trouble. If your pants fall down because they are too *loose,* you'll be embarrassed. You might also be in trouble. You'll certainly be in trouble if you mix up the spelling of these two words.

Media: This word is plural and takes a plural verb for agreement. Television is one *medium,* but newspapers, magazines and television are the *media*.

The *media are planning* major coverage of the election. The *media are changing* the way *they* cover news.

ETHICS

ETHICAL DILEMMA: Should you clean up quotes? If a speaker uses poor grammar, should you fix the grammar?

Ethical values: Accuracy, fairness, sensitivity.

Ethical Guidelines: The Associated Press Stylebook says, "Never alter quotations even to correct minor grammatical errors or word usage . . . Do not routinely use abnormal spellings such as *gonna* in attempts to convey regional dialects or mispronunciations."

The guidelines reinforce the concept that a quote must be someone's exact words. However, what is stylistically correct may not be ethically sensitive. If you are trying to convey that a politician uses poor grammar and if that concept is relevant to a profile or to the person's way of speaking, you may want to use the ungrammatical language. However, if you are interviewing someone who may be an immigrant and does not speak English well, it could be insensitive to quote exactly. Instead of using the exact quote, consider paraphrasing or using a partial quote. Avoid using too many partial quotes because they disrupt the flow of a sentence and cause the reader to wonder what was left out.

Memento/not momento: If you want to give students something to remember at their graduation, you will give them a *memento*. There is no such word as a *momento*, although your graduation might be a *momentous* occasion, meaning it was of great moment or something to remember.

Morale/moral: *Morale* means a mental or emotional attitude; *moral* is the distinction between right and wrong.

> In his ethics course, he studied *moral* reasoning methods, but when he failed the course, his *morale* plummeted.

More than, over: *More than* is better when referring to numbers; *over* is better when referring to spatial relationships, as the opposite of *under*. In some cases, *over* can be used with numbers, such as ages or amounts of money. However, in 2014 AP Stylebook editors decided that *over* and *more than* can now be used interchangeably.

> *More than* 300 people attended the hearing.

> The car went *over* the bridge. He is *over* 20. She earns *over* $400 per week. (This last sentence is acceptable, but so is *more than* $400 per week.)

Needless to say: If it's *needless to say*, don't say it. This is another stupid expression.

None: When you use *none* as in *not one*, use a singular verb. Use a plural verb when you mean *no two or more* or *not any* in a collective sense.

> *None* (*not one*) of these students *is* going to graduate school.

> *None* (*not any*) of the student fees *are* being used for health care.

Nonprofit/not-for-profit: A *nonprofit* organization is not supposed to make any profits, nor is it supposed to have a hyphen. The term *not-for-profit* can mean the same thing. If you are using it as an adjective to describe an organization, join the words with hyphens.

Off of: *Off* is enough. *Off of* is unnecessary and ugly usage.

The manager took 10 percent *off* the regular price.

Part-time/part time: When this term is used as an adjective to describe another word, treat it as one word by hyphenating it, such as your *part-time* job. When you say you work only *part time*, meaning part of the time, use two words.

Passive voice, active voice: Avoid passive voice whenever possible. You are using passive voice when you indicate that something has happened to you or the subject. You are using the active voice when you indicate that you or the subject is doing the action. The action verbs that characterize the active voice have more impact than passive verbs. But sometimes you need the passive voice. Place the most important information first in the sentence, and that will determine whether you need active or passive voice. Active voice is preferable for print media and essential for broadcast media.

Active voice: Three students *received* scholarships.

Passive voice: Scholarships *were received* by three students.

Appropriate use of passive: The serial killer *was sentenced* to death by the judge. (That's probably better than saying "The judge *sentenced* a serial killer to death today" because the emphasis should be on the killer, not the judge.)

Pleaded, pled: *Pled* as the past tense of *plead* is considered acceptable in English usage, but the Associated Press Stylebook considers it colloquial and prefers *pleaded*.

The defendant *pleaded* guilty, but if he *pled* guilty, he would still go to jail regardless of whether the Associated Press style gurus approved of the term he used.

Precede/proceed: *Precede* means what goes before; *proceed* means to go ahead or continue.

Basic reporting *precedes* the advanced reporting course, which you take if you *proceed* in getting your degree.

Prerequisite/perquisites: If you have to take a beginning reporting course before you can take magazine writing, the first course is a *prerequisite*, meaning it is required to precede something. You know that because you have many prerequisites (without hyphens). If you get a good job, you might get some *perks*, which is really an abbreviation for *perquisites*.

Proved/proven: *Proved* is the past tense of an action. *Proven* is an adjective and should be used to describe someone.

You have *proved* that you are ready to graduate.

He is a *proven* leader.

Publicly, not publically: If you want to run for president of the student government, you should announce your intentions *publicly*. Be careful not to commit the common mistake of omitting the *l* from the word.

Restaurateur: No *n* as in restaurant. Think of a *restaurateur* as the person who manages the place where you ate, not a place for an ant.

Seasons: Use lowercase for seasons — spring, summer, autumn and fall. That goes for springtime and summertime too. However, if the season is part of a formal title such as *Winter Olympics*, capitalize it.

Should have, not should of: *Of* should never be used as a verb. Also wrong: *could of* and *would of* in place of *could have* and *would have.*

By the time you are in college, you *should have* learned never to write *should of.*

Stationary, stationery: *Stationary* means something stays the same (note the *a*'s); *stationery* is the paper you use for letters (note the *e*).

The desk bolted to the floor is *stationary*. She used pink *stationery* to write wedding invitations.

Subject–verb agreement: *The verb must agree with the subject. If the subject is* singular, the verb must be singular as well. Plural subjects take plural verbs. Here's why that is not as easy as it seems:

The number of students who drop classes is increasing. The subject is *number*, not *students*. When you have a noun, *number*, followed by a prepositional phrase with a plural word such as *students*, identify the subject. Don't be misled by the phrase. When *number* is the subject, it always takes a singular verb.

The rate of dropouts is increasing. The subject is *rate*, not *dropouts*.

There are fewer students enrolled in the print journalism program. The subject is *students*, not the expletive *there*. Avoid starting sentences with *There*, because you are forced to use a weak verb. Better: Fewer students are enrolled in the print journalism program.

A singular subject, followed by the phrase *as well as*, takes a singular verb. The city budget, as well as the tax proposal, was approved. Better to say: The city budget and the tax proposal were approved.

Everyone, each, either, neither, every take singular verbs. Imagine the word *one* as the subject when you use those words. *Each* (one) of the students *is creating* a Web page. If that sounds awkward, use *All* of the students are creating a Web page.

When a compound subject (two or more subjects) is joined by *and*, it takes a plural verb. The professor *and* the students were sick.

When a compound subject is joined by *or, nor, but, either* or *neither*, the verb agrees with the subject closest to it. *Neither* the mayor *nor* the council members have proposed a solution. The desk *or* the computers have to be sold to raise the money.

Collective nouns such as *audience, jury* and *board* take singular verbs. The *Board* of Commissioners *is scheduled* to meet after the holidays. If that sounds awkward, just say, The commissioners are scheduled to meet after the holidays.

The audience was enthusiastic about the performance.

See other entries for *none, board, everyone.*

Than, then: *Than* is used for comparison; *then* is used for time. Think of *then* and *when.*

That, which: When a clause is essential (or restrictive), meaning the sentence won't make sense without it, use *that*. If the sentence can stand alone without the clause (if the clause is nonessential or nonrestrictive), use *which*. Use a comma before a clause with *which;* don't use a comma to precede a clause with *that.* And don't use either word to refer to people. Use *who.*

The committee *that banned reporters* from the hearing was fined. (What committee was fined? The clause is essential to the meaning of the sentence.)

The Lawrence School Board, *which meets regularly on Tuesdays*, will discuss changing school boundaries this week. (The sentence is clear without the clause telling when the board meets.)

The school board members, *who will vote next week*, were elected to two-year terms. (Use *who* when referring to people.)

Their, there, they're: *Their* means "belonging to them"; *there* means "where" or is sometimes used to begin a sentence; *they're* is a contraction for *they are.*

Students who did not qualify for *their* loans this year said *they're* going to file new applications while *there* is still time.

There is or there are: Avoid starting sentences with these words. They always force you to use the weak *to be* verbs. Turn the sentence around and insert an active verb.

Poor: There are no internships being offered at that newspaper.

Better: That newspaper is not offering any internships.

Toward, towards: Use *toward* without the *s.*

Unique: *Unique* means "one of a kind, incomparable." You cannot have something that is more unique or most unique or very unique. If it's unique, it is beyond comparison or qualification.

Who, whom: *Who* is the subject; *who* does the action. *Whom* is the object and receives the action. These words are confusing in clauses. Try to reverse the sentence or clause and see whether *who* can be the subject. Deciding on the right word is even trickier when *who* or *whom* is the subject of a clause.

Are you the person *who* called me about the job? (Who is the subject of this clause; who does the action; who called.)

Are you the student *who* is seeking the job? (Who is the subject of the clause is seeking.) Are you the student *whom* I hired last week? (Whom is the object of I hired; whom received the action.)

Whom do you wish to see about the job opening? (You — the subject — wish to see whom — the object, the person who receives the action of your wish.)

The personnel director will choose *whoever* she thinks is the most qualified. (She thinks *whoever* is qualified; *whoever* is the subject of the clause *whoever is most qualified.*)

Who's, whose: *Who's* is a contraction for *who is; whose* is a possessive meaning "belonging to whom."

Whose team project was late, and *who's* responsible?

Your, you're: *Your* is possessive, meaning "belonging to you," and *you're* is a contraction for *you are.*

Now *you're* ready to test *your* skill by doing the following exercises.

ZIP code: *ZIP* should be all in capital letters, and code should be in lowercase. It is a trademark of the U.S. Postal Service, and it stands for Zone Improvement Program.

EXERCISES

1 Grammar A–K: Study the grammar and usage tips from A to K, and correct the errors in the following sentences. Not all sentences contain errors; some may contain more than one error. Type the errors and the corrections, or type the entire sentence in correct form if your instructor prefers.

a She felt bad about missing the school board meeting, but her editor fired her irregardless of her excuse.

b We will all join together in prayer for the students who died in the shooting, and we will fly the flags at half-mast.

c It's alright if you miss class for a job interview, you can make up the test tomorrow.

d We'll divide the workload between three students.

e The St. Joseph Board of Commissioners are planning to submit a proposal for a bond issue to pay for road improvements, and they are hoping the election committee will reach a consensus of opinion to put the issue on the ballot.

f I know you are anxious to get this job, but each of the applicants will have a chance to discuss their strengths and weaknesses with the personnel director.

g Based on your writing skills, it looks like you could be a good journalist.

h Each of the students is going to receive a plaque with their diplomas at graduation.

i She was embarrassed that she had less than five answers correct on the quiz.

j After the boss read the report, he gave it to Jim and I to rewrite and said its due back by Monday.

2 Grammar L–Y: Study the grammar and usage tips from L to Y, and correct the errors in the following sentences. Not all sentences contain errors; some may contain more than one error, and some of the errors may include information from A to K. Type the errors and the corrections, or type the entire sentence in correct form if your instructor prefers.

a The people that attended the gay rights rally said it was one of the most unique events the school had sponsored.

b However, the participants in the rally said the media was annoying when they converged on the speakers with cameras and microphones.

c Some of the speakers felt badly that the crowd became unruly and the organizer said he was embarassed when some of the participants complained.

d Needless to say, next year the rally will be planned better.

e None of the five students involved in the fracas is going to be punished.

f The first-place award, that was an engraved silver bowl, was received by the class valedictorian.

g The three top restauranteurs in the city provided food for the banquet, but over 200 people got sick after the event.

h The City Board of Health, that investigates such cases, said the food smelled and tasted well, but they are withholding judgement on the cause of the illness until the food can be tested.

i Irregardless, alot of people were laying on the ground, holding their stomachs in pain.

j The city health inspector wanted to know who he should blame, and he said he was moving towards a solution to the mystery of revealing whose responsible for the food poisoning outbreak.

3 Edit a story: The following poorly written story would never be accepted for publication. Ignore the wordiness, and edit it only for grammar and usage errors. When you retype the story, underline, circle or use boldface to identify the errors, and type in the corrections.

In 1918 William Strunk Jr. produced a little book for his English course at Cornell University, it had a great affect on his students. E.B. White, one of the students who the professor taught, published the book in 1957. Today, the book, that was originally known as "The Little Book," is still having a great effect on writers. Its called *The Elements of Style.* Like

I said, it's still popular, and every writer should have their own copy. It's presently available on the World Wide Web.

Strunk never thought it was alright to use alot of unnecessary words. One of his famous sayings are "Omit needless words". Between you and I, that advice is still good today, and I feel badly that this story is filled with errors that would of made Strunk cringe. It goes without saying that Strunk would have been embarrased if I was in his class. None of these sentences are perfect, and if this was the way a student wrote, Strunk would have issued stern judgement. Poor grades were received by students who wrote this badly.

Their is no excuse for writing badly, Strunk might have said. "Vigorous writing is concise", Strunk wrote. The media does not always follow Strunk's advice. He was the most unique teacher of his time. If your anxious to be a good writer, you'll check out his book online.

FEATURED ONLINE ACTIVITIES: Log on to the MindTap for Rich's Writing and Reporting News to access interactive quizzes based on the grammar and usage you have learned in this appendix.

Glossary

A

Absolute privilege—The prerogative of public officials, including law enforcement officials, to make statements in the course of their official duties without fear of being sued for libel.

Acquittal—Dismissal of a charge against a person accused of a crime.

Action verbs—Words that show the act of doing something.

Active voice—Sentence in which subject is doing the action; usually subject–verb–object structure.

Actual malice—Publishing something knowing it was false or carelessly publishing information without checking whether it was true or false.

Actuality—The equivalent of a sound bite in radio.

Adjudicate—To determine by a judicial action.

Advance (for meetings)—A story written about the agenda, the list of what will be considered in a meeting.

Advance the lead—A lead based on the next step in the story.

Agenda—A plan or list of items to be discussed or done.

Aggregator—Software that compiles websites delivered to you regularly and sent via email or downloaded to a portable media player.

Alien—A term that many groups oppose when used to describe undocumented immigrants; AP Stylebook prefers "immigrants living in a country without legal permission."

Allegedly—Supposedly; an unfounded accusation.

Ambient sound—Background sound that is intended to play while the reporter or anchor is speaking; also called "natural" or "ambient" sound.

Analogies—Comparisons, description of two similar things.

Anchor—The person who reads the news on the set in the studio.

Anecdotal lead—A lead based on a story about a person, place or event.

Anecdote—A brief story about a person, place or event.

Anonymous source—A source who remains unnamed.

Appeal—In legal terms, a request to another court for a decision to be changed.

Appellant—The person who requests the appeal.

Apps—Short for applications; programs to download media, music, games or other Web-based items.

Arraignment—A criminal proceeding in which the defendant is read charges and asked to enter a plea.

Arrest—To apprehend someone in a criminal action.

Assessed value—The value of a property determined by an appraiser for tax purposes.

Assessment—The property value for tax purposes.

Attribution—Credit given to the source of the information.

Audacity—A free software program for recording and editing audio.

Audit—An examination of financial records by qualified inspectors.

B

Background—In reference to quoting a source, information that may be used without attribution.

Backtiming—Exact time in the newscast that a segment will air.

Bail—The amount of money, set by a judge, that the suspect has to deposit with the court to be released from jail pending a hearing or trial.

BBI—Boring but important.

Bit.ly—A URL shortening service; a system to use to shorten a full link on Twitter.

Blocking technique—A method of organizing a story by placing all the comments from one source in one part of the story, then the next source's comments in another block, and so on.

Blog—Short for "Web log," a personal journal or commentary about any topic.

Blogger.com—A Google-owned online publishing service to create and host blogs.

Blotter (police blotter)—A daily record of events or arrests in a police station.

Board (collective noun)—Capitalize with a specific title such as the Anchorage Board of Supervisors, but use lowercase when referring to the board of supervisors.

Briefs—Legal documents presented to the court.

B-roll—Supplemental video to accompany the story.

Build-on-a-quote lead—A lead based on a quote that is used later in the story.

Burglary—Entry into a building with intent to commit any type of crime.

Byte—A unit of computer code consisting of eight bits; a string of eight ones and zeros that make up one letter.

C

Capital budget—Money in a government budget, often raised by bonds and used to pay for major improvements such as the construction of highways or new buildings.

Change of venue—Procedure to seek a change of location of the trial, usually because of too much pretrial publicity.

Character generator—Machine that produces titles superimposed under video to identify the speaker.

Chronology—A sequence of events arranged by the order in which they happened.

Chyron—An electronically generated caption superimposed on the screen of a TV or movie screen; generally text or graphics seen at the bottom; also another name for "character generator," as it was the brand name of the machine that generated these titles.

Circle kicker—An ending that refers back to the lead.

Citizen journalism—Content created by readers and viewers who are not the regular reporters.

Citizen journalist—A person who creates content for a news website but is not a member of the organization.

Civil case—A noncriminal lawsuit, usually a dispute between two or more parties over private property.

Civil suit—A lawsuit charging violations of civil law, often involving property or financial disputes.

Clery Act—A federal law, originally called the Campus Security Act, requiring all colleges and universities that receive federal student financial aid programs to publish an annual report listing three years of crime statistics.

Cliché lead—A lead based on a cliché, a familiar or trite saying.

Clichés—Overused sayings that have become trite.

Cliffhanger—A sentence or paragraph that leaves the reader in suspense; usually used as an ending but can also be in the middle of the story.

Climax—The culmination or intense part of a story.

Closed-ended questions—Questions designed to elicit brief, specific factual answers.

Cloud computing—A way to securely store and retrieve computer information and software on a Web server; the cloud is a symbol for the Internet.

Complaint—A legal document in criminal law that states the charges against the person; in civil cases a complaint lists the issues that start the court action.

Computer-assisted reporting—The use of databases and the Internet for reporting.

Confidentiality—A promise not to reveal the identity of the source.

Conflict of interest—A situation in which a person (or the reporter) stands to gain or has a personal interest that conflicts with the company policy or the public benefit.

Consent agenda—A list of items on the agenda that a board will approve without discussion.

Contempt—Action that disregards the order or authority of the court.

Content provider—A person or company that provides content for a website.

Context—The circumstances that surround an event.

Contrast lead—A lead based on two situations that show comparison or differences, such as then and now incidents.

Convergence—Mixture of different types of media, usually print, audio, video and online.

Conversational style—Writing in a natural way as though conversing with someone.

Copyright—The 1976 U.S. Copyright Act protects everything a person writes the minute the information is offered in "a fixed form," which includes online or print information.

Courtesy titles—Mr., Mrs., Ms., Miss, Dr. or title used before a name as a courtesy.

Cover letter—The letter that introduces yourself and accompanies a job résumé and examples of your work.

Creative Commons—A nonprofit organization that offers several copyright licenses, allowing information creators to share their material under specific rights.

Criminal case—A court proceeding in which the defendant is charged with breaking criminal laws.

Crowdsourcing—Using a large group of people to help gather or produce content with social media.

Crystal-ball lead—A fortune-telling approach; a lead foretelling the future.

Curation—A way of gathering information from the Web and organizing it around a topic to post on a social media site where you can share the material.

D

Data graphics—Graphics to display numerical information.

Database—Collection of information that a computer can organize.

Data-driven journalism—News based on reporting with databases.

Deception—An action involving deceit, lies or intent to fool someone.

Deep background—Information that may be used for background only, but may not be attributed to the source.

Defamation—Injury to the reputation of someone.

Defendant—The person, group or company charged in a court case.

Deficit—Debt based on difference between the money government spends and the money it receives.

Delayed lead—A lead that delays the focus, such as a lead starting with description or an anecdote followed by the focus a few paragraphs later.

Deposition—A formal sworn statement to be used as evidence in a court case.

Descriptive lead—A lead describing a person, place or event.

Dialogue—Conversation between two or more people.

Digital—Signals or data delivered in a series of the digits ones and zeroes that are the basis of computer codes.

Digital delivery—Information delivered online.

Digital First media—Publishing first online in any form of digital media, such as websites, blogs or social media, or on mobile media devices.

Digital recorder—A device that records sound in a technology of pulse codes that are the type of codes used by computers.

Direct lead—A summary lead that gets to the main point in the first sentence.

Direct quotes—The exact words of the source.

Disabled—A general term for a person with a physical, mental or other disability; AP Stylebook recommends using a specific description of the issue.

Discovery—Pretrial examination of a person, documents or other items to find evidence that may be used in the trial.

Dismissal—Order to drop the case.

Disposition of case—How the case was decided.

Diversity—Variety, different forms, a mixture of different types.

Docket—List of cases pending before the court.

Dumb factor—A feeling of reporters who are afraid to ask certain questions because they are concerned that they will appear dumb to the sources.

E

Embedded links—Links to Internet sites written within the text.

Empowerment box—Information from a story set off in a box of facts or information that will be helpful to people such as where to go for aid.

Ethical values—The principles a person considers important to guide behavior.

Ethics—Process of making decisions about the way a person behaves.

External links—Links to Internet sites listed separately from the text in a box alongside or at the end of a story.

Extradition—To move a person accused of a crime from the state where he is residing to the state where the crime occurred and where the trial will be conducted.

Eyetrack studies—Studies performed by several organizations to track how the movement of people's eyes affect reading habits.

Eyetracking—Tracing the movements of people's eyes.

F

Fabrication—The process of making something up, such as a false story in journalism.

Facebook—The largest social network company based on technology that allows people who join the group to interact and share information.

Facts box—A brief list of information from the story displayed in a box above or alongside the article.

Fair comment/criticism—A comment on a matter of public interest, based on facts.

Fair use—A determination of what copyrighted material may be copied without infringement of the law.

False light—A published story or picture that gives the wrong impression and is embarrassing to the person if it was published with actual malice, knowledge that the information was not true.

Federal shield law—A federal law, The Free Flow of Information Act, has been proposed in Congress to protect journalists from revealing their sources if a case comes to court where testimony from the source is needed; however, it has not been adopted at this time.

Felony—Major crime punishable by a sentence of a year or more.

First Amendment—The First Amendment to the Constitution protects religion, free speech and the right of people to petition the government for a redress of grievances.

First-day lead—A lead written as a summary lead, as though readers or viewers were hearing the news for the first time.

Fiscal year—A year determined for budgets or tax purposes such as the year going from July 1 to the next July or from any other 12-month period.

Five W's—Basic questions of who, what, when, where and why.

Flickr—A photo-sharing repository.

Focus—The main idea of the story.

Focus-on-a-person lead—An anecdotal lead that features a description or anecdote about a person in the story.

FOIA—Acronym for "Freedom of Information Act."

Follow-up questions—Questions in an interview that follow after a source's response; how and why are good follow-up questions.

Foursquare—A mobile application with a built-in GPS (Global Positioning System), which can broadcast your position to other people you choose.

Free-choice questions—Asking the source if there are any questions or additional information the source would like to add.

Freedom of Information Act—A law that provides the right to access information from the federal government.

Free-writing—Writing from memory without notes for an initial draft.

Future-action kicker—An ending that tells the next step in the situation.

G

Gender—Male or female; bisexual is not an officially recognized separate gender.

Gender-neutral—Language that does not specify male or female roles; for example, "fireman" would be "firefighter" and "policeman" would be "police officer."

Gigabyte—Storage capacity of 1024 megabytes, or 1 billion bytes.

GOAL method—A reporting technique created by this author especially for profile interview: goals, obstacles, achievements, logistics.

Grand jury—Group of citizens selected by the court to investigate whether there is enough evidence or probable cause that a crime occurred and that the person should be charged, or indicted.

Graphics—Images, maps, charts or other illustrations.

H

Handicapped—AP Stylebook says to avoid "handicapped" or "disabled" unless pertinent to the story; if needed, specific description is preferred.

Hard news—Stories about events that are happening or just happened, such as accidents, crimes or conflicts.

Hard-news lead—A direct lead that summarizes the story.

Hashtag—A word or phrase with the #symbol to identify messages on a topic; used on Twitter to indicate keywords or topics of other tweets.

Headline—The line before the story that summarizes the main idea in order to entice the reader into the article.

Highlights box—A list of main points displayed in a box next to the story.

Homicide—Legal term for killing.

Hourglass structure—A story starting with the inverted pyramid, with the most important information in the lead and then continuing in chronological order.

Hung jury—A jury that cannot reach a unanimous verdict, a requirement in most criminal trials.

Hyperlink—Highlighted word or image that connects to a text, video or image in the Internet.

Hyperlocal—Local news for a small area such as a neighborhood within a community.

HyperText Markup Language (HTML)—The authoring language or formatting for creating documents on the Web.

I

Icebreakers—Questions at the start of an interview to put the source at ease.

Illegal alien—A term considered objectionable by some groups: The AP Stylebook suggests describing the person as "living in or entering the country illegally" or "without legal permission."

Immediacy—Reporting what is happening now or the latest developments.

Immunity—Exemption from liability.

Impact—Influence or affect on someone or something.

Impact lead—A lead that shows how the reader or viewer will be affected.

Incident reports—Records police write about a crime, an accident or other investigation.

Indictment—Recommendation by the grand jury that there is enough probable cause to charge a person or group of people with the crime under investigation.

Indirect lead—A delayed lead that may start with an anecdote or story-telling approach rather than a summary lead.

Infographic—A chart, map, graph or other illustration to visually display information.

Injunction—Order by the court instructing a person, group or company to stop the action that was occurring, such as picketing.

Innocent versus not guilty—The AP Stylebook recommends "innocent" because it is more precise and also in case the word "not" is omitted from "not guilty."

Interactive—Involving users to participate or respond to the information.

Interactive content—Information that allows users to react or respond to it.

Interactivity—The process of involving two or more persons to act upon or transfer communication.

Invasion of privacy—The courts have acknowledged four grounds for invasion of privacy: intrusion, public disclosure of private and embarrassing facts, false light, and misappropriation of a person's name or image without permission.

Inverted pyramid—Story structured with the most important information at the top of the story, followed by supporting points in descending order of importance.

Involuntary public figure—A person who does nothing voluntary to garner attention or to get involved in a public issue, but who finds himself in the middle of a public controversy anyway.

iPad—A tablet computer made by Apple Corporation.

J

Jargon—Language used by a particular profession or group; also a term describing pretentious or unwieldly wording.

Juvenile offenders—Offenders under age 18.

K

Key words—Selected words considered important to a sentence or story.

Kickers—A term for endings in stories.

L

Lead—The first sentence or first few paragraphs of the story to summarize the focus and entice the reader.

Lead quote—The first quote that backs up the lead.

Lead-in—An introduction to a broadcast story.

Lede—An old form of spelling "lead," the beginning of a story, to distinguish it from the lead type that was used to set type before computers.

LGBT—Acronym for "lesbian, gay, bisexual, transsexual."

Liability—Legal responsibility.

Liable—Legally responsible.

Libel—A false and defamatory attack in written form on a person's reputation or character. Oral or spoken defamation is slander.

Libelous—Description of a false and defamatory attack in written form on a person's reputation or character.

Limited public figure—A person who has voluntarily thrust himself into a public controversy to influence the outcome.

Linear—Arranged in a line; a story displayed from beginning to end, unlike nonlinear websites, which can be read in any order.

LinkedIn—A professional network where people post their profiles, usually their business or career information.

List lead—A way to start a story with a few brief examples in parallel sentence structure.

List technique—Method of itemizing a group of phrases or sentences.

Literary journalists—A group of writers who, in the 1960s and 1970s, used the storytelling techniques of fiction for nonfiction newspaper and magazine stories.

Log (crime log)—A list of crimes or police actions.

M

Mainbar—The main story in a news report that is accompanied by other secondary stories called "sidebars."

Manslaughter—Homicide without premeditation.

Matchmaker technique—A reporting technique asking one source to recommend another.

Mean—An average; the sum of all the figures divided by the number of items in the survey.

Media kit—A packet of materials to promote a product, often including news releases, fact sheets about the organization and samples of the product.

Median—An average; the value in the middle of a range.

Microblogging—A short form of blogging.

Microcontent—Headlines, summary blurbs and briefs.

Mill—Unit equal to $1 for every $1,000 that a house is assessed.

Misdemeanor—Crime less serious than a felony; crime punishable by less than one year in jail and/or fines.

Mistrial—Trial that is set aside or declared invalid because of some mistake in proceedings or, in a criminal trial, because the jury cannot reach a unanimous verdict.

Mobile delivery—Information transferred to a mobile device such as a smartphone or tablet computer.

Mobile media—Portable media, usually referring to information on digital devices such as smartphones or tablet computers.

Mojos—Journalists equipped with notepads, cameras, recorders, cell phones and laptop computers, so they can produce news with mobile equipment.

Morality—Codes of conduct regarding behavior.

Motion—Request for the court to make a ruling or finding.

Multicultural sources—Sources from different races, gender, ethnic and cultural backgrounds.

Multimedia—A mixture of media, usually print, broadcast and online.

Multi-screeners—People who view more than one digital device at the same time such as a person who views a TV screen and an iPad or smartphone simultaneously.

Multitasker—Someone who can perform several tasks simultaneously.

Murder—Term for premeditated homicide.

Mystery lead—A lead that teases the reader with a surprise that will be revealed like the solution to a mystery.

N

Narrative lead—A storytelling lead that recounts the event with dramatic action to recreate the event.

Narrative storytelling—A form of writing that recounts a story with dramatic action, so readers or viewers can feel as though they are witnessing the event.

Narrative techniques—Methods of writing with the techniques of fiction such as description, dialogue and dramatic action, so readers can feel as if they are witnessing the event.

Natural sound—Background sound that is intended to play while the reporter or anchor is speaking; also called "ambient sound."

Neutral reportage—A First Amendment protection of the news media to write accusations about a public official or public figure in a public controversy as long as the reporter states them accurately and neutrally; recognized only in 10 states.

Neutrality—Unbiased; not taking one side or another on a matter.

News conference—AP Stylebook preferred term for "press conference."

News director—The person who oversees all news operations at the station.

News release—The AP preferred term for a "press release," a statement distributed to the media by officials or public relations personnel.

Newscast—A news program of a broadcast station.

Nightmare lead—Dream leads with the analogy to a nightmare.

Nolo contendere—Latin for "I will not contest it" (no contest); this plea has the same effect as a guilty plea, but it is not an admission of guilt. It means the person will not fight the charge.

Nonlinear—Information not in a straight line; users may access information in any order they choose.

Not for attribution—The information the source gives as background may be used, but the source may not be identified.

Nut graph—A sentence or paragraph that states the focus—the main point—of the story.

O

Obituary—An article about a person who died.

Objectivity—Ability to be unbiased, fair, without prejudice.

Observation—A technique of using what you witness with your senses, sight, sound, smell and taste.

Off the record—Information from a source that may not be used at all.

On the record—Information that the source agrees may be used in a news story and that may be identified as coming from the source.

One-man-band—A reporter who conducts the interview, shoots the video and produces the story; someone who can do it all.

Online portfolios—A job application posted on the Web, which includes a résumé and links to your website with samples of your work.

Open-ended questions—Questions that elicit quotes, elaboration or longer responses.

Open-meeting laws—Laws that require meetings of public bodies be open to citizens.

Operating budget—Money used to provide services (police, fire, garbage removal and so on) and to pay for the operation of government.

Out (in broadcast script)—The script code for the end of a sound bite.

Overview attribution—A brief statement, followed by a colon, that introduces information from a source without attributing each sentence.

P

Pacing—Varying the rhythm in a story, such as following long paragraphs with short ones.

Package (in broadcast)—Reporter's story that includes narration, visual images and sound bites from sources.

Paid death notices—Announcements of deaths that the publication prints for a fee.

Parallelism—Sentences that follow each other and are worded in the same grammatical order.

Parroting—Writing transitions to a sound bite that copy what the source will say.

Partial quote—Using only a part of a quote in a sentence but also attributing it.

Passive voice—A grammatical construction where the action is being done to the person or object instead of the person doing the action.

Pay wall—A system that blocks access to certain information.

PDF—Acronym for "portable document format," a file form that makes it possible to view the document text and layout on any computer screen with a special reader from Adobe, the maker of this format.

Per capita—The rate per person.

Permalink—A link to a blog post.

Person of interest—The name of a suspect released before actual charges are filed; used when police believe the suspect will soon be charged with the crime.

Personalized journalism—News, blogs or stories that reflect the writer's point of view or his or her own experience.

Pervasive public figure—A legal distinction for a person who has gained prominence in society or who has great power and influence and would therefore bear the burden of proving the information in dispute is libelous.

Pinterest—A free program allowing users to create and post a collection of photos in a collage or "bulletin board" of information to share with people.

Plagiarism—Copying the words of other writers and claiming it as one's own work. Even if the information gathered from other publications is paraphrased, it is plagiarizing if the writer does not attribute it.

Plagiarize—To copy information of others and claim it as one's own work.

Plaintiff—Person who sues in a civil case.

Plea bargain—Agreement between the prosecutor and the defendant (or defense attorney) to accept a lesser charge and a lesser sentence in return for a guilty or no-contest plea.

Plop-a-person lead—Starting a story by focusing on a person who is only mentioned in the lead, but not in the rest of the story.

Podcast—Short for "portable on demand," it is digital media information in audio or video form distributed over the Internet for use on a portable media player.

Point/counterpoint—A story arranged by opposing points of view.

Present tense—Grammatical tense using verbs in the present time.

Press conference—A meeting by officials or authorities to notify the media of news or information; AP Stylebook preferred term is "news conference."

Press release—A statement distributed to the media by officials or public relations personnel; preferably called a "news release" by the AP Stylebook.

Primary source—The original source of information, human or records.

Private figure—In libel cases, a private individual needs to show only that the material was published with carelessness or negligence instead of proving actual malice.

Privilege—In a legal sense, absolute privilege means that public officials can make statements in the course of their duties without being sued for libel, and qualified privilege means the media may print defamatory statements made by people who are absolutely privileged, as long as the information is from a public proceeding or public record.

Probation—Condition in which the person is released from serving a jail sentence if he meets certain terms, such as serving in the community, entering drug treatment or accepting whatever restrictions the judge decides.

Producer—Plans the newscast and often writes teasers and some copy for the anchors.

Proofread—To check a document for accuracy and errors in spelling, grammar and style.

Proximity—Nearness in place, situation or relationship.

PRSA—Public Relations Society of America.

PRSSA—Public Relations Student Society of America.

PRWeb—A press release distribution service.

PSA—Public service announcement.

Pseudonym—A false name, usually used when a person in a story is only identified by a made-up name.

Public domain—Intellectual property rights that are available to the public without copyright restrictions.

Public figures—People may be considered public figures if their

achievements or notoriety place them in the public eye or if they seek attention by voluntarily thrusting themselves into a public controversy.

Public records—Records that are available to anyone from government.

Public service announcements (PSAs)—Advertisements or messages in the public interest that the media broadcast without charge.

Pulitzer Prize—The highest honor in journalism and the arts; a prize named for the 19th century newspaper publisher Joseph Pulitzer, who recommended training journalists at the university level.

Pull quote—A highlighted quote pulled from the story.

Q

Qualified privilege—The media may print defamatory statements made by people who are absolutely privileged as long as the information is from a public proceeding or public record.

Question lead—Beginning the story with a question that will be followed by a focus that relates to the question.

Question/answer format (Q and A)—A way of organizing a story by questions and answers, often used in profiles or explanatory stories.

Quote kicker—Ending the story with a quote from a source in the story.

R

Reader—Story the anchor or radio announcer reads without visuals or sound bites.

Reappraisal—State or local decision to re-evaluate properties in the community, usually to increase their values.

Recognizance—Literally, "recognition." A person may be released from jail based on his own recognizance, meaning the recognition of a previously good reputation.

Reference quote—A partial quote referring to something controversial and backed up with the full quote.

References—Recommendations from people listed by name and contact information in print job applications; but online, "references available on request" is preferred.

Resolution—The solution to a dispute.

Résumé—A summary or brief account of a person's background and accomplishments.

Reverse directory—A directory that lists names, phone numbers and addresses by several means, enabling identification by address or phone number rather than only by name.

Rip-and-read—A broadcast term for taking the wire service release and reading it as it is instead of writing or rewriting the script.

Robbery—Involves stealing with violence or a threat against people.

Role-play—Devising questions to ask if you were affected by the incident or if you were a source.

RSS—Acronym for "Really Simple Syndication," a format used to get information that can be delivered with software that compiles it.

RTDNA—Radio Television Digital News Association.

Rundown—Schedule for a newscast allocating the time for each story and segment, including advertisements.

S

Script—The written manuscript for broadcast stories.

Sections technique—Dividing a story into sections and separating them by a graphic device such as a large dot or a large capital letter.

Seg time—Length of time for a news segment. A brief may be 0:10, or 10 seconds; a reporter's package, including the lead-in by an anchor, may be 1:45—one minute and 45 seconds.

SEO—Acronym for "search engine optimization," which means content designed so it will be displayed prominently by a search engine.

Sexism—Discrimination based on sex.

Sexual orientation—The preferred term of the National Lesbian and Gay Journalists Association, instead of "sexual preference."

Shield law—State law that protects reporters from revealing their sources if a case comes to court for which testimony from the source is needed, but no federal shield law has passed.

Show-in-action technique—Writing description that shows the source or

scene doing something as though it were happening now.

Sidebar—A secondary story that accompanies the main story in a news account.

Simple negligence standard—A rule in libel cases that a private individual needs to show only that the material was published with carelessness or negligence.

Skype—A software application that lets people converse and view each other over the Internet with a webcam.

Slideshare—The site to post and share presentations such as slides created on PowerPoint or other programs.

Smartphones—Cell phones that have software to perform several computer functions such as email and Web browsing.

Snapshot profile—A brief mini version of a profile.

SOC (standard out cue)—Sign-off comments at the end of the story.

Social media—Electronic communication where users share information on websites designed to create online communities.

Social networking—Sharing information among people with common interests, usually online.

Soft lead—A feature or creative approach to the lead, often focusing on an anecdote or description.

Soft news—News that entertains or informs, with emphasis on human interest and less immediacy than breaking news.

SOT—Acronym for "sound on tape."

Sound bite—An audio or video recorded statement from a source.

Stand-up—A part of the story in which the reporter talks on camera at the scene; sometimes at the end of a story.

Stereotype—A widely held belief or image of a person, place or thing.

Storify—A social network service that lets users curate other stories from social media, such as Twitter and Facebook, to create their own stories or timelines.

Storyboard—A group of panels or sketches showing the actions or scenes in a plot, a film or the different sections planned in a website project.

Subheadings—Secondary headlines or headings within a document.

Subpoena—Court order commanding a person to appear in court or to release documents to the court.

Summary blurb—A paragraph or sentence that serves as a secondary headline.

Summary judgment—Procedure in a civil suit asking the court to give final judgment on the grounds that there are no further questions and no need for a trial.

Summary lead—A lead that summarizes the main point of the story.

Summary questions—Basic questions eliciting factual answers, who, what, where, when.

Summons—Document notifying a defendant that a lawsuit or complaint has been filed against him.

Super—Letters, numbers or words produced by a character generator and superimposed over visual images; often used to identify the person appearing on the tape. At some stations, the letters CG—for "character generator"—are used to indicate the super.

Suspect—A person suspected of a crime.

Suspended sentence—Court order stating that the punishment of the defendant will be suspended if certain conditions are met. A person who receives probation gets a suspended sentence.

T

Tablet computer—A mobile computer shaped in a single panel with a touch screen.

Tag—The closing sentence for a TV or radio story or package.

Target audience—A specific group of people within a market at which the product is aimed.

Teaser—A short blurb to entice viewers to tune in or stay tuned to a newscast, usually aired before a commercial break or before the broadcast.

Teaser lead—A lead that uses the element of surprise to entice the reader into the story.

Technorati—An Internet search engine for information on blogs.

Teleprompter—Video terminal that displays the script for the anchor or reporter to read.

Temporary injunction—Court order to stop an action, such as a protest, for a specific amount of time until a court hearing whether the action should be stopped permanently.

Theme—An angle or recurring idea that weaves throughout the story.

Time frame—The period of time in which something took place.

Timelines—A list of events in the order they occurred.

Timeliness—News related to the immediate future or past or to a relevant time.

Times v. Sullivan—A Supreme Court landmark libel case in 1964 that prohibits a public official from recovering damages for defamatory falsehood relating to his official conduct unless he proves that the statement was made with "actual malice," knowledge that it was false or with reckless disregard of whether it was false or not.

Tone—Mood or overall feeling such as light-hearted, happy, somber.

Tort—Civil case involving damages, pain, suffering or other allegations of wrongdoing.

Trackbacks—A method for website authors to be notified when somebody links to one of their sites.

Transitions—Words, phrases or sentences that bridge ideas to go from one thought to another.

Transparency—Openness in regards to communication in government or an organization.

Trends—A general movement or direction in which something is occurring.

True bill—Indictment issued by a grand jury.

Truth defense—In libel cases proving the truth of an allegation is considered the best defense.

Tweet—Short message limited to 140 characters to post on Twitter.

Twitter—A social network that limits messages, called "tweets," to 140 characters and may include links to Web content.

U

Update leads—To write a new approach or a lead that reveals the next step in an action.

V

Verdict—Decision by a jury about guilt or innocence.

Verify—Prove the truth or accuracy of information.

Videotape—Magnetic tape for recording and reproducing visual and audio material.

Vimeo—A free video-sharing website on which members can post videos for noncommercial use.

Visuals—Images or graphics to illustrate a story.

VNR—Video news release.

VO—Voice-over, the anchor's voice over video images.

Vodcast—A video podcast.

Voicer—A story a reporter reads that may contain natural sound but does not include actualities.

Vortex public figure—Same as a "limited public figure," a person who has voluntarily thrust himself into a public controversy to influence the outcome.

VO-SOT—Voice-over with sound bite; the anchor's voice over video and sound bite.

W

Wall Street Journal **formula**—A story organized with an anecdotal lead followed by a nut graph, elaboration and a circular ending with a reference to the lead.

Warrant—Court order directing law enforcement officials to arrest a person or giving them authority to search a premises.

Weather-report lead—A cliché approach of starting with weather such as "It was a dark and stormy night."

Wiki—A website that allows users to add, delete or revise material.

Wordpress.org—Web software offering ways to create blogs and websites.

Wrap—A story from a reporter that may include actualities.

Y

YouTube—A video-sharing site.

Index